THE

1000 FINEST

WINES EVER MADE

Fine

PRODUCTION TEAM

Authors	Pekka Nuikki, Juha Lihtonen, Essi Avellan MW
Photographs	Nuikki
Design Agency	Konsepti Advertising
Graphic design	Teemu Timperi
Editorial Team	Jan-Erik Paulson, Ralf Frenzel, Anne Lepola, Petri Laine, Meri Kukkavaara, William Coates, Gareth Hayes, Markus Natri, Peter Stefanovic, Ricardo Rodrigues, Samuli Ollikainen, Mary Banda, Andrew Caillard MW
Printing house	Printed in Finland by Libris Oy / 2007
Book sewing	Libris Oy
Papers	Multiart Silk 150 g/m2
	Multiart Silk 300 g/m2
Typefaces	Bickham Script MM, DIN FF, Neutra, Voluta Script
Publisher	Oy Fine Publishing Helsinki Ltd
Author´s note	www.fine-magazines.com

ISBN 978-952-99976-0-2

Acknowledgements

We are greatly indebted to all those warm hearted people who have helped us again by generously giving us some of their precious time, knowledge and hospitality.

Actually, the most enjoyable part of our work has been the chance to communicate with you either in person or in writing. Whenever we felt lost or insecure, those moments gave us new inspiration and the support we needed to go on. Our special thanks go to Nora Löfving-Lihtonen, Emilia Timperi and Meri Kukkavaara.

Finally, we would like to mention our good friends Jan-Erik Paulson and Ralf Frenzel, who are the most dedicated wine people we know.

We have taken the daring decision to choose 1000

of the best wines measured by their current drinkability and condition.

We have given points to the wines accordingly, and we have even

given the wines a ranking. Our ranking is based on numerous tasting

experiences by our expert tasting panel, and the consensus that they

have reached on the wines.

The 1000 Finest Wines ever Made

Welcome to the 1000 Finest Wines Ever Made. A trail-blazing buying and drinking guide for fine wine enthusiasts, wine investors and lovers of rare and mature wine. We hope our expertise in fine and mature wines will encourage you to buy and enjoy fine wine. Equally we wish that the notes will help to reduce any risk at purchase and to select the correct time to open your finest bottles.

This comprehensive book rates 1000 best wines of all time – from 1774 to 2006 – according to their current drinkability and condition. Most of the wines in this book are tasted knowing the producer and the vintage. The rating of the wines – using the American 100 points scale – is firstly based on the qualities of the wine at the moment of tasting, and secondly on the history and culture connected with the wine. It needs to be borne in mind that our rating differs a great deal, for example, from the rating system used by Robert Parker or the Wine Spectator. We do not give additional points for the wine's future potential, we base our assessment only on its present quality and ability to give pleasure now, both physically and mentally.

The 1000 Finest Wines Ever Made is the only buying and drinking guide to the best wines in the world – the equivalent of a Michelin guide in gastronomy. This book will be revised and updated bi-annually with the addition of new wines and the deletion of wines that have past their peak.

On the following pages you can read more about us and our philosophy in tasting and appreciating wine. We hope that it helps you to make the most of this one-of-a-kind book!

Helsinki 23.10.2007

Pekka Nuikki
Author and editor in Chief of FINE-Magazines

HOW TO USE THE BOOK

The 1000 Finest Wines Ever Made – To Drink Today

Tasting wine is a personal experience and therefore always subjective. Experience, palate, personal taste preferences, and the personality of the taster play a major role in assessment of wine. Tasting wine is to interact with it. It is therefore important to know who the tasters are, what their preferences and experience of tasting the wines concerned are.

The 1000 Finest Wines Ever Made relies on the judgment of five experienced palates:

PEKKA NUIKKI is one of the leading experts of fine and mature wines. He has published several international wine and art books, most recently Drinking History – Stories of Wines and Vintages from 1870 to 1970 and Château Mouton-Rothschild: Wine and Art 1924–2003. He is the founder and Editor-in-Chief of European, German and Scandinavian Fine Wine Magazines.

Nuikki is an award-winning photographer who has exhibited his artwork all over the world. He is also the luckiest man in the world, having hit seven hole-in-ones!

ESSI AVELLAN MW, is the second ever Master of Wine from the Nordic countries. She was awarded the Tim Derouet Memorial Award and Lily Bollinger Medal for excellence in the Master of Wine examination. Essi Avellan is the Editor of FINE Champagne Magazine. Avellan also contributes to a number of newspapers and wine and food magazines. Her main areas of expertise are champagnes, fine and rare wines.

JUHA LIHTONEN is one of the leading Nordic sommeliers. Lihtonen was awarded Best Sommelier in the Nordic countries in 2003 and he has consecutively won the title of Best Sommelier in Finland. Lihtonen has written several wine books, his speciality being wine and food combinations. Juha Lihtonen is the Editor of European Fine Wine Magazine and Scandinavian Fine Wine Magazine.

RALF FRENZEL is the publisher of Tre Torri top quality gastronomy and wine books and magazines in the German speaking countries. Ralf Frenzel is one of the most famous sommeliers of all time. He has been responsible for wine selections for numerous top restaurants in Europe. He has organised and worked in an astonishing number of the world's most prestigious wine tastings with the world's most renowned wine collectors. He is the Editor of the German FINE Wine Magazine.

JAN-ERIK PAULSON is one of the leading mature wine specialists in the world. His main areas of expertise are Bordeaux and Austrian wines. Paulson has gained fame in the past 30 years for the exclusive fine and rare wine tastings he arranges all around the world. He is also a rare wine merchant at www.rare-wine.com.

The above group of fine and rare wine experts have collected notes and memories of the world's best wines for the most part of their adult lives. They have made fine wine their life and profession. Over 60,000 fine wines have been tasted by this pentad, giving them the perfect background to write such a demanding, comprehensive, and daring book. It took an enormous amount of time to find consensus on the list of 1000 best wines, their ratings and the order that does the wines complete justice.

NUMBER OF TASTING EXPERIENCES   2007/2030 x **73** | D 2 h / G 3 h

Since rare and mature wines are our focus and speciality, the question of bottle variation and storage history plays a significant role. The validity and trustworthiness of this book relies on the vast number of tasting experiences and bottles that have been assessed to give the wine its ranking. Our experts have tasted each wine from one to one hundred times, valuing certainty from a multitude of opinions and bottles. The points given to each wine derive from the best bottle evaluated. We provide information on how many tasting times the assessment is based.

Old and rare wines have been a popular target for wine fraud over the past few decades. As there may be an element of uncertainty about the authenticity of old bottles, we only accept tasting notes from wines of known origin or from wines that have been tasted with similar notes from several bottles that derive from different origins. We will list separately a few wines at the end of the book that clearly would belong to the 1000 Finest Wines Ever Made, but the authenticity of which we have no guarantee.

This comprehensive book rates 1000 best wines of all time – from 1774 to 2006 – according to their current drinkability and condition. Most of the wines in this book are tasted knowing the producer and the vintage. The rating of the wines – using the American 100 points scale – is firstly based on the qualities of the wine at the moment of tasting, and secondly on the history and culture connected with the wine. It needs to be borne in mind that our rating differs a great deal, for example, from the rating system used by Robert Parker or the Wine Spectator. We do not give additional points for the wine's future potential, we base our assessment only on its present quality and ability to give pleasure now, both physically and mentally.

Therefore our points have a tendency to rise when the wine is approaching maturity. To be fair to immature fine wines, we have excluded assessment of red wines produced post-2000. The future updates of this book will deal with those wines as they mature. Recent white wine and sparkling wine launches are taken into account.

One of the greatest strengths of this book is its up-to-date evaluations and tasting notes. Only wines tasted since 2000 are taken into account. The reader can therefore trust the accuracy of the notes and condition of the wines.

In addition to full tasting notes, some essential background to the wines, vintages and producers is given to enlighten the qualities, histories and stories of the fine wines to the reader. As the potential of the wine is not taken into account, we give estimates about future potential and optimal drinking time for each wine in the tasting notes. Uniquely, we also give insight into required decanting times to make the best of each fine wine experience.

READING OUR TASTING NOTES

Our five experts have all contributed with numerous tasting notes in the book. Therefore, the style and focus of the assessment may vary by the individual. Our group of experts has agreed on the most important parameters of the evaluations. We focus on describing the personality and essence of the wine: its acidity, fruit, tannin, structure, depth, and length, all of the factors that affect the wine's balance – and balance in our shared opinion is the most important factor in the quality of a wine.

Unfortunately, even the best wines can be ruined by treating and storing them incorrectly, so the tasting note, if not tasted multiple times, can only apply to the bottle in question and not the wine in general.

Key to our points

100p - Sheer perfection to all senses by every parameter of wine quality – True nature's gift.

97–99p - A near perfect experience. The wine and its history are of a unique genre. As a tasting experience, the wine is extraordinary and unforgettable. Impeccable harmony, complexity and one-of-a-kind personality.

93–96p - An outstanding wine, which is produced with the highest standards of quality, and which gives a balanced and unique experience when enjoyed.

91–93p - An excellent wine that has a refined style, balanced structure and nuanced finesse.

88–90p - A good wine, close to excellent. Harmonious wine but lacks the complexity and personality of an excellent wine.

80–87p - An average wine with less character, intensity, structure, and elegance.

70–79p - A modest and straightforward wine lacking life and harmony.

50–69p - An almost non-drinkable, empty wine.

LEVELS

Ullage

Bordeaux / Burgundy

The level of the wine is the indicator that tells most about a singular wine's condition and its storage history. When a wine ages the evaporation through the cork causes the level in the bottle to drop. The lower the level, the greater the risk the wine is oxidised and spoiled. The level also has a significant influence on the price paid for the wine. In this book the levels mentioned are based on the table presented here:

1. By the neck – the normal level of young wines, and often that of older wines recorked at the estate. Especially good level for wines older than 15 years. Influence on the price of the wine: **full price**.

2. Bottom neck – Good level for wines of all ages. Especially good level for wines older than 20 years. Influence on the price of the wine: **full price**.

3. Top-shoulder – Normal level for wines 15 to 25 years old. Influence on the price of the wine: **- 10–15%**.

4. Upper-shoulder – Acceptable level for wines older than 25 years. An especially good level for wines more than 50 years old. Influence on the price of the wine: **- 20–25%**.

5. Mid-shoulder – A sign of a weakening cork or a warning of a possible deterioration of the wine. If the clarity and color of the wine and the position of the cork are in good shape, the wine is probably in good order, especially if it is more than 60 years old. This is quite a normal level for wines from the late 19th and early 20th centuries. Influence on the price of the wine: **- 30–50%**.

6. Mid-low-shoulder – Already quite a risk, especially for wines not bottled on the estate. This level is not acceptable with wines less than 50 years of age. Influence on the price of the wine: **- 50–70%**.

7. Low-shoulder – Usually a clear sign of already spoiled wine, especially if the wine is less than 80 years old. A wine like this is usually on the market if the wine in question or its label is particularly rare. Influence on the price of the wine: **- 70–80%**. Wines from the late 18th and early 19th centuries make an exception to this rule.

Capsule
Ullage: space
between the cork and the wine.

Since bottles used in Burgundy do not have "shoulders", it is not practical to use the same terms to describe the level of the wine as with the wines of Bordeaux. The level in these burgundy bottles is indicated with centimetres in relation to the cork. The condition of the wine is less affected by the level in the slim bottles of Burgundy than in the shouldered bottles of Bordeaux. For example in a 40-year-old burgundy red wine 5–6 cm can still be considered a good level, and not even an 8 cm drop in the level is necessarily a sign of a wine gone bad, though it has a great influence on the price.

The bottle used in Burgundy is also often used in Rhône, in the Loire valley and in Southern France.

DECANTING

2007/2030 x 73 | D 2 h / G 3 h

Bordeaux / Burgundy

There are moments when we wonder at the praising comments that a wine we have just tasted – now trivial and lifeless – has received in the past from wine experts we respect. Sometimes the reason for this is that the ratings of the wine date back several decades. But time and again we find the reason in ourselves; in our inexperience and ignorance – We may have decanted the wine too early and it has "died", or too late denying it the time to even come to life before tasting.

Longevity is a fine quality in a wine. It can be close to magical when an old vintage is enjoyed at its prime. However, even the best wine is too easily ruined by drinking it at the wrong time, and we are not talking about decades, or even years, but hours and minutes.

In our opinion all mature wines profit from decanting for two reasons. Firstly, to separate the wine from any sediment it may have thrown during its long maturation in the bottle, and secondly to allow the wine to breathe, which allows the wine to develop and show us all its complexities and subtleties. If possible, also see to it that the wine has been in an upright position before decanting for at least a day or two.

There are no hard and fast rules so far as to the length of time needed for a wine to breathe, but because air literally breathes life into wine, and on the other hand also leads to its death, it is particularly important to know how much time to give to a wine in decanter and glass. That is why with each tasting note we mention the time that the wine in question needed in our opinion to breathe and develop to its best. The time we have given is based simply on our own experiences with the wine, and should once again be read as guidance only, not as proved scientific truth.

GLASS TIME

2007/2030 x **73** | D 2 h / G 3 h

With each tasting note we have also mentioned the time that the wine held on to its best qualities in the glass after pouring. Particularly, the wines from the 19th and early 20th centuries awaken to life in a decanter very fast, but that glorious, last breath echoing life and freedom often lasts only ten minutes, even after a short decanting of 5–15 minutes. Tears have not always been far at such occasions, fortunately rare, when we have decanted the wine too early and realised that a wine with 50 dignified years behind it, most lively and delicate right after decanting, has no life left when we started to pour it 45 minutes later into the glasses of our guests, all full of wishful expectation.

The time estimates we have given in this book tell merely of the stability in the glass of the singular wine in question, not that of the estate's wines in general or that of the vintage's.

MOST RECENT TASTING TIME

WHEN TO DRINK

2007/2030 x **73** | D 2 h / G 3 h

Optimum drinking time

Today mature fine wines can be found on many good-quality wine stores' lists. Wines from 1970–1990 are easily accessible, along with recommendations concerning maturity degree and drinking time. But as soon as one goes back further in history than the 1970s the recommendations become more difficult and less in number, and the insecurity of the wine's condition increases. The advice and recommendations we have given in this book rest upon our own experiences of the wine in question, and on our opinion of its lasting potential in future. They are based on the assumption that the wine has been stored correctly and will continue to stay so.

The 1000 finest Wines Ever Made — is a unique book launch from the publishers of the European, German and Scandinavian fine Wine Magazines. In addition to three prestigious wine magazines and this new trail-blazing book launch, we publish the world's only international Champagne Magazine and top quality wine books, such as Drinking History — Stories from Wines and Vintage from 1870 to 1970 and Bordeaux Wine Sights.

The most prestigious wine magazine in the world, fine the Scandinavian fine Wine Magazine — published since 2005 — is expanding into a global media for fine and rare wine journalism.

In 2007 the fine — European fine Wine Magazine — has been launched in English and German reaching over twenty countries world-wide. These exclusive, visually unique, informative and entertaining magazines by new generation of wine experts is published quarterly with 152 pages on the world's finest wines, histories and the people behind them.

Read more and subscribe to the European fine Wine Magazine

The 1000 Finest Wines ever Made
– To Drink Today

The 1000 Finest Wines Ever Made – is a unique book launch from the publishers of the European, German and Scandinavian Fine Wine Magazines. In addition to three prestigious wine magazines and this new trail-blazing book launch, we publish the world´s only international Champagne Magazine and top quality wine books, such as Drinking History – Stories from Wines and Vintages from 1870 to 1970 and Bordeaux Wine Sights.

FROM THE SCANDINAVIAN TO THE EUROPEAN FINE WINE MAGAZINE

The most prestigious wine magazine in the world, FINE the Scandinavian Fine Wine Magazine – published since 2005 – is expanding into a global media for fine and rare wine journalism.

In 2007 the FINE – European Fine Wine Magazine – has been launched in English and German reaching over twenty countries world-wide. These exclusive, visually unique, informative and entertaining magazines by the new generation of wine experts is published quarterly with 152 pages on the world's finest wines, histories and the people behind them.

Read more and subscribe to the European Fine Wine Magazine at *www.fine-magazines.com*

WINES FROM 1 TO 1000

Château Latour 1961. It is a truly
unique, classic and perfect wine.
...ever encountered.
We take a low bow to it.

GRAND V
DE
CHATEAU LA
PREMIER GRAND CRU
APPELLATION PAUILLAC
PAUILLAC-ME
1961
MIS EN BOUTEILLE

OUR UNANIMOUS, highest rating went to the fantastic Château Latour 1961. It is a truly unique, classic and perfect wine. The Latour 1961 has been tasted by us more than 70 times, and only on eight occasions has it not scored a faultless 100 points! No other wine from the approximate 60,000 wines we have tasted, has such an exceptional and perfect track-record as the Latour 1961.

NUMBER 1.

100 p | *1961 Château Latour* (Pauillac)   2007/2030 x **73** | D 1.5 h / G 3 h

Although the year 1961 was not perfect at Château Latour, the wines were! A very rainy winter was followed by an exceptionally warm February. Growth started in the first few days – that is to say a month early. The first half of March was very warm and the first leaves were noted on March 10th. April was unstable and predominantly cold, slowing down growth. The end of May was very cold and on May 29th disaster struck. The flowers were frozen and the sterile grapes dried immediately after; three-quarters of the crop was lost. Only once before has there been frosts in May, in 1945.

July was not good on the whole; overcast with no rain and no sun. In the first three weeks of August the vineyards lacked both water and sun, but fine weather settled in on August 24th and continued without a break until September 28th (almost as dry as in 1949). It rained on September 29th and 30th, and harvest took place from 19th until 28th September. The weather was very hot, which caused problems with vinification. Yields were very poor, as had been expected, so the harvest was short.

Almost all of the bottles we have tasted have been in very good condition with only a few of them top-shoulder or lower. The ideal decanting time seems to be 1.5 hours. This last bottle of Latour 1961 lived up to the romantic memory of our previous experiences. It has a beautiful, dark-red, fully mature colour, which is almost orange on the rim. The scent is sound and open, classic, a perfectly merged bouquet. The presence of fruit was unbelievably rich. This sublimely rich, firm, still quite tannic, full, very long, and abundantly fruity classic blew our well-educated senses of taste into new life. Perfect balance and structure. Time lost its meaning. The sensations we experienced in that moment are almost impossible to describe. What we love most about this Goliath was the endless awe-inspiring finish. Not only was the mouth-feel like drinking liquid silk, but the aristocratic finish of multi-layered Cabernet stayed on the palate for an eternity. The best wine we have ever encountered. We take a deep bow to it.

THE MOUTON-ROTHSCHILD 1945 has been tasted by us more than 30 times, and only on seven occasions has it not scored a faultless 100 points. It has almost as exceptional and perfect a track record as the Latour 1961.

100 p | *1945 Château Mouton-Rothschild* (Pauillac) **2007**/**2025 x 34** | D 2 h / G 2 h

Although the Mouton-Rothschild wines from 1926, 1949, 1959 and 1961 are normally impeccable, the 1945 has always had something extraordinary, which for us is hard to describe without deep emotion. Maybe that something is the longest and richest aftertaste, which keeps coming back again and again, or perhaps it is the fact that it is the "Victory Vintage" that symbolizes the victory of good over evil. We do know that there is nothing quite like a Mouton-Rothschild 1945.

To commemorate the Allied victory, Baron Philippe had the idea of embellishing the Mouton-Rothschild 1945 label with an artwork: on this occasion, a symbolic design intended to celebrate the return of peace. He commissioned this work from a young unknown artist, Philippe Julian. M. Julian submitted several drafts for the label and the final one is based on the "V for Victory", made famous by Winston Churchill throughout the war. This marked the beginning of a series of specially designed labels for each vintage. For each year a different artist was commissioned and the payment was in wine.

The 1945 was tasted nine times during the last twelve months and it proved each time to be a very exclusive moment for our friends and ourselves. The last two bottles were in exceptional condition with fine labels. Levels were almost by the neck, and both bottles were decanted two hours before tasting. Deep, dark and thick colour. Sound and wide-open, huge, incredibly sweet nose of black currant, coffee and eucalyptus. All the pieces came together in perfect balance creating an extraordinary, highly concentrated, luxurious, and prosperous wine with a powerful, everlasting aftertaste.

100 p | *1945 Romanée-Conti Domaine de la Romanée-Conti* (Côte de Nuits)

1995/**2020 x 4** | D 1 h / G 3 h

This wine will remain as a relic of the ancient times of the wine world. Vintage 1945 is the last ever made Romanée-Conti from the ancient Pinot Noir Fin vines dating back to 1585. These vines with their descendants had produced highly esteemed grapes for over 360 years. Thus, it was an inconvenient decision for the board of the Domaine de la Romanée-Conti to renew the historic vines. Unfortunately there was no other option since the disastrous small aphid phylloxera, that had first appeared in Vosne-Romanée in 1882, had finally taken over also the Romanée-Conti and Richebourg vineyards. While most other vinegrowers had grafted their vines to resistant American rootstock decades earlier, the Domaine de la Romanée-Conti had fought against the aphid successfully for over 60 years with carbon disulphide. Apparently the Second World War had taken its toll and there were shortage of everything as well as the carbon disulphide. The vineyards begun to decline during the war and, due to the impulsion of the new partner Henri Leroy, the vines of Romanée-Conti were torn up after the harvest in 1945 and replaced in 1947 with grafted clones. Luckily this harvest became a legend with its quality.

1 · 2 · **3** · 4 · 5 · 6 · 7 · 8 · 9 · 10 · 11 · 12 · 13 · 14 · 15 · 16 · 17 · 18 · 19 · 20

1945
ANNÉE
DE LA
VICTOIRE

the "Victory Vintage" that

symbolizes the victory of good

evil. We do know that

nothing quite like a

Mouton Rothschild 1945...

TOUTE LA RÉCOLTE MISE EN BOUTEIL

1945

Cetë récolte

24 jéroboams numérotés de

1475 magnums numér. de

74.422 bout.&, bout. numr. de

2000 Réserve Château

Cette bouteille porte le N°

Château

Mouton Roth

The severe frosts in mid spring reduced the crop before the growing season had even started properly. The weather changed rapidly to beautiful during the end of the spring, and a hot and dry summer followed. The grapes became super concentrated and the harvest was superb in quality but unfortunately restricted in quantity. It is very difficult to find this vintage available anymore. This vintage only produced 608 bottles.

Fine looking bottle with 3 cm level. Decanted one hour. The wine is very deep, dark and richly coloured with a unique exotic nose of oriental spices, black truffles and plenty of depth – very lively! On the palate a full, unbelievably concentrated and sturdy wine. Chewy, intense and showing not a trace of its age – this wine will last forever! Magnificent in a good old-fashioned way! The best burgundy we have ever tasted.

100 p | 1947 *Château Cheval Blanc* (St. Emilion) 2007/2030 x 53 | D 2.5h / G 2h

The Cheval Blanc 1947 has been tasted by us on more than 50 occasions, but it has scored a faultless 100 points only 27 times. Its track record falls below the Latour 1961s and Mouton 1945s mostly because there are so many variable négociant-bottlings available. And regrettably there are also quite a few frauds around.

The Cheval Blanc 1947 was made from exceptionally ripe grapes with remarkably high sugar content. The blend is about two-thirds Cabernet Franc and one-third Merlot. The harvest was delayed until the last moment raising the alcohol content to 2% above normal.

A good bottom-neck level château-bottled magnum. Excellent appearance with a deep and dark, mature colour. Incredibly pronounced chocolaty, leathery nose resembling port wine. Rich and ripe with great extract. The amount of almost overripe fruit was so appealing that it was hard to resist and not just drink the whole bottle right away. A very gentle and soft wine, almost feminine in character. At the same time so powerful and masculine. It has everything a wine can offer in such a historical and exclusive package that it is challenging to find anything as stunning as it! ...And the celebrated aftertaste. We can still sense it after two long days and nights. A perfect out-of-this-world experience.

100 p | 1900 *Château Margaux* (Margaux) 2005/now x 15 | D 45 min / G 2h

The 1900 vintage can be called the vintage of all times in Bordeaux. It was an absolutely perfect vintage that produced long-lived wines. At Château Margaux the grapes were turned into pure gold. Production was nearly 30 000 cases, which is almost exactly the same as in 1982. This monumental wine is considered to be the wine of the century by many wine lovers. Tasting this wine three times during last year convinced us that there is something magical about it. Excellent looking château-bottling. Good top-shoulder level. Decanted one hour. Still surprisingly intensive tawny colour, the complex and rich aromas burst out of the glass – blackcurrant, butterscotch, farmyard and animal aromas. Intensive medium-bodied taste with moderately high acidity forming a great balance with the silky tannin. Ripe fruitiness is attractively combined to velvety textured tannins, immensely long finish with walnut flavour. The great complexity, youthfulness, and refined muscular structure make this wine sensational. Seems to still have great potential for further ageing.

100 p | *1921 Château d'Yquem (Sauternes)*   2006/2030 x **18** | D 2 h / G 4 h

The harvest of 1921 took 39 days to pick and was the last vintage that the Yquem owner Comte de Lur-Saluces sold in cask. Decanted for 45 minutes, it retained its best characteristics for 3 hours after opening. Bottle was in good condition. Château bottling with top-shoulder level.

Very dark, deep golden colour, although not as dark as the négociant bottlings of the same vintage we had tasted earlier. Fresh, vivid, honeyed nose with hints of crème brûlée and coffee. A magnificent combination of mystery and style. A delicious wine with all the components in place. Ideal combination of acidity and sweetness. Very creamy, intense and multi-layered wine, but at the same time wonderfully light and lively – a fantastic yet rare combination. Clean, soft and unbelievably long aftertaste. Yquem at its best and most genuine.

100 p | *1947 Château Pétrus (Pomerol)*   2007/2015 x **34** | D 2 h / G 2 h

Pétrus 1947 has been tasted with enthusiasm more than 30 times, but only on 19 of them has it been blessed with a perfect 100 points. This is mainly because there are so many variable négociant-bottlings and regrettably also innumerable frauds for sale.

1947 was a legendary vintage on the right bank of Bordeaux. It was extremely hot at the time of harvest and the grapes were so rich in sugar that the winemakers had problems in controlling the fermentation. Many wines had residual sugar and most had high volatile acidity, but this was masked by the richness and concentration of the fruit. The wines were attractive at youth but have lasted extremely well in most cases.

The 1947 Pétrus is a great wine, deep coloured and very rich. There were many négociant-bottlings made of this wine, most being very good. It needs decanting, but will develop rapidly in the glass and last several hours if you manage to control yourself that long. An interesting curiosity is that this wine was difficult to sell shortly after the war. The English importer Avery's of Bristol needed several years to sell their small allocation.

The bottle was in excellent condition. A château-bottling. Decanted 1.5 hours. This celebrated Pétrus had a deep, dark colour and a pleasant, delicious, intensive, and mature nose that reopened our senses of smell. The flavour was truly intensive, abundant and densely fruity. The wine had a structure that resembled port, plentiful in an almost jam-like manner. Splendid balance and elegance. This has the softness and roundness that is typical of the best Pétrus made wholly of Merlot. As a grand wine that remains noble and exceptional, we have always felt remarkably well-off when enjoying this wine.

100 p | *1961 Hermitage La Chapelle Jaboulet Aîné* (Rhône)

2007/2030 x **17** | D 2 h / G 2 h

In 1961 the weather conditions in the Rhône valley were variable – a mild winter, chilly and rainy weather in June and July reduced the crop size, drought in August and a beautiful sunny September brought the rest of the grapes to full maturity. Jaboulet´s vineyards Bessard and Le Meal only yielded one-fourth of their normal crop size – around one tonne per acre, but magnificently intense and concentrated grapes were born.

The bottle was in good condition, ullage was 2 cm. Very dark and youthful looking colour. A sound and wide-open nose of leather and truffles. Decanted 3 hours before serving. Very rich in flavour possessing an astonishing complexity and weight. Perfect harmony and balance now. Still quite a masculine and vigorous wine – will probably last eternally. Impressive length. We were so fortunate to taste this remarkable wine again – all the bottles have been real treasures.

100 p | *1870 Château Lafite-Rothschild* (Pauillac)

2001/2010 x **6** | D 15 min / G 2 h

Our friend had acquired this 1870 Lafite in 1979 at an auction for about £900. It was one of the 41 famous magnums that had laid untouched in the cellars of Glamis Castle for nearly a decade. The wine had in its time been bottled in Scotland by Coningham and had come to public sale for the first time at the Christie's auction of June 24th 1971. The selling price was then £83.

Good top-shoulder level. Decanted only 15 minutes. Our notes were: this Lafite must have been nearly black when it was born, since it still was deep, dark red. Nose was most intoxicating – spicy, pure and strongly seductive. A soft tannin was still present, well balanced with sensations of berries and fruits. A very pleasant, majestic and deeply multi-dimensional wine. The aftertaste lasted until the next morning – and it still lingers in our memories.

Though it reportedly takes more than 50 years for a wine to become drinkable, it was worth the wait at least on this occasion. We are no longer amazed at all those harsh statements that this wine and vintage received in the early 20th century. But we wonder what a truly magnificent wine Lafite must have been in the middle of the last century, for it is still one of the very best wines we have encountered – even at the age of 130!

100 p | *1921 Château Cheval Blanc* (St.Emilion)

2007/2015 x **17** | D 30 min / G 2 h

This is the vintage with which Cheval Blanc made its reputation. Château-bottled, excellent condition with base neck level. Decanted only for 30 minutes (we simply could not wait any longer). A very dark but bright colour with some amber on the rim. Huge, immensely rich nose – opened immediately with lots of exotic fruit aromas, together with chocolate and coffee notes. An unbelievably rich and complex wine. Very thick, warm and multi-layered with sweet fruit and soft, melted tannins that follow all the way through. It was even better

NUMBER 8.

NUMBER 9.

NUMBER 10.

1 · 2 · 3 · 4 · 5 · 6 · 7 · **8** · **9** · **10** · 11 · 12 · 13 · 14 · 15 · 16 · 17 · 18 · 19 · 20

than the first tasting we had from a château-bottling magnum nine years previously. Heavier, richer and a more luscious wine than back then, and even that time we thought it was a masterpiece. The most recent encounter – another château-bottled magnum - was even superior to the previous ones. It was more youthful, richer and had millions of layers – unbelievable. What a privileged job we have!

100 p | *1811 Château d'Yquem* (Sauternes)   2001/2010 x **13** | D 30 min / G 1 h

A wonderful old bottle with top-shoulder level, seemingly in good condition. Re-corked at the château in 1971. Decanted for 15 minutes, it retained its best characteristics for one hour after opening. Surprisingly bright golden colour. Rich, full, elegantly flirtatious nose combining apricots, figs, nuts, and sultanas. Honeyed, velvety and lively, multi-dimensional wine that left a fantastically smooth and long aftertaste. The balanced and fresh, fruity character made us almost speechless. No amount of superlatives can do justice to this incomparable experience. An emotionally moving wine that needs to be sipped very sensitively and slowly. A noble and unique experience.

100 p | *1963 Nacional Vintage Port Quinta do Noval* (Portugal)
2007/2020 x **5** | D 6 h / G 4 h

Quinta do Noval made its reputation with the 1931 Nacional – arguably the most sensational port of the 20th century and certainly the most expensive. Almost as legendary as the 1931 is the 1963 Quinta do Noval Nacional. Vasconcelos Porto, who ran the company for nearly three decades, retired in 1963. He was responsible for the extensive programme of innovation that transformed the narrow old terraces into the wide white-washed ones seen today, allowing better use of space and improved exposure to the sun.

His grandsons, Fernando and Luiz van Zeller, took over the company in 1963. Another extensive programme of modernisation was embarked upon, including new vinification equipment, new vine plantations, and increasing the share of bottlings in Vila Nova de Gaia. In 1963 only some 15% of Noval ports were bottled there. Fifteen years later the figure was 85%.

1963 began with a cold winter heavy in rain and snow. The weather began to dry at the end of April. It was cold and at times rainy until the middle of June. Then July and August took over bringing fine and very dry weather. In September there was again some rain, and after the 10th of September fine weather returned for the harvest.

These two bottles were both in a decent condition. One with label, one without. These precious bottles were brought from England. Decanted for two hours. A very deep, youthful colour. Extremely rich and enormously intense on the nose, starting to open after one hour's decanting. Superbly full-bodied, with a great concentration of black cherry, chocolate and truffle flavours. A very powerful and complex wine, but at the same time one of the most sensuous port wines we have ever tasted – A one-of-a-kind combination of pure magic. A gentle giant of a wine.

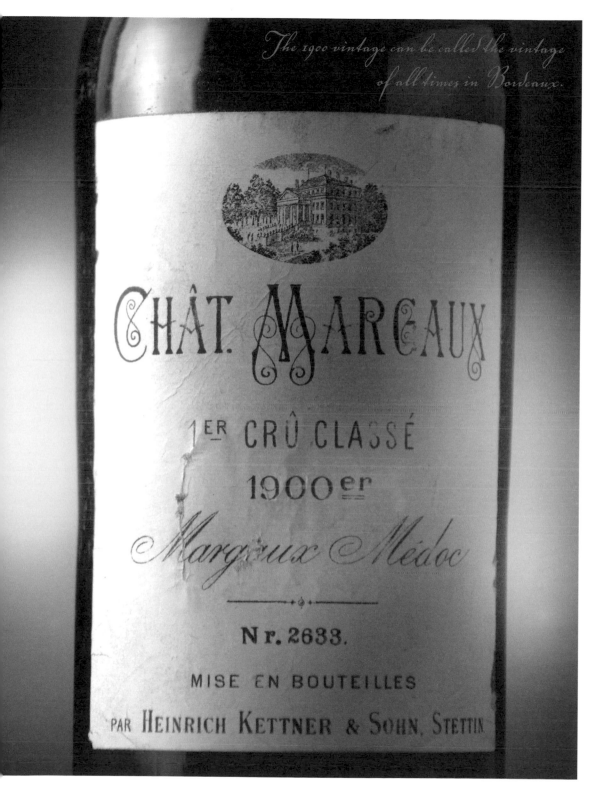

CHÂT. MARCAUX

1ER CRÛ CLASSÉ

1900er

Margaux Médoc

N r. 2633.

MISE EN BOUTEILLES

PAR HEINRICH KETTNER & SOHN, STETTIN.

1961

PETRVS

POMEROL

Grand Vin

Mme EDMOND LOUBAT
PROPRIÉTAIRE à POMEROL.GIRONDE

MIS EN BOUTEILLES AU CHATEAU

The taste has ex-
tremely broad mouth-
feel with elegant qual-
ity, acidity, supple
mellow tannins and
ripe dark fruit aromas.

100 p | *1990 La Tâche Domaine de la Romanée-Conti* (Côte de Nuits)

2006/2025 x 9 | D 4 h / G 2 h

We have only tasted this queen of all wines nine times. But those precious times have been impressive enough to confirm to us that this great La Tâche is also one of the most remarkable wines that Domaine de la Romanée-Conti has ever produced. Time will eventually tell. A beautiful bottle that appears brand new. After two hours' decanting the nose is still closed requiring a few more hours in the glass before it begins to show its whole array of qualities. When it is truly open, the bouquet is one of the most sensational ever. A gorgeously ripe and fragrant nose of dark cherries, raspberries, liquorice, and oriental spices. A full, plump and highly concentrated wine. After five hours it does not show any signs of hardness or tiring fruit. A perfectly balanced and well-structured unity with an absolutely fantastic, and pure, sweet finish. A youthful masterpiece, which might one day find itself on the top of our list.

100 p | *1961 Château Pétrus* (Pomerol)

2007/2020 x 19 | D2h/G2h

Almost every time we have tasted this wine it has left us speechless. On some occasions the wine has been restrained and introvert in style, leaving us quietly wondering whether it is such a great wine at all. On the majority of the times there has been no room for such suspicion, since the wine has been stunningly magnificent. It is a matter of great bottle variation depending mainly on who was the bottler!

Regardless of bottle variation one thing is sure; this wine is a true homage to one of the greatest ladies in the history of Bordeaux – Madame Edmonde Loubat. She became a shareholder of Château Pétrus in 1925. After progressively buying out the shares from the Societé Civile du Château Pétrus, she became the sole proprietor of Pétrus in 1945. By the time of her death in 1961, she had created a status for Pétrus as the Pomerol's most desirable wine.

Our best experience of the 1961 Pétrus was just recently in May 2007 when it was able to reveal its true magnitude. The Pétrus was tasted together with a collection of legends: Cheval Blanc 1947, Lafleur 1947, Romanée-Conti 1943, Mouton-Rothschild 1945, Margaux 1961 and Pétrus 1955. It stood out from its rivals with its incredible power and elegance. A clear, moderately intense, brick red colour. A stunningly pronounced nose, which expanded in the glass. Complex aromas of cigar, cedar wood, smoke, dark chocolate, black berries, teak, and black olives. Such a youthful nose for its age. The taste has an extremely broad mouth-feel with elegant lively acidity, supple mellow tannins and ripe dark fruit aromas. A savoury finish with immense richness. A silky wine with an amazingly youthful style. This wine has scored a full 100 points nine times since we first tasted it in 1989.

100 p | 1928 *Krug Collection Champagne Krug* (Champagne)

2004/2010 x **3** | D 30 min / G 15 min

In 1920´s, Krug Vintage's main market was the UK. There was a practice for the leading wine merchants to reserve their allocation of Krug Vintage, and pay for it, at an early stage, i.e. shortly after bottling and long before shipment – a practice somewhat similar to the en primeur-purchases in Bordeaux. Therefore the 1928 was purchased by the English wine trade in the terrible era of the 1929 recession and the ensueing years building up to the war. However, the combination of the high expectation from experts for this extraordinary vintage, the reputation of Krug, and the limited availability of Krug 1928 aggravated by the absence of good vintages in the early '30s, gave Krug 1928 its great commercial success.

When the war broke out in 1939 Krug still had some significant UK paid reserves kept in cellars, and Joseph Krug wisely decided to buy them back personally to save them from German requisitions. At the end of the war he re-offered what he had saved to the original purchasers, but some of them did not want to take up their full reserve and asked for a substitution, in full or part, with a younger vintage (1937). So he kept for himself whatever was "left over" (what a strange word for Krug!), and this explains why we have been able to taste and follow the extraordinary developments of this stunning wine!

An excellent-looking bottle straight out of the Krug cellars. Not decanted. A clear golden colour. Surprisingly fresh on the nose. Very much alive and looking much younger than expected. Superb concentration, very profound. Gentle, fresh and fleshy wine. There is great personality here. Held up brilliantly, and improved continuously in the glass. This must be the best champagne ever made.

100 p | 1962 *La Tâche Domaine de la Romanée-Conti* (Côte de Nuits)

2005/2015 x **4** | D 2 h / G 2 h

The greatest obstacle of the 1962 vintage has been its role as a successor to the incomparable 1961. On the other hand, the lack of fame has hidden many splendid wines from the general public. This monumental La Tâche was acquired directly from the domain in 1991. It still looked like it was bottled yesterday. The wine proved worthy of its reputation. A splendid, perfect balance between fruit and acidity, which is typical to this vintage. An intense and abundant taste with chocolate and leather, and a full, pleasantly heavy nature. A genuinely elegant and long aftertaste. Truly a great wine.

100 p | *1945 Château Haut-Brion* (Graves)   2006/2010 x **17** | D 2 h / G 4 h

The 1945 vintage produced some of the most memorable Bordeaux. The climate conditions were among the last century's best. The 1945 vintage commands also some of the top prices at auctions, as high as 4,800 € for Pétrus. Most of the first growths sell at around 3,000 € per bottle. Even smaller châteaux such as Pichon-Baron, La Gaffelière, L'Église-Clinet and Cantenac-Brown go easily for 300 € to 500 €.

This legendary Haut-Brion is truly classic Bordeaux that epitomizes complexity. Excellent-looking bottle. Decanted for one and a half hours. Superbly integrated aromas of sweet black fruits, roasted herbs, tobacco, chocolate, and walnuts make it memorable. Its lively, firm texture keeps it fresh to drink. Full-bodied with enormous concentration, masses of fruit perfectly balanced. Tannins are fully integrated and softened. A remarkable taste experience from the start to the solid, smooth finish. This wine has about all one can ask for from a wine of this age.

100 p | *1985 Romanée-Conti Domaine de la Romanée-Conti* (Côte de Nuits)

2004/now x **3** | D 3 h / G 2 h

One of the coldest Januaries in the history of Burgundy was followed by a snowy February. These circumstances ensured the dormancy of the vines, helping them to avoid the early budding risks of spring frosts. Although flowering was delayed, summer arrived free of trouble and the growth cycle got started. One could say that August really made the vintage. A heat wave with constant sunshine and drought concentrated and ripened the grapes extensively. The harvest had already begun at Romanée-Conti on the first day of September.

Excellent-looking bottle. Decanted for three hours. Lovely bright garnet colour. The nose reveals sound and open aromas of violet, cinnamon and blackberry with some toasty new oak nuances. This wine has innumerable layers of graceful yet fully ripe fruit, creating a harmonious interaction of already quite soft tannins and fresh acidity. Excessive weight and extension in the mouth. There is a remarkable balance between all the elements, followed by one of the longest sweet, silky finishes we have ever tasted. This unforgettable Romanée-Conti is already very drinkable, and will easily last through 2020 given suitable cellar conditions.

100 p | *1989 Château Pétrus* (Pomerol)   2006/2040 x **22** | D 3 h / G 4 h

While being an excellent vintage, this year had many challenges. The vines were very much rushing their growth cycle. After April the growth was already three weeks ahead of normal. Early flowering occurred in very favourable conditions and guaranteed a large crop. The summer turned out to be the hottest since 1949. The harvest started already at the end of August, being the earliest harvest since 1893. The hot weather caused some problems in reaching the optimum physiological ripeness. Simultaneously, when the acidity levels started to decline, the sugar levels skyrocketed. This was a more common problem on right bank. Nevertheless, Pétrus turned out to be a success with its edgy austere character.

An opaque, intense ruby colour. Very intense, ripe dark berry nose with spice, truffle and floral tones. Rich medium-bodied palate shows very ripe dark fruit character, moderate acidity and chocolate tones with mineral spiciness. Powerful tannic structure takes a hold on a long concentrated finish. An immense concentration and a great balance guarantees that this still youthful wine benefits from further ageing for ten years or more.

100 p | *1819 Château d'Yquem (Sauternes)*   2004/now x **2** | D 10 min / G 2 h

Decanted for ten minutes. Retained its best characteristics for two hours after opening. Outward condition as expected from a wine of this age. Wine level low mid-shoulder. An old, dusty bottle. Label worn beyond recognition, but the capsule was in good condition and the original cork showed the vintage. Dark, fully mature golden colour. A completely open, clean and rich nose with hints of honey, apricot and peach. A real charmer. A full, creamy, complex wine with indefinite length and depth. An extremely enchanting wine.

100 p | *1947 Château Lafleur (Pomerol)*   2007/2020 x **16** | D 1 h / G 3 h

This picturesque estate produces around 18,000 bottles per year, which is less than half of what its famous neighbour Château Pétrus does. The tiny production and great demand have made Lafleur wines hard to find. When it comes to this legendary wine from a superb vintage, it is almost impossible to acquire. A peculiar thing with Lafleur is that the owners, the Robin family, have been producing this outstanding wine in very primitive conditions – in a barn with poultry and rabbits. This was changed only in 1984 when the barn was dedicated solely to wine production by Marie Robin's cousins, the Guinaudeaus, who took over the estate.

Château bottled with high-shoulder level. Decanted one hour. A moderately deep brick red colour with some cloudiness. Intense youthful nose of ripe red berries dominate the wine: cherries and brambles alongside raisins and floral tones. After a while, more aromas are creeping out: spices, meaty nuances and tar – mainly secondary and tertiary aromas. The full-bodied wine has crisp acidity and loads of dark fruits, cherries and wild strawberries. Tannins are powdery but elegant. The finish of the wine is very fresh and long with a mouth-watering effect. An astonishing satin-like texture!

100 p | *1945 Château d'Yquem (Sauternes)*   2001/2030 x **7** | D 4 h / G 3 h

In 1945 the Sauternes wine area was tormented by a severe cold spell that continued until late spring. In April the weather warmed up rapidly and the short spring that followed was warm and dry. The first vines bloomed at Yquem as early as May 15th (as in 1990). The particularly dry and hot summer months kept this advantage of early growth presaging an early harvest. The dryness of the year is well exemplified by the minimal September rainfall of 13 mm (average at Yquem being 72 mm).

The harvest could now commence on September 10th, and it continued uninterrupted for the next six weeks. However, the Sundays would exceptionally be kept as rest days due to the perfect harvest weather. When the harvest was completed, there were 440 casks of new wine in the cool cellars of Yquem.

Decanted for one hour. Retained its best characteristics for five hours after opening. Bottle outwardly as new. Wine level by the neck. The wine is temptingly golden. A charmingly open, mature and full nose. Still an attractively sweet, lively and multi-layered wine. A soft creamy texture. Excellent balance and a refined aftertaste. A perfect Yquem from a magnificent vintage.

100 p | *1959 Château Mouton-Rothschild* (Pauillac)　2007/2020 x **35** | D 2 h / G 2 h

When the Bordeaux 1959 vintage came into the market, some critics predicted the wines would not age in a good way because of their low acidity and high alcohol. But excellent years such as 1947, 1945 and 1928 were all characterised by low acidity and high alcohol. All of these vintages are still generous to drink, as is this marvellous Mouton.

Excellent appearance, level in the neck. This was, as expected, a gorgeous and approachable wine. At first it appeared quite closed and blank, but after a half an hour it had a sound sensual nose, and became rich and intense. It's all there, and it is graceful and exciting. This is one of those rare "feet off the ground" wines, with an unbelievable presence. When people talk about great claret, this is what they are talking about.

99 p | *1923 Romanée-Conti Domaine de la Romanée-Conti* (Côte de Nuits)

2007/now x **7** | D 30 min / G 45 min

In excellent condition, a rare bottling by Van der Meulen of Belgium. Decanted for 15 minutes, held on to its best qualities in glass for 45 minutes. The Belgian wine merchant Van der Meulen was one of the most renowned and trustworthy wine wholesalers in the first half of the 20th century. All the wine that was sold through them was also bottled by them. They were particularly known for their habit of choosing only the best vintages from the most notable producers. Each lot was tasted barrel by barrel, and only the best ones were chosen. The most famous wines bottled by Van der Meulen were Cheval Blanc 1947, Pétrus 1947 and Yquem 1921.

The vintage 1923 was difficult at the beginning, since the humidity and cold caused retarded flowering. The result was beneficial with uneven fruit set guaranteeing limited yield. The favourable weather during the summer was followed by a partly rainy autumn. Luckily northern winds dried the vineyards and the harvest was finished by the end of September and the beginning of October, turning this into an exceptional vintage producing very complex wines.

The level of this Romanée-Conti was top-notch and the colour was a very dark, beautifully translucent red. The bouquet expressed something so magical, overwhelming with chocolate and coffee and warmth, that it would have melted any heart. Simply one of the most intoxicating aromas ever. The threshold to taste it grew almost too high to overcome. A very roasty, delicate, gentle, and really multilayered and sophisticated wine. As a whole, still almost perfect, but this was at its peak about 20 years ago. The aftertaste was smooth, stylishly seductive. A sensitive experience.

99 p | 1891 Brunello di Montalcino Riserva Biondi-Santi (Tuscany)

2000/now x 2 | **D 15 min / G 1 h**

We found this very dusty and old-looking bottle in a long forgotten cellar in Scotland. According to old cellar books, the seller's father bought it in 1952 along with two bottles of 1888 vintage, which they had consumed with pleasure decades ago.

The level was only mid-shoulder, but it had a promising bright colour and was recorked in 1958. Decanted 15 minutes before tasting. Dark, healthy and even youthful colour. An exquisite, gentle and elegant nose with sherry and caramel flavours. Good weight and concentration. It has a Burgundy-like sweetness, and very soft, delicate tannins. A surprisingly well-balanced and vigorous wine. A bit dry on the palate, but has a fruity and classy, long finish. 1891 Biondi-Santi is just an amazing effort. One of the greatest Italian wines we have ever experienced.

99 p | 1961 Cristal Rosé Roederer (Champagne)   2005/2010 x 3 | D 15 min / G 20 min

The 1961 was a magnificent vintage in most regions of France. Champagne had challenges in the early part of the growing season, but eventually ripening proceeded well and yielded some remarkable wines in below average yields but with attractive richness and structured acidity. This vintage is usually awarded 4 stars in Champagne. The best champagnes of this vintage are very enjoyable today with fine bubbles still alive in these fully mature wines.

Champagne was very different from today in 1961. Surface area under production was 12,033 ha compared to 31,924 ha in 2005. Average grape prices were in the range of 2,90 FrF whereas they were 4,60 € in 2005. Therefore, if one manages to find some well cellared bottles there will be some great deals to be made. Cristal Rosé was one of the most successful and rare champagnes of the year, sheer perfection to our senses.

Excellent bottle with good level. A glossy medium-deep golden colour with a delicate orange tinge. An extremely vinous nose of dried fruits, brioche and nuts. A very light sparkle remains in the wine, but this champagne has such a great structure and texture that one does not miss the sensation of bubbles. A fine acid structure refreshes this lively and rich wine. A refined and velvety mouth-feel with a full-body and a long harmonious finish. A monumental example of champagne's capabilities.

99 p | 1985 La Tâche Domaine de la Romanée-Conti (Côte de Nuits)

2006/2020 x 4 | **D 2 h / G 2 h**

The 1985 was one of the first vintages when the young, dynamic and talented winemaker Hervé de Ferrer was responsible for the entire production at DRC (André Noblet passed away the same year). The harvesting started exceptionally late – on October 6th – at DRC. This was a whole week later than the region's average. This courageous decision proved to be a successful one for the young winemaker. A fantastically stylish and multi-dimensional accomplishment.

The bottle was in fine condition, the level being 2 cm. Decanted for two hours, this deep ruby-red, full-bodied wine is so well balanced that it is difficult to find any imperfection in it whatsoever. A powerful, explosive nose: herbaceous and earthy with ripe black cherry and smoky aromas and a sweet menthol-like edge. This is a big mouthful, a giant of a wine. About as deep and complex as any burgundy we have ever experienced. The flavours are concentrated and expansive. A sweet and silky aftertaste. Aging gracefully, and drinking well now.

99 p | *1989 Château La Mission-Haut-Brion* (Graves)

2006/2035 x **17** | D 4 h / G 3 h

La Mission Haut-Brion estate and its neighbouring Haut-Brion estate are owned by the Dillon family and the wines of both estates have been vinified by the same man, Jean Delmas. However, the wines stand out as being very different. The wines from La Mission are generally speaking more powerful and show more up-front concentrated fruit and tannins than Haut-Brion.

Very deep, ruby red colour with brown tints. Less closed than Haut-Brion from the same vintage. Up-front fruit of ripe cassis and capsicum, floral aromas and hints of butterscotch and toasty spiciness. Concentrated medium-bodied palate with fresh acidity and minerals, firm tannins and intense fruit – all in harmonious balance. The flavours are dominated by toasty and spicy aromas with hints of tobacco and cigar. Long, elegant and discreet finish. A silky wine with very refined and classic style. Still great potential there, and the wine has not even reached its peak yet.

99 p | *1907 Champagne Goût American Heidsieck & Monopole* (Champagne)

2005/now x **3** | D 15 h / G 20 min

In the early hours of November 3rd 1916, off the coast of Finland, the Jönköping, a small Swedish wooden schooner, was stopped by the German submarine U-22. She was carrying 3,000 bottles of champagne, 10,000 gallons of cognac and 17 barrels of burgundy wine, as well as steel products in her hold. Because of the steel products, the commander of the U-22 decided to sink her instantly, but saved the lives of the crew. The vessel went down in less than an hour, remaining untouched at the bottom of the Baltic Sea for more than 80 years.

In early 1997 the wreck was found by a Swedish search team at a depth of 64 meters. The water temperature in the Baltic Sea, hovering around four degrees Celsius, the total darkness and the water pressure at 64 meters had combined to preserve these bottles in immaculate condition for 82 years.

An astonishing, very old looking bottle. Excellent level; decanted only five minutes before tasting. Pale and light, almost youthful colour. Still has some sparkle left. A sweet, fruity, and fresh nose dominated by honey and exotic fruit and raisins. Full and one of the richest champagnes we have ever tasted. It has an amazingly good balance and structure. Not too sweet, even though the Heidsieck Goût American style had a relatively high dosage. Surprisingly long and pleasing wine, which moved smoothly and easily down our throats, leaving a most memorable and historic aftertaste.

99 p | 1990 Romanée-Conti Domaine de la Romanée-Conti *(Côte de Nuits)*

2004/2030 x 6 | D 2 h / G 2 h

This picturesque parcel of La Romanée-Conti was blessed, within the whole of Burgundy, an astonishing vintage. Although the vignerons were hoping for the best, they feared the worst when the vintage faced the unexpectedly warm winter with over 20 degrees Celsius in February and March, encouraging the vegetative growth of the vines. The fears of the vignerons came true when cool and rainy weather took place from April to June delaying the flowering. The fruit set was very uneven, reducing the crop size. Then came the hot summer bringing hope back to vignerons until the long dry season threatened the vines with drought. The early ripening saved the crop and the super concentrated grapes concluded an exceptional vintage. Interestingly enough for La Romanée-Conti, this vintage was not only top vintage for quality but also a record one in terms of quantity for two decades. There were 7,446 bottles made.

Excellent-looking bottle. Decanted for two hours. Deep purple colour, with orange and ruby reflections. Even after two hours' decanting, the wine was slightly closed on the nose, however with some swirling, and little bit of patience everything opened up and blossomed into the most multifaceted and intense bouquet one could long for. Enormous structure but in such a fine balance that despite its substance, the wine shows great elegance and class. On the palate it was marvellously sweet and tasty with plum, strawberry and cherry aromas and flavours that linger indefinitely. This full-bodied and intense wine can be thought of as nothing but a masterpiece.

99 p | 1953 Château Lafite-Rothschild *(Pauillac)*   2007/2020 x 24 | D 2 h / G 1 h

Since Lafite is highly elegant and less massive than most other premier-cru wines, it is also most open to variations in quality, especially in weak years. Particularly from the 1960s until 1975 its quality was often not equal to other premier cru wines. But from the year 1975 on its wines have lived up to their reputation. "The Perfection of Elegance" is a definition many critics connect with Lafite, and this celebrated 1953 Lafite justified this description convincingly.

A perfect looking bottle and the level was by the neck. Decanted for two hours. Attractive, mature brick-red colour. Sound and open bouquet with a hint of mint and sweetness. A soft and pleasing, mouth-filling wine. Incredible elegance and a feminine, classic Lafite with great depth and fragrant finish. Sensitive and multilayered, lingering experience. Tasted 24 times in the last seven years with very variable notes. This vintage shows large bottle variations. At Lafite they needed almost a year to bottle every cask. The best bottles were perfect, but more than a few were already quite one-dimensional and dry. But with a little bit of luck this exquisite Lafite is the best Lafite you will ever taste – a marvellous wine.

99 p | 1959 La Tâche Domaine de la Romanée-Conti (Côte de Nuits)

2000/2020 x 8 | D 1 h / G 1 h

The best burgundies of this vintage, which was one of last century´s finest, are rich and multilayered, so great hopes were set on this particular wine, maybe the most famous of its region.

Both the bottle and the wine seemed to be in perfect condition. Decanted for two hours. Oriental spices, truffles and sweet fruitiness could be sensed in the bouquet. A fascinatingly seductive combination. A very youthful, rich, soft, pure, and elegant wine. Considerably more vital than the colour would have led us to expect. A balanced acidity and intuse fruitiness, long and pampering aftertaste. A gentle but most impressive acquaintance.

99 p | 1945 Château La Mission-Haut-Brion (Graves)

2000/2015 x 19 | D 2 h / G 1 h

On May 2nd in 1945 there was snow in Bordeaux causing a dramatic frost, which destroyed 80% of the crop. The very hot and dry summer produced extremely concentrated grapes. Harvesting began at Château La Mission-Haut-Brion on September 13th and ended on September 23rd.

Decanted for one hour. Good level, bottom-neck. Promising appearance. Deep and dark, mature colour, but surprisingly modest and closed nose. The wine opened up and improved a lot after one hour in the glass. As powerful, big and intense as anticipated. Well-balanced, seamless complexity and intensity. This bottle was close to perfect, and positively worthy of its reputation and very high expectations. Lovely wine that stands out with its great abundance and intense fruit. An impressive experience.

99 p | 1921 Château Pétrus (Pomerol)

2005/2015 x 15 | D 30 min / G 1 h

In its early days – that is to say up until 1947 – this was without a doubt the best Pétrus ever made. We have tasted this rarity quite a few times. The first encounter was from a ´rare´ double magnum, which was unfortunately fake. The others have been château-labelled normal size bottles.

Good looking bottle with château label and capsule. Level was top-shoulder. Decanted only for 25 minutes. Astonishingly dark colour, still practically black in the core. On the nose full, rich with loads of spice and tobacco, over ripe, fat fruit. A seductively deep, chocolate-like sweet fruitiness. On the palate this has a fantastically sweet and well-structured old-vine intensity of flavour. Great depth. Quite big and powerful, yet there is finesse in the form of silky texture, elegant acidity and soft tannins. An absolutely outstanding long and multi-dimensional finish. One of the best Pomerols ever made.

NUMBER 32.

NUMBER 33.

NUMBER 34.

99 p | *1985 Sassicaia Tenuta San Guido* (Tuscany)   2006/2020 x **8** | D 1.5 h / G 2.5 h

The best vintage of the 1980s in Tuscany was by far the 1985. And the best wine of that year in Italy was Sassicaia. This vintage is in a different league from any other Sassicaia ever made, even the legendary 1972. Moderately intense, ruby red colour. Very open and complex nose full of violets, ripe blackcurrants, dark chocolate, cedar wood, spices, and tobacco. Rich medium-bodied palate shows fresh acidity and intense sweet dark fruit alongside ripe velvety tannins. The taste is very concentrated, savoury and long-lasting. A really elegant wine with enough energy to hold well for years or even decades.

99 p | *1982 Château Latour* (Pauillac)   2006/2040 x **17** | D 4 h / G 2 h

A legend of a vintage that is starting to drink very well now. Hot and stormy weather in May and June favoured vegetation and advanced ripening. June and August were magnificent, yielding exceptional phenolic ripeness and high sugar content. The 1982 Latour has it all.

Deep and dark developing red colour. The nose is expressive and rich, filled with blackcurrants, cigar box and oriental spicy notes. Full body and impressive weight. Mouth-feel is structured due to firm but extremely ripe tannic backbone. Refreshing acidity balances the concentrated and thick wine. Long lingering length with well-integrated oak nuances. This wine is still clearly in a phase of constant improvement, opening up with time and showing new layers and angles each time tasted.

99 p | *1978 La Tâche Domaine de la Romanée-Conti* (Côte de Nuits)

2007/2020 x **6** | D 1 h / G 1 h

Another super vintage that had first a cold spring and beginning of summer, which retarded the flowering and overall vegetative growth. Due to this the crop was left relatively small. In the latter part of August, sunny weather finally arrived and lasted until the very end of harvesting, thereby guaranteeing perfect extraction. A high level of tannins and concentration of the grapes. The vintage of the decade.

Fine looking La Tâche. Level was 2 cm. Decanted for one and a half hours. Light dark colour with a tight orange rim. Amazingly youthful nose with aromas of sweet cherries, violets, leather, and spice. Very expansive and feminine wine with flavours of candied cherries, raspberries and liquorice on the palate. This full-bodied wine has a wonderful balance between all the elements. A finely tuned red wine of finesse, superb structure and long, supple finish.

This magnum bottle contained a *special label made for the wedding of Prince Charles and Princess Diana on the 29th of June 1981.*

MOËT et CHANDON à Epernay
Established 1743

Specially shipped to honour
the marriage of
His Royal Highness The Prince of Wales
and Lady Diana Spencer
29 July 1981
Champagne
Cuvée Dom Pérignon
Vintage 1961
Disgorged
1981

PRODUCE OF FRANCE

99 p | *1974 Martha's Vineyard Cabernet Sauvignon Heitz* (Napa Valley)

2004/2010 x **16** | D 1 h / G 3 h

1974 was to California what 1961 was to Bordeaux. A great vintage all over, but the real star and probably the most legendary of all American wines is none other than Martha's Vineyard. It is to us like a caricature of the incredible Mouton 1945. Great eucalyptus nose, fantastically extravagant fruit and so much class. A truly great wine! Brilliant looking bottle with a beautiful, artistic label.

Decanted one hour. Dark brick red with slight signs of oxidation in the colour. Open, clean and wonderful nose of cedar, eucalyptus and mild red fruits. The palate is very attractive and fat-textured, showing soft, lush tobacco, coffee and cedar notes and just enough acidity to provide a charming balance. Seems astonishingly Bordeaux-like. Indeed, very well balanced with near-perfect structure. Very smooth and polished with extremely fine tannins. Exquisite, long and lingering finish. Breathtaking and surely destined for legendary status.

99 p | *1969 Vieilles Vignes Françaises Bollinger* (Champagne)

2004/2010 x **4** | D 15 min / G 30

We tasted this 'living museum' champagne for the first time in the late 1990s, when we had a vertical tasting of Vieilles Vignes Françaises. From those eight vintages – 1969, 1970, 1973, 1975, 1980, 1982, 1985, and 1988 – this 1969 was anything but a 'museum wine' with exceptional freshness and a charming sparkle.

Our notes were then: This rare and historical bottle was in excellent condition. Decanted for 30 minutes. It had a dark, deep, mature golden colour with small streams of slowly rising bubbles. The nose opened into one of the widest champagne bouquets ever encountered, being almost too irresistible. This appeared more like a finest red burgundy. It was mouth-filling, fat and elegant. It has something superfluous, which could not be expressed with any other words than "Vieilles Vignes Françaises". It has the velvetiness of a Cristal, the body of a great Krug and the ripeness and acidity of a Bollinger with a rich and never-ending finish.

99 p | *1966 Montrachet Domaine de la Romanée-Conti* (Côte de Nuits)

2001/2020 x **5** | D 1 h / G 2 h

It was in 1963 when Henri de Villaine's business partner Henri Leroy persuaded him to buy a plot of land of 0,342 ha in the 'new world' for him. This 'new world' was on the other side of the Beaune in the Chassagne-Montrachet district. This plot was located in the highly esteemed Le Montrachet vineyard. Having only made red grand cru so far, this opened a new fascinating world of white wines to Henri de Villaine. Encouraged by the potential, Leroy and de Villaine acquired a second plot of 0,171 ha already in 1965.

In the following growing season of 1966, both men were slightly worried after a difficult beginning. First they had spring hail and then a very poor start for the summer. Nevertheless, the growing conditions improved, and the harvest was carried out in very good conditions.

All three bottles we opened were faultless. Decanted for one hour. A youthful light, golden colour. This is a fantastically vibrant wine. Wide and open nose of lemon, toast and butter layered over exotic fruit and truffles along with a layer of honey and spice. Astonishing concentration and length, giving this wine a strong presence. The wine's viscosity and extract level are unbelievably high. Beautiful to drink now, it should last for a decade or more. Perfectly balanced and structured with one of the longest and purest finishes one has ever experienced.

99 p | *1961 Dom Pérignon Moët et Chandon* (Champagne)

2007/now x **45** | D 30 min / 2 h

This vintage of Dom Pérignon has been tasted several times but this particular bottle was something much more than just a regular one. This magnum bottle contained a special label made for the wedding of Prince Charles and Princess Diana on the 19th of June 1981. These bottles were disgorged late in 1981, carrying more autolysis characters than regular Dom Pérignons of this year.

Bright golden yellow colour with energetic fine bubbles. Very rich nose of milk chocolate, roasted coffee beans and bready tones. Dry, crisp acidity with light-bodied style and vibrant rich mousse. Extremely refined, elegant and opulent wine with toastiness, butterscotch and dried fruit, such as date flavours. Mineral lemony bite at the long finish. A very youthful wine still.

99 p | *1949 Château Mouton-Rothschild* (Pauillac) 2006/2020 x 25 | D 2 h / G 4 h

1949 was the hottest summer ever recorded in Bordeaux. We have always considered the 1949 to combine the structure of 1945 and the richness of 1947. Mouton is the star of the vintage and to us (and Baron Philippe Rothschild), one of the greatest of all Moutons. A lovely wine, eucalyptus on the nose, great fruit and a heavenly balance. This is Jan-Erik Paulson´s "desert island wine". Like him, it is starting to show some age, so do not decant this sensitive wine too early.

The capsule and cork were in excellent condition, but the level was this time only mid-shoulder. Decanted for two hours. The colour was very promising, so we were in quite an optimistic mood. Instantly after opening, the bouquet opened up and was very expansive and complex. From the first sip to the last, this was an absolutely fabulous and grand wine. It has huge, soft and enjoyable tannins with good, jammy fruit beneath. A well-balanced and multi-faceted wine, however, with a slightly high acidity level. At its peak in normal size bottles, but could easily last another five to ten years in magnums. A serious and an intellectually pleasing experience, even from a mid-shoulder bottle!

NUMBER 41.

NUMBER 42.

99 p | 1947 Château L´Evangile (Pomerol)   2004/2020 x 7 | D 1 h / G 1 h

Robert Parker JR once wrote: "Wines such as L'Evangile 1947 can bring tears to your eyes!"

What a discerning person and a gifted foreteller he is - right after the first sip of this divine wine some innocent tears came to our eyes - unbelievable but true.

The wine was, and still is, so dark, so full of life and goodness, so rich and complete that it could be called a wine from heaven. A superb, classic, seductive Pomerol nose. A delicate chocolaty and cedary bouquet. Rich and full with loads of ripe fruit. At this stage bigger, darker and more delicious than Cheval and Pétrus of the same vintage. A great bottle. Best L'Evangile we have ever tasted. Perfectly approachable and drinkable now (decant for at least one hour), but will last for another 10 years or more, if well cellared.

99 p | 1959 Château Latour (Pauillac)   2005/2030 x 33 | D 2 h / G 3 h

Excellent bottle. Level was by the neck. Decanted for two hours. This wine was almost black. A strong, dusty, earthy and cellar-like smell took over the whole room - we were sure that the wine was corked and that was the last thing on the wish list. We decanted the wine and gave it two hours to open. When returning to the room all the impurity had disappeared and a ripe, well-opened aroma full of berries had taken over. A complex bouquet with layers of cedar, leather and hovering flower scent. An abundant, truly massive, still quite tannic yet beautifully balanced wine. Maybe a bit dry and rough on the finish, but only giving it a taste of life!

99 p | 1961 Château Palmer (Margaux)   2006/2020 x 22 | D 3 h / G 2 h

Considered to be one of the greatest vintages of the post-war period, 1961 nevertheless got off to a difficult start with two harsh frosts on April 21th and 29th. Most of the Merlot flowers were frozen to death. But after that short period, the weather could not have been better, although the vines suffered from the very hot, dry summer. The harvest took place under a cloudless sky and a small crop of healthy and ripe grapes were collected. Small volumes and high concentration combined to produce wines of truly exceptional quality. Because there was more technical knowledge and human care in fermentation in 1961 than 1928 and 1945, the wines were very attractive and supple from the beginning, in spite of their excessive tannins. These wines were deep in colour, creamy and consistent.

This lovely looking bottle was found in a small wine-shop in Luxembourg. Château-bottled, the level was low-neck. Decanted for one hour. Very deep, dark and promising colour. The nose was incredible: wide open with an odd but seductive mix of chocolate, truffles, blackcurrant, and caramel-scented aromas. Full, rich and sweet wine with soft and well-balanced finish. Not as deep, fat and concentrated as we were hoping but

one of the best bottles of Palmer from the 1961 vintage that we have encountered. This was very enjoyable and almost as good as its legendary reputation would let one wish. This Palmer is excellent to drink now and will last well few more decades, but our earnest advice is - don't wait, don't sell, just be kind to yourself and enjoy it now.

99 p | *1985 Côte-Rotie La Turque Guigal* (Rhône)   2003/2025 x 2 | D 4 h / G 3 h

Guigal produces three single-vineyard wines from Côte-Rotie: La Mouline (Côte Blonde), La Landonne (Côte Brune) and La Turque (Côte Brune). These three single vineyard wines have become the most sought after Rhône wines in the world. Situated on the Côte Brune, La Turque benefits from full southern exposure and from a complex terroir made up of shale and iron oxide. The debut of La Turque in 1985 was suberb. An excellent vintage with quite a small crop. After a flourishing flowering, the summer was hot and dry. Heat continued into late harvest.

Fine looking bottle. Decanted for two hours. Feminine, perfumed, cherry and herb-scented bouquet with gentle toast and a chocolaty depth. Gorgeous layers of fruit. On the palate powerfully spicy, full of black pepper, satiny ripe cassis, and black cherry fruit, with a full-bodied, silky mouth-feel and a very persuasive texture. Already very good, but should be even more splendid in the near future.

99 p | *1986 Montrachet Domaine de la Romanée-Conti* (Côte de Nuits)
2004/2015 | D 2 h / G 3 h

Domaine de la Romanée-Conti makes only one white wine, the Grand Cru Montrachet from Côtes de Beaune. Le Montrachet vineyard is only 0.67 ha in size and produces around 250 cases annually. The 1986 was an excellent vintage for Montrachet. A cold winter was followed by a rainy spring. The weather improved at the beginning of June, when late flowering took place under near-ideal conditions. A hot summer with some showers. Harvest took place under ideal conditions.

Fine looking bottle. Decanted for 1.5 hours. Open, perfumed bouquet with aromas of apple, citrus, fresh bread, and faint vanilla. Soft, creamy honeyed texture. The wine is exceptionally rich in flavour. Very concentrated wine with great depth and complexity. The very fine acidity carries the lace-like texture into an astonishing, long finish. Drinking divinely.

99 p | *1937 Romanée-Conti Domaine de la Romanée-Conti* (Côte de Nuits)
2000/2015 x 12 | D 1 h / G 1 h

The vintage of the decade in Burgundy escorted this beautiful wine to its existence. The warm season starting from the end of the spring and continuing constantly until the end of the summer was followed refreshingly by scattered rain which brought back life to almost shrivelled grapes.

The bottle was in perfect condition. Decanted for one hour. This wine is already so legendary that we would have been disappointed had it not been totally perfect. Eternal - that is the word that first came to mind when tasting it. Eternal as the temples of ancient Rome and Greece, as the wisdoms of the East, as the beauty of Marilyn...a totally captivating DRC. This has everything one can ask for in a wine. The nose was exotic and enchanting. In the mouth it was incomprehensibly well balanced, multi-dimensional, soft, and silky. Enviably noble and unattainably perfect wine - words fail us.

98 p | *1990 Château Pétrus (Pomerol)*   2006/2030 x **12** | D 2 h / G 3 h

The 1990 Pétrus is a classical Pomerol and a perfect example of the best of the 1990 vintage. Excellent magnum with by the neck level. Decanted two hours. It has a vigorous, bright and dense ruby/purple color, still very youthful for its age. There was a delicious purity of fruit and clean lines on the nose. This beautiful Pétrus unfolds to reveal extraordinary richness and complete symmetry in addition to remarkable flavour depth and persistence. The finish lasted more than a minute and, like everything else in this wine, was gentle and finely balanced. Plenty of tannin remains, and the wine displays a wonderful liveliness and youthfulness. Above all this wine shows great elegance rather than power. Already very delicious and drinkable. The 1990 Pétrus will enjoy easily another 20-50 years of life!

98 p | *1929 Château Haut-Brion (Graves)*   2004/2015 x **13** | D 1 h / G 3 h

The 1929 was extremely hot and dry, the driest vintage since the beginning of the century. It only rained for a short period during the harvest, but then the fine and hot weather came back again. The grapes became very concentrated and the wines characterised by an enormous richness of tannin. Wines slow to mature, but with exceptional structure. This bottle came from the small Cannes auction house Besch.

    Level was high-shoulder. Decanted one hour. The colour was very black, dense and full. Intense, complex nose - round and elegant. This wine has lots of muscle left and it's still quite tannic, and certainly has a long life ahead of it, especially in large bottles. Long, velvety and rich on the palate. Hints of truffles and dark chocolate. Absolutely magnificent. Very enjoyable now or over the next decade.

98 p | *1875 Château Mouton-Rothschild (Pauillac)*   2006/now x **3** | D 45 min / G 1 h

Négociant-bottled. Full level upper shoulder. Slightly cloudy, fairly intensive brownish colour. Intensive, delicious nose - roasted, flowery, leathery, and nutty. Intensive, medium-full and vividly acidic wine. Very soft tannins and a ripe, sweet fruit create a velvety mouth-feel. Long, intensive aftertaste. Very balanced, supple and vivid wine, really enjoyable right now and likely to remain good in the bottle for years.

98 p | 1979 *Clos du Mesnil Champagne Krug* (Champagne)

2005/2020 x 3 | D 20 min / G 1 h

The rarest, most desirable Krug Champagne is Clos du Mesnil. This unique Blanc de Blancs is made entirely from Chardonnay grapes grown in a small vineyard in the village of Mesnil-sur-Oger south of Épernay. A stone wall which dates back to 1698 surrounds the 4.6-acre Clos du Mesnil-vineyard.

Clos du Mesnil's first vintage was 1979. The vines yield just enough Chardonnay in good years to make 1,000 cases. This is a very minute production compared with the other prestige champagnes. The 1979 vintage was very good in Champagne region. Warm spring and fine summer. Good maturation. The harvest took place rather late in the season.

Fine looking bottle. Decanted for 20 minutes. Pale and clean yellow colour. A fabulous bottle, full of life, yet elegant, round and mature. Tiny bubbles, lively persistent mousse. Toasty, delicate and complex mineral bouquet. It has an enormous personality and individuality. Exotic taste with candied fruits, strawberry, coffee, honey, and toasty flavours. On the palate the taste is quite dry and vigorous with super rich and long aftertaste, which went on and on.

98 p | 1989 *Château Haut-Brion* (Graves)

2007/2030 x 29 | D 3 h / G 3.5 h

This is one of the greatest left bank wines from this excessively hot vintage in Bordeaux.

Very intense, opaque ruby colour with brown tints. Moderately close at the beginning with but opens up in the glass beautifully. Great depth, rich and complex aromas with very refined toasty oak nuances. A full-bodied wine with refine firm tannins, mellow acidity and opulent fruitiness. The high level of alcohol is well-integrated and adds richness to the wine. Aftertaste is extensively long and edgy. Charmingly sturdy wine with lovely accessibility now but will develop deliciously over a decade still.

98 p | 1982 *Château Pétrus* (Pomerol)

2006/2040 x 7 | D 3 h / G 3.5 h

A milestone vintage and a milestone wine. Early even flowering was followed by hot and dry summer which continued until the harvest in mid September. This time a great heat wave was ripening the grapes astonishingly fast and especially early-ripening Merlot gained loads of must weight. This is well delivered in the wine. Dense ruby colour with brick red tints. Very intense and complex nose with aromas of black berries, cedar, violets and mint. Rich medium-bodied palate with velvety texture. Great ripe powdery tannins showing a great grip with lovely crisp acidity and broad elegant fleshy fruitiness. Great balance and concentration which is highlighted by mineral bite in the savoury long finish. The wine is not near the greatness it will gain within next 30 years, but still it is drinking wonderfully already now.

98 p | *1911 Vintage Pol Roger* (Champagne)   2002/2010 x 2 | D 5 min / G 30 min

1911 is among the most glorious vintages of Champagne. A rare vintage, which sometimes appeared on the most prestigious wine lists in Paris restaurants but which was above all exported to Great Britain and the United States.

Unfortunately only a small amount of the wines got to the market before the war broke out in August 1914. Thus we were very lucky to have the opportunity to serve this famous wine at The Vine Club's first tasting in Helsinki. There were 12 members present, and though they normally would at this point engage in quite lively and loud discussion, they all sat quietly and focused as in tacit agreement with a glassful of very dark golden yellow wine in their hands.

The magical bouquet of Pol Roger, so soft with hints of nuts, had captivated the whole room. Gradually, quiet comments were heard: full-flavoured, remarkably sweet and tender wine, very good length, delicious flavour, fabulous acidity, and last but not least - love at first taste. A deeply seductive champagne to which one might stay true for a lifetime, and which still has many good years ahead!

98 p | *1959 Château Pétrus* (Pomerol)   2006/2020 x 39 | D 2 h / G 2 h

The Pétrus estate is small, only a little more than 11 ha. The château itself is also only a small building that does not attract much attention. This is typical of Pomerol. Whereas the best vineyards in Médoc were owned by the gentry, affluent financiers and influential wine traders who over the centuries expanded their estates and had impressive manors built on them, the Pomerol estates were much smaller and owned by local families who also lived there and tended them. The phenomenal rise of the fame and price of Pétrus' wines is a fairly recent event. In the beginning of the 1960s they were at the same level as the second or third great growths of Médoc. It was the 1982 vintage that accounts for Pétrus' stellar price increase. In spring 1983 it was sold at premier cru prices, but already a year later the price was more than double that of the other wines. At the moment, Pétrus costs approximately four times as much as Mouton or Cheval Blanc.

Very good-looking négociant-bottling. By the neck level. Decanted two hours. Very healthy-looking colour, bright and vivid. At first the nose was quite closed and modest, but after two hours it opened wide and was very concentrated, cedary and rich. Excellent ripe Pétrus: very full, fruity, warm and elegant. Not as powerful as many other 1959s, but has that individual 'Pétrus excitement' to it, giving it extra finesse and refinement. A well-balanced and fantastic structure. Long, rich and fresh - hard to find any fault with this glorious bottle. The best Pétrus 1959 we had ever tasted. (Nine months later, we arranged a full-size Pétrus tasting to twelve people - 15 vintages. The 1959 beat all of the other great vintages. Even the superb 1947, 1948, 1949, 1970, 1971, and 1989 were left behind by this lovely wine.) These Lafite-bottlings have been outstanding by any yardstick.

98 p | *1982 Château Mouton-Rothschild* (Pauillac)   2007/2032 x **7** | D 3 h / G 2 h

1982 is one of the most legendary vintages for wine connoisseurs. It was not only the wine year of the decade in Bordeaux, but also one of the century's best ones together with the vintages 1961, 1945, 1928, and 1900. The sunny and warm weather produced full, fruity and powerful wines throughout Bordeaux.

Gorgeous-looking bottle with level by the neck. Decanted for three hours. A deep, dark and rich colour. Beautifuly developed complex bouquet with a hint of spices, smoked meat and jammy blackcurrants. This is a full-bodied, spicy and fruity wine with ripe but firm tannins. The vividly acidic taste is complemented by a silky mouth-feel. This intense and well-balanced wine finishes with more than a 90-second demonstration of sweet fruit and silky tannin. A great classic, which will last for many more decades.

98 p | *1928 Château Latour* (Pauillac)   2007/2025 x **7** | D 30 min / G 1 h

The 1928 vintage was excellent for Latour. Weather conditions were encouraging during the whole summer. Big heatwave before and during the harvesting of the very sound and fully ripe grapes. At Latour they made 85 casks of wine. This was for a long time infamous for being an overly tannic wine. However it has mellowed marvellously now.

Excellent Château-bottling. Level was high-shoulder. Dark, deep red colour. On the nose wonderful aromas of blackcurrants, mint, black truffles, plums, and mineral notes. Full-bodied with no hard edges. Still showing remarkable balance between layers of sweet fruit and the softened tannins. The intensity of fruit is remarkable. This is the one of the finest Latour ever, together with the 1929. Delicious to drink from now on through 2020.

98 p | *1959 Château La Mission-Haut-Brion* (Graves) 2006/2010 x **24** | D 2 h / G 2 h

The 'vintage of the century' foretold and baptized before the harvest. After a few false starts, the wines have proved magnificent. Very hot during the harvest, which started on September 23rd and ended on October 3rd at Château La Mission-Haut-Brion.

An excellent magnum. Decanted for two hours. Deep and clear red-brick colour, with aromas of sweet plum fruit, chocolate, blackcurrant, tobacco, and meat. Very open and delicate nose. Very big and muscular style La Mission, like 1955 and 1950. It still has powerful tannins and many layers of sweet, velvety fruit flavours on the palate. Nicely balanced with quite a low acidity. The finish was extremely long and silky. This 1959 may be the best vintage for drinking today and over the next 10 years.

98 p | *1982 Château Le Pin* (Pomerol) | 2006/2020 x **7** | D 3 h / G 2 h

This legendary world's first "garage" wine has existed under the Le Pin name since 1967 when the property owner Madame Laubie had rented her one hectare vineyard to a grower who named it Le Pin à Lalande. The name derives from the pine tree located next to the winemaking facilities. After 55 years ownership of Laubie family and the death of Madame Laubie, the estate was acquired by the Belgic wine merchant family - Thienpont. It was this vintage 1982 that made Le Pin one of the most sought after wine in the world. The small property is located at the edge of the Pomerol plateau. The soil is mainly gravel and clay lying on the iron-rich base. The blend is made mostly from Merlot (92%) and the rest are Cabernet Franc with very moderate yields on 30 hectolitre per hectare.

Wonderful Le Pin! Dark red colour up until the tight rim, no fading. A meaty and fruity complex nose with hints of black fruits and roasted coffee beans. A giant body, rich and smoothly tannic mouthfeel. The pure concentrated fruit starts to show complexity. An incredible finish, this is still on the upswing. Improves over the several hours it is in the glass. Best Le Pin ever!!

98 p | *1929 Château Latour* (Pauillac) | 2001/2020 x **17** | D 1.5 h / G 1 h

Château-bottled, level was top-shoulder. Decanted for 1.5 hours. Deep-coloured with a rich, opulent, well-integrated nose. Surprisingly soft and sweet on the palate. Immensely complex, restrained old vine fruit. Very impressive with a long smooth finish. Vigorous and very classic.

98 p | *1870 Vin de Constance* (South-Africa) | 1998/2020 x **2** | D 1 h / G 1 h

Vin de Constance is the most celebrated and historic South African wine. It was described by Jane Austen as a cure for a broken heart and it was Charles Dickens who wrote that a glass of Vin de Constance "went very well with a home-made biscuit". Vin de Constance was drunk well alongside Château d'Yquem in the 18th century and Napoleon even had it shipped to him whilst he was imprisoned on St. Helena. The verdant Constantia valley, home to the Klein Constantia Estate, is the oldest, most enduring vineyard region in the Cape, first producing wine in 1689.

Very old looking bottle. Bought from Sotheby's. Decanted for 1.5 hours. Deep brown colour with a wide orange rim. Intense nose of honey, spring flowers, crème brûlée and raisin aromas. On the palate quite sweet and warm with flavours of luscious yellow peaches, ripe apricots and honey. Great complexity and balance. Good fruit and high acidity help in retaining some freshness. A long and lingering finish that coats our mouths and never seems to stop. Has held up exceptionally well.

Château d'Yquem

98 p | *1982 Château La Mission-Haut-Brion* (Graves) **2006/2035 x 16** | D 3 h / G 3 h

Wine producers who have been able to retain an even quality from year to year are few and far between. One of the most reliable is Château La Mission Haut-Brion in the Graves region. Some years ago, we had the opportunity to taste the 1982-2002 vintages guided by Haut-Brion's winemaker, Jean-Bernard Delmas. The evenness of the quality was amazing, even the weak and light vintages such as 1991 and 1997 were almost comparable to the outstanding 1989 and 2000.

It is very seldom that such good weather conditions as in 1982 are found. April was very dry and hot. June slightly thundery. A hot summer followed from July 8th onwards. Very hot during the harvest, which began September 15th and ended September 24th. First-rate weather conditions to produce a great wine.

Decanted three hours. Very deep, ruby red with brown tints. Less closed than Haut-Brion with upfront fruit of ripe cassis and capsicum, floral aromas and hints of butterscotch and toasty spiciness. Concentrated medium-bodied palate with fresh acidity and minerals, firm tannins and intense fruit - all in harmonious balance. The flavours are dominated by toasty and spicy aromas with hints of tobacco and cigar. Long, elegant and discreet finish. Silky wine with very refined and classic style.

98 p | *1982 Château Lafite-Rothschild* (Pauillac) **2005/2020 x 9** | D 2 h / G 2 h

This spectacular vintage started off with very early flowering similarly to 1959, 1961 and 1966, indicating a large crop. July turned out unusually hot whereas August was cooler than on average. The heatwave between the 6th and 13th of September nailed the vintage as a legendary one.

A very classic Pauillac. Decanted for two hours. Still a youthful, very dark, ruby red colour. Full-bodied and elegant wine. On the palate it has marvellous flavours of mint, spiced berry fruits, tobacco, lead pencil and minerals, all of which linger very comfortably. Full-bodied, with exemplary extraction of fruit and notable tannins. Rich and big Lafite with a lavishingly long finish. This extensive Lafite will undoubtedly last for another 20 years, but is already very, very pleasing.

98 p | *1990 Château Cheval Blanc* (St. Emilion) **2006/2010 x 27** | D 3 h / G 3 h

Excellent magnum. Decanted for three hours. Opaque dark ruby-red colour. Powerful yet discreet bouquet of ripe fruit, coffee, mint, and mineral scents. Wonderfully rich, thick, powerful, and concentrated wine with layer upon layer of ripe, exotic fruit. The 1990 Cheval is incredibly full-bodied, well-balanced, pure and perhaps slightly more tannic than the 1989. It has an excellent grip and a long, thrilling, fairly tannic finish.

98 p | 1878 Vintage Port Cockburn (Portugal) 2006/2020 x 3 | D 2 h / G 6 h

The mid-19th century was the golden age of vintage port. Numerous port houses were established and many vintages were declared. The last great vintage of these years was 1878, which was undoubtedly the finest vintage of the decade. It was shipped by all shippers. Then phylloxera entered the Douro Valley carrying out its infamous destruction.

Very good looking bottle with Christie's label. Recorked in 1955. Decanted for 30 minutes, which was too short. A very promising dark red colour with only slight amber hues on the rim. The nose opened slowly, but after two hours it was fully open offering spicy plum, black pepper, roasted nuts, sweet fruit, and chocolate aromas. Full-bodied, plenty of grip, flavour and an impeccable balance. The 1878 ports were highly rated upon release, which is no wonder as was well proven by this tremendous bottle from Cockburn's.

98 p | 1928 Vintage Pol Roger (Champagne) 2007/now x 5 | D 10 min / G 40 min

This wonderful vintage of Pol Roger was known as an obsession for Sir Winston Churchill. A case of this, his favourite vintage champagne, was delivered to him by Odette Pol-Roger on his every birthday after the Second World War until 1953 when the vintage finally ran out from the Pol Roger stocks.

The vintage itself started well with an ideal budding season. The spring frosts together with the violent hailstorms caused some damage on the vineyards. The flowering was extended with some millerandage. Preferable weather conditions during the summer and autumn yielded superb quality crop. This vintage has to be considered one of the vintages of the century in Champagne.

Superb looking bottle. Good level. Bright golden colour with lazy small bubbles. Pronounced, elegant nose possesses brioche aromas and a great deal of dried fruits peaches and apricots with delicate hints of creaminess and coffee. Dry and crisp palate with fainted mousse. Very lean and persistent wine with complex, delicate flavours of dried fruits and coffee. Lingering long mineral finish in superb balance. Tasting this wine makes nobody wonder why Sir Winston had fallen in love with this wine. Unfortunately he never had a chance to experience this wine in this lovely mature condition.

98 p | 1792 Madeira Extra Réserve Solera 'Napoléon Réserve' Blandy's
(Portugal) 2006/2060 x 6 | D 3 h / G 3 h

These wines were labelled with Christie's labels and were in good condition, levels at mid-shoulder. They originate back to a time when Napoléon Bonaparte was living in exile on St Helena. He was allowed to receive a pipe of best Madeira. When this pipe arrived he was already suffering of arsenic poisoning. When tasting it from the pipe he felt ill in his stomach and thought it was due to the faulty wine. Thus he refused drinking it and the pipe was delivered back to Madeira by the Blandy family. They bottled part of this pipe in 1840 as a vintage Madeira and the rest they kept for a solera. This solera was bottled in 1957 for Queen Elizabeth II and her husband the Duke of Edinburgh's visit to Madeira.

Bright golden amber medium-intense colour. The nose gives first only volatile aromas but after a while in the glass the wine opens up offering smokey, leathery aromas with almonds and nougatine. Lovely nose! The sweet taste with extremely oily and crisp texture takes hold on the palate. Next one feels the dried fruits on the mid-palate. The long silky finish with warming alcohol shows more oxidation but still in a refined way. The wine leaves a very long aftertaste.

98 p | *1975 Château La Mission-Haut-Brion* (Graves) **2007/2030 x 21** | D 2 h / G 2 h

In 1975 both June and July were very hot. September, on the other hand, was variable. Fair weather went on until the harvest. At Château La Mission Haut-Brion harvesting began on September 25th and ended by October 8th. Everywhere in Bordeaux 1975 produced rich and powerful wines which require a long time in the bottle to develop and soften.

A fine-looking bottle. Level by the neck. Decanted for two hours. Surprisingly mature wine, colour looked very dark but old. Glorious perfumed nose of undergrowth, very dark flavours like earth, tobacco, vanilla and mushrooms. Big and blooming on the palate: coconut and prune. Superb balance of sweet, big tannin and acid. Massive finish and a glorious structure. Excellent grip. The well structured finish lingered on for a very long time. Still a lifetime to live.

98 p | *1945 Château Pétrus* (Pomerol) **2007/2025 x 6** | D 2 h / G 2 h

Pétrus' fame is to a large extent attributable to Madame Edmond Loubat. She bought the estate piecemeal between 1925 and 1945. Madame Loubat had strong faith in the quality of her wines and asked higher prices than any other producer in Pomerol. Jean-Pierre Mouiex was the perfect partner for her. Mouiex was a négociant from Libourne and owned some properties himself. He was successful in marketing Pétrus and catapulted it into global fame. When Madame Loubat died in 1961, Mouiex became part-owner in Pétrus. Today, the Mouiex family owns most of it. The son of Jean-Pierre Mouiex, Christian, has been responsible for winemaking at Pétrus since 1970, supported by Jean-Claude Berrouet.

Good-looking château-bottled wine. Level was top-shoulder. Decanted for one and a half hours. Very healthy-looking dark ruby colour. On the nose quite open and pure with deliciously fruity black olive, violet, herbs and tobacco aromas. While this monumental 1945 sat in the glass, it opened even more and developed a breathtaking perfume of exotic fruits, white chocolate and oriental spices. It has an admirable depth, body, tannin and balance. A very big and refined Pétrus with herbs and jammy black fruits, plum, and dark chocolate flavours. Still incredibly fresh and youthful. A firm, long, delicate, and fragrant aftertaste. This powerful and impressive bottle of Pomerol is at its peak of maturity, but will easily hold another two decades.

98 p | *1982 Château Cheval Blanc* *(St. Emilion)*   2006/2025 x 4 | D 2.5 h / G 3 h

This remarkable vintage ideally ripened the exceptional blend for Cheval Blanc. The blend had 60% Cabernet Franc, 34% Merlot, 1% Cabernet Sauvignon and 4% Malbec. This blend produced a wine of intensive cherry red colour and an extremely elegant and charming complex nose of chocolate, mocha, ripe blackcurrants and hints of butterscotch. The medium-bodied palate is very delicate and classy but concentrated. Chewy wine with vivid acidity and minerality, intense fruitiness supported by firm and ripe tannins. Roasted coffee and chocolate flavours are dominating in a long finish. The immense concentration and the harmonious balance guarantee long ageing potential for this lovely wine.

98 p | *1893 Château Margaux* *(Margaux)*   2001/2010 x 3 | D 1 h / G 1 h

This decade brought relief to the vinegrowers of Gironde who had made almost fatal financial and other sacrifices during the 1880s. The 1893 was the first really good vintage since the unfortunate years of phylloxera and mildew. A wonderful summer with early flowering. Harvest began August 18th - the earliest on record. The crop was almost as large as the great 1875 - 547 544 tonneaux. The wines were very appealing from the start. With age, the lack of natural acidity and grape sugar made some of them a bit sharp and bitter. Prices were also so ridiculously low that by Christmas all the classified growth wines had been sold.

This bottle of Château Margaux came from New York without label and capsule. Otherwise it looked fine – ullage was top shoulder! Decanted one hour. Mature red colour with good depth. Earthy, mature but surprisingly open nose with complexity. Full flavoured, feminine and delicate on the palate. Sweet, gentle but at the same time as classy as an old claret can be. Excellent wine.

98 p | *1917 Unico Bodegas Vega Sicilia* *(Ribera del Duero)*

1999/2010 x 1 | D 1 h / G 1 h

The bottle was in a good condition with top-shoulder level. Decanted for one hour. Dark, old brick colour with bright orange hints. An intense and very expressive nose with aromas of spices, leather and old wood. Really silky and velvety taste. Has great complexity and rich flavours of cocoa, tobacco, vanilla, caramel and wood. Toasty and elegant wine with great acidity that keeps it still alive - what a presence. Long and lingering aftertaste.

98 p | *1978 Hermitage La Chapelle Jaboulet Aîné (Rhône)*

2005/2030 x 3 | **D 2 h / G 3 h**

This legendary wine derives its name from a tiny Saint-Christophe chapel situated in the middle of vineyards almost at the top of the great Hermitage hill. This chapel has belonged to Jaboulet family since 1919. The Syrah grapes used for this flagship wine of Jaboulet come from two vineyards, Bessards and Méal. In 1978 these vineyards among others in Rhône were facing difficult weather conditions. Yields were reduced due to a cool and wet spring. The flowering turned out to be late and it proceeded very slowly. Then came a warm and dry summer not only helping the harvest to survive but to become perfect. A small crop with excellent quality reaching the level of the superb vintage 1961.

Fine looking bottle. Decanted for two hours. Very dark, almost black in colour. Open and exotic bouquet of mineral, pepper, plum, blackberries and leather notes. In the mouth, this 1978 has an overwhelming concentration, exceptional balance and depth, and a superbly long, monumental finish that lasts for more than two minutes. This is the finest La Chapelle made since the legendary 1961.

98 p | *1985 Richebourg Henri Jayer (Côte de Nuits)* **2000/2015 x 6** | **D 1 h / G 3 h**

This 1985 Richebourg was served together with Jayer's famous 1978 Richebourg. The 1978 seemed surprisingly the younger of the two, but the 1985 was superior in many ways. The 1978 was harder with the tannins more apparent and chewy, tasting meatier. The 1985 was fatter and had additional layers of fruit that were lacking in the 1978. The 1985 has a definitely better balance and longer aftertaste as well. Somehow this bottle of 1978 was now much more closed and 'undrinkable' than some previous ones.

Nevertheless, this beautiful 1985 Richebourg is a very full-bodied wine with tannins fully resolved, and as it opens it becomes even more mouth-coating and rich, with denser fruit flavours and another long, long finish. Great wine from a great man!

98 p | *1961 Château La Mission-Haut-Brion (Graves)* **2004/2020 x 32** | **D 1 h / G 3 h**

At Château La Mission Haut-Brion a short period of intense cold at the end of May caused exceptional coulure (the lack of pollinization due to wet or cold weather). A hot summer, but above all very dry (the driest on record). A very fine September yielded a harvest with good maturity and concentration. Harvesting began on September 12th and ended on September 25th.

Pre-auction tasting at Christie's. Low neck level, otherwise like new. Decanted for one hour before tasting. Good, dark, maturing colour. Very wide, rich and intense nose with ripe fruit, tobacco and some oak aromas. Full-bodied and tannic. Big, thick, complex wine with great balance and very long and soft, seductive aftertaste. Serious wine and one of the many much-beloved 1961s. Tasted numerous times with similar notes.

98 p | *1990 Châteauneuf-du-Pape Château Rayas* (Rhône)

2004/2030x **3** | D 2.5 h / G 3+ h

This unique family estate's vineyard of 8 ha were planted in 1922 by Louis Reynaud. Although the family is known for being introvert towards the public, they surely express their fascinating personality through their wines. Their Châteauneuf-du-Pape differs from most of the AOC wines as being a mono-varietal wine from Grenache Noir. The wine that holds 15% potential alcohol most of the years is produced with amazingly low yields of 15-18 hl/ha from vineyards facing north. In this hot and dry year only 2000 cases of Château Rayas were produced.

Clear and brilliant cherry red colour with orange tints. The nose is rewarding with very rich and robust developing aromas of farmyard, a touch of tar and smokiness refreshed by ripe brambles. The wine has a very opulent medium-bodied palate that reflects the aromas detected on the nose. The structure is very refined with round and ripe tannins and a moderate level of acidity. Ripe fruitiness is turned into wild berry flavors with some animal aromas enhanced by a moderate level of volatility. The high level of alcohol is well integrated into the wine leading into a long warm finish. A rich and complex wine possessing a tremendous personality differing from all other Châteauneuf-du-Papes.

98 p | *1961 Château Haut-Brion* (Graves)

2006/2020 x **23** | D 2 h / G 3 h

This spectacular vintage had a rough start due to a cold period at the end of May causing severe coulure. After a poor fruit set in late spring, the weather changed into very hot and dry for the summer, actually the driest on record. Very fine weather in September guaranteed ideal ripeness of grapes and extremely high concentration. The rainfall of this year was almost half the average in Haut-Brion. Both of the two bottles were in good condition.

Decanted for two hours. This is Haut-Brion at its best without a doubt. Very dark, garnet in colour. Gorgeously intense nose - exotic, sweet black fruits and oriental spices. Full-bodied, very well balanced with an excellent structure. This finely concentrated but generously open wine shows a lovely sweet, round and intense ending. A real joy of a wine.

98 p | *1959 Château d'Yquem* (Sauternes)

2005/2030 x **11** | D 2 h / G 3 h

The bottle was in perfect condition. Level was by the neck. Decanted for two hours. Brownish, deep but a bit oxidated colour. On the nose honey, mango and other tropical fruits, roasted nuts, and pine wood aromas. The wine was unbelievably lively and showed no signs of heaviness. Well balanced. Refined, luxurious, elegant, detailed, and sweet with stunning complexity and a lavish finish. Loads of life left.

98 p | *1966 Château Palmer* (Margaux)   2006/2015 x 23 | D 2 h / G 2 h

At the beginning of June, the vines flowered quickly and evenly. After this, in June, the growth was hampered by heavy rain. August was fine but cool, which delayed the véraison and slowed down the ripening process. Fortunately, at the end of August, the weather changed for the better. Warm dry conditions during the whole of September produced ripe and healthy grapes. 1966 wines are classic and long-lived, with fresh acidity and elegant fruit.

Bottle was in A1 condition. Level by the neck. Decanted for one hour. Mature, dark red colour. Quite an old-style nose, but very stylish and sweet with aromas of sweet black fruits. This medium-bodied and concentrated wine shows excellent balance between smooth tannin, wood aromas and sweet, delicious fruit. Rich and silky, a perfect combination of beautiful flavours of autumn berries, fragrant bittersweet fruits and fresh truffles. Sweet, voluptuous and long aftertaste. One of the best old-style Palmer ever made. Only the 1961 is more intense and powerful.

98 p | *1969 Côte-Rôtie La Mouline Guigal* (Rhône)   2006/2010 x 3 | D 2 h / G 1 h

In 1969 nature was very kind to the hard working winemakers in the Rhône. It was no wonder that most of them made excellent and long-lasting wines, and of course Guigal made no exception. To us La Mouline 1969 is the wine of the year in Rhône.

The bottle was in a first-class condition, ullage was only two cm. Decanted for two hours. Highly coloured core and rim. Very strong and spicy open bouquet. Exceptionally harmonious and fat in the mouth with sufficient concentration. Good structure and balance. Lots of ripe, spicy fruit and some rounded and ripe tannins. Excellent, long and solid finish. A comprehensive and truly interesting wine, which seems to have reached its peak.

98 p | *1990 Musigny Comte Georges de Vogüé* (Côte de Nuits)

2004/2020 x 2 | D 1 h / G 3 h

Fine-looking bottle. Decanted for one hour. Excellent, youthful colour. Powerful, open and intense nose. Balanced and already very accessible. Loads of dark and red berries with exotic spices and hints of smoke on the palate. This has grand cru weight and expression. Very classy and uncompromising in style. Finish is refined with a rather sweet, feminine exit of raspberry, ripe red cherry and aromas with spicy mushrooms. Very sexy and charismatic wine with extensive and gracious future.

98 p | *1990 Châteauneuf-du-Pape Hommage à Jacques Perrin*
Château de Beaucastel (Rhône)   2005/2020 x **1** | D 2 h / G 3 h

In 1989, 1990, 1994 and 1995 the weather conditions were so favourable that the Perrins decided to make a special cuvée in honour of their father. The Château de Beaucastel Hommage à Jacques Perrin of those years was made mostly from very old Mourvedre vines yielding tiny quantities of intensely ripe, concentrated fruit. Beaucastel's winemaking philosophy is quite unique: "We try to place the vine in its universe. That is to say relate it to the earth, the animal life and the stars by which it is influenced". Sounds uncommon, but it seems to be working remarkably.

Decanted for two hours. The nose is beautiful, full and evolved: very minty, chocolaty and with an appealing herbal character. There are also tobacco, tea and very deep black and red fruit aromas around. Tannic, rich and leathery on the palate; complex and full with a firm structure. Perfect balance. Not fully drinkable yet, but has a striking future ahead of it.

98 p | *1847 Château d'Yquem* (Sauternes)   2000/now x **13** | D 20 min / G 2 h

This great vintage could be named as the greatest vintage in the history of Sauternes and d'Yquem. It gained great glory and publicity when a Russian Grand Duke Constantine, the brother of Tsar Alexander II, visited Bordeaux in 1859 and placed an order of 1200 bottles of the 1847 Château d'Yquem with the highest price ever recorded at the time. After tasting this wine several times, one can really understand the Duke's actions.

Amber-gold coloured wine with rich honeyed nose. So lusciously sweet and delicate on the palate. Harmonious balance of minerals, acidity and viscous texture forms together a wonderfully integrated immensely long aftertaste. Wine that makes you accidentally swallow your tongue.

98 p | *1990 Chambertin Armand Rousseau* (Côte de Nuits)

2005/2015 x **3** | D 2 h / G 3 h

Domaine Armand Rousseau was one of the first estates in Burgundy that started to bottle and market its wines instead of selling them to négociants. This legendary top quality house owns 14 ha of vineyard in the Gevrey-Chambertin and Morey-Saint-Denis communes. The size of their Chambertin terrain is impressive 2.20 ha.

Decanted for two hours. An appealing fragrant nose of sweet red berries and cherries, with lots of ripeness and mineral complexity. Quite intense: forward yet elegant. The palate is concentrated and rich. Very pure and focused. The fruit and wood notes are perfectly integrated with very smooth, fine tannins. Great balance and class. Work of a genius!

98 p | *1982 Château Pichon Longueville Comtesse de Lalande* (Pauillac)

2005/2025 x 15 | **D 1 h / G 2 h**

1982 was a very important vintage for Bordeaux. It started an era with increasingly well made wines and increasingly high prices. It was a very large vintage as very little crop reduction was used. However, the grapes managed to ripen due to perfect conditions during the harvest. A vintage full of successes. But few wines have been so loved as the Château Pichon Lalande. This was drinking well earlier than most other top wines from the Médoc. However, it has kept its form, giving us wine lovers decades of joy. We have had the pleasure of drinking this soft and lovely wine on several occasions but none more memorable than at a lunch at Restaurant Taillevent in honour of May-Elaine Lencquesaing's 80th birthday.

Bottle in A1 condition. Level by the neck. Decanted for two hours. Very deep colour and with only a hint of amber on the rim. On the nose very open with loads of spice and tobacco over ripe blackcurrant and blueberry fruit. Very promising nose. On the palate this wine has a beautiful balance and solid structure. Very ripe and not too tannic. More muscular and fleshy than Pichon normally is, although very seductive with soft tannin and concentrated, sweet fruit. Terrific length and purity, this truly is a classic. More challenging and harmonious a wine than Pichon-Baron for sure. Drinking surprisingly nicely now, but needs time. Perhaps the best Pichon-Lalande ever made.

98 p | *1970 Château Pétrus* (Pomerol)

2007/2015 x 22 | **D 1.5 h / G 2 h**

Excellent looking bottle, level was by the neck. Decanted for 1.5 hours. More intense and voluptuous than the Pétrus 1971 - very fruity and complex nose. On the palate, much more multi-dimensional and stylish than Pétrus 1971. Has also more structure and muscle. Not nearly as approachable as the 1971 now, but it seems to have better ageing potential. One of the best 'modern' Pétrus.

98 p | *1996 Griotte-Chambertin Claude Dugat* (Côte de Nuits)

2004/2025 x 4 | **D 1 h / G 3 h**

Excellent young Burgundy. Decanted for one hour. Dark and youthful red colour.

Very sound and open bouquet with aromas of dark chocolate, cinnamon, brown mocha, roasted meats and wild berries. There is a lot of elegance and intensity here, yet never arrogant and everything seems to be in the right balance for a long and rewarding future. Expansive, ample and tempting wine. Admirably sensual, enormously concentrated wine with a long and sweet fruity finish. Best from 2007 through 2020.

98 p | *1969 Dom Ruinart Rosé Ruinart* (Champagne)

| 2007/2010 x 3 | D 15 min / G 30 min |

Ruinart is one of the oldest Champagne houses. "In the name of God and the Holy Virgin shall this book be opened..." It was with these words, written by Nicolas Ruinart on 1. September 1729, that the House of Ruinart was officially established. A true entrepreneur, Nicolas Ruinart fulfilled the ambition of his uncle, the Benedictine monk Dom Thierry Ruinart, a close friend of Dom Pérignon, to make Ruinart the premier Champagne house. A resounding success was made possible by the perceptiveness of its initiator, Dom Ruinart, to whom the Ruinart House paid tribute in 1959 by creating the historic, prestigious Dom Ruinart vintage.

This beautiful Dom Ruinart Rosé was in excellent condition. Decanted five minutes. Very deep, dark orange-red colour. The nose is marvellously tuffeed, with raspberries and pure, ripe mineral-rich flavours. Beautiful, vivid, creamy and wide mousse and a mouth-filling weight of rich fruit. Lots of dense, full, exotic flavours and a touch of honey depth. Super concentrated and powerful, yet balanced and gracious. Very young at heart, intense and vigorous wine. One of the best Rosés we have ever tasted.

98 p | *1949 Romanée-St.Vivant Domaine Marey-Monge* (Côte de Nuits)

| 2005/now x 4 | D 1 h / G 1 h |

The label and the capsule had disappeared with the years, otherwise the wine seemed splendid - only 3 cm ullage. A totally sophisticated, elegant bearing. Immensely strong bouquet of ripe blackcurrant and cherry. Seductively velvety, balanced structure - this wine still has many years ahead of it.

Very different from La Tache 1949, much lighter but at the same time it has more dimensions and elegance. The style and elegance are the factors which please my sense of taste, this is an experience we will remember for a long time.

98 p | *1961 Château Mouton-Rothschild* (Pauillac) 2006/2030 x 15 | D 1 h / G 3 h

The vineyard that has caused us most disappointment and sometimes even grey hair, is Château Mouton-Rothschild. Over the past 50 years, the quality of its wines has varied from excellent to disastrous. What is unusual is that the owner of the estate has not changed during that time, and even the winemaker has been the same - Raoul Blondin made the wines at Mouton for half a century, from 1940 to 1990. Even if Mouton-Rothschild has at times produced legendary wines, such as 1945, 1959, 1982, 1986, 2000 and this 1961, the quality in the intervening years has fluctuated far too much. Especially between 1963-1981 the quality was far from the best years in Mouton-Rothschild's history and nowhere close to Premier Cru as this great 1961 is. Everytime we have tasted this wine it has been absolutely magnificent. This last bottle was bought from

NUMBER 89.
NUMBER 90.
NUMBER 91.

Christie's. It was in a very bad condition from the outside. Decanted for one hour before tasting.
Dark, deep and mature colour. Ripe cassis fruit, herbs and sweetness could be sensed in the bouquet.
A strangely seductive combination. Very youthful, rich, soft, voluptuous and elegant wine. Considerably more
spirited and vital than the outside look would have led us to expect. A balanced acidity and tight fruitiness,
long and pampering aftertaste. A gentle but most impressive acquaintance.

98 p | *1929 Richebourg Domaine de la Romanée-Conti* (Côte de Nuits)

1998/2010 x 4 | D 1 h / G 2 h

Excellent weather conditions during the whole year. Very hot summer, especially the end of it. Only three
days of rain in September, but that saved the grapes from too much stress. A big crop was harvested under
perfect conditions.

Very old looking, dusty bottle without capsule. Decanted only for 30 minutes, which was not enought. Very
dark, deep colour, even for the vintage. It took almost 1.5 hours until the bouquet really opened. Marvellous
perfumed nose, very appealing. Lots of chocolate and black fruit aromas. On the palate very full with still
some tannic presence. Very silky and smooth texture. Great concentration.

The best Richebourg we have ever tasted.

98 p | *1978 Romanée-Conti Domaine de la Romanée-Conti* (Côte de Nuits)

2007/2020 x 3 | D 45 min / G 15 min

Extraordinarily cold and wet spring continued until drastic weather change took place in the beginning of
August. The weather changed favourably and grapes ripened ideally, although very late. The result was a very
limited crop with very high concentration in grapes. Truly one of the greatest vintages of the century. The
Romanée-Conti was yielding only 14 hl/ha and 6 535 bottles were made.

Clear, beautiful, cherry red colour with moderate intensity. Immensely complex and wonderfully evolved
nose – full of ripe cherries, leather, hints of violets, earthiness, and spices. On the palate the wine shares
enormous texture! Silky medium-bodied taste with extremely refined elegant tannins and delightfully fresh
acidity. Every drop in the mouth reflects extraordinary concentration of red fruits, spices, minerals, and floral
flavours. The wine seems not to finish ever in the lingering aftertaste.

98 p | *1962 Unico Bodegas Vega Sicilia* (Ribera del Duero)

2003/2015 x 6 | D 1 h / G 4 h

Excellent looking magnum with by the neck level. Decanted one hour. A very classic Unico nose - cherries,
blackberries, vanilla and cedar wood aromas. Still a tannic and youthful wine. Full-bodied with an ideal inherent sense of balance. Very long and complex aftertaste. An absolutely brilliant wine. This great Vega Sicilia
Unico 1962 has potential to live for another decade or more.

98 p | *1990 Château d'Yquem (Sauternes)* 2007/2030 x 23 | D 2.5 h / G 3 h

This wine has become a legend already at its youth. We have tasted this wine on several occasions. Each time it has been charming, although its greatness lies in its exquisite future potential. Bright deep golden colour. Very intense honeyed and botrytised nose still partly closed while giving seductive hints of its complexity. Marmelade and apricots are becoming more pronounced after breathing in the glass. Nose reveals several layers of aromas but not anything like what is to come. The lusciously sweet honeyed taste is lightened up by the crisp acidity. Spicy vanilla tones from barrel maturation adds complexity to the wine. Very concentrated wine with a great length. This wine definitely benefits from further ageing.

98 p | *1985 Clos du Mesnil Champagne Krug (Champagne)*

2007/2020 x 5 | D 15 min / G 1 h

The beginning of the year looked challenging as severe frosts, as cold as -25 °C, destroyed over one tenth of the vines. Early summer was cool and humid, but a warm and sunny July advanced the ripening. Later in autumn the weather remained sunny and warm, producing a 6827 kg/ha crop of very concentrated grapes. The 1985 Clos du Mesnil is one of this single vineyard Blanc de Blancs' greatest vintages. Krug only made 1.240 cases of this complex champagne of great depth.

Decanted 15 minutes. A mature, lavish vintage that makes for a rich, almost fat champagne that is packed with honey aromas and pronounced vanilla, pineapple and creamy flavours. Astonishing combination of lightness and intensity. On the palate firm yet stylish, with plenty of walnut, apple and toast character. It has a refined, silky-smooth structure, broad mousse and a lasting acidity. A sumptuous texture and long, creamy finish complete the package. Wonderful now.

98 p | *1976 Grange Hermitage Penfolds (South Australia)*

2003/2010 x 3 | D 1.5 h / G 2 h

It is safe to say the 1976 Grange comes from one of the top three vintages of the 70s. It has taken the test of time very well as is expected from such faultlessly ideal ripening conditions. The vintage was warm and the Grange still shows high extraction and a big structure. The 1976 is 89% Shiraz and 11% Cabernet Sauvignon aged in new American hogsheads for 18 months. Fine looking bottle with top-shoulder level. Decanted 1.5 hours. Dark, bright, deep red colour. Fragrant nose with hints of over ripeness, rich blackcurrant, minty and vanilla. The palate has a excellent concentration of cherry and black fruits with bags of gentle oak giving a fat, spicy underpinning. The mouthfeel was creamy and it has fine balance. Super intense and long, rich ending. Wonderful to drink now.

98 p | *1959 Château Lafite-Rothschild* (Pauillac)   2007/2020 x 23 | D 1 h / G 2 h

Very good appearance. Decanted for one hour. Healthy, youthful and bright colour. Very classic on the nose with spicy Cabernet notes, cedar wood, chocolate and delicious truffle. The 1959 Lafite is more open, intense and complex than the 1961, which also looks older and has more tannin. Elegant, but ripe fruit, acidity and structure. Well balanced. Surprisingly fat and big wine for Lafite, while very elegant. Long, sweet and intense finish with some soft tannin left. An outstanding wine. Lafite did not make wine of this level again until 1982.

98 p | *1882 Château d'Yquem* (Sauternes)   2005/2020 x 2 | D 30 min / G 2 h

Château bottled. Level mid-shoulder. Clear, deep amber colour. Intensive, classic, youthful nose with honey and wax hint. No oxidised aromas. Intensively sweet glycerol mouthfeel complemented by a host of nuanced flavours – roasted sugar, honey and walnut. Incredible intensity and mouth-filling character with an unending aftertaste. Fantastic bottle.

98 p | *1921 Dom Pérignon Moët & Chandon* (Champagne)

2006/now x 3 | D 10 min / G 30 min

This super vintage in Champagne escorted a new phenomenom to the world of glorious wines. This was the prestige cuvée called Dom Pérignon. This small vintage yielded only 1,400 bottles of the first Dom Pérignon ever.

The bottle was in fine condition. The appearance of a little hazy golden colour with broad watery rim and no bubbles did not promise much. Luckily the nose erased all doubts. Beautifuly developed restrained nose showed dried fruits, figs, seductive toastiness, biscuity tones and a dose of toffee. Crisp and still lovely fresh light-bodied taste with lovely mousse. Toasty finish with restrained fruit of red apples. Very balanced and delicious aftertaste remain at moderate length.

This super vintage in Champagne escorted a new phenomenon to the world of glorious wines. This was the prestige cuvee called Dom Perignon.

Champagne Bollinger

1979 Château Le Pin (Pomerol) 98p

2006/2020 x5 • D 1 h / G 1 h

One could say this wine opened a new chapter in the history of wines being the first so-called garage winery in the world. In 1979 the Belgic Thienpont family purchased 1.6 hectare plot after the death of former owner Madame Loubie whose family had possessed the estate since 1924. From this first vintage onwards the estate became known as Le Pin, named after a solitary pine tree standing on the property. Le Pin is located on the edge of Pomerol plateau on a very poor gravel and clay soil with high iron content. The wine is a blend of 92% of Merlot and 8% of Cabernet Franc. The vines' average age is 32 years and nowadays the two-hectare vineyard yields annually around 6 000 bottles. The vintage 1979 was not superb but turned out well in Pomerol. A wet winter was extended to a wet spring. The growing season was mostly dry and the temperatures remained low. Both Merlot and Cabernet Franc were harvested ideally ripe, resulting into wines with luscious and rich texture.

Moderately dark ruby colour with an orange hue. An intense spicy nose with roasted nuts, lovely ripe plums, fruitcake, and delicate floral aromas along with fascinating evolved leathery and earthy nuances. A lovely concetration on the palate – medium-bodied style with intense red fruit flavours, elegant but still firm tannic structure, and balancing acidity that escorts the lingering harmonious finish. This is a wine with finesse and opulence, which is beautifully exposed now after a decent bottle ageing. The wine is drinking perfectly now but will keep another fifteen years.

1929 Romanée-Conti Domaine de la Romanée-Conti 98p
(Côte de Nuits)

2000/2015 x10 • D 1 h / G 2 h

This was the vintage of the decade together with 1923. The winter turned out to be relatively humid and was followed by rapid vegetal growth in March. The growth was slowed down by mid-April when the weather chilled, even getting icy. The mild and humid weather was retrieved in May causing early flowering. Then again the cooling temperature in June caused the berry set to result in a small crop. Although the summer was very hot, the vines with their small berries managed to avoid unbearable heat stress. The autumn was sheer perfection - mainly dry with much-needed showers before harvest, which was warm and sunny. Harvesting extended over September to the 1st October.

Level was 5 cm. Decanted one hour. Moderately dark red, medium-intense colour with orange rim. The nose is very dense, developed earthy aromas combined with dark berry notes, spices and smoky tones. Very intense and elegant on the palate. Lovely vivid acidity marries delicately ripe fruit. The wine is showing still surprisingly powerful tannic structure. Long persistent lingering aftertaste. A wine in such a great mature shape shouts out for a magnitude of a unique kind.

1928 Vintage Bollinger *(Champagne)* 98p

2005/now x2 • D 1 min / G 15 min

The 1928 was a wonderful Champagne vintage, especially for Bollinger, Pol Roger and Krug. It possesses everything a perfect vintage can wish for. The best wines of this vintage seem immortal. No matter that the carbon dioxide has escaped, these wines have perfect harmony even without it.

The budding went well at Bollinger. The Côte des Blancs suffered from May frosts and violent hailstorms were frequent. The development of bunches during summer went perfectly. Harvesting began on September 28th in the sun and ended in the rain. Extraordinary quality and medium yield: 6 000 kg/ha. In Bollinger's own opinion, 1928 alongside the 1990 and 1996 are the best vintages of the 20th century.

This Bollinger 1928 was a beautifully old-looking bottle. Decanted only for one minute. Still very clear, youthful and bright, golden colour. Crisp and fresh. Very much alive with appealing toasty, yeasty aromas, delicate chocolate, pear and old vanilla notes. Even some very tiny bubbles left. A bold, shameless old champagne. It possesses a definite underlying structure, ripe fruit and a long, extravagant, cream and honey filled finish. Impressive for its vitality and quality. For all the strength and breadth, it's still vigorous and will age even longer.

1967 Château d'Yquem *(Sauternes)* 98p

2002/2050 x16 • D 1 h / G 3 h

The vintage 1967 of Château d´Yquem remains in history as the first Yquem of Comte Alexandre de Lur Saluces. He could not have wished for a better time – the year was most successful in Sauternes.

Decanted for one hour. Retained its best characteristics for three hours after opening. Bottle outwardly in perfect condition. Wine level by the neck. Deep, bright golden colour. Really open, aggressive nose full of fresh, exotic fruit, apricot and fig aromas. Concentrated, solid mouth-feel. Perfectly harmonious structure, fresh acidity and refined sweetness make this wine one of the best Yquems in the last 50 years. An incredibly youthful, round and long wine that really deserves all the attention it gets. A perfect masterpiece by the young Alexandre de Lur-Saluces.

1949 La Tâche Domaine de la Romanée-Conti *(Côte de Nuits)* 98p

2000/2010 x2 • D 1 h / G 2 h

This bottle was in flawless condition, purchased at Sotheby´s of London for 120$ in 1990. The magnificent vintage gave high hopes for this wine. A truly intensive, fully balanced, soft and full flavour. New layers seemed to uncover endlessly. A long, leathery, fruity aftertaste. Youthful both in its colour and nature. Will last nicely for a few more decades of maturation, but without really benefiting from it anymore. After one hour in glass the wine just got better.

1983 *Clos du Mesnil Champagne Krug* (Champagne)   **98p**

2006/2020 x4 • D 15 min / G 1 h

The story of Clos du Mesnil started in 1698 when a 1,85 ha plot in the outskirts of the village of Le Mesnil-sur-Oger was sealed with walls for reasons unknown. The village grew in size and in 100 years the vineyard plot was surrounded by housing. The walls protected the vineyards from being dug up and from being used for housing purposes. The plot landed in the hands of the Krug family, when the brothers were searching for new vineyard acquisitions in the 1970s. A property was being sold in the Côte de Blancs, and as vineyard land was fiercely sought after, the brothers bought the plot without really seeing what they had bought.

When they first saw the Clos du Mesnil, they became very excited by the idea of producing a single vineyard wine. As the plot was not in good condition, Krug had to take the decision to replant it. Therefore, the first vintage of Krug Clos du Mesnil dates back to 1979 when the vines were old enough to produce good wine and when the unique quality of wine from the plot was realised. The Clos du Mesnil is produced in a similar way to the vintage. The plot comprises 6 individual parcels of varying vine ages. Each is picked and vinified separately. Enhancing terroir attributes is the guiding philosophy throughout vine growing and vinification. Rémi Krug stresses that it was not the single vineyard concept that was fascinating in itself. Instead it was the uniqueness of the parcel and its wine; "a diamond one wishes to show on its own". The Krugs always insist that the Clos du Mesnil is a unique wine, but never better than the vintage or the Grande Cuvée. In this massive volume vintage the Clos du Mesnil is however a true diamond of a wine:

Developing bright yellow colour. The floral nose resembling potpourri has caramel, cream and apples in it. Very rich and silky mouth-feel. Pronounced and prolonged aftertaste of toasted bread and roasted nuts. Dried fruits and honey. Perfect steel fresh acidity. The wine developed superbly in the glass. The Chardonnay has just turned into a magnificent creamy and toasted form. At a perfect age now, but will continue to develop well for a number of years.

1970 *Château Latour* (Pauillac)   **98p**

2007/2030 x27 • D 1.5 h / G 3 h

The winter was mild at Latour. Growth started towards the end of March, but the vegetation was affected by frosts at the beginning of April. Early spring was cold. Full flowering was evident on June 15th during a hot spell. July was fine and hot, and the grapes started their slow veraison on the 25th. August was moderate but September was warm with some humidity. A hot spell after the 16th completed the ripening. The vintage began on the 28th in normal temperate weather with some showers. The harvest ended at Latour on October 17th. Quality of the grapes was excellent by every parameter of quality and quantity. According to Latour's own words the wine is today a real "blockbuster".

Excellent magnum. Decanted for two hours before the vertical tasting of 1970s. Ruby red colour with a tiny amber edge. Very expressive and youthful on the nose. Shows plum, truffle, tobacco, and walnut aromas. Full-bodied with fine tannin and a powerful, layered mouth-feel. The finish goes on an on. This gorgeous Latour loses nothing after three hours in the glass.

1976 *Côte-Rôtie La Mouline Guigal* *(Rhône)* *98p*
2003/2020 x3 • D 1.5 h / G 1 h

Very hot and dry year resulted in extremely ripe, concentrated and firm wines. No wonder that Guigal's La Mouline, small parcel on the steep hillside of Côte Blonde, yielded extremely dense wine. Dark ruby colour. The nose is very intense with dark berries, brambles and spices such as white pepper and smoked ham. Very intense, firm and rich wine on the palate with high concentration of dark fruitiness, moderate acidity and ripe rich tannins. Long spicy and toasty aftertaste with floral nuances. Velvety wine drinking beautifully now but will keep for another 10-15 years.

1962 *Grange Hermitage Penfolds* *(South-Australia)* *98p*
2002/2010 x3 • D 1 h / G 2 h

After the legendary 1955 Grange, this is the second most successful Grange in Australian wine shows with its 4 trophies and 20 gold and 10 silver medals. This was the first Grange to be made predominantly from Kalimna (Barossa Valley) rather than Magill (Adelaine) fruit, as well as the first and only Grange to use grapes from the cool-climate region of Adelaine Hills. The 1962 is also one of the three Grange vintages (1952 and 1953 are the others) produced in half (375ml) as well as full (750ml) bottles. A blend of 87% Shiraz and 13% Cabernet Sauvignon.

A copybook season in the vineyard with ideal warmth and fairly dry weather gave a propitious birth to this 1962 Grange. Nice looking bottle, level was by the neck. Decanted for one hour. Sweet, elegant and rich, full-bodied wine. It has lots of sweet fruit backed up by finely grained tannin. Topmost quality and true to its great status. We were privileged to taste this inspiring wine.

1927 *Vintage Port Niepoort* *(Portugal)* *98p*
2006/2030 x2 • D 1.5 h / G 2 h

1927 is one of the most enjoyable vintages of older ports just now. It might also be the best vintage between 1912 and 1936. Because of the high appreciation of this vintage, its prices are very high and availability next to nil. The year 1927 began in the Douro valley with rain, and rains continued for the entire spring until the end of June. The summer was scorchingly hot and dry, and the groundwater reserves filled in the spring came in handy. The harvest was made almost entirely in dry weather. Because of the late-summer drought the harvest was very small, but had extremely high quality. Thirty port houses celebrated the year with a vintage wine. The best of them are velvety, fruity and perfectly balanced entities, which no port enthusiast can resist.

The wine came from the cellar of Dirk Niepoort, and was in fine external condition. Fill level was the best possible. Decanted for 60 minutes. Retained its best qualities in glass for approximately 120 minutes. The wine had a delicate maroon colour. Its nose, on the other hand, was anything but delicate. It opened at once and charmed with its challenging, sweet and dark smell. A very soft and perfectly balanced structure. Delicious and pleasantly acidic, vivid port. Full, sweet and chocolaty mouth-feel. Discernible hints of toffee, plum and slight roastedness at the end of the long aftertaste.

1985 *Vieilles Vignes Françaises Bollinger* (Champagne) 98p

2006/2015 x3 • D 15 min / G 1 h

The 1985 was the number one vintage of the mid-1980s. The relatively small crop of ripe and concentrated grapes produced long-lasting and structured wines. The weather favoured Pinot Noir grapes and therefore it is no surprise that this Bollinger's 'living museum' wine from three Pinot Noir plots shows as one of the greatest champagnes of its vintage.

Fine bottle. Decanted 15 minutes. Very deep, mature looking gold colour. Fresh, lightly creamy and meaty on the nose. In the mouth, the dark fruit was rich and tasty. It has a beautiful, fat, creamy complexity, and its palate was balanced and gorgeous. There were many layers of rich fruit on the palate with white chocolate, truffles and marzipan flavours, along with good lively acidity and dazzling Pinot flavours on its finish.

1937 *Richebourg Domaine de la Romanée-Conti* (Côte de Nuits) 98p

2007/now x1 • D 30 min / G 1 h

This Richebourg 1937 was seemingly in good condition, very dusty and equipped with a wax capsule. The level had fallen only 6 cm, and the colour was promising. We did not dare to decant this delicate wine. In the glass it gave out a tempting bouquet with strong blackcurrant and black cherry nose. On the palate it was heavy, rich and very intense. A well-balanced structure and a notably wide and abundant complexity of flavours. This plentiful wine of a small vintage only got better in the glass, and for obvious reasons did not have time to lose any of its unique qualities. A true surprise and a magnificent experience

1961 *Château Latour-à-Pomerol* (Pomerol) 98p

2007/2015 x10 • D 1 h / G 2 h

1961 was an exceptionally great Bordeaux vintage in all of its wine regions. Low yields due to frost and coulure were followed by perfect conditions up until the harvest. One of the all-time bests. The 1961 Latour-à-Pomerol is extremely rare and extremely good. When tasting any wines from Bordeaux of this tremendously hot vintage, it is common to pick up high levels of volatile aromas. Skillful producers managed to avoid the excess amount of volatility with extra care. One of these was Château Latour-à-Pomerol. This wine needs an hour or so of decanting and grows in the glass all the time.

Wine shows tawny red, bright and moderately intense colour. The nose is surprisingly youthful and delicate for the vintage with complexity deriving from ripe blackcurrant aromas and tobacco. There is a hint of volatility enhancing the complexity of the wine. Moderately high acidity together with firm tannins and ripe dark fruit forms a great mouth-feel and balance, which is well supported by integrated high level of alcohol. The length of the wine is remarkable. A touch of sweetness caused by the high level of alcohol at the very end intrigues you to go for another sip of the wine.

1947 Château Ausone *(St.Emilion)* 98p

2004/2015 x3 • D 45 min / G 1 h

From the early 19th century up to the First World War, Château Ausone produced full-bodied wines with a long life expectancy. It took surprisingly long to recover from the war, more than 50 years, because the Ausone wines returned to their classification quality only in 1976. That is when the young, ambitious and talented winemaker Pascal Delbeck took responsibility for the estate's wines, with dramatic results. Our opinion is that the 1947 vintage was the very last great one at Château Ausone before the 1982 vintage.

Very exquisite and healthy looking château-bottled bottle. Excellent level. Decanted one hour before tasting. Bright, deep and dark colour. Hot, sweet and complex clean nose. Prosperous bouquet. What a mouthful of sweet, ripe and chunky Merlot. Amazingly soft and silky on the palate. Well balanced and still after 55 years quite vigorous and refreshing. Ausone was nearly a perfect wine with its marvellous, long and overwhelming aftertaste. Very accessible now, but will last easily a decade or more. Perhaps the best Ausone ever.

1929 Château Haut-Brion Blanc *(Graves)* 98p

2004/2010 x2 • D 30 min / G 1 h

This rare wine is hardly ever missed when talking about Haut-Brion. It is still amazing how many times it has impressed especially on lesser vintages. Nevertheless, when the vintage is superb as in 1929, it really shows its true colours. Very rare and old-looking bottle. Has a good level and promising, youthful colour.

Decanted 30 minutes. Rich, clean, golden colour. Sound and wide bouquet. Aromas of vanilla, amaretto and nuts on the nose. Palate is brilliantly balanced, rich and silky with creamy texture and lots of citrus and flourishing apricot fruit. Multi-dimensional and oily, with layers of mature fruit and beautifully integrated silky tannin and almost invisible acidity. Fabulous and long, vigorous ending. Very youthful and thrilled white beauty with still some years to go.

1934 Dom Pérignon Moët & Chandon *(Champagne)* 98p

2005/now x4 • D 15 min / G 30 min

The 1934 vintage was a pleasant exception in the quality of Champagne vintages in the 1930s. A healthy and large (10 500 kg/ha) crop was harvested after a fairly unproblematic growing season. Moët & Chandon produced only 1200 cases of this third official vintage of Dom Pérignon. (50% Chardonnay and 50% Pinot Noir blend). This wine really astonished us with its vibrancy and elegance.

Clear golden colour with some refined bubbles left. The gracefully developed and rich nose highlights the wine's complexity - oxidative mushroomy aromas turn into powerful roasted coffee with hints of tiramisu. Dry and crisp on the palate with a delicate mousse. Harmonious finish with smokiness and hints of bitter almonds and oxidative hints. Enjoy now in perfect company. No further ageing recommended.

Very vigorous, but silky and smooth wine all at
once. Like sleeping in silky, but warm sheets.
Balanced and gentle, slightly spicy ending.
Stunning and one of the most memorable
Monfortinos we have ever had.

1941

CONTERNO

Monfortino

EXTRA
BAROLO

1978 Musigny Joseph Drouhin *(Côte de Nuits)*   98p
2005/2015 x2 • D 1 h / G 1 h

Bottle was in first-class condition with 2 cm level. Decanted 45 minutes. Bright, mature colour of ruby with a tight orange rim. Open and promising nose packed with ripe, sweet, cassis fruit, violets and creamed cherry flavours. Powerful and round on the palate. Well structured with perfectly balanced velvety tannins and good, underpinning lively acidity. Very intense and has huge concentration. This Musigny had a big and bold personality with an openhanded character and a vigorous, sweet and long ending. Fully mature but no hurry to drink. Enjoy this between 2007-2012.

1928 Château Léoville-Las Cases *(Saint-Julien)*   98p
2004/2010 x5 • D 45 min / G 1 h

Good deep and dark colour. Charming, fruity and ripe open nose. Very rich and complex - impressive youth for this vintage. Very round and good structure - a dazzling bottle! No rush - will last many more years. Much better than the 1926, which was tasted a few months before - this feels much younger and has better balance and harmony. One of the best Leovilles ever tasted.

1982 Château Lafleur *(Pomerol)*   98p
2006/2025 x5 • D 3 h / G 2 h

The 1982 vintage was something exceptional. Early flowering succeeded very well and a perfect summer spell lasted right until the harvest. The crop turned out to be large with incredible quality. The year earlier Marie Robin had decided to trust her 4,5 ha family business in the consulting hands of J-P Mouiex and his team. Beautiful magnum. Decanted three hours. Dark, ruby colour. On the nose aromas of violets, blackberries, truffles, and exotics fruits. Full-bodied and super intense with sweet, jammy fruit and superbly refined, smooth tannins. Thrilling and well-balanced wine with full-sized and powerful finish. This brilliant Merlot-based wine is already very pleasant but should hold easily for another 15 – 20 years.

1975 Château d'Yquem *(Sauternes)*   98p
2005/2030 x3 • D 3 h / G 3 h

Fine looking bottle, level by the neck. Decanted three hours. Deep yellow colour. Fascinating, open, honeyed, flowery botrytis nose with hints of ripe exotic fruits. The palate is very concentrated with intense, sweet richness and waxy, spicy vanilla and lemon notes. In the glass it really develops. Breathtaking length and cleanliness of finish with the complex package of components persisting for minutes in the mouth. A complex, harmonious wine with good posture.

1978 Chambertin Armand Rousseau *(Côte de Nuits)* 98p
2004/2020 x2 • D 1 h / G 3 h

The 1978 vintage was very good for Rousseau and for the whole of Burgundy. Despite a cold, wet spring and a rainy summer, a welcome change in weather in the beginning of August saved the crop. Warm weather continued until late harvest in mid-October.

Good-looking bottle. Level was 2 cm. Decanted for one and a half hours. A substantial wine, traditional in style but amazingly up to date as well. Very dark and bright in colour. Amazingly ripe and open nose with wild mushrooms, blackberry, cherry, pepper, and cedar aromas. Full-bodied and well balanced with silky tannins and exotic fruit that go on and on. This Chambertin is a grand, sumptuous and concentrated Burgundy that will not get any better with time. Which is good, because it is hard to resist now.

1950 Château Cheval Blanc *(St. Emilion)* 98p
2005/2010 x21 • D 30 min / G 1 h

1950 is an underrated vintage in Bordeaux and in many cases rightly so. This was however an excellent vintage in Pomerol, St. Emilion and parts of Graves. The 1950 Cheval Blanc is very rich, concentrated and youthful. There are a number of different négociant-bottlings of this wine - most are very good. Needs only short decanting time and should be drunk over an hour or so. This Nicholas-bottling Cheval was in mint condition. Level by the neck. Decanted for 30 minutes before tasting. What a colour - more bright and youthful than the 1982 Cheval. Very expansive and open nose with an exotic bouquet of ripe fruit, caramel, mint, and cedar. The Cheval Blanc 1950 is still a gorgeously sweet, opulent and full wine with elegant soft tannins. At this time it presented more texture, structure and concentration than the famous 1947. Extra long and multi-dimensional finish. Very hard to resist now, but should easily last through 2010, at least.

1952 Barolo Monfortino Riserva Giacomo Conterno *(Piedmont)* 98p
2006/2010 x4 • D 1 h / G 1 h

Giacomo Conterno is a celebrated traditionalist in the Piedmont town of Monforte d'Alba and has been one of Barolo's most influential forces since the first vintage of Monfortino in 1920. Both the Barolo Cascina Francia and especially the Monfortino Riserva have literally created the history of Barolo since World War I.

Bottle was like new. Decanted 45 minutes. Very pale, a bit brownish but clean and bright colour. On the nose very sound and rich, ripe and open with lots of tobacco, sweet black fruits and toffee aromas. Quite full-bodied, with ripe, dark fruit and a velvety, firm tannin structure. Very vigorous, but silky and smooth wine all at once. Like sleeping in silky, but warm sheets. Balanced and gentle, slightly spicy ending. Stunning and one of the most memorable Monfortinos we have ever had.

1934 Romanée-Conti Domaine de la Romanée-Conti *(Côte de Nuits)* *97p*
1999/2010 x2 • D 1 h / G 1 h

This 1934 Romanée-Conti was made from pre-phylloxera vines, the proudly named vignes originelles françaises non reconstituées. The old Burgundy vintages from pre-phylloxera vines seem to have had better keeping qualities than their successors have ever achieved. The early twentieth-century vintages are therefore normally much younger-looking and livelier than their heirs at the same age.

Good-looking domaine-bottled bottle, ullage was no more than 3 cm. Magnificent, aromatic and oriental bouquet. Excellent, fully evolved wine. Still quite powerful. Despite its smoothness and elegance. Velvety and lingering aftertaste. Impossible not to adore this wine.

1952 Clos des Goisses Philipponnat *(Champagne)* *97p*
2006/2010 x4 • D 15 min / G 30 min

The bottle was in mint condition. Decanted for half an hour. A bit pale in colour but has a very complex, toasty and fresh Pinot-dominant nose. The black grapes give depth and richness, filling the mouth and staying for an incredibly long period of time on the palate. Great balance of weight and acidity. Silky and soft, a ripe sweetness at the finish. However quite a powerful and meaty wine. Far more suitable for drinking with food than as an aperitif. What a treat!

1895 Red Port Livadia Massandra Collection *(Crimea)* *97p*
2005/2020 x4 • D 1 h / G 3 h

This wine was originally ordered for the coronation ceremony of the last Tsar of Russia Nikolai II held in Moscow in 1896. After the ceremony one thousand bottles were returned to Massandra winery as leftovers. Eight hundred bottles of 1895 Red Livadia Port has now been sold on the world wine market as the Massandra Collection. This bright and clear wine with beautiful maroon red colour has a very intense nose with chocolate and nutty aromas spiced with cocoa. Sweet (RS 80 g/l), medium-bodied structure has a very elegant style with balancing acidity and a well-integrated high level of alcohol. The aftertaste of dried fruit and nut flavours extends in great length. Very rich and intense wine with a charmingly complex structure. It is hard not to fall in love with this wine. Massandra Collection wines can challenge the world's best fortified wines with their extremely appealing intensity and stability. This wine is by far the greatest from the Massandra Collection we have tasted.

1900 Château d'Yquem *(Sauternes)* *97p*
2002/2030 x3 • D 1 h / G 3 h

Noble looking bottle, level was mid-shoulder. Decanted for two hours. A brown, intense goldish colour. The dense, complex nose shows spice, honey, butterscotch, and apricot, without any rough edges: it's very harmonious and appealing. The palate is complex and balanced, with some sweetness still left. Good acidity and a honeyed thick texture. This was a great vintage for Yquem, and it is easy to imagine that 100 years ago this 1900 showed the same promise as the famous 2001 today. Holding well, but we still recommend a few years' cellaring for this beauty.

1926 *Vintage Champagne Krug* (Champagne) *97p*

2006/now x2 • D 15 min / G 1 h

The bottle appeared to be in bad condition, the label was almost gone and the vintage was left almost unknown, only the last number, 6, was left. The colour of the wine was though very clear, and the level was excellent. Decanted for 10 minutes, held on to its best qualities in the glass for about 30 minutes. As always with Krug, one tends to always expect perfection from the wine, and this peculiar bottle with "reserve de Wermach" label did not let us down. This bottle was one of those that the German troops had reserved for themselves to celebrate their great victory. We met Rémi Krug and asked what vintage the wine might be from. He believed that it was from the last vintage that got bottled before the war, i.e. 1926.

The mere thought of enjoying this wine that was in its time meant to symbolise victory was enough to make it magnificent, regardless of its quality. But fortunately the quality lived up to our great expectations. The colour was beautiful golden yellow and clear. The bouquet was very intense, fruity with sophisticated perfume. The bubbles were typical for Krug, small and moving serenely. Almost as if small pearls were rising to the surface to give the wine dignity. The bouquet was so overwhelming that the taste itself seemed a little reserved at first. But after a short lag it mesmerized the taste sense as well giving a truly savoury and abundant taste experience. A perfectly cultivated, multilayered and cool, sophisticated wine!

1945 *Château Léoville-Las Cases* (Saint-Julien) *97p*

2004/2020 x12 • D 1 h / G 1 h

This Leoville was one of the most elegant and stylish wines in the Vine Club's 1945 vintage dinner. There was a super-Bordeaux 1945 flight to finish our third main course. We tasted Latour, Haut-Brion, Lafite, Palmer, and this handsome Leoville together. We started with 1945 Leoville magnum, which was an excellent château-bottling. Level was top-shoulder. Decanted for two hours. Very bright, surprisingly youthful looking colour. Fresh and open nose with intense black raspberries, plum and smoke aromas. The palate, however, was smoother and softer than expected. Very elegant, almost feminine structure. Rich and had excellent balance and a refined, smooth ending. The height of sophistication.

1946 *Cabernet Sauvignon Inglenook* (Napa Valley) *97p*

2002/2010 x2 • D 30 min / G 1 h

This was a warm and high-quality year in Napa Valley with an unusually early harvest that started in mid-August. The bottle had no label, but otherwise in mint condition. Decanted for 30 minutes. Deep, developed, lovely colour. Rich, open and fabulous bouquet very reminiscent of Cabernet aromatics. This is a gigantic and powerful wine, with delicious layers of fruit and rounded tannins. Ripe, chocolaty and exotic full-bodied work of genius with an extended finish. A real surprise, as it was in incredibly good condition for its age. Great fully mature Napa wine.

1950 Château Latour-à-Pomerol *(Pomerol)* 97p

2006/2020 x14 • D 1.5 h / G 3 h

Excellent magnum. Decanted for 1.5 hours. The wine has a youthful, deep, dark red colour. The nose was so rich and forthcoming in ripe black fruit, coffee, cedar wood, chocolate, and truffle aromas. Excellent backbone and grip. Big on palate with superior complexity offering appealing redcurrant, spicy and smoky oak and mocha flavours. This appealing Latour-a-Pomerol has excellent balance and a long, structured finish. Wonderful wine.

1966 Richebourg Jayer Henri *(Côte de Nuits)* 97p

2007/2015 x4 • D 1 h / G 2 h

Henri Jayer is probably the most legendary Burgundian vigneron. He committed his life to pioneering the cultivation and vinification of Pinot Noir. The high concentration of Jayer's wines has charmed many Burgundy lovers. The reasons for the concentration levels are various: not using potassium on the vineyards from the Second World War has yielded smaller grapes with higher proportion of solid matters. Cooler fermentation temperatures and limited amount of rackings are also listed as a secret of the concentration in his wines. Although the beginning of the 1966 vintage was disastrous with spring hail limiting the size of the crop and a series of rainstorms, the weather improved. The autumn was very favourable and the harvest took place in ideal conditions at the end of September making 1966 a very good vintage.

Excellent bottle with 2 cm Ullage. Very pure, bright, dark red colour with good depth. Ripe, full, open nose with breathtaking fruity and earthy aromas. Full of gentle personality and complexity. This is an exquisite wine to respect for its sensitivity rather than strength. Very much alive and voluptuous. Long and rich aftertaste. Finely tuned experience.

1945 Château Latour *(Pauillac)* 97p

1998/2030 x10 • D 2 h / G 2 h

The outside of the bottle was slightly damaged, no capsule and only remnants of the label left. Otherwise it had a healthy looking colour and the level was top-shoulder. Decanted for two hours. Deep dark colour. Open, ripe and spicy on the nose. This wine is even now a real blockbuster with well-expressed fruit and a marvellous purity throughout. Warm, seductive wine without being overly powerful. Very well structured tannin. Certain earthiness on the finish. An absolute tour de force.

1970 Nacional Vintage Port Quinta do Noval *(Portugal)* 97p

2005/2030 x2 • D 3 h / G 5 h

This was the first vintage when almost every port house bottled all their production themselves. Good-looking bottle, bottled by Quinta Do Noval, as always. Decanted one hour. Dark, healthy ruby red in colour with just the slightest browning on the edge. Needs more time in the glass or decanter, but once opened the wine drinks beautifully. Round and supple with excellent grip of fine tannin. Delicious chocolate, berry and plum flavours. Intense, fleshy but not aggressive. Some oriental spices and black pepper here, all with a generous hint of white chocolate and mocha that comes in on the very long finish. We prefer this to the 1975.

1921   *Château Suduiraut* (Sauternes)   97p

2003/2015 x3 • D 1 h / G 3 h

Old-looking bottle with only medium-shoulder level. It had an excellent, promising, bright deep golden colour. Decanted for 45 minutes. From a fantastic vintage in Sauternes, this wine is fabulously exciting, ripe, luxurious and not overly sweet. Classic lively botrytis flavours. Very exotic wine with great balance and harmony. The warm and long finish offers dried fruit intensity along with mineral, honey and tropical fruit complexity. Drink now to 2015.

1988   *Côte-Rôtie La Mouline Guigal* (Rhône)   97p

2005/2025 x9 • D 3 h / G 2 h

Decanted three hours. Immense dark colour, with just slight hues of maturity. The nose has sweet blackberries, toasty oak and a wealth of fruit with a coffee elegance. As it develops it becomes more masculine, offering aromas of meat, earth and iron. The palate has great power controlled by lovely balance. There's a bitter-edged grip and fine acidity. Full, weighty but reserved rather than opulent. Despite over ten years' bottle age, the quality of both vintage and cuvée shine through with great power - this is incredible wine which needs at least another five years or more in the cellar to show its best, and will drink well for a decade or more thereafter. Excellent with potential for improvement.

1962   *Hill of Grace Henschke* (Eden Valley)   97p

2001/2015 x2 • D 30 min / G 1 h

Hill of Grace has a rare pure fruit resonance that captures the warp and weft of an historic single vineyard originally planted in the 1860s. Ancient genetic Shiraz vines, many over 140 years old, are planted on red clay soils overlain by sandy and silty loams interspersed with gravels. The wine speaks profoundly of place and is the quintessential Eden Valley Shiraz. Partial barrel fermentation in a combination of new American and French oak and 18 months maturation bring further complexity and harmony.

Fine, recorked bottle with perfect level. Decanted one hour. Good, healthy dark colour, no sign of ageing. Showing nuances of dried blackberry, vanilla bean and coffee in the nose. On the palate the wine offered plentiful flavours of vanilla, black cherry fruit, tar, and dark chocolate. A good marriage of sweet fruitiness and vibrant acidity. Silky tannins and a textbook balance enhanced a long, solid finish. Still very fine.

1961   *Château L´Evangile* (Pomerol)   97p

2005/2020 x3 • D 1 h / G 2 h

Decent looking château-bottling. Level by the neck. Dark and deep, fairly youthful colour. Lovely complex and a very fragrant, vigorous nose of fresh blackcurrants and cedar with a peppery note. Dazzling silky texture on the palate, with pleasing balance and acidity. A wine of real depth, fat structure and breadth. The soft tannins and oak were well integrated decades ago and the overall impression is sweet fruit driven. Long, aromatic and elegant ending without being too biting. A rich and solid claret.

1952   *Château Cheval Blanc* (St.Emilion)   97p
2005/2020 x14 • D 2 h / G 2 h

This must be the best price-quality ratio Cheval Blanc that can be found. The vintage was very good overall in Bordeaux but especially on the Right Bank. A warm spring and hot summer from June until the end of August ensured good vegetative growth to the vines. Only the cold September ruined the dreams of outstanding quality. This wine has been always delicious when tasted.

Deep, clear brick red colour already indicates the richness of the wine. Powerful still elegant nose reveals ripe dark fruits: mainly blackcurrants, dark chocolate, coffee, and spices. Almost full-bodied taste, it is very opulent and fleshy with velvety texture. Tannins are gentle but firm and the finish is very balanced. The wine is drinking perfectly now but has the qualities to keep for another decade. But why wait, since it definitely will not improve any longer.

1971   *Vintage Champagne Krug* (Champagne)   97p
2005/2015 x4 • D 15 min / G 30 min

What a vintage! It gave the worst case scenario for vine growers throughout the growing period. Spring frosts were followed by storms in May. Hot and humid weather caused uneven flowering. Severe hail storms in June were followed by a stormy and rainy August. Just when vine growers were about to loose their faith, mother nature turned their frustration miraculously into celebration. September brought hot and dry weather saving the suffering vines and vine growers. The crop was small and fierce selection was a key part in producing top wines. The quality in these cases has been outstanding.

Decanted for 15 minutes. Quite deep, bright golden colour. An attractive nose of truffles, nuts, coffee, honey, and vanilla aromas. The palate was full and harmonious, with beautiful purity and structure. 1971 Krug has a prosperous personality and loads of character. An exquisite wine to drink now.

1967   *Barbaresco Sorí San Lorenzo Angelo Gaja* (Piedmont)   97p
2007/2010 x5 • D 30 min / G 1 h

Both bottles were like new. Decanted 1 hour. This first vintage of Sori San Lorenzo absolutely ranks with the finest wines in Italy. The best and most delicious bouquet we have ever experienced in Italian wines. Superbly fragrant, perfumed with minerals, exotic black fruits, toasty vanilla, truffles, and hints of white chocolate. Refined and stylish despite its full-bodied, prosperous personality. Extremely long and round, velvety tannins and a ripe fruity aftertaste. An emotional wine with great strength and refinement. Drink now to 2010.

1959 *Corton-Charlemagne Domaine Louis Latour* (Côte de Beaune) *97p*
2000/2010 x3 • D 1 h / G 1 h

A very fine and reliable white Burgundy vintage. Generally Louis Latour's Corton-Charlemagnes are rich and warming wines with a lot of temperament.

The bottle was in a superlative condition and ullage was only two cm. Bright, lovely deep-golden colour. Open, sweet, spicy and flavourful nose. One did not want to take one's nose out of the glass. Prosperous, well balanced, intense and multi-faceted wine. As good and big as expected. A real joy now, but the good fruit and dense structure makes us think this may be even more breathtaking in the future.

1971 *Comtes de Champagne Rosé Taittinger* (Champagne) *97p*
2005/2010 x2 • D 15 min / G 20 min

Bottle in excellent condition. Tasted with Richard Juhlin at his home. According to him, this is supposed to be one of the best rosés ever made, and he was so right, as usual. Not decanted. Bright, salmon rosé colour with plenty of slowly climbing bubbles. Intense toasty nose with brioche and creaminess. Lovely tones of strawberries. Very gentle and intense rosé. Dry and crisp on the palate with wonderful mouth water-ing mousse and creamy strawberry flavours lasting long in lingering harmonious aftertaste with depth and finesse. What a first-rate rosé from the best Champagne vintage of the 1970's!

1988 *Côte Rôtie La Turque Guigal* (Rhône) *97p*
2004/2025 x9 • D 2 h / G 2 h

Bottle was in A1 condition. Decanted for two hours. We have had this splendid La Turque many times over the last years. It has always been a very satisfying, straightforward, big wine and excellent particularly with food. Very good, deep, almost black colour. The open nose shows nice smoky, peppery and spicy tenderness. On the palate it was still a bit too tannic and alcoholic, but only a little. Huge in size. Great grip and structure. Breathtaking in its potential. Strong, rich and complex finish. Needs time and patience.

1969 *La Tâche Domaine de la Romanée-Conti* (Côte de Nuits) *97p*
2006/2020 x8 • D 1 h / G 1 h

In 1969 at Domaine de la Romanée-Conti the summer was especially hot. The September was wet and cold. Maturation, however, was first-rate, and the wines were tannic and had an excellent future ahead.

Bottle was in good condition, and level was 3 cm. Decanted 45 minutes. Deep, dark red colour. Nose was very lively and open with aromas of mint, tobacco, dark chocolate, and ripe fruit. A quite big and opulent wine with beautiful balance. The ending has well-behaved roundness and length. Seductive wine with fresh acidity and finesse.

NUMBER 142.
NUMBER 143.
NUMBER 144.
NUMBER 145.

Domaine de Chevalier tasting

1986   Château Lafite-Rothschild (Pauillac)   97p

2005/2025 x24 • D 3 h / G 2 h

Although 1986 yielded the biggest crop since the World War II, this vintage has been the underdog compared to the vintage 1985. 1986 started with a mild winter that was followed by a damp and cool spring with a delayed bud-break. May and June turned out well with good flowering period and the weather continued very hot and dry the whole summer, making the grapes very concentrated and thick-skinned. Refreshing showers were welcomed in September but violent storms with heavy rain took their toll on the ultimate concentration and quality of the grapes. Nevertheless, the weather got better again and the harvest was done in superb weather.

Deep, intense red colour with orange tint on the rim. Nose develops temptingly in the glass starting from rich cassis, tar and cedar notes and then moving into complex and intense aromas of coffee, spices and violets. Full-bodied mouth-feel is completed with very firm and marked tannin, moderately high acidity compared to other first growths of the vintage and extensively rich fruit intensity of cassis, figs and plums. The long finish is highlighted with a range of appealing aromas of violets, coffee and dark chocolate. A very aristocratic and subtle wine with many more years if not decades to come.

1990   Château Haut-Brion (Graves)   97p

2005/2020 x22 • D 2 h / G 2 h

At Château Haut-Brion the winter was warm and budding started exceptionally early. The start of the spring was cold but summer was especially hot and dry. Little rain in September allowed an abundant and very healthy crop to ripen. Harvesting began September 4th and ended September 28th.

A wonderful magnum. Decanted two hours before tasting. Deep, youthful colour. Marvellously open and fragrant nose of ripe fruit, mineral, tobacco, and spicy oak. Silky and velvety with superb concentration. This has the most wonderful purity and depth of fruit. Fat and rich wine with medium acidity. Very forward and nicely balanced. Lovely, perfumed, long, spicy and elegant finish. Almost as good as the legendary 1989 Haut-Brion.

1976   Cabernet Sauvignon Special Selection Caymus (Napa Valley)   97p

2004/2015 x3 • D 1 h / G 1 h

The bottle was damaged from the outside, but happily the inside was almost pure gold. Decanted for 45 minutes. Wonderfully deep and complex, as rich in colour and aroma as it is on the palate. Classic Caymus flavours on the nose - herb and black cherry, ripe plum, aniseed, and earth notes. Full-bodied, with tobacco, vanilla and liquorice aromas and a velvety mouth-feel of concentrated tannins and superb fruit. Impressive depth and layers of complexity. The tannins turn silky on the long, persistent aftertaste. Caymus 1976 is an impressive example of amazingly mouth-watering thirty-year-old Napa Valley Cabernet. This wonderful wine will last for another decade.

1928 *Château Suduiraut* (Sauternes) 97p
2002/2010 x2 • D 1 h / G 3 h

Old, dusty bottle with a tight capsule and a branded cork, no sign of label whatsoever. Level was high-shoulder. Decanted for two hours. Warm, golden colour. Very rich, honeyed and sound bouquet with apricot and peach aromas. A real charmer - a creamy, soft, crisp and fat wine with all the three dimensions of length, breadth and depth in order. Superb balance. The best Suduiraut we have ever tasted. This solemn wine seemed as perfect now as it is ever likely to get, so just take pleasure in this pure gold!

1950 *Château Pétrus* (Pomerol) 97p
2005/2025 x8 • D 1 h / G 2 h

Miserable looking château-bottled bottle, but the level was by the neck. Mature, healthy-looking colour. Very fragrant and intense nose that has hints of blackberries and vanilla oak. Extremely smooth and silky, but at the same time fantastically massive and thick, almost too good to be true. A generous Pétrus that is very complex and harmonious. Ready of course, yet enough depth to last. A stunningly mature wine that, thrilled the mind as much as the palate. This wine can easily live on for at least two more decades.

1989 *Meursault 1er Cru Charmes Comtes Lafon* (Côte de Beaune) 97p
2007/2015 x4 • D 2 h / G 2.5 h

This was a year of a tiny crop (20 to 30 hl/ha), very ripe grapes and great concentration. In 1989 a generous winter lead into early bud break in spring. The hot summer with a dry and sunny autumn resulted early harvest. Meursault Charmes is the largest and best known vineyard in Meursault. Its rich cold clay soil has a good capacity of retaining water beneficial on hot vintages like this. On the other hand the limestone is known to benefit further ageing compared to other premier cru sites in Meursault. According to Dominique Lafon, these factors guarantee a long ageing potential for their wines of 1989.

Intense bright yellow colour. Pronounced nose is full of buttery aromas, nuts and ripe pineapple aromas with toastiness. Dry and moderately crisp wine with great intensity and fatness. Elegant toastiness and long opulent finish. Very enjoyable currently but will keep another 6-8 years.

1941   Unico Bodegas Vega Sicilia *(Ribera del Duero)*   97p
2001/2010 x2 • D 2 h / G 1 h

It seems nearly impossible to find Unico outside mainland Spain. So every time we return from a trip to Spain it is tempting to carry along some hard-earned bottles. This rare 1941 Unico was found in Barcelona and its condition was almost equivalent to new.

Level was by the neck. Decanted for two hours. Very dark, mature brown colour with only hints of red left. Intense and very expressive nose with aromas of eucalyptus and peppermint. Surprisingly feminine wine on the palate - smooth and soft taste. To some extent lighter than many other vintages. However, the marvellous acidity keeps the wine fresh and very much alive. Sensitive and fragile wine with fantastic structure and balance. Silky with a long, rich finish. Definitely one of the greatest Unicos along with the 1942, 1957, 1962, 1968, 1970, and 1985!

1929   Château Pétrus *(Pomerol)*   97p
2001/2015 x11 • D 30 min / G 1 h

Many wine critics consider this vintage to be the best since 1900. This handsome and rare Pétrus was first-rate proof of that. Château-bottled with top-shoulder level. Decanted for one hour. Good depth, with quite a mature hue. Certainly not the darkest wine from this gloomy coloured vintage. The nose is mystical and fascinatingly seductive. Sound and open with ripe fruit and gentle tannin. It combines style and class with exotic flavours of black cherries, coffee and cedar. A fabulously thick, soft and mature mouth-feel. Intense and rich port-like aftertaste. This is a very good Pétrus indeed and one of the best wines of the vintage.

1929   Chambertin Joseph Drouhin *(Côte de Nuits)*   97p
2002/2010 x4 • D 1.5 h / G 1 h

The bottle was in quite a decent condition. Ullage was only 3 cm and it was Drouhin-bottled. Decanted for one and half hours before tasting, it still needed almost two more hours to open completely. Very good, dark and deep colour. Hardly any sediment. Great depth and complexity. Round, soft, rich, and big wine - has more concentration and weight than Leroy´s Chambertin 1929, which was a feminine and modest wine. Fabulous length and perfect balance. Currently at its peak, but should hold there for at least five to seven years. One truly wishes that they would still make more red Burgundies like this controversial wine: gigantic and powerful, but at the same time so velvety and persistent.

2000   Trockenbeerenauslese No. 10 Welschriesling   97p
"Zwischen den Seen" Alois Kracher *(Burgerland)*
2006/2030 x3 • D 30 min / G 3 h

A great vintage in Burgenland. The crop was very high in quality but regrettably low in quantity. The concentration in sweet wines was amazing as in this nectar-like TBA wine.

Vinified in the traditional way in large vats as Kracher's "Zwischen den Seen" is always, this particular wine presented Kracher's most concentrated TBA wine of the vintage.

Golden yellow colour with very high viscosity. The nose is extremely rich and honeyed with intense apricot and honeysuckle aromas. Lusciously sweet with residual sugar of 399,6 g/l. Syrupy texture is delicately balanced with crisp acidity (7,8 g/l). The alcohol level is naturally a very low 5,5 %. Pure, lean and intense wine with enormous lingering finish. Lovely now, but no hurry to drink up for 20-30 years.

1975   *Château Lafleur* (Pomerol)   *97p*

2003/2015 x14 • D 3 h / G 2 h

Fine-looking bottle. Decanted for three hours. Very deep red colour. At first the nose was a bit quiet with lightweight touches of menthol, mineral, spice, and sweet cedary flavours. After four hours it became fully opened. Immensely concentrated, almost too dense. Still very tannic, but has massive reserves of sweet, luscious fruit. Great depth and power. Superb purity. Substantial, very long and exotic ending. We would never hesitate to drink this black beauty now. But if possible do not touch the bottle until 2020, you will be rewarded. Perhaps the wine of the vintage in Bordeaux.

1947   *Château l´Eglise Clinet* (Pomerol)   *97p*

2001/2015 x11 • D 1 h / G 2 h

First-rate looking bottle with high-shoulder level. Decanted one hour. Inspiring dark, healthy colour. Full-bodied and wonderful in its complexity and structure. This charming Pomerol continues to demonstrate rich, thick, sweet flavours and aromas that range from black berries, ripe plums, chocolate, and truffles. Sound, velvety and long. An excellent effort, and as good as the impressive 1921 and 1949. Wonderful now, but will last at least one more decade.

1958   *Unico Bodegas Vega Sicilia* (Ribera del Duero)   *97p*

2007/2015 x4 • D 1 h / G 2 h

This 1958 vintage dates back to the "dark period" in Vega Sicilia's glorious history. The farm was purchased in 1952 by the Prodes seed company who evitably were more interested in the farming operation than wines. The difficult Prodes period lasted until 1966, but even in those financially tight times magnificent wines were born. Medium-deep developing garnet colour. The slightly volatile nose is tart, with sour cherries, chemical nuances and earthy tones. The wine opened up magnificently in the glass revealing aromas of salted liquorice and raisins. Lively velvety mouth-feel with warming alcohol influence. This wine has passed its peak but it will keep moderately well for a number of years.

1990   *Richebourg Domaine Leroy* (Côte de Nuits)   *97p*

2005/2020 x5 • D 2 h / G 2 h

Decanted one and a half hours. Giving and lush, the 1990 Richebourg shows an opaque purple colour and intense aromas of blackberries, fresh herbs, plums, and spices. The wine offers a powerful, muscular body, with velvety texture, sweet, big tannins and very long, persistent finish. Powerful yet harmonious, the 1990 promises a long life in the bottle.

1955   *Vintage Champagne Krug* (Champagne)   *97p*

2004/now x2 • D 15 min / G 30 min

A large-sized crop was harvested in this first underrated vintage. The wines have proven to be highly long-lived and harmonious. Many are drinking magnificently today with well preserved, elegant and subtle fruitiness, and lively acidic backbone. Krug Vintage is one of the masterpieces of this vintage. Very promising appearance. Decanted for 15 minutes. The colour is still quite light, with touches of bright gold and bronze. An exotic nose of freshly baked bread, warm butter, nuts, and soft vanilla aromas. Very high in acidity. The taste is magnificently concentrated and developed. Well balanced with an exquisite silky-smooth structure. The 1955 Krug has a wonderful exotic richness and concentrated aftertaste, which is close to perfection. A very hearty and charming wine.

1949   *Château Latour* (Pauillac)   *97p*

2006/2025 x21 • D 2 h / G 2 h

Fine looking bottle, level was high-shoulder. Decanted for two hours. Very good, dark and deep colour. Still complex and rich on the nose. Full and masculine wine that has more appeal than Lafite 1949. Great concentration of sweet fruit, leather and tobacco. The delicious flavours are enhanced by attractive layers on the complex mid-palate. Rich and elegant Latour with great intensity and balance. A concentration of fruit and, though fairly low in acidity, the tannins do just enough to leave it quite fresh and grippy. Superbly long, smooth and enduring finish. As always it showed no sign of getting tired, needing another decade to hit its peak. A great bottle of Bordeaux!

1985   *Château Haut Brion Blanc* (Graves)   *97p*

2002/2025 x3 • D 1 h / G 2 h

Decanted one hour. Deep, beautiful golden colour. Open and exotic nose with buttery, melon, nut, and interesting fruit aromas. This rich, beautifully balanced and silky wine has fantastic ripeness of honeyed fruits and intense velvety texture. Very good integration of acidity that is still breezy and palate-refining into the long, very focused and sheer finish. Excellent definition and very lively. This is a white, long-distance runner. Will last at least two more decades.

1982   Château Margaux (Margaux)   97p

2006/2020 x3 • D 3 h / G 2 h

Fine-looking magnum. Decanted for two hours. We were very impressed when we first tasted this wine almost 15 years ago. Since then we have been just as impressed every time we have tasted it. This, the most recent magnum tasted, makes us feel even more impressed, for the wine is truly hitting its peak now. Every bit as full-bodied and vigorous as we recall from earlier tastings. Well-balanced and full of meaning. Still remarkably young and intense, displaying the depth and extract of this fine vintage and this eminent property. A solid wine with generous flavours of black fruits, coffee, cedar wood, and cigar leaf. A long, bit sweet and elegant finish that goes on and on alluring the palate. A reliable choice.

1947   Dom Pérignon Moët & Chandon (Champagne)   97p

2006/now x3 • D 5 min / G 20 min

A fabulous looking bottle. Decanted for only five minutes. Clear, bright golden colour. Tiny, vivid bubbles make up the fine mousse. Elegant and complex nose with a hint of coffee and nut aromas. Smooth and creamy, nicely balanced structure. Very full-bodied and rich with a mature, fresh and long finish leaving a satisfying impression on the palate. Full of life, this wine has held very well.

1991   Ermitage le Pavillon Chapoutier (Rhône)   97p

2006/2020 x4 • D 2 h / G 2 h

The Pavillon vineyard has a surface area of about 4 ha. Its geological composition is characteristic: the soil is made up of a fine layer of deposits on a granite ground. In 1991 after a severe pruning the grapes were harvested at full maturity. The 80+ year-old vines gave a very low yield: 10hl/ha. Vinified by Michel Chapoutier, Pavillon 1991 went through a long maceration that lasted for more than 5 weeks. Bottle like new. Decanted for two hours. Open and broad nose with intoxicating aromas of violet, ink and smoke. Rich and full-bodied with wonderful concentration. Long and balanced with superb acidity. This powerhouse should last for two decades or more.

1973   Krug Collection Champagne Krug (Champagne)   97p

2007/2015 x3 • D 15 min / G 1 h

Krug is known for the very pricey high-quality vintage champagnes they mature in their cellars for 6-10 years before introducing in the market. Krug Collection is a series of their best old vintages stored in the estate's own cellars for 15-40 years until their "second life" begins. The bottles are then given numbered metal plates and sold in very small quantities.

The magnum we opened was outwardly in perfect condition. The wine was youthful and its fill level first class. Decanted for 10 minutes. Retained its best qualities in glass for approximately 45 minutes. In our opinion, this is one of the best Krugs of the 1970s, with only the 1979 vintage reaching the same level. When we tasted the same vintage a few months ago, the experience was different. Then it was an ordinary vintage bottling in a normal-sized bottle. Although the wine was the same in both cases, the recorking had been made 16 years later to the benefit of the Collection. The 1973 Collection we opened now had a clearly more youthful and fuller feel to it.

Light golden colour. Small bubbles moving up slowly in tight strings. Really elegant, multi-dimensional nose with hints of nut, toffee, mint, and vanilla. Really full and dense mouth-feel. As if you were enjoying velvety smooth thick cream blended with light toffee and layers of tropical fruit - a very intensive and pure taste experience. The broad mousse with a wide scope caressed the palate gently and peacefully. A refined long aftertaste. A balanced and noble champagne.

1990 Côte-Rôtie La Landonne Guigal *(Rhône)*   97p
2003/2020 x2 • D 3 h / G 2 h

Decanted for three hours. This was very, very good. A fascinating combination of elegance and power. At first it did not give much on the nose, but after two hours it really opened up: intense ripe dark fruit, a touch of caramel, some herbs, and a bit of vanilla aromas. On the palate this is full, clean, hot, showing a firm tannic structure and nice acidity. Everything suggests it will age well. Fine structure and well balanced as La Landonne always is. Constant power from beginning to the end. Firmer than the La Turque and not as sweet. A great effort.

1947 Château Calon-Ségur *(Saint-Estèphe)*   97p
2006/2015 x23 • D 1 h / G 2 h

Two centuries ago Calon was under the ownership of Marquis Nicolas-Alexandre de Ségur, owner of chateaux Lafite and Latour. He was also the president of the parliament of Bordeaux. Seemingly de Ségur preferred Calon to his other famous properties, and he is reputed to have stated "I make wine at Lafite and Latour, but my heart is at Calon". The heart publicized on every label of Calon-Ségur commemorates this saying today. Just as the de Ségur lost his heart to Calon, so did we.

This 1947 Calon was the most generous and sumptuous Calon-Ségur we have ever tasted. Château-bottled with heart on the label. Level was by the neck. Decanted for 2 hours before dinner. Dark, deep colour. An intense, open bouquet with plenty of fruit. Very chunky and loaded. Superb ripe fruit with admirable intensity of flavour. Finely balanced with a long, soft and very graceful aftertaste. Big-hearted wine.

1961 Grange Hermitage Penfolds *(South Australia)*   97p
2001/2010 x3 • D 1 h / G 1 h

This very hot and dry year ended up in a moderately small crop, thus a rare vintage to see on markets nowadays. This year the blend had 88% Shiraz and 12% Cabernet Sauvignon. The grapes came from Magill Estate,

Morphett Vale and Modbury Vineyard from Adelaide region, Kalimna Vineyard from Barossa and Coonawarra. This beauty was reconditioned by Penfolds in London. Ullage was topped up with reserve wine and re-corked.

Decanted for one hour. Very dark mature colour. The nose was very cedary and Bordeaux-like, with leather and eucalyptus notes. Also fresh butter and American oak on the nose. Very generously textured and nicely balanced. It has a particular sweetness of almost overripe fruit and a body almost like old Port. Very persuasive blend. On the palate it was a big, rich and intense wine with lovely sweetness of alcohol, balanced acidity and plenty of length. Definitely one of the best Granges ever made.

NUMBER 170.

1928 *Château Pétrus* (Pomerol)   *97p*
2007/2025 x3 • D 30 min / G 1 h

This vintage yielded a large crop with ups and downs in quality. Some succeeded and some have faded in the long run. Although Château Pétrus had not yet gained its superstar reputation, the signs were there of what was to come.

Still moderately intense, clear, brick red colour. Very complex and rich nose with extensive amounts of aromas. Ripe dark fruits, toastiness, roasted coffee, pencil shavings, and beef stock. The crisp palate has lost its most intense fruit but it still shows great amounts of ripe red berry flavours. Tannin structure has smoothened although the wine is still astringent reflecting the hot vintage. The finish is very mineral and savoury with rustic and austere aftertaste. The wine will not benefit from further ageing but it is to be adored now.

NUMBER 171.

1962 *Romanée-Conti Domaine de la Romanée-Conti* (Côte de Nuits) *97p*
2006/2020 x5 • D 1.5 h / G 1 h

This wine must have been one of the most hidden treasures of the wine world. It really showed the dark side of Pinot Noir by being closed down for many years. In this case it closed down for four decades! All this time it was considered a lesser wine until it finally bloomed in the beginning of the Millennium.

This bottle was in excellent condition. Decanted for one and a half hours. The bouquet was youthful, eager and leapt in your face. Quite leathery and spicy, with dark fruit. A clear and very well balanced wine. It kept on evolving in the glass positively. A beautiful and unique wine that still has many years left.

NUMBER 172.

1928 *Château d'Yquem Sauternes* (Bordeaux)   *97p*
2007/2020 x2 • D 45 min / G 2 h

This Cruse bottled Yquem had been optimally cellared by one owner only. Therefore the bottle and its label were in perfect condition. The colour was charming medium deep and bright amber. The sound and fragrant nose was explosively charming with apricot, crème brûlée and herbaceous aromas. The nose promised a lot but the palate exceeded all those expectations: extremely fine and lively, all elements in an admirable harmony. An all experienced wine that gave a softly sweet taste of great depth and complexity. It is fully mature but very much alive, promising the wine further 10-15 years aging capacity. We were taken by its grace.

1975 R.D. Bollinger *(Champagne)*   97p

2007/2015 x3 • D 15 min / G 45 min

Yet another remarkable proof of the potential of the 1975 vintage. This variable vintage has produced some very fine champagnes. The best, such as this Bollinger R.D., have aged with grace and possess outstanding youthfulness and liveliness today.

Beautiful deep golden colour. Lively small-sized bubbles freshen up this concentrated wine. Rich and nuanced toasty nose. Hazelnuts, dark fruits and mushroomy notes. The elegant and complex nose is complemented by a matching palate. Firm acidic backbone and outstanding fruit intensity. Fine-grained, elegant and soft mousse. Long brioche like flavour at the end invites you to take another sip of this mature and charming wine. Buy it when you see it.

1961 Château Pichon Longueville Comtesse de Lalande   97p
(Pauillac)   2005/2015 x7 • D 1 h / G 2.5 h

Fine looking magnum. Level was top-shoulder. Decanted one hour. Moderately deep garnet colour with orange hue. Extremely elegant and delicate nose with spices, mint, soy, cigar box, and ripe blackcurrants. Medium-bodied wine shows an exquisite elegance thanks to its vivid acidity, silky tannins and supple ripe black fruit character. Spicy cinnamon and ginger flavours combined with elegant cedar and leathery aromas. Incredible persistence and overwhelmingly balanced lingering finish. Elegance par excellence.

1959 Riesling Trockenbeerenauslese Scharzhofberger Gold   97p
Capsule Egon Müller *(Mosel-Saar-Ruwer)*
2000/2020 x3 • D 2 h / G 2 h

This noble bottle looked like new with the shining gold capsule topping it. Decanted for two hours. A bright and deep golden colour. Sound and perfumed nose with flavours of honeyed fruit, tropical fruits, mangoes, and pineapples. Rich, layered with well-integrated acidity. This was a powerful, velvety-textured and explosively prosperous wine. Dry, multi-dimensional, warm and long, full-bodied finish. Very much a top wine, but so is the price tag.

1990 Hermitage J.L Chave *(Rhône)*   97p

2005/2020 x3 • D 2 h / G 4 h

A true masterpiece by Gérard Chave. Chave is known for opting for blending Syrah from their 15 ha vineyards on the Hermitage hill. Their philosophy is against single vineyard wines since blending guarantees more complexity in the wine. In this superb wine this is clearly indicated by the tremendous complexity. Syrah from Bessards gives rich fruit intensity and concentration to the wine while Méal more depth in flavours and bouquet. Rocoules adds finesse in structure and length along the floral tones. L'Hermite contributes peppery earthy tones and colour. Péléat gives wildness and firmness in structure whereas Diognières provides colour and the savoury tastiness. Gérard Chave himself has compared this top vintage to 1952 and 1961.

Fine looking bottle. Decanted for two hours. This beautiful Hermitage has a deep, dark and seductive colour. On the nose amazing aromas of blackberries, vanilla, herbs, and refreshing minerals. The palate was remarkably rich and long and less tannic than expected. The finish was super-long and pure with pleasant sweetness and rich, earthy flavours. This is the essence of Syrah with a long life span ahead.

1966 Krug Collection Champagne *(Champagne)*   97p

2003/2010 x2 • D 10 min / G 1 h

This second life launch of Krug bears no discorgement date on it. The wine is exactly the same as the regular vintage but it has been aged in the Krug cellars undiscorged. As this wine shows, it is a great concept that proves the true potential of the top wines of Champagne. The 1966 was an exciting vintage in the region despite the early scepticism due to the January frosts, frequent summer hail and a disturbed blossoming. The average yield remained at 7000 kg/ha but the perfect harmony was not disrupted by these challenges.

Fine looking bottle with excellent level. Decanted for ten minutes. Clear, bright bronzing colour. It has a gorgeous, open nose full of flowers and exotic fruits. There was a sweet playfulness as well as elegance and a smooth personality. Lots of sweet citrus, honey and vanilla flavours. Very smooth and satin-like, but vigorous and flavourful as well. Long, creamy aftertaste. This 1966 seemed to be a particularly smooth and elegant vintage by Krug Vintage standards.

1959 Blanc de Blancs Pol Roger *(Champagne)*   97p

2003/2015 x2 • D - / G 30 min

At Pol Roger the year 1959 was notable for its exceptional conditions. The budding was excellent, the flowering took place over an extended period but was problem free. Healthy, well-formed bunches were able to profit throughout the summer from long hours of sunshine. The harvest started on the 10th of September under ideal conditions. The 1959 was a healthy vintage of the highest standard, rich, lively and much-renowned. An exceptional year in the history of Champagne, which was hailed at the time as the finest vintage since 1893. Very fine quality wines, with an expectation from the outset of above-average longevity: a year which compensated fully for three successive fallow years between 1956-1958.

Fine looking bottle with perfect level and colour. A honeyed, rich, full-bodied, and seamlessly balanced wine. Surprising energy and tight fruitiness complemented well this elegant wine, so soft and silky on the palate. A grand wine that still has a long future ahead!

1971 *Château Pétrus* (Pomerol)   97p

2006/2025 x12 • D 1.5 h / G 2 h

The cold and rainy spring generated a small crop, which was pampered by sunny and warm summer and autumn. Pomerol enjoyed the outstanding vintage. It was this particular vintage that Christian Moeuix introduced green harvesting on his 11,5 hectare vineyards. This new and unseen method in Pomerol was not tolerated by his fellow growers who condemned him along with the local priest who considered this as destroying the Lord's bounty. Obviously this method was beneficial since Pétrus has proven to be by far the best wine produced this year in Bordeaux.

Moderately intense, tawny bright colour. The nose is open with elegantly developed richness showing ripe dark fruits - plums, black currants and brambles, floral tones - violets, tobacco, mocha, and hints of vanilla. The palate is rich and voluptuous. The texture is silky with lovely acidity, mellow tannins and ripe black fruits. Exquisite harmony and suppleness charmed by lingering long finish. A wonderful wine with powerful character, marvellous depth and great intensity suggesting it will keep still easily 20 more years.

1964 *Chevalier-Montrachet Les Demoiselles Louis Jadot*   97p
(Côte de Beaune)

2004/2015 x2 • D 30 min / G 1 h

Healthy looking bottle. Ullage was 3 centimeters. Decanted for one hour. Beautiful, bright medium-gold colour. Wide and sound toasty bouquet. Very rich, creamy and elegant on the palate. Great length and complexity. Almost everything about this wine was perfect. Yet it was not as commanding and luscious as DRC Montrachet 1966, but really not far away. One of the tastiest and loveliest white burgundies from the 1960s.

1923 *Veuve Clicquot Ponsardin* (Champagne)   97p

2004/now x5 • D 10 min / G 1 h

This beautiful old Veuve Clicquot had arrived the day before tasting after spending a peaceful 60 years in ideal surroundings - the damp cellars of an Austrian castle. It arrived uncleaned and covered with a thick layer of dust and dirt. Beneath the dust the bottle was in top condition. The champagne itself looked clear, its ullage being by the tin foil. A real surprise caught us when we opened that 80 year-old wine - the cork popped with such a loud sound that we cried out in delight. And that was of course met with amazement on nearby tables. Well, they did not know the age of this particular wine.

In 1923 the harvest was of good quality but small in size, and it took place exceptionally late in the season. Veuve Clicquot of this vintage has a truly fresh, rich apple-like bouquet. Its clarity, golden yellow colour and numerous youthful bubbles spoke rather of an age of twenty years. On the palate a rich, smoky creaminess supported and gave body to those lively bubbles. The youthfulness and balance of this remarkably full and sophisticated wine surprised us very positively. Without a doubt one of the best champagnes from the 1923 vintages.

1921 *Niersteiner Riesling Hermannshof* (Germany)　　　　*97p*
2003/2010 x2 • D 30 min / G 1 h

The bottle was recorked in 1999. Decanted for 30 minutes. The bouquet of this deep, golden yellow wine was most seductive. We do not remember having sniffed any other white wine as long! The anticipation of its taste grew higher with every moment, with the fear of disappointment waiting, but the fear was unnecessary. This perfectly matured, well balanced, multi-dimensional wine plentiful with citrus fruit and with a pleasant, roasted touch to it was a most charming experience. Perfect harmony, length and finish - excellent quality!

1979 *Vintage Champagne Krug* (Champagne)　　　　*97p*
2006/2018 x9 • D 10 min / G 1 h

The 1979 vintage Krug was one of the greatest Krugs that we have ever had. Almost as good as the outstanding Clos du Mesnil 1979. Decanted for ten minutes. Bright, light golden colour. The nose was incredibly fresh, with lots of exotic fruit and warm nutty aromas. The palate was fantastic and sensual. Great complexity full of white chocolate, spicy yellow fruit and butter flavours. This classically well-balanced Krug has firm structure with great finish bursting and sparkling with refreshing minerals.

2001 *Kiedricher Gräfenberg Riesling Auslese Robert Weil* (Rheingau)　　*97p*
2006/2030 x4 • D 30 min / G 2 h

Bright yellow developing colour. The expressive nose is stylish and intensely fruity: dried fruits, apricots, honey. Some delicate petrol notes are starting to emerge. A perfect harmony of oily texture, marked acidity and rounding sweetness. Firm textured wine with high minerality that brings elegance to the wine. A long lasting fruity and layered aftertaste. The wine drinks exceptionally well now but has the harmony and structure to age for two more decades.

1982 *Château Haut-Brion* (Graves)　　　　*97p*
2006/2030 x9 • D 2 h / G 2 h

This dream vintage was turned into liquid gold also at Château Haut-Brion. The dry and hot spring was followed by an extremely hot July reaching the temperature of 40°C. The season continued hot and dry over the harvest.

Intense ruby red colour with orange brown tints. Opulent, rich, smoky, and powerful nose full of ripe dark fruits and delicate spiciness from the oak. Highly concentrated palate with medium-bodied structure shows vivid acidity and rich, ripe fruitiness – black currants, blueberries and brambles. Velvety tannins are firm but deliciously ripe. The long aftertaste is escorted with delightful minerality. Concentration and elegance are the most expressive words to describe this delicious and harmonious wine which will easily keep another 25 years.

1945 *Château Grand-Puy-Lacoste* (Pauillac) *97p*

2001/2015 x5 • D 2 h / G 2 h

The origin of the property is very old, since the first mention in official documents appears at the beginning of the 16th century. The estate extends over 225 acres in a single unit to the south of Pauillac on a rise, which is the origin of its name "Grand-Puy". M. Lacoste gave his name to the Château when he bought the property and kept it until the epidemic of phylloxera at the end of the 18th century. Its reputation comes from M. Raymond Dupin, a legendary figure in the Medoc wine world, who was proprietor until 1978.

Excellent looking négociant-bottled magnum. Level was high-shoulder. Decanted 1.5 hours. Full, very hopeful and youthful colour. Perhaps a little quiet on the nose, but otherwise there was plenty of elegance around. Fantastically rich, a little on the dry side, but very aromatic and voluptuous. Previous bottles were more fruity and more forceful. But there is still some length, complexity and spicy aromatic flavours for enjoyment. The finish is positive and quite long. This magnum was not the best example of this excellent wine, at least all the château-bottled wines that we have tasted have been better in every way. At best, a very good and enthusiastic example of this classic Château.

1953 *Cristal Roederer* (Champagne) *97p*

2001/2010 x3 • D 30 min / G 1 h

This 1953 Cristal was in remarkably good condition. Made from 60% Pinot Noir, 40% Chardonnay. Decanted 30 minutes before tasting. Highly irresistible exotic and sweet, floral nose. Delicate, creamy - lots of class on the palate. It has a beautiful silky seduction and gentle, soft finish. Taste went on and on. Great champagne that has held extremely well.

1928 *Château Margaux* (Margaux) *97p*

2003/2010 x12 • D 45 min / G 1 h

The 1928 Margaux had a marvellous nose with astonishing perfumed fruit and smooth tannic presence. Best supporting aroma nominations included chocolate, blackberries, tobacco, and earth. This bottle was by Barton-Guestier bottling with upper-shoulder level. Decanted 45 minutes. It has a divine nose. The palate is pronounced and classic Margaux all through. Very rich wine with great balance and finesse. Perfumed and luxurious finish. This bottle had great freshness and vividness. Drink now.

1991 *Proprietary Red Wine Harlan Estate* (Napa Valley)   97p

2003/2020 x3 • D 1 h / G 2 h

Decanted for one hour. The 1991 Harlan is a fabulous wine that more than lives up to its hype, if not exactly its ludicrous price tag. The nose shows the utmost complexity and meticulousness of all the wines that evening. What a great mix of flavours: red cherries, damp earth, smoked meat, blueberries, dark plums and currants, minerals, sweet tobacco, and a sophisticated dose of toasty oak. The texture was incredibly rich and meaty for a '91, more so than one normally tastes in a wine from that vintage. Very massive and intense wine with an elegant and super ripe finish. Delicious now.

1964 *Clos des Goisses Philipponnat* (Champagne)   97p

2000/2010 x2 • D 30 min / G 30 min

The Clos des Goisses is a unique champagne. It is produced from the grapes of one single vineyard in only the best years. It is given all the time it needs to mature in the spacious Roman-built cellars of the estate. Clos des Goisses is matured for at least ten years before its launch on to the market. The quantity produced is small for a champagne, on high-yielding years only 2,000 - 3,000 cases, and in some years the whole output remains in some hundreds of cases. In 1964 the production was 3,000 cases.

An excellent looking bottle. The cork opened easily making a lively sound. Bright golden colour. Lots of complexity and class on the nose. Tiny, lively bubbles. Extremely rich, round and complete champagne. Mellow, smooth and very elegant. A long, fat and complex aftertaste that lasts forever. A very special champagne!

1997 *Cabernet Sauvignon Screaming Eagle* (Napa Valley)   97p

2004/2025 x7 • D 2 h / G 3 h

Lovers of big and powerful cult wines from Napa Valley will be thrilled with this already very enjoyable to drink vintage. Fine looking bottle. Decanted for four hours. Screaming Eagle 1997 has a very youthful appearance, with a brilliant, deep, purple-red colour. There are powerful, complex and very exciting aromas of blackberries, violets, sweet vanilla, as well as a toasty oaky overtone. Very intense and super concentrated wine with a thick and mouth-filling structure. This multi-dimensional wine has a very long, silky aftertaste of spice and very ripe cassis fruit. The 1997 is a real treat to drink now, but there is no haste whatsoever, since you can easily keep it for 5-15 more years.

1947 *Château Mouton-Rothschild* (Pauillac)   97p

2004/2020 x19 • D 30 min / G 2 h

1947 was an amazingly good vintage of very ripe, full and age-worthy wines. This Mouton looked like new. Cork and capsule in fair condition. A deep, very impressive colour, even brighter than the 1949 Mouton. Fabulous ripe, rich fruit, sweet vanilla nose. On the palate it was well balanced, very concentrated, not as complex as hoped, but had beautiful smoothness and structure. Soft tannins and sweet ripe fruit created a deliciously flirtatious taste experience, reflecting quality in the form of a long and balanced aftertaste. Held in the glass for an hour and a half without drying up. A wine that has certainly survived the test of time.

1964 Vintage Champagne Krug *(Champagne)* 97p
2007/2015 x3 • D 15 min / G 45 min

A full five star vintage that can boast on the keeping potential as well as the full-bodied and structured nature of its wines. The best 1964s are very lively and enjoyable today. And due to the fairly high yields averaging 8 900 kg/ha there was good supply that kept the prices reasonable. This is a recommendable vintage if one wishes to enjoy mature champagne without taking too big risk.

Very developed golden colour with amber tints. No bubbles detected. The nose is rich and round with dried fruits, apricots and nutty aromas. Dry, crisp and medium-bodied wine that develops amazingly in the glass. Flavours are getting richer and more complex as well as oxidated. Mineral finish with mint chocolate flavours. Charming and very appealing wine that may still age in perfect conditions. However, no improvement to be expected.

1985 Cabernet Sauvignon Special Selection Caymus *(Napa Valley)* 97p
2004/2015 x2 • D 2 h / G 1.5 h

Decanted two hours. Medium-intense, bright ruby colour with tawny tints. Intense ripe dark fruit nose of brambles and black currants combined deliciously with smoky and toasty coffee aromas. Full-bodied taste is voluptuous but still sophisticated. Ripe dark fruit intensity of cassis, plum compote and cooked brambles. Very well balanced with toasty oakiness and refine firm tannins. The finish is lingering long enhanced with lively acidity. Wine is surprisingly youthful still. The youthful condition encourages also for further ageing. To drink the wine now decant well in advance for at least 2 hours.

1890 Vintage Port Burmester *(Douro)* 97p
2007/2025 x3 • D 30 min / G 3 h

Slightly hazy pale ruby red colour. The nose is stylish and roasted with raisin and honey nuances. The palate is extremely lively and harmonious. Perky acidity lifts up the wine and the sweetness level feels just perfect. Long-lasting palate of dried fruit flavours and nuttiness. Fully mature wine that will keep for another 10 to 20 years due to its harmonious character and fruit intensity.

1966 *Château Pétrus* (Pomerol)   97p

2006/2020 x3 • D 1 h / G 2 h

In 1966, Michael Broadbent was invited to revive the wine auctions at Christie's after a closure of decades. The first Christie's wine auction had taken place exactly two hundred years before, in 1766. The recreation of the wine auction could not have been better timed. The market was growing and the people who had invested in wine then would get enormous profits in the future. The auctions at first focused on the best wines of Bordeaux, which even today constitute approximately 70% of the wine sold at auctions.

The 1966 Bordeaux vintage is an excellent one for classic wines. The wines combine the typical features, style and quality of Bordeaux wines making them elegant and balanced. Most of them are still in fine condition today. Many of the best wines may still benefit from cellaring if kept correctly. However, the general principle is: drink now or sell.

The theme of the dinner was Number Six. Our host Oliver Bernard had chosen wines whose vintage ended with the figure six. The last red wine before Château Coutet 1906 was a Pétrus 1966. Outwardly in good condition, appropriate for its age.

Fill level top shoulder, estate bottled. Decanted for 45 minutes. Retained its best qualities in glass for approximately 60 minutes. The decanting had opened the wine beautifully. The nose in the glass was open and charming with lots of berries, vanilla and a touch of cellar. The mouth feel was extremely delicate. The soft, full wine was so delicately perfect that it required the taster to really concentrate and put his mind and soul into the venture. The wine was not as aggressively full as Pétrus often is. An intellectual, multilayered and balanced wine. The aftertaste lingered on the palate for a long time.

1997 *Masseto Tenuta dell'Ornellaia* (Tuscany)   97p

2007/2015 x4 • D 3 h / G 2 h

Masseto is a pure Merlot wine produced by Tenuta dell'Ornellaia since 1986. It is often referred as the "Pétrus of Italy". In 1997 an early spring encouraged early bud break but a frost in mid April and rains in the end of April did not promise a good start. Then May brought very warm and dry weather to Bolgheri. Summer was hot and the harvest took place in ideal conditions between August 25th and the first week of September. Due to the dry and hot weather grapes remained small with thick skins. Thus the crop was very limited but high in quality.

Opaque ruby-purple colour. Powerful and intense nose with loads of blackcurrants, fresh herbs, smoke, green capsicum, and pine needles. Full-bodied structure with intense ripe dark fruit with refined firm tannins and herbaceousness. Very classy, long, mineral finish is delicately rich and harmonious. The wine has still very good potential for further ageing.

1990 Château Montrose *(Saint-Estèphe)*   97p

2006/2025 x7 • D 2 h / G 3 h

Moderately intense developing brick-red colour. Rich and robust nose attracts with plenty of nuances. Developing farmyardy aromas with a nice mixture of primary and secondary aromas of black currants, black olives, cedar, teak, pencil shavings, and hints of capsicum. Medium-bodied mouth-feel expresses vivid acidity with a mineral twist, firmly marked tannins and ripe moderately intense fruitiness with dark fruit flavours. Charming finish with great balance. The wine has many years to evolve and is just turning into its second life.

1964 Unico Bodegas Vega Sicilia *(Ribera del Duero)*   97p

2003/2010 x2 • D 2 h / G 2 h

This is supposedly the second best Unico of the 1960s, right after the grand 1968 - at least according to most critics. We place the 1962 Unico side by side with the 1968 and before the 1964. The bottle had arrived straight from the estate's cellars and was in excellent condition. Although the wine in front is still quite reserved and seemed to have saved its best qualities for the darkest hours of the evening, it already showed promise with its clear, dark red colour.

Some two hours after decanting the wine finally opened and released a soft and roasted bouquet tinged with vanilla and flowers. Very ripe, concentrated and aromatic nose. Full, firm and quite tannic on the palate. Some soft wood nuances. Very good grip, remarkable depth of flavours that keep appearing one after another. This is and will be a very voluptuous wine. Perhaps one of the best Unicos ever.

1959 Vintage Champagne Krug *(Champagne)*   97p

2002/2010 x2 • D 30 min / G 30 min

The bottle was outwardly in A1 condition. Its colour was lighter than 1959 Pol Roger's but the bouquet was clearly stronger, more intense and with a subtle perfume to it. The bubbles were small and elegant, so typical of Krug. The nose was superbly giving. Compared to the open nose, the wine felt at first a little reserved on the palate. However, after a short delay it almost exploded in the mouth giving an extremely aromatic and abundant tasting experience. A perfectly cultivated, layered and refined wine!

Hill of Hermitage 1

1989 *Château Lynch-Bages* (Pauillac)   97p
2006/2020 x17 • D 2 h / G 3 h

Excellent magnum. Decanted two hours. Fine, opaque purple colour. Dense, ripe, powerful nose with notes of roasted herbs, smoky, toasty oak and sweet currants. Overflowing, fat body and well rounded with oaky, earthy and spicy cassis flavours. Good ripe tannins and high acidity. A huge and rich wine, almost as good as Haut-Brion 1989, but not as elegant and refined. Soft tannins and good acidity. Long finish with flavours of leather, cassis and tobacco. Firm and complex, this is drinking amazingly well now, but should go on for another 15 or 20 years.

1997 *Cabernet Sauvignon Bryant Family Vineyard* (Napa Valley)   97p
2006/2030 x5 • D 4 h / G 3 h

Bryant Family Vineyard is located on Pritchard Hill, high above Lake Hennessy in the Napa Valley. Ever since its instant success release in 1992, the Bryant Family has produced a string of highly rated wines through the 1990s with the help of the cult winemaker Helen Turley.

Bottle like new. Decanted for 4 hours. Almost black colour. On the nose wide and open with aromas of blackberries, dark chocolate and espresso. This is a profound, inky wine that has the perfect expression of Napa Cabernet Sauvignon. Massively structured and loaded with glycerin. The fruit really came out at a huge-sized, pronounced finish.

1975 *Clos des Goisses Philipponnat* (Champagne)   97p
2006/2010 x3 • D 10 min / G 30 min

Philipponnat, a medium-sized champagne house, is famous for its single vineyard luxury cuvée Clos des Goisses, and deserves the credit for being the first major producer of a single vineyard champagne. The vast 5.5 ha parcel of Clos des Goisses in Mareuil-sur-Aÿ must be the most beautiful vineyard in Champagne. The steep slope overlooks the river, and the exposure is so phenomenal that the wines manage to attain a 1-1.5% higher level of alcohol every year compared to the regional average. The history of the plot is complex. The difficult period of phylloxera, the First World War and the following depression brought the plot from Montebello to the hands of Philipponnat in 1935. Production of single vineyard wine had already begun at that time. The wine was labeled as Vin des Goisses until 1959. The vineyard consists of 14 different plots with various planting dates. Initially it was planted with 50 percent Chardonnay and 50 percent Pinot Noir, but over the years most of the replanting has been done with Pinot Noir, that now comprises over 60 percent of the total. Stringent selection takes place at the blending phase conducted by blind tastings. Only part of the wine from the parcel ends up in the Clos des Goisses wine. Their ideology of winemaking is to produce great "wine", not sparkling wine. Clos des Goisses is produced from very ripe grapes, picked at separate dates. Lutte Raisonnée is practiced to maximize the terroir expression. Malo-lactic is mostly avoided and the wine never acidified nor chaptalised, a rarity in Champagne.

The hot vintage of 1975 produced a small, very concentrated harvest. Bright, golden yellow colour. Rich and voluptuous nose with toasty, roasted coffee flavours and delicious aromas of toast and apricot marmalade. Big palate with crisp acidity, rich honeyed fruitiness, toasty, round and complex taste with long mineral finish. Gracefully developed wine ready to be toasted on special events!

1998   Château Le Pin *(Pomerol)*   97p

2005/2030 x3 • D 3 h / G 2 h

Decanted three hours. A deep, purple wine showing no sign of age. A rich, inviting nose of roasted nuts, black cherries and vanilla. Full-bodied, fleshy and opulent entry with fruitcake, ripe black fruits and cherry-like flavours, but it was not really giving much away yet. Firm, velvety-textured with layers of concentration and well-integrated tannins. Good acidity carried through into a sensational, fat and long finish. Well balanced wine with a high level of dense tannin. This might be as good as Le Pin 1982 in the near future. Starting to drink well now, but outstanding in 5 to 15 years.

1994   Cabernet Sauvignon Hillside Select Shafer Vineyards   97p
(Napa Valley)   **2003/2020 x6 • D 1 h / G 2 h**

Vintage with loads of rain in California. Nevertheless Cabernet Sauvignon did very well. This is one of the great examples. These Cabernet Sauvignon grapes enjoy the great hillside location in Stags Leap District known for its wines' especially generous tannins.

Decanted one hour. Moderately intense garnet colour with mahogany tints. Very complex developing nose - creme de cassis, cedar, cigar, lead pencil. Rich full-bodied taste stands out being very ripe and intense but at the same time very elegant. Ripe pure cassis flavours are married with lovely velvety tannins and delicate acidity. Very refined and stylish - resembling Médoc style with its richness and elegance. Extremely well-balanced long aftertaste. Aristocratic wine.

1947   Vintage Port Graham's *(Portugal)*   97p

1999/2020 x2 • D 1 h / G 3 h

Fine looking bottle with perfect level. Decanted only one hour. The 1947 Graham was as pleasant as it promised: very intense, deep and dark colour. The palate is very fresh and vigorous with good acidity. Complex and classy. This is a very noble wine. Sweet, but not too much. Still has a great future ahead - excellent.

1993   Chardonnay Lorenzo Vineyard Marcassin *(Sonoma)*   97p

2002/2015 x4 • D 1 h / G 3 h

Helen Turley, the winemaker of Marcassin, is America's most famous consulting winemaker. At the same time she is a very traditional winemaker. Her simple philosophy is: find great vineyards, farm them precisely, limit crops, make sure the grapes ripen fully-even if it leads to higher sugar levels than many winemakers prefer- and ferment using natural yeasts.

Sometimes unfussiness is the best way to create fine wines, like this beauty. Decanted 45 minutes. Striking wine, opulent, concentrated Chardonnay, the best bottle we have tasted from this small estate. After

30 minutes of aeration, the wine opens and develops beautiful richness and complexity with spicy aromas of pineapple, hazelnut and butter. Well brought-up structure with a subtle tannic bite, surrounded by soft creamy texture. This 1993 Marcassin shows brilliant balance and surprisingly stylish finesse. The long intense and lingering finish with fresh, lovely ripe fruit. A super result.

1997   *Nacional Vintage Port Quinta do Noval* (Portugal)   *97p*

2006/2050 x4 • D 6 h / G 3+ h

Winter began very cold in 1997 and snow covered the whole Quinta for some time. This hadn't happened in more than three decades. In February and March temperatures were very hot, rising to 29 degrees Celsius. Blooming occurred a month earlier than in 1996, with the temperature above 20 degrees and almost no rain. This provided excellent conditions for good maturation. The rain compensated for the lack of water in the soil in April and May. The below average temperatures reached normal levels by the end of June. Ripeness became excellent due to the hot days and night breezes in August and September.

It sounds unreal but after tasting this extraordinary wine several times, it offers something indescribably superior to the other tremendous vintages such as 1931, 1963, 1970, and 1994. Very intense, deep purple colour. Rich spicy nose with incredible depth and concentration. Aromas of liquorice, coffee and ripe blackberries. Sweet full-bodied taste with intense dark fruit flavours and a very silky but firm tannic structure. Wine is in perfect balance with moderately high acidity and a well-integrated high level of alcohol. Overall a fleshy wine with superb balance and length. Drinking amazingly well already now but is saving its best for decades to come. Only 1200 cases were made.

1964   *Richebourg Domaine de la Romanée-Conti* (Côte de Nuits)   *97p*

2001/2020 x2 • D 1 h / G 1 h

It was only on the third attempt that we managed to get ourselves a bottle of this Burgundy in an auction. This is the Burgundy with perhaps the best reputation out of all 1964s. Its demand seemed to be far greater than the supply, and we had underestimated the development of its price in the previous auctions (the starting price was 240€).

1964 produced very full and long lasting wines in Burgundy and this Richebourg only confirmed our opinion. A fine looking bottle with 4 cm level. A delightfully rich, plentiful, round, and masculine wine. A silky texture, quite tannic and strong nature, with tight sweet fruitiness. Somewhat dry but elegant aftertaste. We decanted the wine two hours before tasting, which was apparently too early since the wine did not seem to last more than thirty minutes in the glass. A nearly perfect experience however.

1921   Le Montrachet Bouchard Père et Fils *(Côte de Beaune)*   97p
2000/2008 x3 • D 30 min / G 1 h

This one had 4 cm ullage and the bottle was in a fine condition. Gorgeous, bright golden colour. Waxy, vanilla and honeyed nose. This is a lovely, forthcoming, full, and attractive wine. On the palate rich, nutty, steely, with underlying sweet fruit. Excellent character and in wonderful condition.

Very enjoyable and bottles with good level will last a few more years.

1990   Château Latour *(Pauillac)*   97p
2005/2025 x9 • D 3 h / G 3+ h

Extraordinary warm winter encouraged the early bud break. Apparently the early start was slowed down by a cold period mid spring. At the end of May the weather got sunny and hot again and the summer continued this way. Intense heat and drought formed a great threat for vines. Ripening turned out to be very uneven causing a prolonged harvest period at Latour. However, waiting patiently for optimal maturations paid out superbly.

Deep, dark violet colour. Pronounced nose with tremendous depth and complexity. Black currants, blackberries, cedar, black olives, dark chocolate, liquorice, and cigar with hints of violets. Very concentrated medium-bodied palate with great volume. Very firm super smooth tannins, vivid acidity and deliciously ripe elegant fruitiness of cassis and blackberries. Toasty and spicy oakiness with complex range of flavours supports discreetly the fruit. The wine seems to have an almost never-ending finish. Although the wine offers all this now, it will certainly offer double pleasure after a decade or two or even three. If you have only a bottle or two of this, it is worth waiting patiently.

1996   Bollinger Vieilles Vignes Françaises *(Champagne)*   97p
2007/2020 x4 • D 15 min / G 2.5 h

This vintage has been generally assessed potentially as the best vintage of the century together with 1955 and 1928. The winter was cold and dry with some frost occurring still in mid April. The extensive warm and dry summer was interrupted by rainstorms in mid August. The weather improved in September with dry and sunny conditions. The days remained warm and the cool nights guaranteed ideal acid levels in the grapes. This 100 percent Pinot Noir wine derives from rare ungrafted pre-phylloxera vines from three small vineyards owned by Bollinger. The vineyards cover slightly less than 0.6 hectares. Vineyards are nursed with ancient methods and vinification relies on ageing in 205 litres small oak barrels. After the second fermentation the wine was aged for five years before disgorging. In 1996 the total production was 2,600 bottles. Wine holds 7-9 grams residual sugar. This vintage was launched with a new label designed by an Englishman Lewis Moberly aimed to reflect the same spirit as Bollinger R.D.

Moderately pale, straw yellow colour with lively bubbles. Really fresh and opulent nose offers ripe apple aromas combined with smoke and hints of wild red berries and depth from yeastiness. Rich and intense medium-bodied palate with crisp acidity and creamy mousse. Touch of smokiness and lovely yeastiness adds texture and complexity to the vivid freshness of apples and red berries. Long lingering mineral finish with firmness and power expressing the potential of the wine. The wine will be moving on to its second phase within next five years showing more tertiary flavours and will develop beneficially for at least another 15 years. Nevertheless, the wine delivers enormous pleasure already now with its youthful energy and vibrancy.

1996 *Astralis Clarendon Hills* (South Australia) *97p*

2005/2015 x5 • D 2 h / G 2 h

This flagship wine of Clarendon Hills is one of the most refined style Syrahs made in Australia if not the most refined. Over 70 years old Syrah vines produce extremely small yields of two tons per acre in clay soil rich in iron and gravel. The vinification is done in a very natural way in open tanks at fermentation temperatures of up to 32°C. No cultivated yeasts are used. Ageing in French barriques for 18 months without any filtration or fining.

Dense ruby colour. Powerful complex nose with great dose of pepper, ripe raspberries and brambles with smoky and bacony aromas. Full-bodied wine has immense power and concentration between jammed dark fruit, rich ripe tannins and refined acidity. Incredibly long spicy, smoky and chewy finish. Sheer power with style and many more years to go.

1945 *Vintage Champagne Krug* (Champagne) *97p*

2006/now x5 • D 10 min / G 1 h

A superb bottle with perfect label and capsule. Level was as good as ever. Decanted 20 minutes. This is a great 'victory' champagne that can and should be spoken of only in terms of superlatives. It has a healthy, deep golden colour. On the nose flavours and aromas exploded wide open right after decanting - lots of generous citrus, nuts and honeyed toasty aromas, all coming together in an almost cream-like texture. It still has some tiny bubbles left. This full-bodied and commanding wine has almost perfect balance and heavy, multi-layered structure. At the end all those grand flavours and aromas lingered for an extremely long time. Krug 1945 is superb now and will hold comfortably a few more years.

1964 *Barolo Monfortino Riserva Giacomo Conterno* (Piedmont) *97p*

2006/2020 x6 • D 1 h / G 1 h

Bottle was in excellent condition with top-shoulder level. Decanted one hour. Scenic nose: delicate, eerie notes of cedar and chocolate, earth and game, with wild violet notes and a subtle black fruit core. Fabulous sweetness of fruit on the palate with super-ripe cassis, spices, coffee, and mushrooms. Lots of energy. Complex and multi-layered wine with a great balance and pure, vigorous ending. A wonderful wine drinking perfectly now, and one of our greatest Barolo experiences.

1995   Cristal Rosé Roederer *(Champagne)*   97p
2006/2020 x4 • D 20 min / G 1 h

This is one of the rarest prestige champagnes as barely one thousand bottles were produced. The wine is based on the blend of 70% Pinot Noir and 30% Chardonnay from the best crus.

Bright, very pale salmon rosé colour with very refined bubbles. Charming and elegant but still closed on the nose with a touch of orange peel and jasmine aromas. Dry, crisp acidity and very delicate rich mousse in the palate. Very intense taste with lingonberry and wild strawberry flavours. Long lingering mineral finish of outstanding elegance.

1994   Nacional Vintage Port Quinta do Noval *(Portugal)*   97p
2005/2040 x8 • D 3 h / G 3 h

Quinta do Noval Nacional holds the record price for a bottle of port. In 1988 the Graycliff Restaurant in the Bahamas sold a bottle of 1931 Nacional for 5,900$. Nacional 1931 also holds the record as the most expensive port ever sold at auction, fetching 1,100$ at a Christie's auction in London in 1988. A year later, the same wine sold privately for 2,500$ through London-based fine wine merchants, Farr Vintners. In 1991 a bottle fetched 3,800$ in New York, where it was auctioned at a charity event by Michael Broadbent of Christie's. In 1997 a case of the newly released 1994 Nacional was sold for 5,250$ by Sotheby's of New York, a record for a young Vintage Port. More recently, a bottle of 1963 Nacional has been sold in Portugal for 5,000€.

Fine-looking bottle. Tasted at the Quinta do Noval. Decanted two hours. Very fine young port. Deep ruby-black colour. Full-bodied and dense showing powerful tannins, but opening to reveal its astonishing depth, length and balance. On the palate you will find crushed berries, tobacco, chocolate, and espresso coffee aromas. Sweet with masses of fruit and tannins. Grips your mouth totally but in a gentle way. The wine has a terrific backbone, structure and a very long, velvety finish. It will last forever.

1990   Château Margaux *(Margaux)*   97p
2005/2030 x12 • D 2 h / G 3 h

Decanted two hours. Intense, dark, purple colour with a tight rim. Wonderfully sweet and concentrated, powerful nose with aromas of ripe cherries, blackcurrants and vanilla. It is lush and cedary with earthy flavours and notes of incense and violets. Not a super concentrated wine but one with impressively sweet fruit beautifully balanced with fine tannins. Elegant and harmonious. The palate is well structured and full with lovely smooth tannins and nice, dark earthiness under the sweet fruit. A great wine with a long and hot aftertaste. Built for development.

1963 Vintage Port Taylor Fladgate (Portugal) 97p

2007/2020 x2 • D 3 h / G 3 h

The 1963 was one of the greatest wine vintages in Portugal, unlike in France. In France it was disastrous-a summer so wet and sunless that many of the great vineyards, such as Château d'Yquem and Château Cheval Blanc, sold their entire harvest as vin ordinaire.

Fine bottle. Decanted three hours. This is what class is all about in vintage port and especially in the 1963 vintage. This sophisticated dark purple wine shows a spectacular open nose, with blackberry, espresso coffee, cedar, and cherry perfumes. Full-bodied and marvellously sweet, with intense aromas of raisin, dark chocolate, raspberry, and a hint of earthiness. Gorgeous, rich, well balanced and with soft tannins that tickle your palate on the long and hot, fruit-dominated end. Complex and very fine. A shining vintage Taylor, which compares positively with the great 1948 and the stunning 1945.

1945 Vieux Château Certan (Pomerol) 97p

2003/2040 x3 • D 30 min / G 1.5 h

This famous neighbour of Château Pétrus has been owned by the Thienpont family since 1924. The historical estate existed already before the French Revolution and thanks to its long history it has carried Pomerol's reputation longer than any other estate. It had been the flagship wine of Pomerol a few centuries before the legendary Pétrus took the number one position. The estate is located on the high plateau of Pomerol where its soil constitutes from gravel and clay with little sand on topsoil and iron-rich clay in subsoil. Thanks to the gravel Cabernet Sauvignon and Cabernet Franc are planted in higher proportions at Vieux Château Certan than at any other Pomerol estate. This also makes the taste of Vieux Château Certan very different from other Pomerols.

The 1945 vintage was a great one but very limited due to a severe frost in May. The vintage was otherwise outstanding and yielded very tannic wines for long-term ageing. Thanks to the blend of slowly mellowing Cabernets, Vieux Château Certan requires a long time to reach the optimum ripeness.

Moderately dark ruby colour. Very refined nose with earthy tones, leather, horse saddle, ripe blackcurrants, cedar, and hints of mint. Elegant medium-bodied structure, still firm tannins, lively acidity and pure black fruit flavours. Very elegant, long lingering finish shows complexity and sophistication. The wine is very appealing to drink now but it will improve even over three more decades.

1996 Château Margaux (Margaux) 97p

2006/2035 x15 • D 3 h / G 3 h

An extreme year in Bordeaux with unsettled weather conditions throughout the summer. Great temperature fluctuations from hot to cool and stormy showers in between. Médoc was able to avoid the heaviest rains. The dry and cool weather in September lasted for three weeks until rains hit the area again. In Château Margaux it is paradoxically assumed that the heavy rains actually helped to finish the ripening of Cabernet Sauvignon, like in the year before. At Margaux 1996 is considered a dream vintage, so overwhelmed are they of the quality of this wine.

Deep ruby, almost opaque colour. Extremely refined nose with many layers – blackcurrants, cedar, cigars, tobacco, roasted coffee, hints of capsicum. Restrained medium-bodied palate shows moderately high acidity, refined powdery tannins and deliciously ripe black fruit character. The concentrated texture holds elegant touches of spicy and toasty oak flavours. Long lingering mineral rich finish. Aristocratic style of Margaux par excellence. Truly classic wine benefiting from further ageing for a decade or two but is lovely already.

1900   *Colheita Niepoort* (Portugal)   *97p*

2000/now x3 • D 2 h / G 3 h

Big year both in quality and crop. Delicate wines with balance although less colour and structure than in most classic vintages. It snowed in the region in February and March. The warm weather only got to the region at the end of July. The harvest started in the third week of September.

Excellent bottle. Gift from Dirk Niepoort. Decanted two hours. Bright, moderately deep brick red colour with brown tints. Pronounced clean nose with deliciously rich - cacao, chocolate, roasted nut, almonds, and dried fruits. Sweet medium-bodied palate with delightfully refreshing acidity, maderized but still intense flavours of dried fruits. The alcohol is integrated extremely well in the palate. Long sticky finish. Like a sweet that you just do not want to finish, ever. This Colheita 1900 offers a great deal of structure. Layers of complexity rush over the palate with delightfully smooth texture and yet it is still such a vibrant wine considering its age.

1988   *Cristal Roederer* (Champagne)   *97p*

2007/2030 x16 • D 20 min / G 1 h

Roederer blends its prestigious Cristal from 60-65 base wines based on blind tasting only. The blend comprises of 55% Pinot Noir and the remaining part is reserved for Grand Cru Chardonnay. Cristal's splendour originates in the vineyards as Roederer still owns a lion's share of the vineyards that produce Cristal. Over 25-year-old vines from own parcels produce base wine of 1 degree more potential alcohol compared to the purchased grapes. One of Cristal's secrets is in its non-maloed nature. Roederer seeks the highest possible acidity, which combines well to the perfectly ripe fruitiness of their wines.

The 1988 vintage started a 3-year consecutive span of great vintages. The acidity in the powerful and fruity wines of this classical year makes them very fine and long-lived. As Cristal is a true vin de garde, this magnificent 1988 is still waiting to reach its full potential.

Fruit-driven, nutty and citrus nose with layers and layers that show after some time in the glass. Some development especially in the nose but the palate remains slightly restrained but packed with future potential. Razor-sharp acidic spine brings elegance and a feeling of lightness to this very concentrated wine with amazing length and depth.

1919 Vouvray Haut-Lieu Moelleux Domaine Huet *(Vouvray)* 97p
2002/2015 x3 • D 10 min / G 2.5 h

Clear, moderately intense, golden amber colour. Powerful, intense and rich nose with mushroom aromas of truffles and chanterelles. Partly oxidative apple aromas remind of Calvados. Medium-sweet and medium-bodied palate is harmonized by crisp acidity, intense rich fruitiness. During the ride the palate experiences complex characters from refreshing minerality to lively fruitiness of apples, lemons and grapefruit. In the aftertaste oxidative and volatile balsamic characters integrate well with the wine's mushroomy aromas. Wine is drinking very well and has potential to keep many more years. The most unique white wine experience!

1975 Château Pétrus *(Pomerol)* 97p
2006/2020 x6 • D 3 h / G 2 h

This hot year in Bordeaux is reflected in this wine's firm, mouth-coating tannins and less delicate but rich and ripe aromas. Moderately intense ruby colour with garnet red tones. Rich, overwhelming liquorice flavours with ripe blackcurrant nose. On the palate this rich medium-bodied wine is surprisingly crisp and fresh with intense, fleshy ripe fruitiness and subtle tannins. Long, ripe and round finish. Very New World wine by style. Appealing and enjoyable wine today.

1976 Salon *(Champagne)* 97p
2006/2015 x3 • D 15 min / G 1.5 h

One of those special occasions when this magnum was popped open was at Pekka Nuikki's joyful Cheval Blanc dinner at Hirvihaara Mansion. This particular vintage was the 31st vintage ever made of this adorable wine. Fine looking bottle. Beautifully bright yellow colour with golden tints and refined energetic bubbles. Very intense nose with hints of mushroom aromas but still youthful with green apples, bread and creamy tones. Crisp, medium-bodied taste had an adorable creamy mousse and persistence with a lemony bite on the palate with great length. A superb start for an exclusive seven course menu!

1989 Romanée-Conti Domaine de la Romanée-Conti *(Côte de Nuits)* 97p
2006/2035 x2 • D 2 h / G 5 h

In 1989 winter was mild and there was no frost at all. Perhaps one of the warmest winters seen, but spring frost did some damage at the bottom of the Domaine´s vineyards. The summer was very warm and dry. The harvest started early for the period: September 20th, the earliest date since 1976. The sugar content was very high. Large quantity and quality met together like the year before and also the year after. Decanted 1.5 hours. Has an amazingly intense and attractive bouquet: full, smoky and meaty with lots of sweet raspberry flavours. Very rich, opulent and well balanced on the palate. Has a thick texture and lots of power in its finish. Very complex and concentrated wine. This was a youthful if not truly immature wine that needs lots more time in decanter or better yet, in cellar to reach its peak. Grand vin.

1945 *Barolo Monfortino Riserva Giacomo Conterno* *(Piedmont)*   97p
2006/2015 x3 • D 30 min / G 1 h

Bottle looked like new. Decanted 30 minutes. Fine, full, vigorous colour. Ripe, fat and minty on the nose. Youthful, very rich and concentrated. Even more so as it developed in the glass. Elegant, full-bodied, balanced palate, with some spicy tannins providing structure. This is a really excellent bottle. Great complexity of fruit. This is quite a serious example of Monfortino. Lots of life ahead of it.

1966 *Clos des Goisses Philipponnat* *(Champagne)*   97p
2004/2020 x2 • D 20 min / G 1 h

Clos des Goisses is a unique champagne in the whole Champagne region. It is made from a single "clos", a walled vineyard owned exclusively by Philipponnat. The vineyard consists of steep hillsides facing south and it has a total surface area of 5.5ha. On the average 15,000 to 20,000 bottles are produced on vintage years. Its grape varieties are predominantly Pinot Noir, with the rest planted exclusively in Chardonnay. Clos des Goisses is always a vintage wine; it is vinified according to the tradition upheld by generations of cellar masters and aged for almost ten years in the cellars.

Fine looking bottle with 2 cm level. Decanted 20 minutes. Surprisingly young light gold colour. Tiny bubbles. Softly honeyed nose with amazingly complex aromas: chocolate, caramel, ripe pear, melon, and apple fruit flavours. Absolutely perfect balance in the mouth. Very full and extensive. This goes on and on. Long delicious aftertaste, not too sweet or dry. Exceptionally fine.

1971 *Grange Penfolds* *(South Australia)*   97p
2004/2015 x3 • D 1 h / G 2 h

This vintage of Grange Bin 95 Shiraz has been highly rated for almost 30 years now after beating the best Rhône wines at the Gault-Millau Wine Olympiad in Paris in 1979. The inventor of Grange and a legendary winemaker, Max Schubert, has said that this is the Grange of his lifetime, a wine, which fulfils the ambitions of Grange. The blend is 87 percent Shiraz and 13 percent Cabernet Sauvignon.

The colour is moderately deep with brick red tones. Very intense nose with ripe dark fruit aromas and vanilla flavours mixed attractively with smoke, bacon and cedar aromas. Full-bodied and intense with refreshing acidity, rich set of ripe meaty tannins and fleshy ripe fruitiness of dark fruits. Mid-palate shows elegance of oak with chocolaty and mocha flavours. Long intense finish. Truly breathtaking wine drinking well now but keeping for a few more years.

1990 *Hermitage Cuvée Cathelin J.L. Chave* (Rhône)   *97p*

2004/2025 x2 • D 4 h / G 2 h

This is a controversial wine in Chave's wine range since Chave's philosophy is to make one red Hermitage from the best Syrah grapes from various parcels. However, this wine is a special cuvée on top of their regular Hermitage. This is the first vintage of this rare flagship wine. It is named after their family friend and artist, Bernard Cathelin who has designed the label of this lovely wine. Chave has made just over 100 cases of this rich and exclusive wine.

Decanted four hours. Inky purple coloured with undertones of magenta. The 1990 Chave's top cuvée showed aromas of blackberries, smoked liquorice, plum, and fresh vanilla, with hints of spices and black truffles. A giving, almost mind-blowing entry is followed by intense flavours and super concentrated body. Finished with lingering, sweet tannin and pronounced spiciness.

1991 *Masseto Tenuta dell'Ornellaia* (Tuscany)   *97p*

2005/2015 x5 • D 2 h / G 2 h

This vintage had a promising start with good conditions during the flowering and optimum berry set in mid June. Then the weather cooled down and the rains came. Merlot grapes matured three weeks later than usual reflecting the still coolness of the vintage.

Moderately intense tawny colour. Delicate nose with herbaceous nuances along with cedar, plum and cherry notes. Medium-bodied wine with moderately high acidity, restrained fruit with plums and blackcurrant notes. Firm tannins and herbacious spicy flavours dominate during the long aftertaste.

1955 *Cristal Roederer* (Champagne)   *97p*

2006/2010 x3 • D 10 min / G 45 min

Cristal is one of those rare champagnes that truly blossom after long bottle ageing. It almost hurts to consume Cristal too young, since it really reveals its true character after 20-30 years of age and evolves beautifully decades after that. This wine is again a great proof of that. The vintage 1955 turned out to be a superior vintage that resulted in a large crop of excellent quality grapes.

Golden bright colour with small quickly evaporating bubbles. Intense and complex nose that has opened wonderfully. Touch of toastiness, nuttiness, dried fruits, apricots, and apples with honeyed overtones. The still crisp and vinous taste shows lesser mousse but really intense and concentrated minerality combined with nutty dried fruit characteristics. Lovely long finish with lemon tart and brioche flavours. Drink up with good company!

1969 Cristal Roederer *(Champagne)*   97p
2007/2010 x9 • D 10 min / G 45 min

Yet another example of the greatness of Cristal. Attractive golden colour. Steady stream of tiny slow bubbles. Ripe and mature delightful nose. Layered and charming aromas of honey, toast, rosemary, and caramel. Sheer perfection in the glass with a soft mousse refreshing the rich mouthful. A wonderful acidic backbone with real grip. Enticing flavours of ginger, cinnamon and chicken tikka. A seamless, chewy wine that invites you to taste it and to keep on sipping it.

1945 Hermitage Delas Fréres *(Rhône)*   97p
2003/now x2 • D 45 min / G 1 h

In 1945 Northern Rhône was sharing the joy of whole of France. Not only were they celebrating the end of the Second World War but also an extraordinary vintage. The only downside was the small crop. This fabulous Hermitage has a deep developing mahogany colour with orange tints on the rim. Still surprisingly fresh, complex and seductive nose with blackcurrants, chocolate and mint aromas. The wine possesses lively acidity, firm ripe tannins and intense fruit with an elegant lingering finish with flavours of chocolate, cassis, spices, and violets. Amazingly youthful wine with great concentration.

1953 Château Pichon Longueville Comtesse de Lalande *(Pauillac)*   97p
2006/2030 x3 • D 1h / G 2 h

Fine-looking négociant-bottled magnum. Decanted 45 minutes. Deep, royal purple in color. On the nose intense flavours and aromas of currants, tobacco, raspberries, and spices. This sweet, smooth and multi-layered wine unfolds on the palate seemingly endlessly with supple, refined flavours of sweet cherries, raisins, cedar, spices, and minerals. Indeed, very rich and long. This magnum had a slightly acidic finish but showed plenty of ripe, delicious fruit and elegance.

1947 Le Montrachet Van der Meulen *(Côte de Beaune)*   97p
2003/2010 x5 • D 1 h / G 1 h

In 1947 the grapes were covered with botrytis exceptionally early, so this wine also received a beautiful, golden yellow colour and tasted almost like a dry Yquem. There was oak and caramel in the bouquet, and also tight fruitiness. This rich, balanced, full, and dark wine did not leave much to hope for. As the night grew older, the wine just got better in the glass. It is one of the best Montrachets we have ever tasted from a 1947 vintage. A perfectly balanced and elegant wine.

1990 *Vieilles Vignes Françaises Bollinger* (Champagne) 97p

2004/2020 x7 • D 15 min / G 1 h

The 1990 Vieilles Vignes Françaises came from the Clos Saint-Jacques, Chaudes Terres and Croix Rouges plots cultivated in the ancient layering method. The production process follows the regular Bollinger pattern with only the cuvee being utilised followed by fermentation in old 4 to 40 year old oak barrels or inox. The wine is regularly chaptalised and goes through the softening malo-lactic fermentation. During its 6-7 month stay in barrel the wine is racked twice but no battonage is carried out. After bottling in April the second fermentation takes place in 10-11°C over a long period of time. Regularly a bottle of VVF spends 5-12 years in the Bollinger cellars before being discorged. The dosage of 7-9 g/l brings harmony to this special wine, which gets to rest for a further 3 months in the cellar after recorking. This recipe created yet another successful VVF in 1990.

A deep, yellow colour turning into gold. A vivid, rich and powerful wine with complex aromas of mushrooms, autumn apples and brioche. Extremely intense, firm and rich mouth-feel. Full-bodied and balanced wine with enormous length. Starting to open up but will give its best after ten years.

1792 *Madeira Bual* (Portugal) 96p

2005/2020 x7 • D 2 h / G 2 h

Fine looking bottle with excellent level. Decanted two hours. Surprisingly smooth and gentle considering its age and over 20 percent alcohol content. Gorgeous, structured and vivid Bual, with loads of candied pear, maple syrup, vanilla, honeyed milk chocolate, and cream flavours. Long, creamy and delicious. Finish was still quite fresh and filled with walnuts, spice and orange marmalade notes. This old beauty is drinking beautifully now and has the potential for cellaring until 2020.

1896 *Château d'Yquem* (Sauternes) 96p

2007/2010 x6 • D 1 h / G 2 h

Decanted for 30 minutes. Retained its best characteristics for one hour after opening. Bottle outwardly as new, recorked at the estate in 1967. Wine level top shoulder. Very dark, but clear colour. The bouquet was really modest at the beginning, but after about 45 minutes the wine was totally different. It transformed into an intoxicating combination of caramel, overripe exotic fruit and honey that overwhelmed the room. Surprisingly full, creamy and silky wine with the same kind of velvety smooth, almost tangible softness as the 1811. Good balance and structure. Even the aftertaste included fresh, sweet fruit and sprightly acidity. A surprisingly elegant wine that appeared much younger than we expected.

NUMBER 238.

NUMBER 239.

NUMBER 240.

1900   *Veuve Clicquot Ponsardin* (Champagne)   96p

2006/now x2 • D 10 min / G 20 min

Superb looking bottle with good level. Some haziness in the golden amber colour, no bubbles apparent. Developed rich nose with apricots and dried fruits, waxiness and mineral tones. Moderately dry on palate with some residual sugar detected. Intense and concentrated taste with moderately high acidity and minerality. Long lemony aftertaste. Not a very complex wine but very persistent and gracefully matured. Champagne like a noble lady.

1989   *Château Pichon-Longueville Baron* (Pauillac)   96p

2006/2030 x5 • D 2 h / G 2 h

First-rate bottle. Decanted two hours. Impressive dark, youthful colour. Muscular, open, vigorous nose. Full bodied and wonderful in its complexity and structure. This handsome Pichon-Baron continues to demonstrate rich, fat and commanding flavours and aromas of wild blackberries, ripe plums, cassis, and vintage leather. Sound, heavy and long. A good effort, even better than the well made 1982, or soon to be great 1990. Drinkable now, but will last at least two more decades.

1864   *Château Lafite* (Pauillac)   96p

2000/2010 x3 • D 30 min / G 1 h

This superb wine derives from one of the best vintages of the 19th century. Excess amount of heat during the growing season can be felt in this wine in the moderately high level of alcohol and very ripe almost sweet fruitiness. Fine looking bottle with Christie's label. Level was mid-shoulder. Decanted 30 minutes. The colour is amber red with plenty of fine sediment. The nose is surprisingly intense with spice and cigar notes. Even hints of blackcurrants can be sensed. Medium-bodied palate possesses sweet dark fruit and spicy ginger tones and moderately high acidity. High alcohol adds roundness and sweet tones to the moderately long mineral finish. Delicious wine, drinking very well still!

1890   *Gran Reserva 890 La Rioja Alta* (Rioja)   96p

2002/now x1 • D 30 min / G 1 h

A dirty and dusty, fascinating looking old bottle. The level was top-shoulder and it was decanted for 30 minutes. Dark, bright and healthy colour. Sound, elegant and soft, chocolate and vanilla nose. The nose leads to even softer and more chocolaty palate. A surprisingly multi-dimensional and complex wine. The tannins were already fully softened and we did not find it too acidic at all. It was a rather dry and well-balanced wine. It had a powerful sherry-like aftertaste with a slight touch of excess alcohol. The overall pleasure produced on the palate by this historical wine was a great experience.

1924   *Château Latour* (Pauillac)   *96p*

2007/2015 x13 • D 30 min / G 1.5 h

The vintage 1924 was not outstanding although a very good one. Poor spring, which was followed by miserable rainy summer. Luckily ideal weather conditions in September turned the misery into happiness for the winegrowers and saved the vintage.

This wine was tasted blind and it overwhelmed all of us with its energy. The condition was extraordinary suggesting a much younger wine. The wine showed astonishing suppleness and vividness from the nose to the long aftertaste. Good bottle with top-shoulder level. Bright, still moderately intense mahogany red colour. The tremendously intense, rich and complex nose is marked by sophisticated style of the left bank. Nose shows roasted coffee, blackcurrant leaves, herbs, and chocolate. Very seductive nose. Moderately high acidity together with ripe, refined and elegant tannins forms a firm structure to the wine. Acidity and tannins form a balanced chewy taste that lasts for long in the supple lingering aftertaste. What an aristocrat! Drinking perfectly now but a well-kept bottle will keep over a decade.

1955   *Château Mouton-Rothschild* (Pauillac)   *96p*

2007/2015 x9 • D 1 h / G 2 h

One hour of decanting had opened this lovely-looking 1955 Mouton wonderfully and its nose in the glass was forward and charming with lots of berries, vanilla and a touch of cellar. The mouth-feel was extremely refined. The opulent, full wine was so delicately perfect that it required its taster to really concentrate and put his soul into the exercise. The wine was not as aggressively full as Mouton sometimes is, but if you dare to close your eyes with this wine to see better, the result is almost a religious experience. An intellectual, multilayered and balanced wine.

1896   *Vintage Port Cockburn* (Portugal)   *96p*

2005/2020 x6 • D 2 h / G 4 h

One can only close the eyes and imagine what sensations this wine raised in the mouths of three influential leaders when they were organising the new European and Asian borders after the Second World War in Yalta in April 1945. Winston Churchill, Josef Stalin and Franklin Roosevelt may not have analysed the wine specifically but it must have been extremely appealing, since 60 years later it is still very impressive.

Moderately pale bright brown colour. Very rich nose of sweet ripe plums, dark berries and buckthorn berries enhanced with chocolate tones. Intensely sweet, mellow tannins and moderate level of acidity with nuts and dark chocolate flavours. Warming long finish. A very balanced and charming wine.

1997 Merlot Pahlmeyer (Napa Valley)

96p

2005/2020 x2 • D 1 h / G 2 h

Deep garnet red colour. Very intense toasty, nutty and chocolaty nose with loads of ripe dark fruits - blackberries, dark plums. Full-bodied, immensely rich and extracted wine with super ripe and intense dark jammy fruit, big velvety tannins and still enough acidity to balance it all. The toasty oakiness adds sweet exotic spicy flavours that remain long in the warming aftertaste. A big wine with many years to go.

1964 Château Latour (Pauillac)

96p

2006/2015 x24 • D 2 h / G 2 h

We have tasted Latour 1964 more than ten times in the last decade, and it has always been a first-class claret (all the bottles have scored 92-96 points). On the last occasion in 2006 it was still very vigorous and a lovely wine, maybe even better than ever before.

Excellent looking bottle with base neck level. Decanted for two hours. Very youthful and deep bright colour. Rich, ripe and open nose with earthy and black fruit and truffle aromas. Perfectly balanced, rich and full wine, which has been developing beautifully throughout the last 15 years, building more and more intensity and complexity. It is now a multi-dimensional, fat, thick, chocolaty wine with long, attractive, slightly tannic aftertaste. A harmonious wine with a long and glorious future to come.

1929 Château Cheval Blanc (St.Emilion)

96p

2007/2010 x13 • D 45 min / G 1 h

Last time we drank this beautiful Cheval Blanc we were having dinner at Domaine de Chevalier. We tasted it blind and it was fairly uncomplicated to guess the vintage. It possessed the characteristic sweetness and charm of the 1929 vintage. Still very fresh and lovely. Decanted one hour. Very harmonious and balanced. On the nose rich aromas of ripe fruit, tobacco and minerals. Full-bodied, with a fabulous balance of lovely, rich fruit flavours and silky texture and just enough grip to keep it alive. Plenty of white chocolate and smooth coffee flavours on the finish. Drink now.

1959 Château Haut-Brion (Graves)

96p

2004/2020 x11 • D 30 min / G 1.5 h

Great vintage in Bordeaux, yielding very concentrated and ripe fruity wines this being one of the greatest examples. Moderately intense brick red colour. Pronounced and ripe nose of blackcurrants and violets enhanced with complex bouquet of horse stable, earthiness and smoke. Very concentrated, rich and mellow full-bodied taste, delicious minerality with balancing acidity and firm tannins. Long leathery aftertaste with great intensity and harmony. The wine has reached its peak but will keep over a decade.

1861 *Château d'Yquem* (Sauternes)   *96p*

2005/2010 x3 • D 15 min / G 1 h

Not so fine looking négociant-bottled Yquem. Hardly any parts of the label left and the capsule was missing. Level was only low-shoulder. Decanted 15 minutes. Dark almost bronzed golden in colour. Sound and open bouquet with a luscious, still intense botrytis nose along with flavours and aromas of crème brûlée, tropical fruits and sweet caramel. Quite a lot of charm and freshness but not as intense and long as 1811 or 1819. Still some good acidity and fruit left. Considering the poor condition of the bottle, it has held surprisingly well. A real treat!

1982 *Château Léoville-Las Cases* (Saint-Julien)   *96p*

2006/2020 x24 • D 2 h / G 2 h

The Saint Julien appellation is situated in the very heart of the Médoc. Eleven Classified Growths cover the great majority of the vineyards in Saint Julien. The wines are said to be both powerful and elegant, concentrated and suitable for laying down. But even so each wine remains unique.

This Leoville was an excellent condition. Decanted three hours. Very deep, dark, mature colour. Quite youthful on the nose - aromas of blackcurrants, violets, and truffles. A wonderful concentration of fruit and flavour, a still powerful, complex and rich well-balanced wine. There are deep seams of fruit in this wine and a wonderful balance and complexity finishing in long aftertaste mellowed by toasty vanillin oak. Very feminine and refined. This Leoville is excellent to drink now, but can last well for a few more decades.

1812 *Château Lafite* (Pauillac)   *96p*

2006/now x3 • D 15 min / G 30 min

Although it sometimes takes more than 50 years for a wine to become enjoyable, the wait was in this case worthwhile - those sceptical opinions that this strongly tannic wine and vintage received in the middle of the 19th century can now be understood. But how marvellous and brilliant this Lafite must have been 50 years later, at the beginning of the 20th century, since it still is one of the best Lafite we have encountered - even at the age of almost 200 years!

A château-bottled bottle of 375 ml in good condition. The colour of the wine and the level were both excellent. Decanted for 15 minutes. Held well in glass for approximately 45 minutes. This Lafite must have been almost black when it was born, since the colour was still deep dark red. The nose was most intoxicating - spicy, pure and strongly seductive. Intensive, but the velvety tannins and quite high alcohol content were still present, though now well in balance with the abundant, jam-like fruitiness. An extremely pleasant, majestic and multi-dimensional wine that had a long, soft aftertaste one could still feel lingering in the mouth the next morning.

1924 Château Haut-Brion *(Graves)* 96p

2000/2010 x2 • D 1 h / G 1 h

A bit of an overrated vintage. In general the wines are sound, rather full-bodied, smooth, elegant, charming, and still very drinkable. A decent-looking château-bottling. Level was top-shoulder. Decanted 45 minutes. This ethereal, complex Haut-Brion showed lovely intense spice, meat and cedar aromas and flavours, with dried fruit and earthy notes. Still lively and long on the finish.

1922 Unico Bodegas Vega Sicilia *(Ribera del Duero)* 96p

2002/2010 x1 • D 1 h / G 1 h

This rare Unico looked very old indeed, but had an admirable top-shoulder level and both original label and capsule. Decanted 30 minutes. Very dark, almost black, deep and a healthy looking colour. The bouquet was slightly weak in the attack, but when it gradually opened up during the first 30 minutes in the glass, it was amazingly powerful, sweet, ripe, and leathery. No rush! Incredibly youthful and fresh. It has a good structure, sweet fruit and great acidity. The taste was smooth and balanced which emphasised the feeling of harmony. This 1922 Unico was a round, delicious wine with silky tannins and lovely length. A truly fine wine with excellent keeping power.

1947 Brut Impérial Moët & Chandon *(Champagne)* 96p

2005/2010 x3 • D 15 min / G 20 min

Very good vintage in Champagne. Early flowering in June, pleasant growing conditions in the summer, record amount of sunshine in August and favourable weather conditions during the harvest. If this vintage left something to wish for, it had to be a bigger crop. Due to the small crop, it makes it difficult to find bottles from this wonderful vintage anymore.

This was an outstanding wine as an aperitif: appealing yellow-gold colour with few fine bubbles. The rich and fragrant nose seemed very youthful. Absolutely complete wine with creamy, toasty flavours and fresh acidity still in balance - enormously full and intense with perfect harmony.

1995 Vina El Pison Artadi *(Rioja)* 96p

2000/2015 x3 • D 1 h / G 2 h

Decanted 1 hour. Prominent nose with smoky oak, dusty, earthy, mushroom and cherry aromas. Full-bodied with an appealing big structure. On the palate very smooth with good fruit and acidity. Brilliant balance here: very Pomerol style with a leafy edge. Excellent follow-through. It's drinking very well now!

1964 *Nacional Vintage Port Quinta do Noval* (Portugal) *96p*

2006/2020 x4 • D 3 h / G 4 h

Bought directly from Noval's shop in Oporto. Decanted three hours. Bright red, deep ruby-garnet colour with orange reflections. This still young-looking, full-bodied and intense wine shows that extraordinary and very seductive combination of being simultaneously muscular and feminine. Very smooth and silky on the palate. The dominating flavour here is black cherry, but over that you will find graceful layers of chocolate, cedar wood, smoke, and sweetness. Long, warm and refined aftertaste. Ready now, but no rush.

1990 *Clos des Corton Faiveley* (Côte de Beaune) *96p*

2006/2010 x4 • D 1 h / G 2 h

Decanted 45 minutes. The nose was very deep and brooding, classic Corton with dark fruits, iron and cedar. Very rich on the palate, a thick texture and lots of power on its finish. There were deep seams of fruit in this wine and wonderful balance and complexity. This has lost its initial thickness but will probably develop into a very interesting wine: all the components are there. A very attractive modern wine that reflects its origins.

1900 *Château Léoville Poyferré* (Saint-Julien) *96p*

2004/now x3 • D 30 min / G 30 min

1900 was an amazingly good vintage of very ripe, broad and age-worthy wines. This Léoville-Poyferré had top-shoulder level and cork and capsule still in fair condition. Very deep, striking bright colour, even more brilliant than the 1900 Lafite. Amazing ripe, rich sweet fruit, caramel and black cherry aromas on the nose. Sound and open. On the palate it was nicely balanced, very concentrated and surprisingly fresh. Has complexity and beautiful smoothness with sweet tannins. It is an unbelievably seamless, classic and elegant wine. Held in the glass approximately 30 minutes without drying up. Another ingenious wine that has confidently survived the test of time.

1976 *Clos de Vougeot Leroy* (Côte de Nuits) *96p*

2004/2010 x11 • D 1 h / G 1 h

Even though the 1976 vintage was only average in Vosne-Romanée, this Leroy wasn't. The winter was mild, dry and there was no frost. Beautiful long, hot and dry summer. Early harvest. Decanted 45 minutes. This Clos de Vougeot is showing unexpectedly well now. But you need to let it breathe and sit in the decanter at least 45 minutes before tasting. Very good colour for a 1976. Moderately fat, intense and sweet on the nose. Good structure and balance. A fresh, round and complex wine with good fresh fruit. Very good grip. Not as faded as I thought from the nose at first. A very charming and positive wine with youthful acidity and a long, sweet finish.

1885 *Sherry Amontillado González Byass* (Jerez)   96p
2002/2010 x1 • D 1 h / G 2 h

This fantastically old-looking, dusty and badly damaged bottle has been in the custody of the family of our friend for a very long time. His grandfather is believed to have bought it in the early 1910s from Berry & Brothers. It is believed to be one of those famed bottles that Mr. Berry bought from the legendary Royal Cellar's public auction in 1901.

Decanted 45 minutes. A surprisingly pale and light colour for an old Amontillado. A sound and wide open bouquet that really filled the room. Rich and smooth, velvety and luscious wine. Not a huge, powerful and alcoholic wine. Vigorous, alive and dry. This was a warm-hearted wine with grace and elegance.

It has been said that King Edward kept a hundred bottles of sherry for every one that he authorized to be sold at that auction - what a wise King he was!

1921 *Château Latour* (Pauillac)   96p
2005/2015 x13 • D 30 min / G 1 h

The hottest year since 1893 caused severe problems in the vineyards with shrivelling grapes and in the cellars vats overheating during the vinification processes. Château Latour was nevertheless able to create a big wine with lovely texture.

Moderately deep, tawny colour with brown tints. The nose is intense and ripe with great extraction. Sweet aromas of ripe black fruits and cooked vegetables enhanced with hints of spiciness and violets. On the palate the wine shows its great extraction and power. Broad texture is formed by sweet black fruit flavours that are being pushed by the high alcohol. A firm and big tannic structure balances the ripe fruit although the acidity level remains moderately low. Long savoury finish. A voluptuous wine with intensive power forming a more fleshy and meaty wine than a refined and elegant one in style. Drinking beautifully now but will keep for another five to ten years.

1985 *Barbaresco Sorí San Lorenzo Angelo Gaja* (Piedmont)   96p
2005/2019 x6 • D 1 h / G 1.5 h

Bright, moderately pale tawny red colour. Vibrant floral nose with brambles, cherries, spices, and a touch of waxiness. Racy acidity with softened tannins gives a vivid structure to the wine. Sweet fruit flavours of root vegetables and ripe cherries. Silky long aftertaste is highlighted by floral aromas.

Romanée Conti
VIGNE ORIGINELLE FRANÇAISE NON RECONSTITUÉE
Produced by
Villaine & J. Chambon
ANNÉE 1943
Seuls propriétaires
Bottled in France

1986   Château Mouton-Rothschild *(Pauillac)*   96p

2007/2030 x35 • D 5 h / G 2 h

The bottle was in a superb condition. Bright, lovely deep and dark colour. Surprisingly open, oaky, spicy, and flavourful nose. A prosperous, well-balanced, intense, and multi-faceted wine. As good and big as expected. A real joy now, but the good intensity of fruit and firm structure makes us think this will be much more breathtaking in the future.

1996   Maya Dalla Valle *(Napa Valley)*   96p

2005/2019 x2 • D 1 h / G 2 h

This super premium single vineyard wine is made from a blend of Cabernet Sauvignon and Cabernet Franc from Maya vineyard in Oakville district. The production of Maya is only 500 cases annually and it has been made since 1988. Wine is aged in 70-80 percent new French oak.

Deep ruby garnet colour. Rich and intense nose of dark fruits, blackcurrants and black cherries with delicious dose of smokiness and liquorice. Very rich and refined full-bodied taste with silky tannins and vivid acidity. Ripe dark fruitiness is combined with spicy, tar and liquorice notes.A fleshy wine with elegance and great length. A lovely youthful wine with supple silky texture and good concentration. Drinking deliciously already but will evolve gracefully for the next 10-15 years.

1950   Château l'Eglise Clinet *(Pomerol)*   96p

2004/2010 x12 • D 2.5 h / G 1 h

Exceptional château-bottled magnum. Level by the neck. Decanted 1.5 hours. Very deep, fresh and vibrant colour. The nose was still a bit closed, but after another hour in decanter it was filled with fragrance: coffee, white chocolate and floral nuances. On the palate there is a breathtaking sweetness of fruit and soft tannins. Has a good depth and complexity as well. Quite a long, creamy and fat aftertaste. Very fine but not as exhilarating as the famous 1921 or 1947. It has held extremely well and still has plenty of years left.

1898   Grand-Chambertin Gresigny *(Côte de Nuits)*   96p

2006/now x2 • D 30 min / G 1 h

This bottle was in sound condition, and the level was 8 cm below the cork. In our experience, old Burgundy bottles with levels from 4 to 8 cm below the cork can still contain high-quality wine, and very often they actually do. It must be remembered that the original fills varied because there was no accuracy of a modern bottling line. So we did not pay much attention to this wine's level! To us good colour is a more important sign of a sound wine. In the case of this Grand-Chambertin it was very fine and mature. A lovely fragrant nose of menthol. This is a surprisingly vigorous and complex wine: one can even claim that it is youthful. Very rich with a fine acidity. Amazingly good for the vintage. This wine has good positive energy, and is worthy of its name - a grand wine!

1969 Vintage Champagne Krug *(Champagne)* 96p

2007/2010 x2 • D 10 min / G 30 min

Old looking bottle. Level was 5 cm and colour was pure and youthful. Decanted ten minutes. On the nose still very fresh, full and perfumed, like cherry blossoms at first, then developing into baked sour cherries in pastry. Few bubbles were present with wide and energetic mousse. Great depth of fruit and balance. Fantastically complex and long, and with a touch of mint chocolate. Not quite as fine as the 1971 but still lovely to drink.

1950 Château La Mission-Haut-Brion *(Graves)* 96p

2006/2015 x16 • D 1.5 h / G 3 h

Fine looking château-bottling. Top-shoulder level. Decanted two hours. Intense ruby colour with maroon tints. Extremely ripe cassis nose with delicate flower aromas, capsicum and a touch of butterscotch. Full-bodied structure enjoys a moderate acidity, intense dark fruit and fine concentration. This wine turns out to be still very youthful and it will likely gain rich complexity with further ageing.

1985 Côte-Rôtie La Mouline Guigal *(Rhône)* 96p

2005/2020 x2 • D 2 h / G 2 h

Decanted 1.5 hours before dinner. Full, complex, open nose with bright, herbacious fruit and some animal character. Dense and peppery on the palate. This is full-bodied, herbacious and complex with spice and leather notes. Well balanced with firm tannins and complex spicy ending. This is drinking quite well now, but obviously has some years to go. Mouth-wateringly delicious.

1966 Dom Pérignon Rosé Moët & Chandon *(Champagne)* 96p

2001/now x11 • D 15 min / G 1 h

All the six bottles were in good condition with perfect levels. A developed orange-hued deep golden colour. Elegant light effervescence left in the wine. Rich and pronounced nose of toast, mushrooms and honey. Marked acidity on the palate. Fruitiness remains high enough to balance it. However, slight drying of the wine is evident. Full and round wine with a long toasty finish. Drinking very well now but declining slowly.

1874 Château Lafite-Rothschild *(Pauillac)* 96p

1999/now x2 • D 30min / G 15min

Top-shoulder, decanted 30 minutes before tasting. A deep, dark, hale, and hearty looking colour. Enormously rich and mature nose with some sweetness and black fruit. Opened instantly, then faded almost straight away. It only lasted 15 minutes in the glass, but during that short time the wine was exceptional. It reminded us a lot of Clos Vougeot 1821, which acted exactly in the same way and was also an amazing wine during those few moments.

Those 15 minutes were glorious and lifelong. This 1874 Lafite had a fabulous complexity and intensity, and at the same time it was a very sensitive and fragile wine. What a sophisticated and refined moment. We were very fortunate to share this unique moment with our best friends - a grand moment, a grand wine.

1945   *Château Lafaurie-Peyraguey (Bommes)*   *96p*

2001/2015 x3 • D 2 h / G 2 h

Excellent condition and level was by the neck. Decanted two hours before tasting. Brilliant deep-gold, bright and warm colour. Fabulous honeyed nose, open, soft and complex. Good acidity and structure, but not as fat and complex as Yquem, but a very close match. Excellent length and finish. A lovely and joyful experience.

1945   *Château Lafleur (Pomerol)*   *96p*

2004/2015 x15 • D 1.5 h / G 2 h

Quite old and damaged-looking bottle with only the remains of the label and capsule left. Château-bottled with top-shoulder level. Decanted at first for only 30 minutes, which was not enough. 1.5 hours would be the most favourable decanting time. Full, vigorous colour. Fine, very concentrated and intense nose with nuances of cedar, dark chocolate and eastern tobacco, but a core of ripe, sweet blackberries. The palate has elegance with a wonderful minerality giving a very clean, vigorous impression. Rich, full and lovely to drink. Quite honest and powerful wine. It is not as exotic and stylish as 1947 or 1950, but has an excellent, long finish. Still has a fine future.

1959   *Château Palmer (Margaux)*   *96p*

2007/2015 x9 • D 2 h / G 1 h

At Château Palmer, flowering took place in excellent conditions thanks to a fine mild weather in the spring. July was hot and dry with exceptionally high temperatures. The dry weather continued in August and this led to widespread vine stress. As a result, the ripening process slowed down considerably until some welcome rainfall came in mid-September. Throughout the harvest the weather remained fine and dry.

A good-looking château-bottled magnum. Level was high-shoulder. Decanted two hours. Full, healthy and vital colour. Voluptuous, rich and youthful on the nose. Real class and complexity. Beautifully soft and round on the palate. Well-structured with nicely balanced tannins and impressive underpinning acidity. Loads of blackcurrant, sweet fruit and gentle spiciness. Very inviting, rich and long. This beauty will still hold up for a decade or two.

1945 *Château Calon-Ségur* (Saint-Estèphe) 96p
2003/2010 x11 • D 1 h / G 2 h

This is one of our much-loved Châteaux and the vintage is not bad either. We opened this bottle to celebrate Christmas 2003, and it was the best Calon-Segur 1945 we have ever tasted (tasted 10 times previously). It was Château-bottled and the level was top shoulder. Dark colour to the rim. Delicate, yet an intensely clean, vigorous nose. Very full, long, and ripe on the palate with good fruit extract and backbone. Still tannic. A tremendous bottle!

1992 *Chardonnay Alexander Mountain Estate Marcassin* (Usa) 96p
2005/2015 x5 • D 30 min / G 1 h

Decanted 30 minutes. With its light gold colour, this wine reveals a tight nose with white flowers and candied citrus fruits. Its dense and lively palate conceals pears, peaches and gorgeous butterscotch fruit. This wine has high minerality and it is one of the most concentrated and complex Marcassins we have ever tasted. Long, hot and fresh finish. Will probably benefit from a few more years in the bottle, although wonderful right now.

1953 *Château Mouton-Rothschild* (Pauillac) 96p
2007/2020 x25 • D 2 h / G 2 h

Excellent bottle with by the neck level. A healthy, fresh-looking mature colour. Very delicate and sensitive wine with sweet concentrated flavours of red fruits and chocolate. The best characteristics of this wine were its elegance and its faultless mouth feel, decadently silky and classy. A very fragrant and smooth wine, almost as great as the 1955 Mouton, which merely has a slightly better balance and complexity, but they both share the same very long and concentrated finish. At 54 years of age, this Mouton is at its peak now, but should easily live on for at least one more decade. A genuinely classic and vigorous Mouton.

1988 *Salon* (Champagne) 96p
2006/2020 x11 • D 10 min / G 2 h

Bright, pale yellow colour with vivid small bubbles. Extremely elegant and complex developing nose. Walnuts, buttery aromas with cream and ripe pear aromas. Crisp acidity with a strong mineral structure form a backbone to this delicious champagne which has expressive mousse and creamy intense taste and a long walnutty finish. A beautifully aged elegant wine with great potential for further ageing.

1995 *Cabernet Sauvignon Herb Lamb Vineyard Colgin* (Napa Valley) *96p*
2004/2020 x2 • D 2 h / G 2 h

Fine-looking bottle. Decanted two and a half hours. Almost black in colour. On the nose very open and intense with hints of spice, pepper, currant, plum, and wild berry aromas and smooth new oak. So full-bodied and commanding that one tends to think of it as concentrated, but maintaining a sense of well-balanced elegance and finesse. Still powerful tannins tend to hide the black cherry, mocha-vanilla and mineral flavours. The finish is well-balanced, distinctive, chewy, immense, and very flavourful.

1988 *Vintage Champagne Krug* (Champagne) *96p*
2007/2010 x12 • D 20 min / G 1 h

Clear, bright, yellow colour with really lively bubbles. Intense nose is powerful with rich toasty and mineral notes reminiscent of gunflint and ashes. Crisp acidity with mouthfilling mousse on palate. Very rich and round texture with ripe apples. Great finesse and firm minerality and lingering subtle finish. An opulent wine with power and elegance.

1988 *Romanée-Conti Domaine de la Romanée-Conti* (Côte de Nuits) *96p*
2004/2020 x2 • D 2.5 h / G 2 h

Moderately deep, ruby colour with tawny tints. Ripe but restrained dark fruit nose with perfumed tones of violets and musk. Somehow mystically powerful and seductive nose. Crisp and firm acidity takes a grip on the rich medium-bodied palate. High level of masculine tannins is hidden partly under extracted ripe fruitiness of dark berries - wild strawberries, blackberries and boysenberries. A very powerful experience with rich floral and musky/spicy tones in the lingering finish. A very charming wine with more to come in the future.

1937 *Colheita Quinta do Noval* (Portugal) *96p*
2006/2020 x5 • D 1 h / G 2 h

Quinta do Noval Colheita is produced from a single vintage, matured in cask for at least seven years and bottled on demand. It combines finesse and elegance with creamy, nutty characteristics and like vintage port will take on the style of the harvest year. Increasingly rare, these wines are the supreme expression of the old tawny ports. The wine is made entirely from grapes of Quinta do Noval near Pinhão, in the heart of the Douro Valley. Colheitas spend their entire life in the barrel until the moment of bottling, which takes place only as and when an order is received. The grapes were trodden by foot and fermented in the traditional 'lagares' of the Quinta, where a disciplined and intense treading is essential for a good final result.

We had the privilege to enjoy this wine at Noval. The varietal composition is traditional with Touriga Nacional, Tinta Roriz and Touriga Francesa predominance. This wine demonstrated the charm and harmony of a great mature Colheita. Dry fruit, hazelnut and almond nose is expressive but smooth and fine. The palate has a silky texture and a complex range of subtle nuances: spices, vanilla, figs, burned wood... Persistent aftertaste and perfect harmony. In a perfect phase now but no hurry to drink up.

1927 *Vintage Port Cockburn* (Portugal)   *96p*

2001/2020 x2 • D 2 h / G 2 h

Cockburn has historically declared vintages less often, selecting only those years that fit their more elegant style - from which this very old looking bottle gave an excellent performance. Decanted three hours. Impressive, dark colour, slightly darker and deeper than Graham's. The huge, sweet nutty nose exposed plentiful aromas of liquorice, spices, black fruits, and white chocolate. Great balance. It exhibited rich, sweet, medium-bodied flavours, great elegance and length finishing with grace. Excellent bottle, but perhaps it does not quite possess the richness, complexity and fragrance of the 1908. This surprisingly youthful Cockburn will provide impressive drinking for years to come, although it is perfect now.

1997 *Solaia Antinori* (Tuscany)   *96p*

2006/2025 x5 • D 30 min / G 2 h

Solaia was one of the forerunners of the Super Tuscan category seeing daylight in 1978. Antinori's Tignanello had been a mainly Sangiovese based wine with some Cabernet Sauvignon. Solaia has majority of Cabernet in the blend, a style that was to become very popular in Tuscany. The 1997 vintage was legendary in Tuscany. Frost in April limited the size of the crop but contributed to quality. The ripe super vintage's characteristics were well evidenced in Solaia 1997.

Deep, dark, purple youthful colour. Rich and voluptuous nose of blueberries, boysenberries, dark chocolate, and vegetal notes. The nuances increase over time with liquorice and tobacco complementing the layered character. Full-bodied with ripe fruitiness and smooth firm tannins. Intense and mineral wine with impressive body-weight and length. A super vintage for Solaia that is starting to see its peak, but will develop positively until 2025.

1955 *Dom Pérignon Moët & Chandon* (Champagne)   *96p*

2006/2010 x3 • D 10 min / G 45 min

Fine bottle with good level. Decanted ten minutes. A very pale, light colour with a steady spray of fine, small and intense bubbles. Wide and overwhelming bouquet. Massively full-bodied and powerful wine. This is even richer than Krug 1955, but lacks some freshness and fruitiness. But what an elegant Montrachet-like wine!

1995 Pingus Dominio de Pingus *(Ribera del Duero)* *96p*

2004/2020 x3 • D 1 h / G 3 h

The first vintage of Pingus. This could be Peter Sisseck's 'dream come true' incarnation. Tinta Fina grapes for this wine come from 5 ha of vineyards with vines over 60 years old.

Very deep, ruby intense colour. Powerful toasty nose with concentrated ripe fruitiness. Complex aromas of ripe wild strawberries and plums, coffee, spices, bacon, and violets. Full-bodied rich, velvety texture on palate with moderately high acidity, intense firm tannins, very rich dark fruitiness, and toasty spiciness. All in great balance topped with great length and huge concentration. This wine has not yet shown its full potential.

1997 Cristal Roederer *(Champagne)* *96p*

2007/2020 x8 • D 30 min / G 2 h

The 1997 vintage has been suffering throughout its existence from its unfortunate destiny of being the successor to the superb 1996. It was a good year with less structure but charming fruitiness offering enjoyable purchases for mid-term drinking. Cristal is never a wine that comes around young, and the 1997 is no exception.

Bright yellow colour and small-sized energetic bubbles. The nose is somewhat closed. Aromas of green apples and green asparagus and some yeasty notes are detectable. Mouth-filling mousse and refreshing firm acidity. Aromas of lemon and herbs complement the rich body. Edgy finish with high mineral and green aroma character. A closed wine that requires more years in the bottle to open and show its full potential.

1990 Hermitage La Chapelle Paul Jaboulet Aîné *(Rhône)* *96p*

2006/2025 x6 • D 2 h / G 3 h

A majestic wine and excellent vintage, comparable to the quality of 1961. This was an extremely dry and hot summer followed by much favoured rain in August. The harvest took place in very good conditions and the results were superb. This wine could be listed as one of the flagships of the vintage.

Very intense, almost inky colour. Pronounced and complex nose is full of ripe dark fruits, black berries, blackcurrants and blueberries. Very intense floral and spicy aromas shows smokiness, bacon, tar, liquorice, and lovely hints of violets. The palate is very intense and fleshy with supple but firm tannins and vivid acidity. The ripe intense fruitiness shares flavours of blueberries and blackberries. Lovely spiciness and tar flavours take hold on mid palate while bacon, liquorice and pepper notes will escort the long lingering finish. A big but astonishingly elegant wine that shares lovely drinkability now but will keep wonderfully for decades still!

291

1929 Banyuls Grand Cru (Banyuls) 96p

2006/2040 x4 • D 30 min / G 2 h

It was Jan-Erik Paulson who found this unique fortified wine. There was only one barrel left available of this Grenache Noir and Carignan-based wine made by co-operative wine producers in the Banyuls area 80 years ago. It was just bottled in 2000 and those 300 bottles disappeared rapidly into the world markets. Bright, medium-intense maroon colour. Rich and intense nose with prunes, raisins, orange peel marmalade, jammed cherries, and nutty aromas. A sweet full-bodied wine with gentle acidity, mellow tannins and well-integrated high level of alcohol (17%) forming an oily texture on the palate turning into silkiness in a long lingering finish. A surprisingly concentrated and lovely wine with an exquisite balance.

1986 Bâtard-Montrachet Louis Jadot (Côte de Beaune) 96p

2004/2020 x2 • D 15 min / G 45 h

This appealing wine derives from the vintage of the challenges. A cold weather in winter was followed by a cold and wet spring. The summer enjoyed ideally warm and sunny weather conditions until the heavy storms rolled over the area in late August and September causing severe rot problems. Towards the end of September the weather improved and the harvest ended as a large one and especially good for whites. Jadot nailed the vintage with their wonderful Bâtard-Montrachet.

Moderately intense, bright and deep yellow colour. Intense nutty and beautifully developed nose with butter, spices, pineapple, and truffles. Dry and crisp palate with sophisticated richness of tropical fruits, butter flavours and oakiness. Concentrated, complex and harmonious taste with mineral, spicy, smoky, and vanilla flavours. Opulent and subtle long lingering finish. A white wine with power and concentration to age still easily another ten years, if one just has patience to wait. For the ones that cannot, the wine offers great pleasure already now.

1959 Chambertin Domaine Leroy (Côte de Nuits) 96p

2005/2015 x3 • D 30 min / G 1 h

Decent looking bottle with 3 cm ullage. Decanted 45 minutes. Medium-deep, a bit brownish but bright colour. The nose was immediately appealing with plenty of sweet fruit, mushrooms and truffles. Well balanced with low levels of tannin. On the palate it has plenty of those sweet fruit, tobacco and chocolate flavours. Rich, ripe and concentrated. A really delicious wine that has great complexity and medium-long, soft and stylish finish. Absolutely perfect to drink now.

1996 Cuvée Elisabeth Salmon Rosé Billecart-Salmon (Champagne) 96p

2006/2020 x3 • D 10 min / G 1 h

Billecart-Salmon is one of the constantly rising and growing stars in Champagne. The purity and intensity of its wines has much to do with the double settling of the must and a particularly cool fermentation temperature (13 °C). Partial oak fermentation of the vintage wines brings complexity and a smooth silky texture. Therefore it is no surprise that the magnificently ripe, fruity yet acidic vintage 1996 also produced a great Cuvée Elisabeth Salmon Rosé.

Since its first vintage 1988, this Rosé has consistently been one of the best in Champagne. It is made of an equal blend of Chardonnay and Pinot Noir with an addition of Mareuil-sur-Aÿ red Pinot Noir.

Intense and medium deep salmon rose colour. Delicate nose with red fruit of cherries and raspberries with a dash of citrus. A very delicate and balanced taste with delightful elegant acidity, great density and, rich creamy mousse. A harmonious wine with opulence and finesse. Without a doubt one of the best roses of the vintage.

1959   *Grands-Echézeaux Domaine de la Romanée-Conti* (Côte de Nuits) *96p*
2004/2010 x2 • D 45 min / G 2 h

In 1959 a big crop was expected from the beginning. Indeed the yields were remarkably generous, but at the same time the fruit was fully ripe. The summer was dry and not too hot, with just a little rain at the beginning of September. The 1959 are normally rich and complex like this Echezeaux.

The DRC Grand Echézeaux 1959 we enjoyed here was in excellent condition. Ullage was 3 cm from the cork. What a huge depth and complexity! A fruity, rich, fleshy, and round stylish wine. This is much finer than the modern-day Echézeaux. Superb concentration and lovely, harmonious long finish. Drink in ten years.

1964   *Château Pétrus* (Pomerol)   *96p*
2001/2010 x21 • D 2 h / G 2 h

Handsome magnum. Excellent level, wine was almost touching cork. Decanted 1.5 hours. Very impressive, youthful, vibrant colour. Open and sound nose with tobacco, exotic spices and mushrooms.

Almost too sweet and round on palate. Very gentle and harmonious Pétrus. Layers of flavours. Acidity and tannins are well integrated. Dangerously easy to drink. Lots of intense fruit underneath. After an hour in glass it became even slightly more full and tender. Has very good grip and length at the end. This is really very fine.

1979   *Clos des Goisses Philipponnat* (Champagne)   *96p*
2006/2010 x5 • D 10 min / G 1 h

Deep developed golden colour with elegant effervescence in the glass. The nose is wide open and appealing. Mature aromas of honey, bruised apple and burned sugar. The palate is consistent with the nose. Full, rich and perfectly ripe. Attractive linear acidity gives the wine a firm backbone for few more years of aging. At peak now.

1992 Maya Dalla Valle *(Napa Valley)*   96p

2003/2015 x4 • D 2 h / G 2 h

In 1983, Gustav and Naoko Dalla Valle began planting vines on the hillside east of Oakville, overlooking Napa Valley. Their vineyards produce first-rate quality grapes, resulting wines of great structure, complexity and balance. Gustav passed away in 1995 and Naoko Dalla Valle, with winemaker Heidi Barrett, continues the legacy of Dalla Valle wines. Dalla Valle Vineyards produces two wines - the proprietary red wine Maya, named after the owners' daughter, and Napa Valley Cabernet Sauvignon. Production at Dalla Valle has dropped from 1993, mainly because of the phylloxera damage to the vineyard, and the following replanting. The production in 1993 was around 40% less than that in 1992. The 1992 Maya is made of 55% Cabernet Sauvignon and 45% Cabernet Franc.

Excellent bottle. Decanted two hours. Good, deep saturated red colour. This still very youthful wine offers up subtle but strikingly sweet blackberry fruit, oak, mineral, and spice aromas. Full-bodied, a powerful, firm intensity, a multi-layered texture and richness. Still quite tannic, nevertheless it is skilfully balanced, with a long, voluptuous finish. Although it is already more accessible than we would have thought, it is a good candidate for 10-20 years of maturation.

1990 Riesling Loibner Vinothekfüllung Emmerich Knoll *(Wachau)*   96p

2005/2010 x12 • D 45 min / G 3 h

This is probably the greatest dry white wine ever made in Austria. It is a complex wine with enough structure and backbone for long ageing. This has been the clear winner at two major blind tastings where it was tasted next to the best Chardonnays, including the elite from Burgundy, of the same age. Decant an hour before drinking. Luxurious and concentrated, with mineral, pineapple, spice, and vanilla notes displayed on the extensive, complex and firm palate. A very good and long, intense finish. Drink now through 2015.

VINO FINO
DE MESA

Elaborado con uvas: Cabernet Sauvignon, Malbec... ...y albillo

MARCA

VEGA-SICILIA
"UNICO"

COSECHA 1966

Medalla de Oro y Gran Diploma
Feria de Navidad de Madrid
Medalla de Oro y Gran Diploma
Exposición Hotelera de Barcelona
Gran Premio de Honor
Exposición Internacional de Barcelona

R. Sanidad n.° 30.1.500/VA - N.° embotellador 2342 - Conten... ...rado alcohólico 13,5°

Esta cosecha se ha escogido para ser embotellada este año y consta de 96.000 botellas.

El número de esta botella es el ... 70947

BODEGAS VEGA SICILIA, S. A.
El Presidente

VALBUENA DE DUERO (Valladolid) España

1978   Château La Mission-Haut-Brion (Graves)   96p
2007/2010 x18 • D 2 h / G 2 h

In our opinion it is La Mission-Haut-Brion which produced the best Bordeaux in the challenging year of 1978. Decanted three hours. Deep, developing colour. The nose is stylish with leather, dark berries and a roasted complexity of aromas. The palate is extremely fine and harmonious. Tannins are admittedly very firming, but there is enough fruit to match up. This balanced and pleasurable wine is at a great age for drinking today. But it has the structure to keep at least for another 10 years.

1982   Unico Bodegas Vega Sicilia (Ribera del Duero)   96p
2005/2015 x2 • D 30 min / G 2 h

Developed, deep and clear ruby-red colour. The nose is fragrant and beautifully nuanced with tart berry aromas, herbs and farmyard notes. The classic and elegant, almost feminine style continues on the palate. Medium-bodied, delicate and silky mouth-feel. Layered aromatics and a long delicious finish.

1931   Garrafeira Niepoort (Portugal)   96p
2006/2015 x2 • D 45 min / G 4 h

An exceptional Garrafeira from Niepoort. Bottled in 1938 and decanted in 1975. 1931 was an exceptional year, but one when most houses declared no vintage. The vintage produced fruity and tannic wines, with a lot of ageing potential. The winter was dry and the summer unusually cold. In September the temperatures rose and some rainfall helped with slow maturation. The harvest started in late September, with perfect weather conditions.

Fine looking bottle. Developed tawny-hued colour. Mature nose of dried fruit, almonds, fresh cherries, and toffee. Silky, smooth and elegant - perfectly harmonious mouth-feel. Astonishingly delicate and attractive!

1999   TBA No.10 Welschriesling Nouvelle Vague Alois Kracher   96p
(Neusiedlersee)   **2006/2025 x3 • D 1 h / G 2 h**

This vintage was astonishing all over Austria. The weather conditions were perfect with no frosts in spring. A dry and warm flowering period was followed by a warm rainy summer until the weather turned into a mild and sunny autumn ensuring the best possible conditions for ripening. Among other regions Neusiedlersee succeeded well with botrytis appearing on the grapes at the right time. Alois Kracher, the king of sweet wines, was also relieved by this. He managed to produce a broad range of TBA collection wines, in its entirety 10 cuvées.

This most concentrated wine of the year with residual sugar of 345,6 g/l reflected perfect golden bright colour with a pronounced, extremely intense nose of honey and apricot marmalade. The sweet fruit tones were elegantly in balance with complexity through 22 months of French oak barrel fermentation authentic to the Nouvelle Vague line. Lusciously sweet taste with crisp acidity and amazing concentration filling the whole mouth. Spicy toasty oak aromas are in perfect balance with intense fruitiness. A amazing finish that lasts for ages!

1966   Dom Pérignon Moët et Chandon *(Champagne)* 96p
2006/now x7 • D 15 min / G 1 h

Fine looking magnum. Decanted 15 minutes. This is probably one of the most appealing Dom Pérignons at the moment. Very alive with a beautiful and intense structure. It has a fine, yeasty nose that is clean and fresh, yet has good richness and minerality. The palate is balanced between very stylish, intense fruit and a rounder creamy character. The mousse is fine and broad, and it has plenty of fresh acidity without being at all sharp. A wonderful champagne that offers real finesse and a long attractive ending.

1989   Château La Conseillante *(Pomerol)* 96p
2003/2015 x2 • D 2 h / G 2 h

Level and colour were naturally first-rate. Decanted two hours. On the nose, a very distinctive tobacco scent but not much fruit or any other aromas present. In the mouth, the fruit is more round and ripe; significant tobacco and tannin flavours on the mid-palate. Closed now, but excellent balance and silky tannins.

1937   Tavrida Black Muscat Massandra Collection *(Crimea)* 96p
2006/2010 x4 • D 30 min / G 3 h

One of the great fortified wines from famous Massandra cellars in the Crimean peninsula. Very intense, tawny brown colour with fine sediment. The nose is extremely intense with honey, ripe plums and peachy fruitiness, herbaceous with mint and eucalyptus. Taste is full-bodied and rich with a highly viscous texture full of sweet preserved fruits, honey and a delicious fresh acidity. Moderate 13% alcohol level and 200g/l residual sugar are in great balance with this delicate rich wine. This wine will most likely keep well for years, or even decades still, but is perfectly lovely to be drunk now.

1937   Château d'Yquem *(Sauternes)* 96p
2005/2015 x2 • D 45 min / G 2 h

The 1937 was a fine vintage in Sauternes. The bottle was just like brand new, recorked at the Château in 2001. Excellent level and promising colour. Decanted for one hour. Deep burnished gold, clean and bright colour. Sound and open nose with rich botrytis and honeyed-caramel sweetness on a background of tropical fruits, caramel, coffee, and toasted bread. Flourishing, rich, fat, and intense with good botrytis fruit. Smooth, gentle and a notably long finish of delicious spicy fruits. Clean, sound and ripe, perhaps a bit dry. The acidity is to a certain extent low, otherwise a perfect wine. Will hold, but will not improve. This is difficult to resist.

1998 *Bâtard-Montrachet Romanée-Conti* (Bourgogne) **96p**

2006/2015 x1 • D 1 h / G 2 h

Only a few people in the world know the existence of this superb wine. DRC owns almost 0.2 ha of Bâtard-Montrachet in the Chassagne-Montrachet district. The grapes are picked together with Le Montrachet although vinified separately. DRC produces only around two barrels of Bâtard-Montrachet yearly. This produces 600 bottles, which are reserved solely for private use.

The wine was tasted in November 2006 at DRC's bottle cellar when a French journalist from our group kindly insisted that this wine be tasted. After a little persuasion, cellar master M. Bernard Noblet decided to crack open this peculiar wine. Bright yellow colour with a very herbaceous, minty nose exposes mineral and toasty aromas. Intense full-bodied wine, with very crisp acidity and a long lingering mineral aftertaste, is enhanced with spicy tones. A superb and charming wine!

1990 *Cristal Roederer* (Champange) **96p**

2007/2020 x22 • D 15 min / G 1 h

The very warm March quickened the blooming and, due to this, the area suffered from some spring frosts. Irregular pollination and incomplete fruit development were problems. Good weather with intense heat and precipitation at the right moments assured an exceptional maturation. Alcohol and acidity levels were exceptional, yields substantial. A top vintage by any measure! This vintage was very successful at Cristal too producing wine with great ageing potential but an instant charm.

Deep, developing, light yellow colour. Classic nose with refreshing floral aromas combined with ripe apple fruit. Very fresh and crisp palate with youthful character. Delicate creaminess softens the racy acidity. Very long mineral finish. A truly classic wine with great potential.

1908 *Vintage Port Cockburn* (Portugal) **96p**

2005/2030 x3 • D 1 h / G 3 h

1908 was a plentiful vintage that produced some excellent wines by the 26 houses that declared it. Cockburn's made perhaps its greatest wine of the century. Winter was quite normal. April and May followed without too much heat and the vines progressed adequately. June and July were promising, neither too hot nor with too many showers. Autumn was warm with just a touch of rain. The conditions were quite similar to the vintage of 1896.

A very old looking, dusty bottle. Decanted only for 30 minutes. Very deep, clean and sound colour. Great depth, fleshiness and complexity with a mythical sweetness, and the aromatics here are dazzling! Seems sweeter than most mature Cockburn. Refined and well balanced. Full-bodied and very pure, with a long, fruity, maple syrup aftertaste. A big but vigorous and very harmonious wine.

2001 Kiedricher Gräfenberg Riesling Eiswein Robert Weil *(Rheingau)* 96p
2006/2015 x3 • D 45 min / G 1 h

Deep golden viscous eye. Pronounced nose of sweet dried fruit characteristics: honey, raisins and floral notes. The palate is lusciously sweet masking the high acidity. A full-bodied wine with an oily texture and a never-ending finish. This wine is drinking well already now. However the sweetness and firm acidic backbone guarantee at least two more decades' bottle aging capacity.

1952 Brut Impérial Moët & Chandon *(Champagne)* 96p
2004/2010 x3 • D 10 min / G 40 min

The bottle was disgorged a few months ago, and was - as expected - in excellent condition. Bright gold colour, good depth. Expansive, magnificent, ripe, and fruity bouquet. A fine palate with tiny, lively bubbles. Great length, balance, and fine complexity. Clean, creamy, buttery, long, and slightly sweet aftertaste. Fresh. Still vivacious. An exciting wine from a very difficult vintage.

1996 Barolo Briccho Rocche Ceretto *(Piedmont)* 96p
2001/2020 x3 • D 2.5 h / G 3 h

Exquisite single vineyard Barolo with bright, deep, ruby colour. Classic Barolo aromas of brambles and violets are enhanced with charming toasty, gamey, bacony, and spicy aromas. A full-bodied, powerful wine with firm refined tannins and chalky minerality combined with crisp acidity. Intense dark fruit and moderately high alcohol rounds up the palate and the wine has a long, lingering finish with beautiful balance.

1929 Château Cos d´Estournel *(St.Estèphe)* 96p
2004/2010 x1 • D 1 h / G 1 h

Château-bottled. Level was top-shoulder. Decanted 45 minutes. Good, deep, dark colour to rim. Cedary, spicy, sweet Cabernet nose. Round and rich. Good bottle. Has lots of excellent fruit and good acidity. Not the biggest wine from this splendid vintage, but was in very good shape and solid to drink now. Elegant and somehow touchy ending. Good reminder of great days gone by, awe-inspiring, but definitely not for further cellaring.

1983 Château Margaux *(Margaux)* 96p
2005/2025 x9 • D 1.5 h / G 2 h

If there is a vintage that can be declared as the success of one appellation in Bordeaux, then this is it. Margaux enjoyed a perfect harvest this year, which started off with a very rainy spring, but turned then into a very hot and dry flowering period in June. The rest of the summer was almost tropical with a hot and humid climate. Margaux appellation succeeded amazingly, avoiding the heaviest storms in August, which were ravaging in other Médoc appellations.

Moderately deep garnet colour. Elegantly developed complex nose offers blackcurrants, cedar, roasted coffee, pencil shavings, and earthiness. Medium-bodied taste has a rich velvety texture formed by ripe black fruit and firm ripe tannins. The acidity level is moderate but the rich mineral taste adds finesse and length in the long finish. Astonishing wine with elegance and class. Keeping still over ten years but drinking lovely now.

1988 *Dom Ruinart Rosé Ruinart* (Champagne) 96p
2007/2020 x8 • D 10 min / G 1 h

This Dom Ruinart is one of the most mouth-watering rosé champagnes in the world. Orangey pink colour with lively bubbles. The nose delivers a beautiful range of developed aromas, ripe wild strawberries, prunes, and round toastiness. The mouth-filling creamy mousse holds the same flavours as the nose. The texture is satin-like and very subtle with an adorable finish.

1996 *Grande Cuvée Billecart-Salmon* (Champagne) 96p
2006/2025 x2 • D 15 min / G 1 h

The Grande Cuvée is always an impressive wine and more so in this greatly structured vintage. This Chardonnay and Pinot Noir based wine has been made on the best years since 1982 exclusively at Grand Cru vineyards. Until 1996 it was rarely sold outside France. In fact, it is the same wine as the Cuvée Nicolas Francois Billecart but with an additional 2 years on the lees. Billecart-Salmon's signature cleanliness and harmony are present in this magnificent wine that is already drinking superbly but possesses great future potential.

Very intense and pronounced creamy and toasty nose. Highly concentrated taste with an elegant touch of oakiness. Very velvety texture shows pure power and unique leanness at once. Delightfully refreshed by super crisp acidity. A big champagne to be consumed with dishes rather than as an aperitif just on its own. Drinking beautifully now but will take further bottle ageing.

1945 *Vintage Port Graham´s* (Portugal) 96p
2007/2015 x1 • D 2 h / G 5 h

1945 was a very good vintage in Douro Valley, the best since 1935. The year was very dry with a hot summer. "The vintage started on September 6th. The weather throughout was exceptionally hot. In spite of the heat it was only during two days that high temperatures were registered in the lagares, and precautions had to be taken." - Ronald A. Symington.

Bottle was without label and capsule, but level and colour were excellent. Decanted 2 hours. This may be one of the greatest Graham´s vintages ever produced. It is still amazingly youthful and firm. Bright, vigorous colour. Very rich, velvety bouquet. Fat, fruity and awfully charming. Still sweet and powerful with massive depth and concentration. Marvellously intense fruit. Almost as good as the legendary Taylor's 1945, which has even more complexity and acidity. Excellent soft and silky, long finish. Very fine indeed!

1934 Château Coutet (Barsac) 96p
2003/2015 x7 • D 45 min / G 2 h

Tasted well over five times. Lots of variations in colour from rather pale to a lovely deep amber. But the taste has always been the same - wonderfully creamy and rich.

Bottle was in excellent condition, level by the neck and château-bottled with the original capsule and a branded cork. Decanted 30 minutes. Perfect deep, rich amber colour. Appealing, fragrant, and honeyed bouquet. Opened up fully in the glass after one hour. Extremely rich, fleshy, and almost fat, balanced by its excellent acidity. Hot and long finish. There was like an entire, warming sun inside the bottle.

1937 Barolo Monfortino Riserva Giacomo Conterno (Piedmont) 96p
2007/now x2 • D 1 h / G 1 h

This lucky bottle was in prestige condition. Decanted one hour. A paler and lighter colour than we expected, but the bouquet was very intense, complex and spicy. This was a marvellous Barolo, really elegant and silky with many layers of sweet fruit and tannins covered by richness and extract. Well-balanced and not nearly as hard and robust as the 1945 vintage. It has good length and wonderful aftertaste – exhilarating to drink.

1959 Carte d´Or Brut Champagne Drappier (Champagne) 96p
2005/2010 x4 • D 15 min / G 1 h

This exquisite bottle came directly from Drappier's cellar. While the new vintages mature in the cool darkness of the Reims cellars, the large bottles and old vintages like this 1959 are prudently lined up in the 12th century cellar constructed in Urville. The old bottles are still predominantly turned by hand in the old method of remuage.

This small company has a long history. The Drappier family has its roots in the 17th century, when Rémy Drappier was born and became, like Nicolas Ruinart, a merchant draper in Reims. But it was not until 1808 before one of the ancestors of the Drappier house, Louis, settled in Urville and began to develop the vineyards. Drappier was President de Gaulle's favourite champagne, which was no wonder, since Drappier has always been a very quality-minded house. Today, André and his son Michel preside over the destiny of the house, and three Drappiers of the next generation allow them to hope that more history shall be made. This 1959 Carte d´Or Brut 1959 champagne is from vineyards situated in Urville, and it has been made from 90% Pinot Noir and 10% Gamay selection massale de Champagne. Only the cuvée has been used to produce this lovely champagne. After a natural decantation by gravity, 50% of the blend is fermented in demi-muds (large oak barrels). Egg whites have been used for the fining during the cold temperatures of winter (5°C to 8°C).

This bottle was disgorged in 2003 and it had a youthful appearance. Decanted for 30 minutes. Deep, gold and seductive colour. Tiny bubbles. Clean and fresh with charming fruit. Lively, crispy and complex. This wine is extremely rich, creamy and very long. It also has the typical power of the vintage. It has always given us the most enjoyable experience - a surprisingly good, big-hearted champagne!

1959 Scharzhofberger Riesling Auslese Egon Müller 96p
(Mosel-Saar-Ruwer) 2005/2010 x5 • D 45 min / G 1 h

The Müller family and their seven hectare Scharzhofberg vineyard in Wiltingen, Mosel are known to produce one of the best Rieslings in Germany. On a vintage like this, the exclusive slate based vineyard produces unique Riesling grapes. This legendary vintage in Germany had glorious and hot weather conditions with extraordinary dryness from summer to autumn yielding grapes with extremely high sugar levels.

Bright, moderately pale yellow colour. Seductive, pure and intense nose with ripe peach and passion fruit aromas, petrol and hints of lemon. Medium-bodied wine with dry taste of ripe fruits - peaches and passion fruit and apricots. Lack of botrytis has helped the wine to maintain its sublime freshness. The wine is pure and straightforward in style with a lingering mineral finish showing less complexity but more sincerity of a genuine top quality Mosel Riesling. Drink up and purify your mouth and mind!

1959 Dom Pérignon Moët et Chandon (Champagne) 96p
2006/now x16 • D 10 min / G 30 min

Fine looking bottles with good levels. A pale yellow colour and lack of bubbles did not promise much. The totally modest, almost fruitless and lifeless nature of this wine was reflected in the faces of my guests as a disappointment, and the short, dry and somehow odd aftertaste did not improve matters. Previous experiences have been similar. Only four times has the wine met our expectations and deserved its reputation. Bottle variations are surprisingly frequent. Tom Stevenson said that one reason for this is that the defective bottles have warped necks. As a result the cork cannot close the bottle airtight. This unusually great uncertainty about the content's condition does not encourage one to purchase this fine vintage, although at its best the wine is superb and a 'unique' experience.

1945 Vintage Bollinger (Champagne) 96p
2005/now x2 • D 10 min / G 30 min

The celebration of the end of Second World War in early summer 1945 was restrained in Champagne by a very difficult growing season. The vintage got started early with good budding. Then the frosts in April damaged especially Ambonnay, Bouzy and Trépail districts causing damage to 75 per cent of the vineyards. This was followed by couloure and millerandage. In July the region faced drought while in August heavy rains were followed by insect and parasite problems and then rot in vineyards. The harvest took place in beginning of September yielding a very small crop. The quality turned out to be superb though.

Moderately pale, golden colour with refined lazy bubbles. Opulent and expressive nose shows dried fruits, apples and apricots, toasty aromas, walnuts and truffles. Medium-bodied and crisp taste with faint mousse. Very lively and supple texture with dried fruits, hints of lemon and toasty flavours. Lingering finish with great harmony. Sipping this now, it is difficult to see this balanced, harmonious wine being made in the area, which was devastated by the war and forces of nature. One can only feel twice as privileged to be able to drink it now.

1977 Vintage Port Taylor Fladgate (Portugal) 96p
2001/2025 x4 • D 2 h / G 2 h

This vintage really took its time to form since the wet winter, cold spring and cool summer did not encourage the vines to work well. But by the beginning of September there were signs of improvement. The high temperature during the rest of the month made this autumn the hottest since 1963.

Fine-looking bottle. Decanted five hours. Dark, purple colour with very pronounced and intense nose of fruitcake tones, anise, plum, liquorice, dark fruits, blackberries, and coffee. Full-bodied, moderate acidity and big tannins are dominating this relatively young port. On the palate very ripe, jammy dark fruitiness and violet flavours are accompanied with loads of spices, liquorice, smoke, and espresso flavours. A high level of alcohol is very well integrated into the wine prolonging the youthful, spectacular aftertaste. This should remain as it is until 2020.

1966 Château Lafleur (Pomerol) 96p
2006/2030 x4 • D 2 h / G 2 h

Absolutely fine-looking magnum with by-the-neck level. Decanted 1,5 hours. Wonderfully deep and rich colour. Sound and open, very fragrant and complex nose. Magic! We are more and more convinced that this is one of the finest wines of the vintage, if not the finest! Very rich and velvety texture with good acid and discreet tannin level. Great balance and extract. A superb wine with an astonishingly long and graceful ending. No rush to drink this divine bottle.

1966 La Romanée "Réserve du Paul Bouchard" Bouchard Père & Fils
(Côte de Nuits) 2007/2015 x2 • D 1 h / G 1.5 h 96p

This Grand Cru vineyard is the smallest appellation in France with the size of only 0.85 hectares lying on the moderately steep slope with limestone-clay soil and chalk crumbles just few metres from the legendary Romanée-Conti vineyard. This monopole vineyard has recently changed hands back to Vicomte Liger-Belair family after being long-term contracted to the exclusive use of Bouchard Père & Fils. In 1966 the vineyards faced damaging spring hail and a poor beginning of the summer. Luckily the weather conditions improved gradually towards the autumn and the harvest was completed in ideal conditions. The yield was high in quantity as well as in quality. Excellent bottle with 2 cm level. Decanted one hour. The appearance is moderately intense with hazy cherry red colour and tawny rim indicating mature age. Beautifully intense and opulent nose delivers root vegetables, wild strawberries and ripe brambles. Youthful but with lovely bouquet of tertiary aromas appearing. Dry, vivid acidity with elegant tannins and ripe red fruit flavours form satin-like texture that stands out moderately long in a very balanced aftertaste. A perfectly mature, extremely supple wine with delicious taste ideal for immediate pleasure, but will keep still another ten years.

1994   *Janus Pesquera Alejandro Fernández* (Ribera del Duero)   96p
2003/2015 x3 • D 2 h / G 2 h

Clear, deep, tawny colour. Pronounced, rich, complex, and developed nose. Vegetal and earthy aromas of farmyard and cooked root vegetables. Touch of burnt chestnuts and sugared almonds, pencil shavings, cinnamon and even beef stock aromas. Crisp acidity, stalky tannins and a savoury taste with roasted almond aromas are dominant. A restrained style wine with great length and incredible finesse.

1974   *Barolo Granbussia Riserva Aldo Conterno* (Piedmont)   96p
2006/2015 x1 • D 30 min / G 1 h

First class bottle. Level was by the neck. Decanted only 15 minutes. Well-developed, bright, medium-deep browning colour. Sound and open nose with great expression of mint and chocolate, blackberries and earthy notes. The mouth-feel is surprisingly well balanced, silky and smooth, firmed charmingly by ripe tannins and refreshing acidity. This wine is now harmonious and evolved but will not keep and improve any longer.

1998   *Hill of Grace Henschke* (Eden Valley)   96p
2005/2025 x2 • D 2 h / G 1.5 h

A great vintage for producing elegant but intense wines thanks to the long growing season and overall moderate temperatures. This tiny plot of pre-phylloxera Shiraz yielded quality-wise a wonderful crop.

Very intense and deep garnet colour. Pronounced and rich nose with plenty of ripe dark fruits, dark chocolate and sweet spices. Concentrated and complex full-bodied palate possesses very ripe and intense dark fruitiness of plums and blueberries. Rich smoky and peppery finish with tarry and herbaceous notes. Very refined, firm and chewy tannins and concentration of fruit and acidity give a promise of many years to come, but excellent to drink now.

1983   *Riesling Clos Ste. Hune Domaine Trimbach* (Alsace)   96p
2001/2015 x2 • D 45 min / G 1 h

Fabulous vintage in Alsace. One of the warmest winters, wettest springs and driest summers in history. Bright, clear, straw yellow colour. The nose is distinctive Riesling with loads of minerals, lemon and a touch of peach. Very pronounced petrol aromas indicative of development. Refreshingly crisp acidity and minerality are enhanced with lemon and green apple flavours. Medium-bodied structure with long lingering finish with tangy minerally grip. This wine has aged gorgeously but still shows the energy to keep another ten years.

1985 Corton-Charlemagne Leroy (Côte de Beaune) 96p
2007/2015 x6 • D 1 h / G 2 h

The year 1985 has become known for its abundant and elegant white wines. Decanted one hour. This bright yellow wine from Leroy charmed with its aromas, and one got swept away by plentiful vanilla, flowers and elegant fruit. The taste corresponded to the bouquet - it was round, soft, with concentrated fruit and a fair amount of acidity. A very pleasant experience that left a longing to taste this wine again.

1942 Vintage Veuve Clicquot-Ponsardin (Champagne) 96p
2005/now x2 • D 10 min / G 30 min

The 1942 Veuve Clicquot was feminine and fun, a bit of a mystery to us, and we all kept coming back to it over and over again. All the other vintages gave us a kind of 'excellent wine' pleasure, but this 1942 gave us something more - a hint of a smile perhaps. We actually do not know why this 1942 brought a smile on our faces. Our generous notes were:

Excellent looking bottle with a healthy golden colour. Decanted 30 minutes. Surprisingly lively with tiny, slowly running bubbles. It had a lovely, flowery, feminine and perfumed nose with lots of vanilla and tropical fruits. It opened beautifully in the glass. It had splendid richness, length and excellent acidity with a touch of sweetness. Very gentle and powerful at the same time - hard to describe. It went up and down in the mouth like a roller coaster - there were moments of just enjoying the ride and moments when you just wanted to scream for the excitement. This 1942 Veuve Clicquot was one of the biggest positive champagne surprises we have ever experienced. What a ride!!

1900 Château Ausone (St.Emilion) 96p
2003/now x2 • D 15 min / G 30 min

This Ausone in a half bottle is a living proof of the top quality clarets' capability to last for an immensely long time. It stood out as the oldest and one of the best 20th century clarets out of the twelve wines tasted in a fine and rare tasting.

The level was upper shoulder. Cloudy, medium-intense, tawny colour with an orange rim. Pronounced classic St. Emilion nose with plenty of aroma layers. Sweet ripe vegetal aromas enhanced with mint and smoke characters. After a while vegetal characters were joined by cherry and fried bacon aromas. Surprisingly intense. Medium-bodied taste was showing still moderately intense fruitiness and sweet tones in satin-like texture. Mouth-watering acidity and almost non-existent tannins were balancing the wine extremely well.

Penfolds

Grange

BIN 95

VINTAGE 1989   BOTTLED 1990

Grange is generally recognised as Australia's finest red wine and has earned international acclaim. This great wine developed by Max Schubert, commencing with the 1952 vintage, is made from premium Shiraz grapes grown at select vineyards in South Australia and matured in small casks prior to bottling.

During an extensive tour of the Bordeaux region of France in 1951, Max Schubert studied numerous wine-making practices that have now become an integral part of Penfolds wine-making technique. He also observed the practice of maturing wine in new oak casks, a method previously unused in Australia. The development of Grange represented the beginning of a new era in Penfolds red wine-making tradition.

This knowledge combined with Max Schubert's foresight, skill and dedication has resulted in Grange, the definitive Australian red of style wine, acknowledged to be amongst the world's best.

A really appealing and seductive wine, being more rich and round than refined and elegant. An astonishing experience!

1995   *Château Mouton-Rothschild* (Pauillac)   96p

2006/now x3 • D 4 h / G 2 h

Great dark red colour with slight lightening around the rim. Almost opaque. Rich and open bouquet with exquisite aromas of spices, black fruits and new oak. On the palate the wine still boasted aggressive tannins, with an almost fleshy structure. It was rich and spiny, possessing excellent acidity with flashes of fruit and earth. Good intensity and some ripe, sweet fruit were already present. A substantial finale, hard tannins still holding firm, great length pooled with class and freshness. Already an amazingly satisfactory wine with lots of life ahead. A pure Bordeaux drinking pleasure!

2001   *Château d'Yquem* (Sauternes)   96p

2007/2040 x5 • D 1 h / G 3+ h

A unique vintage in Sauternes. Moderately hot weather in summer, sunny cool autumn and some rains just before the first harvest guaranteed a big botrytis year with very ripe grapes but still fresh acidity. Residual sugar level is amazingly high for Sauternes (150 g/l).

Bright, golden colour. Incredibly complex nose with extremely seductive aromas of nuts, roasted coffee beans, apricots, a touch of wax, and new oak. A lusciously sweet, very concentrated nectar-like taste, which is well balanced by fresh acidity. Mouth-feel is silky sweet with high glycerol. Aromas in the long finish stand out as orange peel, apricots and cinnamon flavours. A gorgeous wine with unbelievable finesse, richness and concentration to be shared in decades to come.

1962   *Nacional Vintage Port Quinta do Noval* (Portugal)   96p

2007/2025 x3 • D 1 h / G 4 h

The bottle was in perfect condition and was opened for us. Decanted for only 30 minutes, but, regardless of this short decanting time, the nose was already wide and fully open with intense, dark, and concentrated fruit flavours. A healthy, fresh looking, dark ruby colour. Massive and intense wine with sweet concentrated flavours of prunes, figs and chocolate. The best characters of this wine are its elegance and faultless mouth-feel, which was decadently silky and rich. A very ample and smooth wine, almost as great as the perfect 1963 Nacional, which merely has a slightly better balance and complexity, but they both share the same very long and lingering finish. At 42 years of age, this port is at its peak now, but should easily live on for at least two decades more. A genuinely classic Noval Nacional.

1959   Château Lafleur *(Pomerol)*   *96p*

2007/2015 x3 • D 45 min / G 2 h

A hot vintage in Bordeaux. The cool, clay rich soil in Lafleur coped well with the heat and yielded extremely ripe but still fresh Merlot and Cabernet Franc grapes to this wonderful wine.

Very dense, dark cherry red colour. Extremely appealing nose with a full range of exotic spices, flowers, ripe plums, blackcurrants, smoke and earthiness. Medium-bodied, opulent and harmonious palate with lovely firm acidity and smooth tannins. Intense earth, roasted coffee and ripe blackberry flavours are escorted with a persistent mineral finish. A sensual and very elegant wine, despite the hot vintage. The wine is wonderful at the moment and will keep at this level probably a decade more before starting to decline.

1976   Dom Pérignon Moët & Chandon *(Champagne)*   *96p*

2007/now x8 • D 20 min / G 1 h

Fine bottle with good level. Decanted 30 minutes. The nose had already something magical about it. The heaviness of the wine itself included ultra-light seduction, the depth had something interesting on the surface, and the sensitive generosity was moving, in one word - magnificent. Underneath, a very balanced, tight and fruity structure started to reveal an endless amount of new layers that one could sense, but not one of us could determine them more specifically. One of the best Dom Pérignons ever, a true surprise!

1949   Château Haut-Brion *(Graves)*   *96p*

2001/2008 x2 • D 1 h / G 2 h

Fine looking bottle with bottom-neck level. Decanted two hours. Very dark, vivid colour. Opulent and flattering complex nose with tobacco, earth and dusty blackcurrant aromas. Full-bodied, charming with an almost chocolaty richness. Minerals and hints of smoke offer an astonishingly long and enchanting finish. Not as profound and gigantic as the famous 1945, but very good indeed.

1999   Pingus Dominio de Pingus *(Ribera del Duero)*   *96p*

2006/2025 x3 • D 3 h / G 2 h

Tasted at the Bodegas. Decanted 30 minutes. Very deep, rich purple colour. Commanding and intense nose with loads of blackberries, fresh herbs, coffee, truffles, and toasty new oak. Massive in the mouth with a luxurious texture, very sweet tannins and herbaceousness. A very masculine wine with a showy personality in addition to a massive, concentrated ending. The 1999 Pingus will almost certainly put on flesh to rival the great 1995 during ageing. This mind-blowing wine can be drunk between 2015 and 2025.

1966 Vintage Port Quinta do Noval *(Portugal)*   *96p*

2007/2020 x11 • D 2 h / G 5 h

This is one of our favorite ports from 1966. We have tasted it a number of times and it has never let us down. This bottle was in perfect condition. Decanted 2 hours before tasting. This is one of the most feminine, soft and stylish 1966s. A dark colour and lovely, fruity nose. Very charming, elegant, full, intense, and rich port. Lively and long ending - perfection now. This excellent port is still a bargain at auction - buy and drink it now, you won't regret it.

1949 Château d'Yquem *(Sauternes)*   *96p*

2001/2025 x7 • D 45 min / G 2 h

A wonderful Yquem. Good-looking bottle with upper-shoulder level. Decanted one hour. Unexpectedly light and pale in colour. Soft, sweet peaches, cream and fruit on the sound and open nose. 1949 Yquem was fantastically seductive, almost overemotionally sweet and rich. Packed with honey, ripe pineapples, vanilla, crème brûlée, and dried apricot flavours. This passionate Sauternes has layers of luxurious fruit, excellent balance and an immense, lingering aftertaste. At its peak now. A dream of a wine. Will age very well.

1961 Château L´Angelus *(St.Emilion)*   *96p*

2005/2015 x3 • D 1 h / G 2 h

Gorgeous double magnum. Level was bottom-neck. This gigantic wine was served on a boat while at sea, so there was no opportunity to decant the wine, but the bottle was opened at least five hours before dinner. Excellent, dark, vivid colour. Intense nose, fruits melting in hints of truffle, dark berries and exotic spices. Full and very rich, port-like wine. Good acidity. Slow developing, full of ripe fruit and creamy texture. Lovely sweetness of soft tannins. Not a bit astringent. Long lasting and splendid finish.

1879 Seppelt Para Liqueur Port Barossa Valley *(Australia)*   *95p*

1999/2040 x1 • D 2 h / G 1 h

Seppelt 100 Year Old Para Liqueur Vintage Tawny is the most remarkable of wine curiosities. It is an Australian heritage wine in a bottle, a direct link to the colonial past. For 125 years Seppelt has been laying down puncheons (475 litre barrels), arguably making it the longest unbroken collection of wine vintages held anywhere in the world.

Clos de Vougeot

This excellent looking bottle came from Langton´s Fine Wines Australia Auction some years ago. Decanted three hours. A very deep brown, almost black colour. The bouquet was immediately wide and sound, very tempting with burnt coffee and hot chocolate aromas. This was the thickest port-style wine we have ever tasted. A very rich, smooth and concentrated wine with some exotic fruit characters. Nicely balanced and the warm, strong alcohol came through giving a powerful kick to this eternal wine. Hot, long and bittersweet aftertaste. A much more refined and well-made wine than we were expecting. A thought provoking wine!

1964   Château Cheval Blanc (St.Emilion)   95p

2005/2020 x21 • D 1 h / G 2 h

One of the biggest harvests since the Second World War, this is considered overall to be very good, especially in southern Médoc and on the Right Bank. Cheval Blanc was one of the most successful châteaux in Bordeaux this year.

Developing, moderately intense tawny colour. Opulent and restrained nose with sweet fruit tones, cedar and spices. Ripe tannins still have a good grip on the medium-bodied palate with a mineral twist. A dose of volatile acidity adds a nice edge to the ripe fruit and delicate finish. Wine performs still nicely, chunky and elegant with alcohol level at a modest 12%.

1986   Château Léoville-Las Cases (Saint-Julien)   95p

2006/2020 x12 • D 1.5 h / G 2.5 h

The vintage 1986 yielded the biggest crop since the Second World War. The vintage started late due to the cool and poor spring. The hot and dry summer was very promising until the September rains ruined the expectancy of an excellent vintage. Northern parts of Médoc managed to avoid the heaviest rains and were able to produce the best wines of the vintage. The greatest estate in Saint-Julien, Château Léoville-Las Cases, succeeded well.

Deep, ruby red colour. A very refined and complex nose with cedar, blackcurrants, black olives, and toasty spiciness. Rich medium-bodied palate with moderate acidity, firm tannins and ripe fruitiness. Highly concentrated wine with spicy cigar box and floral flavours. A rich and intense finish with gently mouth puckering tannins. Drinking charmingly now but still has attractive potential, thanks to its sturdy tannic structure.

1989   Vintage Champagne Krug (Champagne)   95p

2007/2010 x9 • D 15 min / G 1.5 h

Very rich and developed deep yellow colour showing lively bubbles. Beautifully developed nose is full of biscuits, brioche and broad toasty aromas. Fresh acidity balances the ripe, toasty and creamy character of the wine. Broad, nutty and bread flavoured finish with lemony mineral twist. A really opulent champagne - less elegance and more richness. An extremely delightful wine for drinking now!

1964   *Musigny Domaine Leroy* *(Côte de Nuits)*   95p
2000/2015 x2 • D 1 h / G 2.5 h

Musigny Grand Cru grows some of the best grapes in the entire Burgundy. Its terroir is much more complex than Clos de Vougeot lying just below of it. Musigny is known for its super elegant and feminine characteristics, but this hot vintage gave this fine "lady" some extra muscle that has given an extra dimension to it and structure lasting. A great wine from the legendary Leroy.

Intense ruby red colour with orange rim. Such an elegant and complex nose full of ripe red fruits, anise and flowers enhanced with refined earthy aromas and spiciness. Rich medium-bodied palate with great grip of minerals, vivid acidity and smooth powdery tannins. Satiny texture with charming floral flavours, brambles and wild strawberries in lingering long finish. Drinking splendidly now but will keep another eight to ten years.

1937   *Musigny Comte Georges de Vogüé* *(Côte de Nuits)*   95p
2007/2010 x2 • D 30 min / G 1 h

Dirty, old-looking bottle. No capsule and the ullage was as low as seven cm. Cork was also very dry and powdery. Our hopes were not very high, but we were positively surprised. Medium deep brick red colour. Ripe, full, open nose with breathtaking fruit aromas. Full of personality and complexity. This is a fabulous old wine, with a soul of fruit flavour. Very alive and voluptuous. Long and positive aftertaste. It stunned us all!

1973   *Vintage Champagne Krug* *(Champagne)*   95p
2006/2015 x3 • D 15 min / G 1 h

This was a hot vintage that raised expectations. However, heavy rain in September caused a lot of damage by generating rot and dilution. Nevertheless, the richness of fruit combined with high levels of acidity has proven this to be a vintage, which matured well. Many 1973s are still showing magnificently, Krug being the prime example.

An extremely delicate bright orange hue. Hardly any bubbles detected. Very vinous nose with cranberries and strawberries. The palate shows a very intense dried fruit flavour enhanced with toasty and brioche flavours. Although the mousse is weak, the crispiness and delicious freshness forms a great elegance to this moderately rich champagne. The lingering finish is velvety and immensely long.

1952 Château La Mission-Haut-Brion (Graves) 95p
2006/2015 x22 • D 1 h / G 2 h

La Mission-Haut-Brion made some mind-blowing wines in the 1950s together with the grand 1950, 1953, 1959 and even the superior 1955. This is a very good example of the high eminence of this significant Château. Bottle in good condition, top-shoulder. Attractive dark red colour. Wonderfully, sweet, cedary open nose. Very elegant, fruity and slightly tannic – a masculine style of wine (more so on the palate than on the nose). Well-balanced, complex with a good backbone. This wine will keep for quite some time – no rush.

1929 Château Montrose (Saint-Estèphe) 95p
2000/2010 x13 • D 1 h / G 2 h

Good-looking Château bottling. Level was by the neck. Decanted 1.5 hours. Very deep, clear and full of promise with a red colour. Intense, compelling and complex bouquet of herbs, dark chocolate, cassis, lead pencil, and cedar. Very full-bodied with quite low acidity. Excellent ripeness and mature, soft tannin. A classic example of Montrose. Well-made and still youthful. Subtle and serious with good backbone on the finish. This very elegant and energetic wine will last well over a decade or two.

1906 Romanée St. Vivant Bouchard Père & Fils (Côte de Nuits) 95p
2004/now x4 • D 1 h / G 2 h

This bottle of wine from a truly magnificent vintage had spent almost a hundred years in peace in the cellar of an Austrian castle. The level of the wine had dropped an unusual amount - 11.5 cm - so expectations were not very high, even though a good friend of ours had recommended the wine to us.

The colour looked promising but there was a strong strange element in the bouquet - a hint of medicine seemed to obscure almost all of the other elements of the nose. After two hours in a glass this peculiar smell faded and gave way a little, and the bouquet started to correspond to the palate. A very balanced, elegant and surprisingly fruity, abundantly perfumed wine, which surprised us with its excellence. The aftertaste lingered in the mouth as well as on the mind for an unprecedented length of time, leaving a memory of a particularly pleasant and unique experience. Taste-wise, it is a good example of the well-known femininity of the RSV. A wine that underlines the significance of storage conditions and the producer.

1961 Château Gruaud-Larose (Saint-Julien) 95p
2002/2020 x23 • D 2 h / G 3 h

These three magnums were in textbook condition. Levels were all by the neck. Decanted two hours. Deep, garnet purple colour with ruby and amber highlights. This remarkably rigorous wine holds an exciting youthfulness. Full-bodied, concentrated and with a bouquet scented with sweet blackcurrants, roasted herbs, chocolate, and cedar, and with strong flavours that linger well on the palate. It has a multi-layered thick texture and an intense, warm and long ending. This vigorous and delicious wine is perfectly ready for drinking now in either regular or magnum format bottles. In regular bottles count on it to continue to age well for an additional 10 years and in magnum bottles it should cellar nicely until 2025.

1953 *Vintage Champagne Krug* (Champagne) 95p

2006/2010 x3 • D 15 min / G 1 h

Bright and beautiful medium deep golden colour with lazy bubbles. Creamy fully ripe developed nose. It charms with sweet aromas reminiscent of crème brûlée, apricots, apple compote, and pears. Dry palate is filled with a very refined mousse, crisp acidity and lemony mineral tones. Very persistent long finish.

1955 *Château Pétrus* (Pomerol) 95p

2007/2015 x8 • D 1 h min / G 1 h

Fine looking Château-bottlings. Clear, bright, dark mahogany colour. Deep intense nose with ripe dark fruits has even a hint of preserved brambles. Rose petals, dark chocolate and spiciness highlight the rich nose. Refreshing acidity combined with firm velvety rich tannins and very ripe dark fruit form a beautiful balance in the medium-bodied wine. This less delicate, more rustic style Pétrus is extremely appealing with its very good firm grip in the long aftertaste.

1982 *Vintage Champagne Krug* (Champagne) 95p

2007/2018 x4 • D 15 min / G 1 h

A marvellous high quality vintage with the biggest crop ever. Compared to the previous year it was three times bigger. Almost pale straw yellow colour with fine vivid bubbles. Developing, creamy nose with nutty and smoky characters with a zesty tinge. Delicate mousse on the dry, crispy, light-bodied palate is showing a lemony twist with a delicious finish of walnut flavours.

1969 *Belle Epoque Perrier-Jouët* (Champagne) 95p

2004/now x3 • D 10 min / G 30 min

This attractive bottle was looking fantastically old and had some thin layers of dust on it, which made it appear somehow even more elegant and grand than the new ones. Made from 50 percent Chardonnay and 50 percent Pinot Noir. Decanted 30 minutes.

A deep honey-gold colour. Had lots of tiny, lively bubbles running eagerly to the top. The bouquet was immensely full, rich and wide with flavours of ripe pear, flower and honey. Very fresh and youthful wine. Lighter and not as creamy as we expected, but has great balance and marvellous complexity on the palate. Although the balance between grapes was equal by numbers, here the Chardonnay holds command of the taste. Pinot Noir, which normally brings the body and richness to the wine, was now overrun by the Chardonnay's enormous finesse and elegance. The finish was round and insistent. A master blend of elegance and lightness.

1975   *Unico Bodegas Vega Sicilia* (Ribera del Duero)   95p

2006/2010 x3 • D 1 h / G 2 h

This was a vintage prior to the Álvarez family period. 1975 was not a successful vintage in many regions but Spain and the Ribera del Duero made a delightful exception. It is, in fact, known as one of the great historical vintages of the house. The wine perfectly lived up to its reputation being harmonious and powerful as well as youthful.

Clear and deep ruby-red colour. The nose is astonishingly youthful revealing black cherry, lingonberry and smoke aromas. Oak nuances are still slightly noticeable and the delicate yet complex nose is enriched by tobacco notes. A medium-bodied, feminine and very elegantly harmonious wine. A firm tannic backbone supports the persistent and flavourful wine.

1912   *Colheita Niepoort* (Portugal)   95p

2006/2020 x2 • D 3 h / G 2 h

In August 1912 the Douro valley and its inhabitants were facing a massive heat wave, which guaranteed a superb vintage. The high quality was confirmed by the 25 shippers who declared this vintage. It became the vintage of the decade resulting in full-bodied wines with concentration and balance of fruit and tannins. Also an exceptional year in both quality and the quantity produced. Clear, moderately pale, cherry red with lime green rim. A rich, lean and complex nose: chocolate, nuts, almonds, beef stock, menthol, and dry fruit tones. A sweet, delightful acidity, although partly affected by the volatile acidity. Medium-bodied palate with dried fruits, apricots and plums. Chocolate and coffee flavours in long warming finish.

1992   *Vintage Port Taylor Fladgate* (Portugal)   95p

2004/2030 x5 • D 7 h / G 3 h

An excellent-looking, perfect bottle. Decanted seven hours before the tasting. Full-red, almost black, bright colour. Very open nose full of raisins, minerals, blackcurrants, and spice aromas. This is still a very young and unformed wine, but what a great future lies ahead. Fabulously multi-layered and concentrated with an already strong harmonious and well-balanced structure. A very stylish and complex wine with great richness and huge body. Powerful, long and firm aftertaste. As good as one can ever hope for a port of this age.

1934 Château Latour *(Pauillac)* 95p

2004/2010 x5 • D 30 min / G 1 h

Old-looking, château-bottled bottle. Level was top-shoulder. Decanted 30 minutes. Very deep ruby colour with just some browning. On the nose lovely, sweet cassis fruit and classic cedary, pencil shaving complexity with an attractive sweetness of alcohol and developed fruit. Smooth as silk on the palate with opulent fruit and firm tannins evident. Quite firm body and complexity with mineral nuances, bitter cherry and blackcurrant. Delightfully long, plump, supple, and pure. Perhaps the wine of the vintage.

1921 Vintage Pol Roger *(Champagne)* 95p

2001/now x2 • D 30 min / G 1 h

This good-looking Pol Roger was filled to the upper neck. Decanted 30 minutes. Unexpectedly pale, but lively looking light gold colour. First a hit odd, old straw nose, but after another 30 minutes it opened wide and was full of chocolate, honey and cream flavours. The taste was wonderfully joie de vivre and full of energy. Not very sweet, but not dry either. Has a very fat and strong body, almost too big and commanding a wine for champagne, but well balanced and fully harmonious. Wine with substantial charm and an excellent, multi dimensional, long, crispy aftertaste. It is a very good aperitif, but also excellent with food!

1924 Château Mouton-Rothschild *(Pauillac)* 95p

2007/now x3 • D 1 h / G 1 h

Excellent-looking bottle with the label in mint condition. Level top-shoulder, decanted just one hour before tasting. Very good, dark, deep, and mature colour. Intense looking. A fabulous, decadent nose of blackberries, mint, earth, and tobacco. Opened fully in 15 minutes. The palate was beautifully balanced with fresh acidity and, like all the great wines, got better and better in the glass. The tannins were smooth and spirited. A complex and elegant wine with multilayered fruits and a long, clean finish. Unquestionably a top class Mouton. An epochal wine in many ways!

1981 Mount Edelstone Henschke *(Eden Valley)* 95p

2007/2015 x9 • D 2 h / G 3 h

Mount Edelstone 1981 was made from 100 percent old-vine Shiraz. The Mount Edelstone vineyard was planted in the 1920's in a rich sandy loam soil on the eastern slopes of Mount Edelstone, (meaning gemstone) near Keyneton, high in the Eden Valley region of South Australia. The 70-year-old dry-grown vines are low yielding, producing intensity of colour, spicy fruit flavours, great complexity, and palate length. Handpicked, made using traditional winemaking techniques and matured in small oak barrels, the Mount Edelstone wines have received awards at National Wine Shows every year since 1956. The 1981 vintage will be remembered for the hottest, driest summer since 1939, which put the vines under severe water stress and which was only relieved by rain on the first day of autumn. This was then followed by pleasant, cool, dry weather, which allowed grapes to ripen under more favourable conditions than those experienced in the hot, earlier vintage areas.

A fine looking bottle with by-the-neck level. Decanted one and a half hours. Very dark, ruby colour. On the nose rather spicy with intense blackberry, earth, dark chocolate, and cedar aromas. Quite immense and powerful on the palate with first-class structure and hints of pepper, prune, liquorice, and vanilla flavours. Rich in style and wonderful texture with silky tannins and a very long, warm finish.

1938   Ai-Daniel Tokay Massandra Collection *(Crimea)*   95p

2006/2010 x4 • D 30 min / G 3 h

Moderately intense, tawny brown colour with yellow tints. Full of sediment. The very delicate and refined nose is seductive with a touch of herb and toast aromas. Extremely concentrated honeyed sweet taste (RS 260 g/l) is balanced delightfully with crisp acidity and a well-integrated high level of alcohol (16%). Full-bodied wine with great elegance in aftertaste.

1974   Monte Bello Ridge *(Santa Cruz Mountains)*   95p

2005/2010 x4 • D 1 h / G 2 h

Monte Bello is a wine to fall in love with. Both bottles were faultless. Decanted 45 minutes. Rich in flavours and colour. Open and fresh bouquet of currant, mineral, spice, tart, leather, and black cherry aromas. This gorgeous and silky wine combines softness and weight in ways that are utterly elegant. A wonderful balance and structure with mature flavours of dried plum, mushrooms and spicy black cherry. Lovely, intense and rich finish. This Monte Bello has already been fully mature for a decade and will not last for another.

1887   Vintage Port Graham's *(Portugal)*   95p

2005/now x1 • D 2 h / G 1.5 h

Excellent looking bottle with good level. Decanted two hours. Moderately intense, cloudy, developed colour with red tints. Pronounced partly oxidized nose with almonds, nuts, prunes, figs, and spices. Sweet mouthfilling texture possesses spicy aromas with dark chocolate and raisin notes in long warming aftertaste. Very well balanced harmonious wine full of life and spirit.

1975 *Cristal Roederer* (Champagne)   95p

2006/2020 x3 • D 15 min / G 1 h

There is a lot of variability in the 1975s. The vintage witnessed a late bud break and hot summer weather. Lack of direct sunshine postponed the harvest, which averaged fairly high at 9,082 kg/ha. There was attractive fruit intensity and high acidity, which should account for long-lived wines. Cristal alongside Clos des Goisses are in a remarkably youthful form today with no rush to open them.

Clean, pure and fruity attractively developing nose. Fresh, spicy and bready aromatics. Lightness of autolysis characters combined with a lemony tartness makes the wine appear incredibly youthful and lively. Small-sized bubbles on the mousse contribute to the feeling of roundness. Elegant, charmingly fruity wine with an acidic spine that can age harmoniously for another 10 years or more.

1988 *Cristal Rosé Roederer* (Champagne)   95p

2001/2020 x3 • D 45 min / G 1 h

Roederer, which is one of the few producers in Champagne vinifying the rosés by the saignée method, has again managed to macerate a beautiful light salmon rose colour to this unique champagne. Very delightful nose with strawberries and biscuits, also hints of toastiness. Very crisp light-bodied wine with persistent and mouth-capturing mousse reflects a marked minerality and lovely brioche flavours that are enhanced by delicate strawberry aromas. Long, lingering finish.

1999 *La Tâche Domaine de la Romanée-Conti* (Côte de Nuits)   95p

2006/2030 x8 • D 4 h / G 2 h

Dense ruby-red colour. Nuanced and pure nose of raspberries, strawberries and black cherries highlighted with minerals. Some still unintegrated yet stylish oak on the nose. Ripe attractive and powerful fruitiness on the palate. The fine tannic structure is in perfect harmony with the smooth silky texture. Well-structured and intensely fruity wine with enormous ageing and quality potential. In a very drinkable phase at the moment.

1970 *Vieilles Vignes Françaises Champagne Bollinger* (Champagne) 95p

2002/2010 x2 • D - / 45 min

This was a very good vintage despite the wet summer causing worries to the growers. Luckily the autumn was favourable resulting in some very good vintage wines like this one.

Pale golden yellow colour with refined vigorous bubbles. A very intense and complex nose showing great depth - dried fruits, ripe apples, smoke, and spices. Charmingly rich palate with vivid acidity, moderate mousse with lemony bite and broad texture full of ripe apples, nuts, smokiness, and exotic spices. An opulent and vigorous wine with a long lingering finish. Drinking perfectly now, but will still keep for few years.

1969 *Le Montrachet Domaine Leroy* (Côte de Beaune)   95p

2002/2015 x4 • D 45 min / G 1 h

Maison Leroy is one of the most esteemed négociant establishments in Burgundy over the past one hundred years. Leroy family has become well known as the half-shareholder of Domaine de la Romanée-Conti since 1942 and - within the last 15 years - from Madame Lalou Bize-Leroy's ambitious and superb domaine wines. Still the négociant house, Maison Leroy, is superior to any other négociant keeping the stocks of several million bottles of fine and mature wines in their cellar. This rare wine is one of the jewels of this cellar deriving from the greatest white wine plot in Burgundy and from an outstanding vintage. In 1969 the winter started mild and was followed by a wet and cold spring delaying the bud break. The sunny and warm summer ripened the grapes thoroughly. The cold wet period in early September turned luckily into fine weather in the beginning of harvest in October causing no damage to this reduced crop. This vintage yielded outstanding whites better in quality compared to reds in Burgundy.

Bright, moderately intense, golden yellow colour. Expressive nose with charmingly oxidative character - smoke, ripe tropical aromas, spices, sweet waxiness, and honeyed overtones with truffles. Dry and still crisp medium-bodied palate with oily texture. Ripe tropical flavours mixed with spices and mineral flavours. Long, very integrated and well-balanced finish with seductive sweet tones. Still a wonderful wine, at its peak now. A slow decline is soon to start.

1957 *Romanée-Conti Domaine de la Romanée-Conti* (Côte de Nuits)   95p

2007/2010 x2 • D 45 min / G 25 min

Fine bottle with 4 cm level. Decanted 45 minutes. Bright, medium-intense, dark cherry red colour. Complex and opulent nose with spices, toastiness, leather, and vivid floral aromas. Broad, medium-bodied taste with refreshing acidity. Wonderfully silky texture makes the wine very stylish but with great density. It falls, however, slightly short of vividness and harmony. Glorious wine for drinking now but not for much longer!

1995 *Cabernet Sauvignon Bryant Family Vineyard* (Napa Valley)   95p

2005/2020 x2 • D 2 h / G 2 h

Bottle was like new. Decanted two hours. The colour is dense and dark. The nose is powerful and open with a good complexity. The huge scents of black fruits, creamy oak, liquorice, plus exotic spices are all there. At first, the volume of the tannins have a tendency to overwhelm the fruit in the mouth, but after two hours in the decanter the wine became more fruity and balanced. Bit by bit the silkiness and multi-layered structure of the wine emerges, dominating the end of the tasting. Its finale is very long and powerful. Very good already, but will certainly be better in a few years.

1990 Clos des Goisses Philipponnat *(Champagne)* 95p

2005/2025 x5 • D 30 min / G 1 h

The Clos des Goisses single vineyard parcel is situated in the 99 percent 1er Cru Mareuil-Sur-Aÿ. This south to southeast facing steep slope has the maximum inclination of 45 percent giving it a very particular micro-climate. The 70 percent Pinot Noir and 30 percent Chardonnay blend comes from vines that are 30 years old on average, planted at 8,300 vines per hectare. Massal selection used to be the replanting method but clonal selection is utilised. Over recent years the share of Pinot Noir has increased on the parcel with PN 779 being the favoured clone. The ripe vintage of good acidity level produced yet another spectacular Clos des Goisses. This great Clos des Goisses was supplied straight from the Philipponnat´s cellar.

Intense yellow colour with golden tints and tiny energetic bubbles. Rich, complex, yeasty nose with white peaches, ripe apples and honeyed overtones. Dry and crisp, full and rich on palate. A very complex and big wine with delicious brioche flavours. Lingering, long, yeasty finish with mineral tones. Drinking well already but is still a baby on its journey.

1959 Château Gruaud-Larose *(Saint-Julien)* 95p

2005/2015 x14 • D 1 h / G 2 h

Château-bottled. Level was high-shoulder. Decanted one hour. Exciting, youthful purple colour. Really dense. Very deep, heavy, gloomy nose of almost stewed black fruits and some chocolaty richness, lovely cedar and mineral components and liquorice notes too. Certainly luscious palate with mint, eucalyptus, blackcurrant fruit, and firm tannins. A complex wine with great length and fine acid structure. An excellent, rigorous and loaded Gruaud-Larose.

1996 Cristal Roederer *(Champagne)* 95p

2007/2030 x5 • D 30 min / G 1 h

A dream-come-true vintage combining volume (10 356 kg/ha), ripeness and remarkable acidity. This is as structured and long-lived as it gets, near immortal. Another positive characteristic is that there are still 1996s around to buy and stock for years to come. Every Cristal vintage requires time, but usually, one should allow the 1996 a further 5-10 years in the cellar. As Cristal has not gone through malolactic fermentation, the acidity is phenomenal and to the liking of all high acidity champagne lovers.

Persistent and fine small-sized bubbles in the glass. The nose is pure, pronounced and with some signs of development. Ripe fruitiness, lemon, brioche, and ripe apple aromas overwhelm the taster. The palate is fresh and tart, slightly tight and closed still, but with remarkable concentration and length. This will undoubtedly develop into one of the best Cristals ever made.

1959   Château Margaux *(Margaux)*   95p

2007/2020 x11 • D 1 h / G 3 h

Handsome magnum with by-the-neck level. Decanted one and a half hours. Magnificent, complex perfume and wide-open nose. We have had this wine numerous times before from 750ml bottles with a similar, open and superb nose. A full and somewhat feminine wine with soft, gentle tannins. Good balance and long on-going aftertaste. Will not improve, but will last well, especially in bigger-sized bottles. A charming wine, we were very happy that this was not our last one!

2004   Montrachet Domaine Ramonet *(Côte de Beaune)*   95p

2006/2015 x3 • D 30 min / G 1 h

Noël Ramonet produces only a few barrels of this splendid wine from his 0.25 hectare plot at Le Montrachet vineyard. The wine is treated with 100 percent new oak and has, as all of Ramonet's wines, an extremely expressive and opulent style compared to Lafon's or DRC's Montrachets. Although this vintage did not receive great applause due to its cool and wet summer, it was saved by a miraculously dry and sunny September with a drying north wind. Not the vintage for long term ageing but well suited for mid term drinking. The best whites, like this one, are drinking perfectly now already.

Bright yellow colour with lime tints. Round and rich, ripe tropical fruit aromas with sweet tones compli-mented marvellously the spices and toasty coffee aromas. Extremely intense, explosive dry palate reveals enormous complexity with fresh fruits, roasted coffee and mint flavour. Very rich buttery texture with a linger-ing long mineral finish. Drinking beautifully now but will evolve delicately within the next five years.

1968   Martha's Vineyard Cabernet Sauvignon Heitz *(Napa Valley)*   95p

2000/2010 x2 • D 1 h / G 1 h

This 1968 is a wine of great reputation and fame. After the famous cult-vintage 1974, it is one of the most sought-after wines from California. Fine-looking bottle. Decanted one hour. Top shoulder. Deep red colour. Open, forthcoming cedary and eucalyptus nose. Great fruit extract, balance and multi-layered structure with lingering velvety aftertaste. A delicate and historic wine.

1979   Sassicaia Tenuta San Guido *(Tuscany)*   95p

2006/2010 x6 • D 30 min / G 45 min

This very good vintage ripened Cabernet Sauvignon grapes perfectly in Bolgheri. Bright, moderately light brick red colour. Intense, ripe and developed nose dominated by cedar, pencil shavings and cigar aromas. Restrained palate, with mouth-watering acidity, ripe red fruits and sour cherries, supported by silky tannins. Medium-bod-ied style with great concentration and wonderfully elegant long finish. One of the most elegant Sassicaias ever.

1959   Château Cheval Blanc *(St.Emilion)*   95p

2006/2015 x19 • D 1 h / G 2 h

All four bottles were in excellent condition. Bottled by P. Bouillon. Decanted one hour. Deep, dark, brick red colour. Very rich and ripe fruity nose. Plums, dark fruits, spices, chocolate, coffee, and toastiness. Full-bodied opulent palate with very ripe dark fruitiness and round tannins. High level of alcohol adds power and sweetness into the rich, spicy and toasty finish.

1966   Vintage Port Graham´s *(Portugal)*   95p

2000/2020 x3 • D 2 h / G 3 h

The bottle was in a decent exterior condition, the level was by the neck. Decanted three hours before tasting. Very dark, deep and opaque in appearance. Wide and open nose with lots of violets, minerals and tobacco aromas. A full-bodied and sweet, intense port. Nicely balanced, elegant and flawless mouth-feel. What a smooth and suberb finish. Great quality. A noble, yet forward, port.

1987   Proprietary Red Wine Dominus *(Napa Valley)*   95p

2002/2020 x3 • D 2 h / G 2 h

The rainfall this year was half the average. A very warm early summer turned into a moderately warm ending enhancing the grapes to obtain their crisp acidity. Winemaking was classically non-interventionist. Blend of 88 percent Cabernet Sauvignon, 9 percent Cabernet Franc and 3 percent Merlot. The wine spent 14 months in French oak, of which 25 percent were new.

A medium-intense garnet colour with tawny tints. Very concentrated, ripe blackcurrant nose with plums, cedar and spicy aromas. Medium-bodied palate reveals moderately high refreshing acidity, firm tannins and herbaceous dark fruity aromas of cassis and plums mixed with hints of mint. Long and admirably balanced finish with spicy oak character. Drinking well now but will easily keep another decade.

1961   Château Ducru-Beaucaillou *(Saint-Julien)*   95p

2004/2010 x22 • D 2 h / G 2 h

Excellent château-bottling with top-shoulder level. Decanted one hour. Bright brick red colour. A bursting, versatile, intensive nose with hints of spice, white chocolate and plenty of bouquet from ageing. Full-bodied, fairly complex taste with good dimension and balance. A very long, finely tuned and elegant ending. This is excellently enjoyable right now.

1990 *Cabernet Sauvignon Special Selection Caymus* (Napa Valley) 95p

2007/2020 x5 • D 2 h / G 3 h

Truly an outstanding wine. Being restrained in style, the wine benefited from being in the glass for a long time. Dark, medium intense ruby colour. Extremely intense, concentrated and youthful nose shows very dark aromas - dark cherry liquor, roasted sesame seeds, dark chocolate, and hints of coconut. Mint and cassis aromas stand out after the wine has opened up in the glass. Very weighty and intense mouth-feel. Refined, velvety and sophisticated tannins form a harmonious backbone to the wine with the fresh and crisp acidity. Intense dark fruitiness reveals plum and blackcurrant notes. Moderately high alcohol is integrated so well that it is hard to even detect it from the concentrated taste. Long, elegant finish. Wine is drinking well now, if decanted well before. Otherwise will reach its optimum in 15 years from now.

1961 *Château Pavie* (St.Emilion) 95p

2004/2010 x3 • D 1 h / G 1 h

Decanted two hours before. Hardly any sediment. Good, deep, maturing colour. Lovely fruit. As full, rich and intense as we recalled. Elegant, complex and soft wine - for our taste this is a perfect wine to drink now. At its peak, but should easily hold for at least four to five years.

1994 *Riesling Trockenbeerenauslese Achleiten Prager* (Wachau) 95p

2007/2010 x3 • D 30 min / G 1 h

Deep, developing golden colour. Expressive and forward nose of honey, dried apricots, white flowers, and petrol. Luscious palate that is refreshed by a linear, firm, acidic backbone. Oily mouth-feel and great body weight. Still a very youthful wine that is starting to develop. Primary aromatics of Riesling and botrytis prevail. However, this wine has potential for prolonged aging due to its power, structure and grip.

1952 *Château l´Eglise Clinet* (Pomerol) 95p

2003/2010 x11 • D 30 min / G 1 h

Fine looking Château-bottling with upper-shoulder level. Decanted 30 minutes. A bit light and pale in colour. Intense, silky, coffee-edged aromas and berries and blackcurrant fruit. There was a little dark chocolate and vanilla depth present as well. The palate was really very concentrated and grippy with super gentle tannins wrapped around a rock-hard core of red fruit. Well balanced with medium-long, dry and slightly skinny finish. Very elegant and with a good structure; however, we found this less rich and complex than previous vintages (1947 and 1950).

NUMBER 389.

NUMBER 390.

NUMBER 391.

NUMBER 392.

NUMBER 393.

1937   Dom Pérignon Moët et Chandon (Champagne)   95p

2006/now x1 • D 30 min / G 1 h

This 1937 was a marvellous bottle, full of life and pleasure. It has tiny lively bubbles and a sound, open yet complex nose. Rich, long and compound. Extremely well made. A complete and enjoyable champagne that has held very well. We have never underestimated the keeping power of Dom Pérignon. What a thought-provoking wine!

NUMBER 394.

2000   Riesling Loibner Vinothekfüllung Emmerich Knoll (Wachau)   95p

2005/2010 x2 • D 45 min / G 2 h

Developing golden colour. Intense, completely ripe fruitiness of acacia, tropical fruits and lemon. The palate is consistent with the nose. Attractive minerality and high acidity bring great elegance to the wine. Perfect combination with the ripe fruitiness and balanced high alcohol. At a great drinking age today, but the wine will keep well for many more years.

NUMBER 395.

1955   Vintage Bollinger (Champagne)   95p

2006/now x2 • D 15 min / G 45 min

Excellent-looking bottle with good level. Decanted 15 minutes. Golden yellow, small pieces of sediment and weak sparkle. The nose is evolved and complex with a touch of yeasty flavours and toastiness. A very crisp and fresh taste stands out, a bit racy even. Long, minerally and lemony finish with a firm grip. Shockingly youthful wine considering it is over 50 years old!

NUMBER 396.

1994   Riesling Smaragd Steinertal FX Pichler (Wachau)   95p

2006/2010 x3 • D 15 min / G 45 min

Franz Xaver Pichler is the highly admired Grüner Veltliner and Riesling producer whose wines are considered to represent the best of Austria. This is the result of the almost 80-year research of clones and possession of the unique wine sites in the eastern part of Wachau Valley. All wines are made in large vats avoiding reductive winemaking and cultivated yeasts. The Steinertal vineyard is located at the foot of Loibner hill where the Riesling vines have laid their roots in deeply deposited primitive rock capable of delivering wonderful mineral finesse into the wine. The 1994 vintage was the hottest vintage Austria had ever experienced. Rain in June and July boosted the vegetative growth while the rest of the summer's weather was dry and hot, concentrating the grapes heavily.

Moderately pale, straw yellow colour. Very persistent pure Riesling nose dominated by a strong influence of mineral aromas with underlying intense flavours of ripe white peaches, preserved orange and hints of fresh lemon. A full-bodied palate for whites is very expressive with racy acidity enhanced with mineral finesse. Intense fruitiness forms more body to this extremely persistent wine. Together with a high level of well-integrated alcohol, the wine forms a broad texture accompanied by a long lingering mineral finish with lemony bites. A wonderful Riesling wine to be enjoyed now.

1955 Brunello di Montalcino Riserva Bionti-Santi (Tuscany) 95p

2007/2020 x6 • D 30 min / G 2 h

Fine-looking bottle. Re-corked at the estate. Top-shoulder level. Decanted only 30 minutes. Clear, medium-intense ruby colour. Very intense, partly closed, restrained nose is dominated by resin-like herbaceousness - sage and hints of horse saddle indicating ageing. Medium-bodied palate shares crisp acidity, supple tannins and moderately intense raisiny sweet fruitiness with hints of plums. Very concentrated taste with a lingering finish. Lively wine that can still keep for another 10 years.

1949 Château Pétrus (Pomerol) 95p

2004/2010 x11 • D 1 h / G 2 h

Château-bottled. Top-shoulder level. Decanted 1 hour. A very elegant, soft and even fruity wine. What bothered us, though, were the still harsh tannins, which made the wine a little tight and slightly imbalanced. We have not yet met these qualities in other Château-bottled Pétrus 1949 that we have tasted. These are qualities that one would not expect to meet in a Pétrus. An impressive experience, especially to many of our friends for whom this was their first Pétrus - not a bad vintage to start with, though it did not quite meet our highest expectations!

1953 Krug Collection Champagne Krug (Champagne) 95p

2007/now x4 • D 15 min / G 1 h

Covered in dust, an old-looking bottle without a label. Otherwise in brilliant condition. Decanted 15 minutes. Very deep but bright gold colour. Not as dark as 1955. Toasty, creamy and buttery nose - opened immediately. Petite lively bubbles. Fat, complex and quite sweet. As rich and full as 1955, but a bit more like a dessert wine. Long and youthful. Excellent, far-reaching champagne. Eternal!

1978 Sassicaia Tenuta San Guido (Tuscany) 95p

2006/2010 x4 • D 1 h / G 1 h

The 1978 was not only a very good year in Piemond, but also in Tuscany, where the first three months of the year were cold and wet. Poor start, but then spring came early and summer was warm but not terribly hot. Fine growing season. Small, a good quality crop.

Bottle was in A1 condition. Decanted one hour. Deep dark, youthful colour. Very Bordeaux-like nose. Spicy, minty, ripe black fruit and hint of oak. Exceptionally full, refined and has very good acidity. Loads of fruit. A big, overwhelming and serious "old style" Sassicaia with a long, velvety ending. No wonder, that Sassicaia 1978 got 20/20 scores from the judges at an international Cabernet tasting organised in London by Decanter.

1945 Richebourg Louis Gros *(Côte de Nuits)* 95p

2005/2015 x1 • D 45 min / G 1 h

Very old-looking, dusty bottle with only a miscellany of the label left. Level was excellent at 3 cm and colour was very bright and sound. Decanted 45 minutes. Charming bright-red colour. Sound and wide-open bouquet with well-developed ripe fruit, truffles and chocolate flavours. No trace of oxidation. Forceful rather than delicate but with a seductive balance and a firm but smooth tannic structure. This is very classic Burgundy; as powerful, rich, deep, ripe, and harmonious as one could hope for. Ready now but the wine will continue to age well for another 10 years.

1994 Riesling Rangen de Thann Clos St Urbain Zind-Humbrecht 95p
(Alsace)

2003/2010 x2 • D 10 min / G 30 min

Zind-Humbrecht's position in Alsace is considered parallel to DRC's in Burgundy. The Humbrecht family has cultivated the same vineyards for almost four centuries. They have been bottling their wines since 1947 and nowadays they are known also as the leading biodynamic winery in Alsace. The secret of their wine is based on the exclusive sites, very restricted yields and high planting densities. The vinification process of their wines bases in natural processes from the natural yeasts to intervened fermentation.

This two hectares Clos St Urban vineyard is located in Rangen de Thann Grand Cru site. This most southern vineyard site of Alsace was known for its quality already in the Middle Ages. The vines of 15 and 40 years of age are grown on terraces on an extremely steep hillside of 70 degrees on a carboniferous soil of volcanic rock, particles of sandstone and volcanic tufa.

Moderately light yellow colour. Very intense nose with tremendous concentration and complexity revealing petrol aromas, smokiness, Granny Smith apples, and citrus with hints of exotic fruits and spices. Dry, crisp acidity, oily broad texture with intense fruit topped with honeyed overtones. A concentrated wine with long lingering finish full of mineral flavours. A rich, refined and impressive Riesling with balance and persistence. A beautiful wine from a lesser vintage making wine wonderful for drinking now. At its peak but will still keep for few years.

1965 Unico Bodegas Vega Sicilia *(Ribera del Duero)* 95p

2002/2010 x2 • D 2 h / G 2 h

In Vega Sicilia the harvest started at the beginning of October in dry and warm conditions. The quantity was high for this vintage and total production of Unico was 91,000 Bordeaux bottles and 2,000 magnums. The 1965 Unico was made from Tinto Fino (Tempranillo) 75%, Cabernet Sauvignon 20% and Merlot 5%, and was commercialized from 1984 to 1987 in Bordeaux bottles.

This wonderful and rare magnum was released to the market in 1989, and was in textbook condition. Level by the neck. Decanted two hours before dinner. Brilliant, fairly deep, bright, youthful colour. Sweet fruit, truffles, and American oak on nose - sound and wide, open bouquet. A fresh, rich and concentrated wine with sweet fruit flavours and soft tannins. Very elegant and gentle to drink. Chocolaty and smooth, welcome finish. Ready now and will not gain from any further ageing. A delicious and complete Unico. This is certainly the best of all those red wines made in 1965.

1984 Zinfandel Dickerson Vineyard Ravenswood *(Napa Valley)* 95p
2001/2010 x3 • D 45 min / G 1 h

Medium-deep developed brick red colour. Pronounced spicy nose with jam and roasted aromas and black-berries. Full body and medium acidity. The wine has remained surprisingly fruity and firm for its age. Long fruity finish with a slight alcoholic and spicy burn. At its peak and will no longer improve. Definitely not a wimpy wine.

1964 Dom Pérignon Moët et Chandon *(Champagne)* 95p
2006/now x7 • D 30 min / G 2 h

Bright, golden colour with slow, small, pearl necklace bubbles. Very delicate, complex and youthful nose. Distinctive lovely aromas of toastiness, roasted coffee, toffee, creaminess, and dried fruits. Very crisp and dry on the palate with rich mousse. Medium-bodied champagne with moderately intense dried fruit flavours and rich mineral tones. Long lingering finish is greatly balanced, elegant and silky in style. One of the richest style Dom Pérignon ever made.

1953 Château Haut-Brion *(Graves)* 95p
2001/2015 x8 • D 2 h / G 2 h

A good dark colour to the rim, showing a little age but excellent appearance. Spicy, open, forthcoming, cara-mel-sweet nose. It has typical earthy, tobacco-like Graves taste. A surprisingly soft, elegant, round, and velvety wine with great balance, and a long and multi-layered aftertaste. A wine of distinction and class.

1943 Romanée-Conti Domaine de la Romanée-Conti *(Côte de Nuits)* 95p
2007/2015 x4 • D 1 h / G 2 h

This elegant wine contains very unique features as being the last DRC wine made from ungrafted rootstocks. Clear, bright brick-red colour. Very developed medium-intense nose shows very complex and vivid aromas from ethereal, herbaceous, willow tree aromas to earthy and perfumed aromas with dark chocolate nuances. A dry, crisp and light-bodied wine with silky texture due to the ripe mellow tannins. Mineral flavours and ripe cherries with long savoury finish shows very good intensity still. A real charmer.

1955 *Château La Mission-Haut-Brion* (Graves)   95p
2007/2015 x10 • D 2 h / G 2 h

Fine looking Van der Meulen bottling. Level was top-shoulder. Decanted one hour. Now celebrating a half-century since its harvest. Excellent dark and youthful colour. This very rich and nicely balanced wine remains remarkably young and interesting. Full-bodied and packed with sweet fruit and soft tannins, its long finish is refined and silky. A benchmark for the vintage. Elegant and eminent, the wine is now as ready as it is ever going to be.

1953 *Château Margaux* (Margaux)   95p
2001/2015 x2 • D 3 h / G 2 h

The fantastic month of August, very hot and dry, decided the privileged fate of this vintage. September was normal, and it rained a little during the harvest, but it was too late to affect the quality of the grapes, which were already ripe and concentrated. This vintage is one of the greatest from Château Margaux; it expresses, in a particularly perfect way, the genius of its terroir.

Moderate intensity of garnet-tawny colour. Amazingly fresh, seductive floral nose with ripe red fruit and beautifully evolved bouquet of leather and earthiness. Medium-bodied palate is very stylish and restrained in style. Mineral and moderately acidic structure is well-balanced with ripe red fruitiness and smooth tannins. Mid-palate and finish shows more earthy and leathery flavours with some tobacco and cedar. A very elegant and delicate wine with lingering classy finish. Drinking perfectly now.

1985 *Chevalier-Montrachet Leflaive* (Côte de Beaune)   95p
2007/2015 x6 • D 1 h / G 3 h

Fine bottle. Decanted 45 minutes. Pale, medium-golden yellow with distinct green tinge. Very refined nose. Flowery bouquet, with buttery, pecan and walnut aromas and restrained creamy oak. Beautiful sweetness as it strikes the palate. Ripe fruit is buttery-edged with greengage and citrus favours. Taste is firm and endless with beautiful layers of fruit and unctuous texture, giving a real succulence on the mid-palate. The commanding finish has good length through a lively acidity. A charming wine now, but should cellar very well.

1953 *Château Cos d'Estournel* (Saint-Estèphe)   95p
2003/2012 x4 • D 2 h / G 2 h

Good-looking château-bottling, and the level was high-shoulder. Decanted 2 hours. A deep, dark and healthy colour. Beautifully developed bouquet with a hint of leather, smoked meat, exotic spices, and blackcurrants. This is a full-bodied, meaty, spicy, and fruity wine with non-aggressive tannins. This intense and well-balanced wine finished with more than a 90-second demonstration of sweet fruit and silky tannins. A great wine, which will last for another decade. Tasted four times with similar notes.

1949 Château Lafite-Rothschild (Pauillac) 95p
2005/2025 x18 • D 1 h / G 1 h

Tasted 18 times with consistent notes except for two occasions. Decanted one hour. Medium rich, youthful and classic Bordeaux with lovely aromas of cassis, blackberry, black truffles, and dark chocolate. Medium to full-bodied, velvety-textured, elegant and pure with lovely ripe fruit, silky tannins and a long, fulfilling finish. A beauty, not a beast.

1975 Nacional Vintage Port Quinta do Noval (Portugal) 95p
2006/2030 x2 • D 3 h / G 2 h

Mature medium-intense colour. Elegant developing nose of dried fruits, red berries and fine spiciness. The palate supports the harmony of the nose: fine-tuned and layered wine with relatively light body but balanced acidity and alcohol. Far from being a blockbuster vintage, this wine charms with its class, feminine style and admirable harmony. At its peak or very near, but will easily keep for over a decade

2003 Scharzhofberger Riesling Auslese Egon Müller 95p
(Mosel-Saar-Ruwer) **2006/2020 x4 • D 1 h / G 2 h**

Attractive bright yellow colour. The nose is open and filled with sweet ripe fruitiness and mineral elegance. The palate is consistent with the nose: apples, lemon and apricots. Some noble rot marmalade hints. The oily texture is refreshed by the lively and firming acidic backbone. A long, stylish and intense wine that is very youthful yet drinking well. The peak is to be expected in 10-15 years time.

1961 Barbaresco Angelo Gaja (Piedmont) 95p
2007/now x3 • D 30 min / G 1 h

This legendary vintage was extremely hot in Piedmont. The ripe Nebbiolo grapes were turned in gold in Gaja's winery. The Midas was Agnelo Gaja's father who made this wine one of the greatest Barbarescos ever made. Moderately pale bright ruby colour. Nose is very intense, complex, spicy, and sound. Instead of being a big and massive Barbaresco, this was a really elegant and round wine with layers of sweet fruit and juicy tannins covered by richness and extract. A well-balanced wine with good length and wonderfully harmonious aftertaste. An exhilarating wine to drink now!

1961 Comtes de Champagne Taittinger (Champagne) 95p
2005/2010 x3 • D 15 min / G 1 h

Fine-looking magnum. Decanted 15 minutes. Pale golden yellow colour with fine slow bubbles. Complex, oxidative aromas with mineral tones. Dry, crisp, ripe, and rich in style with nutty and dried fruit aromas. Creamy texture combines beautifully with its mineral finish. A true charmer with creamy richness.

1949   *Château Cheval Blanc* (St.Emilion)   *95p*

2005/2015 x23 • D 45 min / G 1.5 h

A huge wine from this extreme vintage. Rainy and cold flowering period reduced the size of crop. An extreme heat wave of 43 °C shortly after was followed by storms ending in fine weather during the harvest. This was (again) a superb Cheval Blanc vintage.

Good château-bottling with upper-shoulder level. Decanted 45 minutes. Deep, intense and bright mahogany colour. Rich nose of ripe dark berries and plums also spices with mineral tones. Ripe fruit flavours give a sweet twist to the wine that has moderate acidity and ripe softened tannins. Long elegant and supple finish. Very appealing now, but will keep a few more years.

1952   *Château Pétrus* (Pomerol)   *95p*

2007/2015 x7 • D 1 h / G 2 h

This Pétrus came from Sotheby's of London and was in excellent condition. Top-shoulder level château bottling. Fully mature, bright colour. Wide, fat and straightforward nose, which opened up immediately. Full, voluptuous and opulent on the palate. A surprisingly gentle, round, soft, and nicely balanced wine. Long and strikingly persistent after-taste. This unquestionably is our kind of wine and it still has some years ahead of it. A recently tasted Van der Meulen bottle was even better. It had a bit more richness and fruitiness - tremendous wine.

1953   *Château Cheval Blanc* (St. Emilion)   *95p*

2006/2015 x16 • D 2 h / G 2 h

Bottle was in excellent condition. Level was by the neck. Decanted only half an hour before tasting, which was definitely too short - it needs to breathe at least two to three hours before drinking.

A first class, bright, surprisingly youthful colour. Round and rich, aged bouquet. Strikingly modest and simple wine at first, although it was very elegant and stylish right from the start. But after breathing three long hours in a glass, it became like another wine. Rich and full with lots of fruit and energy. A well-balanced, convincingly sophisticated and grandiose wine. Be patient and you will be rewarded. Tasted many times from different bottlings with almost similar notes.

1990   *Barolo Cannubi Boschis Luciano Sandrone* (Piedmont)   *95p*

2006/2025 x4 • D 2 h / G 2 h

The vintage 1990 marks the beginning of a new era in Italian wine production. Modernisation and new innovative producers made their final breakthrough in this outstanding vintage. Hot and dry summer with cool night time temperature created wines of high quality and perfect phenolic ripeness. The third good vintage in a row in Piedmont!

Luciano Sandrone is one of the heroes of the Italian wine renaissance having contributed significantly to the modernization of Piedmont wines. Sandrone bought his first vineyard from the Cannubi hill in 1978. It was tiny in size - less than a hectare - but large enough to start lifting Sandrone on to the Piedmont wine map. 1990 was a successful vintage for the single vineyard Barolo Cannubi Boschis.

A developed, glossy medium-deep browning colour. The nose is lifted and nicely maturing; great expression of tar and roses, roasted and earthy notes. The mouth-feel is silky and smooth, firmed attractively by ripe tannin and refreshing acidity. This wine is harmonious and evolved today but no doubt will keep and improve for another decade.

1921 Château Sigalas-Rabaud *(Sauternes)* 95p

2003/now x3 • D 1 h / G 3 h

Very old-looking bottle with no label, but the colour and level were very promising. Original cork and capsule. Decanted one hour. Dark brown but bright colour. Fabulously rich, floral and creamy bouquet. Very sweet, fat and concentrated. In spite of its admirable age, it was filled with jammy fruit, with bags of fruit exploding in the mouth. Good balance and structure. Elegant and smooth, yet quite powerful and warm with good acidity. This Sigalas-Rabaud offered everything this great vintage is famous for!

1996 Celebris Rosé Gosset *(Champagne)* 95p

2006/2015 x4 • D 15 min / G 2 h

A major part of Gosset Celebris' appeal lies in its character as champagne that has not gone through the malolactic fermentation. It has been an essential element of the history of the house's champagnes and helps them age gloriously. The 1996 was a vintage of superb acidic backbone. In the Gosset Celebris Rosé one can really sense the structure and grip of the vintage.

Elegant orange-hued colour. Lively small-sized bubbles last well in the glass. The nose is fruit-driven and elegant with spicy notes and dried fruit and brioche aromas. An intensely fruity palate with a lovely silky mouth-feel and good weight. Sublime acidity refreshes the round and rich palate. The length is long and harmonious. A long and glorious future lies ahead of this already enjoyable luxury cuvée.

1998 Château Mouton-Rothschild *(Pauillac)* 95p

2006/2030 x7 • D 2 h / G 2 h

Good, dark and deep colour. Quite open and clean, gentle nose with hints of cassis and coffee aromas. Fleshy, sweet wine with soft tannin, but still has a lot of character and complexity. A very vigorous and elegant wine, but unquestionably lacking the charm and roundness to be one of the greatest Moutons. Warm and satisfying finish. Considering it was an 'off' year, the wine was a surprisingly good and one of the best wines of this weak Médoc vintage.

1927 Vintage Port Fonseca (Portugal)   *95p*

2001/2020 x3 • D 2 h /G 1.5 h

The vintage 1927 was difficult from grape ripening perspective. It was not at all that promising until the very last tine ten days before the harvest. Without this period the vintage would had failed, but now it became declared by 30 shippers and embraced as the best vintage since 1912. This was a glorious year also for Fonseca's owner Manuel Pedro Guimarãens who returned back to Portugal after having fled from there earlier in an empty port pipe because he supported the losing side in the Civil War.

Moderately deep mahogany colour. Intense and opulent nose of preserved blackberries, liquorice and spices with herbaceous notes. Sweet, intense and concentrated full-bodied palate with lovely supple tannic structure and velvety texture. Ripe blueberries and blackberries, smoky and liquorice in flavours. Long minty finish with surprising youthful character ensuring the wine has still ageing potential left for over ten years.

1941 Romanée-Conti Domaine de la Romanée-Conti (Côte de Nuits) 95p

2004/now x2 • D 30 min / G 1.5 h

The level of wine had lowered only 4cm and both the capsule and the cork seemed to be in good condition. The information found on the cork confirmed the origin of the bottle.

The colour of the wine was already a little brown and muddy, but the bouquet had something so magical to it - overflowing chocolate, coffee and warmth - that it would have melted any hardened heart. One of the most intoxicating and overpowering bouquets we have experienced - indeed to bring oneself to taste it became almost too hard! A very roasted, old pinot style, delicate and gentle, slightly over-matured wine. Fading but lots of charm and length. Nevertheless, even after five hours in the glass the bouquet still swept us off our feet. The second bottle, which we tasted in 2004, was in much better condition. Very vigorous and long. An extraordinary and fantastic experience.

1820 Guilherme Vintage Port (Portugal)   *95p*

2007/now x2 • D 45min / G 1.5 h

This must be one the best vintages from the early days of vintage ports. The first port wine had been bottled only few decades before. This vintage yielded extremely rich and ripe grapes resulting in areally high concentration and delicious sweetness in the wines.

Excellent looking bottle with good level. Decanted 45 minutes. Moderately pale orange- tawny colour, little hazy. Extremely appealing nose with delicious sweet raisin aromas with plums and dates. Spices and orange peel are pushing through as volatile flavours. Peculiar sweet mouth-feel with high concentration. The acidity and tannic structure are moderately low but the wine as a whole is still in a wonderful harmony. Extremely well preserved wine.

1919   Clos-de-Vougeot Grivelet-Gusset *(Côte de Nuits)*   95p
2001/2008 x1 • D 45min / G 1 h

This Clos de Vougeot has a clean, mature dark red colour. Ullage was 5 cm. Delicate, charming old Pinot-nose. Subdued, sweet and complex. There is lots of charm and attraction here - seductive. A classic wine that is very soft, round and inviting.

1917   Castillo Ygay Bodegas Marqués de Murrieta *(Rioja)*   95p
2000/now x2 • D 15 min / G 15 min

The oldest and the best Castillo Ygay we have ever tasted. The bottle was in a respectable condition, and the level was top-shoulder. This is one of those peculiar wines which should be drunk very soon after opening. Otherwise you will lose that magnificent and complete taste which is there during those precious first 15 minutes. Very refined and complex with full-flavoured rich fruit. An old-fashioned, chocolaty, fat, and voluptuous wine but fading very rapidly with massive loss of flavours and depth. A well spent 15 minutes.

1997   Clos-St. Denis Domaine Dujac *(Côte de Nuits)*   95p
2007/2020 x3 • D 1 h / G 2.5 h

Domaine Dujac was known until 1967 with the name of Domaine Graillet. Under the new ownership it has become one of the modern estates in Burgundy. The owner Jacques Seysses has introduced plenty of new viticulture and vinification techniques in the production. Seysses has cultivated six different clones of Pinot Noir for this wine, which are grafted in three different rootstocks on the Clos-St.Denis Grand Cru. The vineyards are treated organically and the vinification procedures occur as naturally as possible with no de-stemming, natural yeasts and no clarification.

Moderately intense, developing cherry red colour with a little hazy appearance. Pronounced and developed nose with animal, horse saddle and sweaty aromas with intense aromas of red berries. Broad and elegant medium-bodied mouth-feel with intense silky texture and complex flavours. Red berries, cherries, animal and floral flavours rise up in long chalky mineral finish that is underlined with high level of alcohol. Surprisingly ready to drink now and the wine actually delivers more maturity than expected. A very fine experience!

1911   Le Chambertin Clos de Bèze, Louis Jadot *(Côte de Nuits)*   95p
2005/now x3 • D 1 h / G 1 h

Wonderful bottle with 4 cm level. Decanted one hour. Dark, mature evolved colour. Fair amount of sediment. Very sweet, gentle and intense old-Pinot Noir on both nose and palate. Very forward and mature. Certainly plenty of finesse in here. Lots of extract and ripe, intense, sweet fruit. Long and appealing finish. A charming old wine!

1935   *Château Filhot* (Sauternes)   95p

2003/2020 x2 • D 1 h / G 1 h

This southernmost, classified second growth Sauternes estate has a colourful history under the ownership of one family since 1709. The founder, the advisor of Bordeaux Parliament Romain de Filhot, died the year after he founded this estate. The family married into the well-known Lur-Saluces family. The 1935 vintage was controversial. Sauternes faced less favourable weather conditions that year, but it did not dim the mood in Château Filhot since the château was just being acquired by a lady, Thérèse de Lur-Saluces alias Comtesse Durieu de Lacarelle, and the wine got an elegant female touch. This can be sensed in this lovely honeyed wine, which shows some oxidation in its amber colour. The developed nose expresses waxy and honeyed aromas due to the Semillon domination. Light and elegant botrytis aromas reflect the vintage with style. A moderately sweet and medium-bodied wine shows liveliness with its vivid acidity while dried apricots, spices and honeyed notes highlights the finish of the wine. A very balanced and elegant Sauternes drinking well now.

1934   *Robert Weil Beerenauslese* (Germany)   95p

2007/now x2 • D 1 h / G 3 h

This wine was enjoyed at the Robert Weil winery with Wilhelm Weil himself on a beautiful January Saturday. After a relaxed tour of the estate and a tasting of a selection of the 2004s and 2005s, Robert Weil made an excursion into the cellars to search for this lovely rarity. We sipped it with great enjoyment and appreciation. Deep golden colour and highly viscous texture. A developed raisiny nose filled with floral and petrol notes as well as apricots and marmalade deriving from botrytis. Soft, silky mouth-feel is sweet but not luscious. Fresh steely acidity makes the wine appear very lively and enjoyable. Very attractive and persistent palate. An elegant mature Riesling at a very interesting age, however no hurry whatsoever. Opened up and developed positively in the glass.

1996   *Château La Mondotte* (Saint-Emilion)   95p

2007/2020 x5 • D 3 h / G 3 h

Decanted 3 hours. Full of fruit, oak and tobacco on the nose. Very ripe up-front fruit, a taste of olives and tobacco on the mid-palate. This is a huge endeavour from the Proprietor Count de Neippberg. Unbelievably harmonious, with the tannin and alcohol in correct balance. Fantastic mouth-feel with long and soft aftertaste. Ready to enjoy but will last.

1927   *Romanée-Conti Domaine de la Romanée-Conti* (Côte de Nuits) 95p

2005/now x2 • D 20 min / G 40 min

This vintage is generally one to forget due to the weather conditions that were the worst of the 1920's. However, luckily there are always exceptions. Again the miraculous vineyard of La Romanée-Conti was capable to yield grapes that turned into lovely wine.

Fine bottle with 5 cm level. Pale, brick red orangey colour. Delicate earthy nose with sweet vegetal character, raspberry aromas and faint hints of violets. Dry, light-bodied wine with moderately high acidity and slightly coarse tannins. Moderately intense red fruit and root vegetable flavours balance the tannic structure nicely. The wine has not the great length but the finish is harmonious and pleasing. Be aware of bottle variations and drink up the wine in the first proper event possible.

1918 Château Rausan-Ségla *(Margaux)* — 95p

2003/now x1 • D 30 min / G 30 min

These twelve bottles of Rausan-Ségla were definitely worthy of their high prices, which were paid for eagerly! They were château-bottled, in outstanding condition and with levels at top-shoulder or better.

Incredibly youthful, bright colour for its age. Great cedary, chocolaty, clean, and open nose. Very long, smooth and generous wine. Round and full of life - what a splendid surprise! This is a classic example of the importance of good storing conditions. These bottles had been lying untouched from the year 1922. We still have five of them left - thank goodness for that!

1996 Cuvée Sir Winston Churchill Pol Roger *(Champagne)* — 95p

2007/2020 x7 • D 30 min / G 2 h

The vintage of the decade, 1996 introduced a new packaging for Cuvée Sir Winston Churchill. Having long been dressed in black, Sir Winston Churchill's memory is from now on celebrated with a navy blue/purple labelling after one of his military outfits. The change did not affect the content of the bottles and the 1996 is indeed a glorious tribute to Churchill. This structured, ripe and intensely fruity vintage will make up one of the best Cuvée Sir Winston Churchills ever made. Almost as eternal a wine as the memory of the man himself. Moderately pale yellow colour with lively bubbles. Rich is the nose as well, with ripe fruity and toasty aromas that set this wine's nose near perfection. Very rich, round and ripe taste is enhanced by monumental acidity. Promising young wine with great harmony. A great future ahead, although very enjoyable already now.

1959 Unico Bodegas Vega Sicilia *(Ribera del Duero)* — 95p

2002/2010 x2 • D 45 min / G 3 h

A dusty, almost unrecognizable bottle was found in a wine shop on a small side street in Barcelona. The seller assured us it was an Unico from 1959. The level of the wine was high-shoulder, colour was dark red and clear, and since the price was also right, the bottle travelled with us to Helsinki.

We opened it a few years later in a Vine Club tasting, and the cork proved the vintage right. The bouquet was not so typical to Unico; sweet, raisiny and surprisingly youthful. On the palate the wine felt heavy, generously intensive and exceedingly chocolaty. This most vivid and vital wine was very well balanced and multidimensional enough to be given the mark 'great'. It seemed to even improve in the glass, and was at its best two hours after the decanting. An experience worthy of its reputation!

2000 *Riesling Unendlich FX Pichler* (Wachau) 95p
2006/2015 x2 • D 30 min / G 2 h

The top of the line Riesling of FX Pichler is a blockbuster of a white wine. Deep developed golden colour. Pronounced nose of very ripe aromatics of flowers, petroleum and lemon. The packed mouth-feel is velvety and round, however refreshed by the benchmark steely acidity. Very high concentration of fruit and. as the name promises a near-unending finish. Ripe fruitiness makes the wine very enjoyable right now, but the superb structure will keep the wine for at least a further decade.

1959 *Riesling Oestricher Gottesthal Ferdinant Pierot* (Germany) 95p
2002/2010 x4 • D 15 min / G 1 h

Fine-looking bottles with respectable levels. Decanted twenty minutes. Fabulous pale lemony colour with a definite tinge of green. The nose was sound and broad with some perfumed, flowery nuances, a touch of honey, olive, and pronounced petrol aromas. On the palate it was extremely youthful, with high acidity and very subtle, wonderfully honeyed fruit underneath. Good weight and initial impact. Charming balance and intensity with a long and a bit spicy aftertaste.

1950 *La Tâche Domaine de la Romanée-Conti* (Côte de Nuits) 95p
2007/now x2 • D 1 h / G 1 h

Handsome, old handmade-looking bottle. First-rate condition, ullage only 3 cm. Decanted 1 hour before serving. Fresh, spicy and open nose. Fat, rich, loaded with fruit and exotic aromas. Still had some rounded tannins left. Great extract and fruit intensity. No faults. A very stylish, vigorous wine. This was a pleasant surprise.

1996 *Three Rivers Shiraz* (Barossa Valley) 95p
2005/2020 x3 • D 4 h / G 2 h

This is an utterly gorgeous wine that seduces and bombards the senses, suggesting a deep emotional connection between winemaker and the vineyard landscape. The unusually thick-skinned Shiraz is sourced from Chris Ringland's dry grown vineyard planted originally in 1910 on shallow skeletal granite sandy loams over underlying clay on the edge of the Barossa Valley (but technically in Eden Valley). The wines are painstakingly handmade in open fermenters and regularly plunged to extract colour, flavour and tannins. After basket pressing, fermentation is completed in 100% new French oak hogsheads. A period of up to 40 months oak maturation follows to achieve optimum complexity and balance between oak and fruit. The very limited release Three Rivers is about opulence, flamboyance, richness and concentration.

The 1996 vintage showed aromas of cassis, coffee and truffles against a fat texture of sweet tannins and already round, rich fruit. This very concentrated and superbly balanced wine offered flavours of vanilla, earth and blackberries. Long and very intense finish. This was a charming and very promising young wine.

1997 *Grüner Veltliner Smaragd Ried Loibenberg Emmerich Knoll 95p*
(Wachau)   2005/2020 x3 • D 1 h / G 2 h

The house of the Knoll family is located in the village of Unterloiben in the Wachau. The family has run the estate for several generations. Today, an Emmerich senior and an Emmerich junior are in charge, and both agree that what is needed to make notable wines, is great attention in the vineyards, and as little intervention as possible in the cellar. Knoll wines age fabulously and Knoll has consistently been one of the top Austrian producers over a period of decades. The flagship wines of the estate are the Grüner Veltliner Smaragd Vinothekfüllung, and Riesling Smaragd Vinothekfüllung.

Decanted one hour. Very lovely nose, clean and pure. The palate has a lovely weight and texture with really impeccable balance. Very intense and rich. The botrytis component seems to be less apparent in this, than in the other Grüner Veltliner Smaragds. Very powerful and stylish. There is a great sense of elegance and serenity here, with enormous length.

1985 *Romanée St Vivant Domaine de la Romanée-Conti* 95p
(Côte de Nuits)   2002/2015 x4 • D 2 h / G 2 h

An extremely cold winter destroyed more than 250 ha of vineyards in the Burgundy area. A part of La Tâche vineyards was also devastated, and it was replanted the next year. After the severe winter, the rest of the year was thought to be close to perfect, and the wines became particularly flirtatious and bounteous. The tannins became soft and stylish.

The bottle seemed to be in good condition. Decanted two hours. The bouquet is pleasantly perfumed. The wine was still quite tannic, slightly one-dimensional and closed - but still balanced and peaceful. Requires at least 4-5 years' further maturation.

1961 *Vintage Champagne Krug* (Champagne) 95p
2006/2012 x2 • D 15 min / G 2 h

Beautiful magnum with perfect level. Golden yellow colour with lively bubbles. Wonderfully appealing nose full of creaminess and elegance. Peculiar rich mushroom-like nose with walnuts adds a great deal of complexity to the wine. Lovely, crispy taste with very elegant rich mousse enhances the flavours of apples, citrus, biscuits, and minerals in the lingering long aftertaste.

1976 *La Tâche Domaine de la Romanée-Conti* (Côte de Nuits) 95p
2007/2015 x6 • D 1 h / G 1 h

The hot summer in Burgundy produced shrivelled grapes with substantially high skin-to-pulp ratio. This yielded wines with a firm and robust taste profile. This was the case also with this wine, of which only a total of 2,115 cases were produced.

Slightly cloudy, cherry-red colour with orange tints. The rich, developed nose gives soft ripe cherry flavours and a great deal of woody spicy notes. The taste is very crisp with moderate intensity of ripe dark fruitiness. Tannins and woody flavours are taking a strong grip on the long aftertaste. The wine gives gradually more flavours after being in the glass. Nevertheless, after half an hour the wine started to lose its edge. A lovely wine to be enjoyed no later than now!

1940   *Romanée-Conti Domaine de la Romanée-Conti* (Côte de Nuits) 95p

2004/now x2 • D 45 min / G 2 h

Very old-looking bottle. Good label and level. Decanted 45 minutes. The colour was deep, mature and a little cloudy. The nose was exotic, smoky, almost over-mature. In the mouth: full-bodied, rich, spicy, and round. Classical and multi-layered long aftertaste, which appears almost sweet. A fully mature classic Romanée-Conti.

1961   *Château Margaux* (Margaux)   95p

2007/2025 x7 • D 1h / G 2 h

The superb 1961 vintage begun with a spring frost and due to a cold spell that was followed by very exceptional "coulure" reducing the crop size drastically. Luckily the wonderful weather conditions with hot and dry weather during the summer enabled this small crop to reach really extraordinary ripeness and concentration.

Dark, deep and youthful colour. The nose is very complex, elegant and fragrant bouquet with layers of ripe fruit, flowers and oak. On the palate the wine is wide open and expanding. Refined, gentle tannins and soft and silky texture. A multitude of flavour nuances. Rich and harmonious wine with smooth and elegant tannins. A well-balanced and elegant wine that is mature, but there is no hurry. The aftertaste is impressively persistent.

2002   *Bâtard-Montrachet Domaine Ramonet* (Côte de Beaune)   95p

2007/2015 x3 • D 3 h / G 2 h

2002 was a super vintage for the Montrachets. The cold winter had ensured that the dormant vines had a good rest. The bud break and flowering occurred as normal but the following drought caused a water deficiency for the rest of the season. After some welcomed rain in September, the dry and cool northern wind and sunny weather dried the grapes guaranteeing a high concentration.

Bright yellow colour with green tints. Rich and fresh aromatic nose with an intense menthol aroma. Lovely crispy acidity with persistent minerality forms a firm backbone to this concentrated wine. Very broad mouth-feel with moderately intense fruit on the mid-palate. Lingering, long, elegant finish with beautiful spiciness from the oak. A delicate and opulent wine with years ahead.

1995 Château Margaux *(Margaux)* 95p

2003/2025 x9 • D 2 h / G 3 h

A very good year on the Bordeaux Left Bank. Mild winter and spring with substantial rains were followed by an early vegetative growth and beautiful weather conditions during the flowering. The summer was hot and extremely dry, in fact the driest in 20 years.

These fine looking bottles were decanted for two hours. Moderately intense, ruby garnet colour. Very sophisticated and promising, restrained nose. A seductive touch of roasted coffee and toastiness. The palate reveals real class and plenty of density. Medium-bodied palate has subtle structure. Aristocratic acidity and minerality with restrained but concentrated ripe fruitiness of blackcurrants with black olive tones. The structure is completed by dense and firm tannins. Well-integrated, delicate toasty oak flavours take hold on the palate with a long finish. Truly subtle and classy wine drinking well already now but will improve during the next ten years.

1928 Dom Pérignon Moët & Chandon *(Champagne)* 95p

2005/2010 x2 • D - / G 45 min

This officially second-ever made Dom Pérignon, was tasted blind in Pekka Nuikki's wine photography exhibition's opening in Helsinki in 2005. It had a developed golden colour with refined yet vibrant bubbles. The nose was full of roasted coffee aromas with scents of butter and spices. Crisp, opulent and mouth-filling wine with good mousse that managed to trick us into guessing the vintage to be from the fifties. An absolutely astonishing and gracefully aged wine with a beautiful, light-bodied style and an elegant toasty finish.

1934 Château Pétrus *(Pomerol)* 95p

2006/now x2 • D 45 min / G 30 min

1934 Pétrus looked fascinating to us. There were only the remains of the label left and no capsule whatsoever, but it had a branded cork with all the much-needed information. Level was top-shoulder and it was decanted one hour before tasting. The colour was quite cloudy and unhealthy looking, but the nose was incredible; wide open with an odd but seductive mix of chocolate, truffles, blackcurrant, and caramel-scented aromas! Full, rich and ripe wine with soft and well-balanced finish. Not as deep, fat and concentrated as the best Pétrus from the 1940s and 1950s, but one of the best Bordeaux from the 1934 vintage we have ever tasted. This was very enjoyable.

1900 Château Léoville Las Cases *(Saint-Julien)* 95p

2004/now x3 • D 20 min / G 40 min

Old, quite damaged-looking bottle. Négociant-bottled, level was a bit better than mid-shoulder. Considering the not so promising looks, what a glorious deep colour and round, open nose. Beautiful fragrance, with a slightly floral, delicate redcurrant fruit, earthy flavours and plenty of cedar finesse. The palate has lovely

weight and richness, with blackcurrant fruit, a touch of mellow coffee and cedar flavours. Very ripe and seductive. A bit dry and short, but otherwise an amazing wine. This must be even more pleasant from a better bottle.

1998 TBA No.13 Chardonnay Nouvelle Vague Alois Kracher *(Wachau)* 95p
2005/2050 x4 • D 1 h / G 3 h

This is one of the most concentrated wines Alois Kracher has ever produced with residual sugar over 400 g/l. Clear, intense golden colour. Explosive nose with huge intensity of ripe yellow fruits, honey and botrytis with hints of pencil shavings and cedar. A taste of extreme. Lusciously sweet and dense like syrup, with a mouth-filling texture and full-bodied structure, which are well balanced with a high level of acidity. The rich apricot marmalade and intensive fruitiness marry beautifully with spicy toastiness of new oak. An extremely long, super-concentrated finish.

2002 Montrachet Domaine de la Romanée-Conti *(Côte de Beaune)* 95p
2006/2030 x3 • D 2 h / G 3 h

Difficult weather at flowering time led to a small crop and small sized berries with high quality. This year DRC made 2,321 bottles of Le Montrachet. Bright yellow colour with golden tints. Very intense and complex nose full of ripe fruit aromas, pronounced toastiness, and spicy aromas with a touch of peppermint and melted butter. A dry, medium-bodied wine with crisp acidity and mineral and lemon tones. The very toasty taste is balanced with ripe fruits. A long buttery aftertaste and a very concentrated wine.

1896 Le Chambertin Louis Jadot *(Côte de Nuits)* 95p
2005/now x7 • D 30 min / G 2 h

Good-looking bottle with 2 cm level. Decanted 30 minutes. We have had this wine several times in the past twelve months. Each time it was a spectacular and surprisingly youthful wine - generous and mouth-watering, with an unexpected aromatic dimension and character. This last bottle was remarkably opulent, still youthful and showing only a small sign of a brown edge in its colour, and a fragrant nose of cedar, volatile acidity, white chocolate, and fruitcake-like spices. On the palate it has a gentle, harmonious texture and lovely sweetness. The tannins are sweet and smooth, but it still has a firm backbone that gives it depth and structure. With any ancient vintage differences in quality is the rule, but these particular bottlings were all excellent.

1947   Château d'Yquem *(Sauternes)*   95p
2004/2015 x5 • D 2 h / G 2 h

Re-corked at the château. Excellent level and appearance. Decanted two hours. Deep golden colour with an orange tint. Sound and open floral, pineapple, and tropical fruit-scented bouquet. Full-bodied and concentrated, with ripe, fat apricot and lemon flavours. This 1947 has great richness and length, finishing with a rich butter, caramel flavour and honey. Very delicious and not overly sweet.

1994   Proprietary Red Wine Dominus *(Napa Valley)*   95p
2004/2020 x3 • D 1 h / G 2 h

This wine is in many ways unique. It was the first vintage of Dominus produced under the exclusive ownership of Christian Mouiex. Secondly, it was an amazing vintage considering the extraordinary growing season at the Dominus estate. The growing season from bud break to harvesting took 186 days! This is one of the longest seasons in history of any quality red wine-producing region in the world. The wine has a very intense, deep, brick-red colour. Rich, complex nose holds a developed bouquet of truffles and horse saddle aromas, spices and smoke with intense ripe dark fruit aromas. The wine is full-bodied on the palate with muscular tannins, ripe intense dark fruitiness and balancing moderate acidity, with well integrated alcohol adding richness to the long finish. Cedary and spicy oak aromas add complexity to the palate. A well matured and concentrated wine which has many years ahead of it.

1950   Château Lafleur *(Pomerol)*   95p
2007/2015 x12 • D 1 h / G 2 h

Château-bottled. Upper-shoulder level. Decanted 1.5 hours. Dark garnet colour with noticeable amber tints at the edge. This thick, sweet, cedar, mocha, and black fruit-scented wine possesses massive, chewy flavours and pronounced vanilla character. Smooth and generous. The wine still has some tannin to lose, but wonderful to taste now. Plump but seductive on the finish. Still in fabulous condition and it is capable of lasting for 10-20 more years.

1978   Cabernet Sauvignon Volcanic Hill Diamond Creek *(Napa Valley)* 95p
2000/2010 x1 • D 1 h / G 1 h

Fine-looking bottle. Level was by the neck. Decanted one hour. Good, healthy dark colour. Gorgeous nose: delicate, fat and sweet. Fabulously strong Cabernet-grip on the palate, with super-ripe cassis, lots of spices, coffee and cedar pushing through. Ripe and rich. The follow-through is soft and elegant with sweet, ripe tannins and enough acidity. Peaking now and will no longer improve.

2000 *Château Pétrus* *(Pomerol)*   *95p*

2006/2045 x4 • D 4 h / G 3 h

What could be a more perfect start for the new millennium than the 2000 vintage, already described as legendary? The weather conditions caused concern early in the year. A warm, humid summer led to fears of mould. The warm, dry June however, put everything right. The final success can be attributed to the perfect weather all the way from late July to the beginning of October. Just the perfect amount of rain and the warmer-than-usual weather created concentrated grapes with thick skins. All vintage 2000 Bordeaux wines typically have an intensive fruitiness, plentiful aroma, high glycerol content, and powerful, ripe tannins. These are absolutely balanced, full-bodied wines that will be at their best only after decades. The starting prices of the wines have been so high that they cannot be considered notable investments.

All four bottles were as good as new. Decanted for four hours. Dark and deep colour. Surprisingly wide and open nose with loads of wild blackberries, smoky grilled meat, liquorice, and white truffle aromas. Solid and firm. Very powerful, almost too gigantic a wine with sweet tannins and a multilayered texture. The massive, super intense finish lasted forever. In our judgment this is fuller and more intense than the great 2005 and has better structure than the outstanding 2003. A very good start for the new millennium from Pétrus. Only 2,600 cases of this Millennium Pétrus were made.

1947 *Château Lafite-Rothschild* *(Pauillac)*   *95p*

2007/2010 x11 • D 1 h / G 2 h

These 1947 Médocs have matured much faster than the 1945s and some of them are now past their prime, but not this Lafite. The previous five bottles have all been in immaculate condition, just like this one — bright deep colour and perfect top neck level.

Decanted one hour before. Charming, mature, wide yet ripe fruit impression of classic Pauillac on the nose. This is an elegant, soft, chocolaty wine with some tannin left. Well-balanced and long, dawdle aftertaste. Some people have said that Lafite 1947 can be inconsistent, because in those days they used to bottle each barrel separately rather than as an assemblage. These six bottles and the five previous ones have all been similar, so we have been fortunate? This wine is at its absolute peak now.

1971 *Mas La Plana Torres* *(Penedès)*   *95p*

2005 / 2010 x 2 • D 30 min / G 45 min

Really adorable wine. Medium-intense brick-red colour. Rich and ripe Bordeaux style nose with cassis, capsicum and mint complemented with sweet spicy notes deriving from 24 months ageing in American oak barrels. Round, medium-bodied velvety texture with mellow tannins, moderate acidity and ripe fruitiness with plenty of dark fruits. Opulent, long finish with appealing elegance. Drinking very well still.

Château La Mission Haut-Brion Garden

1989 *Echézeaux Domaine de la Romanée-Conti* *(Côte de Nuits)* **95p**

2006/2015 x3 • D 2 h / G 2 h

A brilliant vintage, especially for Burgundy reds. Long, warm and sunny summer ripened the grapes earlier than normal, guaranteeing high sugar levels and ripe tannins.

Clear medium-intense brick-red colour. Seductively sweet and perfumery aromas with ripe red fruit, flowers and spices. Medium-bodied palate with crisp acidity, firm tannins and ripe fruitiness with red fruit aromas, all in good balance in the long structured finish.

1990 *Dom Ruinart Rosé Ruinart* *(Champagne)* **95p**

2007/2020 x2 • D 10 min / G 50 min

The 1990 cuvée of Dom Ruinart Rosé is made up of 83 percent Grand Cru Chardonnay. The remaining 17 percent is red Pinot Noir wine which gives this wine its delicate orange-hued look. The outstandingly ripe and perfectly structured 1990 made a magnificent Dom Ruinart Rosé. Moderately pale salmon-red colour and slow tiny bubbles can be detected from the wine. Very vinous nose with delicate aromas of ripe lingonberries and strawberries. Dry, moderately crisp and velvety rich taste resembles Burgundy Pinot Noir. Ripe wine with gracious acidity and beautiful elegance. Delightful wine to be drunk now, but will keep easily for another ten years.

1945 *Château Latour-à-Pomerol* *(Pomerol)* **95p**

2006/2015 x4 • D 15 min / G 1 h

This super vintage yielded this beautiful wine under the surveillance of the estate's owner Madame Loubat, who was also the owner of Château Pétrus at that time.

Medium-intense brick-red colour. Pronounced meaty nose with aromas of ripe blackcurrants, truffle, mocha, and chocolate. Very complex and rich medium-bodied palate with vivid acidity, firm tannins and ripe blackcurrant flavours. Earthy and smoky flavours in mid palate add lovely complexity, which is highlighted in the long aftertaste. A harmonious wine with a great balance.

1897 *Château Latour* *(Pauillac)* **95 p**

2005/now x2 • D 15 min / G 30 min

Négociant-bottling. Fill level high-shoulder. Decanted 45 minutes. Cloudy, delicately medium deep brownish-orange colour. Medium strong nose with matured nuances and hints of bouillon, root vegetables and animally tones. Lively, acidic, medium-full, and intensive taste accentuated by firm powdery tannins. The taste also has some boiled root vegetable and balsam flavours, typical for such a mature wine. A multilayered, firm and intensive fully matured wine with some years ahead of it but no improvements expected!

1947 Barolo Riserva Borgogno *(Piedmont)*   95p

2007/2020 x6 • D 1 h / G 1.5 h

Clear, medium-intense red colour. Very pronounced and complex nose with nuts, antique wood, smoke, violets, and animal aromas. Medium-bodied wine with still firm tannins, crisp acidity and ripe cherries, figs and dates. Amazingly youthful taste for its age with long astringent finish and velvety texture. Great Barolo from a great vintage!

1995 Barolo Monfortino Riserva Giacomo Conterno *(Piedmont)*   95p

2006/2020 x3 • D 2 h / G 2 h

Only for very good vintages, the selection of the best Nebbiolo grapes is kept apart to produce "Barolo Riserva Monfortino". This wine variety undergoes a different fermentation (no temperature control and longer maceration) and a longer ageing in classic Slovenian oak large barrels. After winemaking, the wines are decanted into oak large barrels, where they rest before bottling. The ageing Monfortino lasts, as a minimum, 7 years.

First-class bottle. Decanted two hours. Dark ruby colour. Fantastically sweet bouquet of minerals, truffles, smoke, and dark fruits. It has beautiful harmony and elegance all the way through the nose and palate. The palate really does show lovely balance with fine but dense tannins and vivid acidity supporting loads of black fruits and liquorice. The wine is full-bodied and fleshy, concentrated with sweet fruit, copious alcohol, and a seamless finish, which lasted an exceedingly long time. It can even be drunk now, but will be better with an additional 10-15 years of cellaring. Magnificent Barolo!

1998 Ermitage L´Ermite Chapoutier *(Rhône)*   95p

2006/2030 x3 • D 2 h / G 3 h

Chapoutier's small L'Ermite vineyard on top of the Hermitage hill around the chapel yields a tiny crop of Syrah from 80 year old vines grown on poor granite soils. The name of the vineyard derives from the memory of Henry Gaspard the knight of Stérimberg, who returned wounded from the Crusades in 1235 and was donated land on the hillside of Hermitage by Anne of Castille, Queen of Spain. The third vintage of L'Ermite1998 was a hot year resulting in an early harvest and low 15hl/ha yields. A hot and dry summer was complemented by an ideal amount of rain during the autumn and the stressed vines were able to produce very concentrated and healthy grapes.

Decanted three hours. There was fabulous perfume, cherries, spices, minerals, and pure exotic fruit. Still wired and with high levels of tannin and a fairly low-level of acidity. The palate was still youthful with lots of striking minerality, weight and excellent, wild fruit. Well-balanced and a fresh ending. It will need more time, a decade at least.

1974   Barolo Riserva Borgogno *(Piedmont)*   95p

2007/2010 x3 • D 1 h / G 2 h

Outstanding vintage, with a large high quality crop in Barolo. Excellent appearance. Level was 2 cm below the cork. Decanted one hour. Clear, moderately pale tawny colour. Developed and intense nose expresses ripe figs, dates and raisins, forest vegetation, autumn leaves and mushrooms. Medium-bodied palate shows high acidity, muscular tannins, rich, ripe dark fruit, and very high concentration in the long finish. An opulent wine typical of Borgogno's traditional style with meaty and robust texture.

1989   Barbaresco Sorí San Lorenzo Angelo Gaja *(Piedmont)*   95p

2004/2015 x4 • D 1.5 h / G 2 h

Medium-intense cherry-red colour. Delicate spicy nose with cherries, dark berries and floral aromas, mainly violets. Crisp acidity together with firm tannins take a grip on the palate. In the mid-palate, medium-intense fruit flavours such as cherries push further, balancing the racy taste of the wine. Delicate long finish highlights tannins together with floral aromas. Balanced medium-bodied wine drinking superbly well now, but will keep well for another ten years.

1995   Clos de l'Obac Costers del Siurana *(Priorat)*   95p

2004/2015 x2 • D 2 h / G 2 h

The uniqueness of this wine compared to other Priorat super wines is based on its elegant, less powerful style. This intense, almost opaque, dark ruby coloured wine offers a beautiful range of aromas - ripe dark berries, wild strawberries, blueberries, brambles, violets, and spices such as anise. Mouth-filling, rich, elegant texture formed by ripe tannins and intense fruit. Fruit intensity is generous but not over-extracted. Oak adds extra complexity to the wine's flavour profile in a very elegant way. Long finish with concentration. Charming style and thus a very special Priorat.

1994   Masseto Tenuta dell'Ornellaia *(Tuscany)*   95p

2004/2020 x3 • D 3 h / G 2 h

Decanted one hour. Very dark colour. A deep and profound Merlot wine that exhibits intense berry, mint and cassis aromas and flavours. Flavourful but very elegant and refined; wonderful silky tannins and marvellously fat, intense, long, and luscious finish. Very drinkable now, but will last a few more decades.

1999 Côte-Rôtie La Mouline Guigal *(Rhône)* 95p

2006/2030 x4 • D 4 h / G 4 h

La Mouline located on the Côte Blonde side is privileged to represent the first single vineyard Côte-Rôtie of Guigal, established in 1966. Unlike La Landonne this wine carries 11 percent Viognier to complement the Syrah. Due to the limestone rich soil and Viognier grapes, La Mouline expresses delightful feminine subtlety.

Decanted three hours. Rather dark, deep colour. Medium-strong, slightly closed nose with a ripe, spicy fruit profile. The youthful and full-bodied taste is characterised by nice acidity, ripe and surprisingly elegant tannins and a fairly strong, sweet fruitiness. Overall this is a very balanced wine with good complexity and promising future.

2000 Barolo Sarmassa Roberto Voerzio *(Piedmont)* 95p

2007/2030 x4 • D 4 h / G 2.5 h

Medium deep colour that is showing some development. Expressive and charming nose of violets, tar, cherry, and liquorice. Still very young in character. Perfumery seduction continues on the palate. Medium bodied palate with crisp acidity and firm, powdery tannic backbone. Elegant and seductive in style. Surprisingly open already. However, this Barolo has the power and balance to age magnificently for an another decades.

1931 Warre Vintage Port *(Portugal)* 95p

2003/2020 x3 • D 4 h / G 4 h

Beautiful, old-looking bottle in excellent condition. Decanted four hours before tasting. Deep red colour, fading to tawny at rim. Spicy nose of chocolate, black coffee and subtle vanilla notes. On the palate sweet flavours of raisins, wood smoke, oak, and a hint of bitter bark. Good acidity and balance with a long and smooth finish. Very enjoyable and fully mature now.

1934 Colheita Niepoort *(Portugal)* 95p

2007/2025 x2 • D 3 h / G 3 h

The 1934 vintage produced exceptional quality fruity and mature wines. The winter was dry and the spring was rainy. Very warm summer and some rainfall in September. The harvest started in the beginning of October with ideal climatic conditions. This is a magnificent example of what a mature Colheita should be like. Excellent bottle. Decanted three hours. Bright, moderately intense mahogany colour. Nose is very complex and powerful showing moderate development. Nose offers various aromas that range from flowers, nuts, coffee and toastiness to intensive chocolaty aromas. Sweet, full-bodied taste, with vivid acidity, intense fruitiness, ripe round tannins, and well-integrated high alcohol. An attractively lively wine with a refined long finish.

1996 *Chambolle-Musigny 1er Cru Les Charmes Domaine Leroy* *94p*
(Côte de Nuits)
2006/2030 x4 • D 1 h / G 3 h

A true piece of art made by the queen of biodynamic viticulture. Madame Lalou Bize-Leroy produced only 805 bottles of this seductive wine in this fabulous vintage.

Deep, almost opaque ruby colour. Absolutely lovely open nose showing the transition phase of the wine from the first life to the second one. Still lovely, fresh and delicious floral red berry nose with Asian spices and seductive oak aromas. On the other hand, the earthy aromas with truffles are giving an indication of the development. Medium-bodied, intense and concentrated palate with satin-like texture. Crisp acidity, velvety tannins and refined fruit flavours are combined with elegant spiciness and oak flavours. A lingering long mineral finish. The wine is drinking adorably now but will still have a great future for decades.

1795 *Madeira Terrantez (Portugal)* *94p*
2005/2040 x8 • D 1 h / G 3 h

This fully mature wine shows the immortality of a great Madeiras extremely well. Moderately pale with slightly hazy amber colour and olive green tints. The nose is explosive and ethereal. Nutty with touches of burnt sugar. The intense, moderately sweet palate is highlighted with pronounced acidity. A touch of hazelnut, chocolate and caramel flavours in the long, mouth-warming aftertaste. An astonishing Madeira from a top vintage!

1966 *Hermitage La Chapelle Paul Jaboulet Aîné (Rhône)* *94p*
1998/2015 x5 • D 1 h / G 1 h

Excellent bottle. Decanted one and a half hours. Impressive dark colour. Full bodied and wonderful in its complexity. This lovely La Chapelle continues to demonstrate rich, thick, elegant flavours and aromas that range from blackberries, ripe plums, chocolate, and leather. Sound, chunky and long. A good effort, but not nearly as good as the impressive 1961 or soon to be great 1990. Ready now, but will last at least one more decade.

1892 *Clos-des-Ursules Louis Jadot (Côte de Nuits)* *94p*
2003/now x2 • D 30 min / G 1 h

This Jadot was another treasure from a long-lost Belgian cellar. The bottle looked very old, but the original château capsule and cork were in excellent condition. Ullage was only 3 cm. This wine had a very fine and deep colour for its age. A rich, fragrant and wide, complex bouquet, which got better and better in the glass and was still very alive after three hours. A delicious, opulent, overripe old classic Pinot Noir taste. Beautiful acidity. A surprisingly rich wine that gave a sweet impression. Chocolaty, and fleshy, elegant aftertaste. A complete wine and a very good example of the importance of first-class storage conditions.

1999 Romanée-Conti Domaine de la Romanée-Conti (Côte de Nuits) *94p*

2005/2040 x4 • D 2.5 h / G 3+ h

For any Burgundy lover this ought to be the benchmark wine of modern times. Biggest crop of all time with outstanding quality. Its appearance expresses the ripe grapes with a very intense, deep ruby colour. Powerful spicy nose with ripe brambles, blueberries and wild strawberries with hints of flower aromas and liquorice. Extremely concentrated medium-bodied mouth-feel. Firm acidic backbone and pronounced ripe tannins are wrapped up with a good concentration of ripe dark fruits and spicy aromas. Lingering long and refined wine with a masculine character. It just won't do any justice to the wine to open it yet. Keep it at least for another decade.

1988 Château Mouton-Rothschild (Pauillac) *94p*

2006/2015 x5 • D 2 h / G 2 h

Good dark and deep colour. Appealing and open fruity nose. Very rich and complex. Fantastically round, full, meaty, intense, with a good structure - a dazzling bottle! No rush - it will last many more years. Appeared to us to be superior to the 1989, which we tasted on the side - this feels much younger and has better balance and harmony. Perhaps the wine of the vintage.

1871 Château Gruaud-Larose (Saint-Julien) *94p*

2002/now x4 • D 15 min/ G 45 min

Bottled by Sarget, level was top-shoulder. Very full, deep and mature colour. Not much sediment. Decanted 15 minutes before tasting. The nose opened after 30 minutes, and the bouquet was very elegant, fragrant, aromatic, and chocolaty. A rich, soft and very tender wine with exquisitely charming fruit and balance. An absolute masterpiece for 45 minutes, after which it started to dry out. An unforgettable magnum, which will last in our memories.

1989 Clos des Goisses Philipponnat (Champagne) *94p*

2006/2010 x5 • D 20 min / G 1 h

The Mont de Mareuil, where this splendid single vineyard lies, has been under vines at least since the early 16th century. Under the Ancient Régime, most of its vineyards were the property of the Viscount of Aÿ and Mareuil, who was none other than the Duke of Orleans. It was sold after the Revolution to the House of Bouché, a wine dealer in Mareuil. Bouscé raised the walls around the vineyards making it a 'clos' after the phylloxera crisis, the Clos des Goisses was acquired by Philipponnat in 1935, who gave it its current physiognomy by completing the system of stairs for water evacuation and by consolidating its monopoly through buying up parcels that had been dispersed during revolutions and crises. It immediately became the guarded crown jewel of the Philipponnat.

Faintly developed, pale colour. A ripe, fruity nose: fresh with a full, young-at-heart character. Thoroughly firm acid structure and concentrated fruitiness. Ripe apple hints, but the total aroma spectrum was not yet fully developed. A mineral-like, crusty mouth-feel and a very long aftertaste. Fine already, but one should have patience to store it at least for another decade.

1976   R.D. Bollinger *(Champagne)*   *94p*
2007/2020 x7 • D 20 min / G 1 hour

Extremely hot and dry vintage yielding concentrated wines. This late disgorged wine expresses the vintage well. Golden-yellow colour with modest amount of small bubbles. Very complex and rich nose with strong yeast aromas. Lovely Bollinger style with ripe apple notes combining well with the smoky aromas. Dry and crisp wine with delicate mousse and edgy acidity. Great depth of flavours thanks to the long ageing "sur lie". Lingering long, spicy, smoky, and lemony mineral finish. Drinking superbly now, but will keep easily over a decade more.

NUMBER 486.

1928   Château Haut-Brion *(Graves)*   *94p*
2004/2010 x4 • D 1 h / G 2 h

Bottle in fine condition. Top-shoulder level. Decanted one and a half-hours. Dark brick red in colour, with tobacco and cherry character. Powerful yet refined, with luscious aromas and flavours. Full-bodied with excellent concentration. Aromas of black and red cherries, and red currants. The wine lingers comfortably and generously on the palate.

NUMBER 487.

2000   Château Le Pin *(Pomerol)*   *94p*
2006/2025 x3 • D 5 h / G 3 h

Decanted six hours. Very dark and deep in colour. The nose showed high toned black fruit, smoke, soft vanilla oak, minerals, and a note of coffee. On the palate it had a good concentration of fruit balanced by some soft tannins, but the wine finished surprisingly rapidly. The structure was alright, but there was still something missing. It just generally lacked excitement. But definitely the second best Pomerol of this great vintage, right after Pétrus.

NUMBER 488.

1904   Colheita Niepoort *(Portugal)*   *94p*
2004/2010 x2 • D 1 h / G 2 h

A hot, dry summer. The grapes ripened well. Quite a big crop harvested on the 24th of September. Colheitas are single-vintage tawnies aged in a cask. The minimum age requirement is 7 years, but the tradition at Niepoort is to let the wine age several more in the casks before bottling.
This first-class bottle came directly from Niepoort's own cellars. Decanted only 30 minutes before dinner.

NUMBER 489.

Lovely amber colour. Intense, wide, raisiny nose. Full, intense, nutty, and sweet, yet with lively good acidity. Great grip and complexity. Full of life. An ageless, noble Colheita.

1928   *Livadia White Muscat Massandra Collection* (Crimea)) 94p

2006/2010 x2 • D 1 h / G 3 h

These two bottles were bought from Sotheby's famous Massandra Auction. They were in perfect condition. The colour was surprisingly black, deep and very promising. A flowery, spicy nose of ripe raisins. Amazingly fresh and viscous, full-bodied wine. A very rich structure with subdued Muscat flavours - well balanced. Long and clean finish. This is an elegant and velvety thick wine - a fine experience. Smooth and almost too easy to drink. Enjoyable now but there is no rush.

2000   *TBA No.8 Welschriesling Alois Kracher* (Burgerland) 94p

2005/2025 x5 • D 1 h / G 4 h

Rich golden yellow colour with very high viscosity. Honeyed, floral nose with sweet spiciness and apricot marmalade. Luscious (RS 314,2 g/l), rich, honeyed, full-bodied wine with an oily texture and crisp acidity. Although the wine is sticky, the fresh acidity lightens the heaviness caused by high residual sweetness. Long harmonious finish.

1904   *Vintage Port Dow's* (Portugal) 94p

2005/now x6 • D 1 h / G 2 h

These two good-looking port bottles were purchased from Christie's about 12 years ago. The first one was served at our Vine Club's '1000 points dinner' approximately six years ago. Then it was almost perfect with an enjoyable, lively fruitiness and complexity complemented by a long, warm and silky ending. We assumed then that this wine would last forever. So it was quite an unpleasant surprise to find out that the second bottle - which was of an identical shape and form as the first one - was a fairly feeble wine. Although the colour looked as dark and deep as before, that glorious and most attractive bouquet from the first bottle was completely gone, and it was now very plain and simple. A rather undemanding, unattractive port without the class and finesse of the first one. The third occasion when we had the opportunity to taste it was in London in 2005. Yet again a satisfactory bottle (same bottling as before) with a very dark colour, plenty of fruit and flavours, a little less powerful and aggressive than the first one, but it had plenty of charm. Long and well balanced with lots of life ahead of it.

1982   Gran Reserva 890 La Rioja Alta *(Rioja)*   94p

2007/2015 x14 • D 1 h / G 1 h

The flagship wine of the famous and highly esteemed old school Rioja bodega La Rioja Alta. The vintage of the decade in Rioja yielded this opulent and elegant wine with a moderately pale developed tawny colour. Medium-intense, ripe. plummy nose with wood, coconut and caffe latte aromas. Moderately high acidity together with refined firm tannins and very ripe fruit flavours form a persistent, mellow and juicy taste. Not a very complex wine but well balanced and a pleasant experience. Drinking well now and showing potential for further ageing.

1999   Côte-Rôtie La Landonne Guigal *(Rhône)*   94p

2006/2040 x3 • D 6 h / G 2 h

The head of the family company, Marcel Guigal, has praised this vintage as the greatest vintage of his lifetime. La Landonne was the second single-vineyard that Marcel Guigal launched in 1978. It took over ten years for him to purchase the entire plot in pieces from 17 different landowners. This 1.8 ha vineyard is located in Côte Brune and represents the biggest in style of three single vineyards with 100 percent Syrah aged four years in new oak.

Opaque, purple colour. Rich and concentrated nose of spices, smoke, bacon, liquorice, jammed brambles, and toastiness. The full-bodied palate and big ripe tannic structure integrate well with the intense dark fruit flavours and moderately high acidity. A long finish with very pronounced toasty oak aromas. Very concentrated and powerful wine with charming robustness and amazing potential for further ageing.

1966   Château Laville Haut-Brion *(Graves)*   94p

2007/2015 x3 • D 1 h / G 1 h

A wonderfully mature white Haut-Brion from the house's outstanding period. Extremely nuanced and uniquely charismatic nose. A mixture of herbs, spruces, wax, petrol, and surprisingly pronounced fruitiness. Balanced mouth-feel with great depth of fruit and lively acidity. Rich oily texture and long waxy aftertaste. A vivid and exciting wine full of life. Peaking now but will easily keep for another 5 to 10 years.

1945   Château L'Evangile *(Pomerol)*   94p

2004/2008 x6 • D 1.5 h / G 1 h

The beautiful magnum was in good condition with top-shoulder level. Decanted 1.5 hours. A dense, deep, dark red colour. Intense, almost overripe Merlot nose, perhaps a little old fashioned, but in a good way. Lots of raspberries, minerals, truffles, and chocolate flavours. Rich and fleshy. An explosion of ripe fruit and concentration. Long, classy and well balanced. The wine was very fine indeed, if not great. Beginning to fade a little, and should be drunk up.

1937   Château Rieussec *(Sauternes)*   *94p*

2003/2010 x4 • D 2 h / G 1 h

The year 1937 was warm and dry. In the Sauternes area the harvest gave a splendid crop and this lovely Rieussec is one of the very best examples of it. The bottle was like new, excellent level and promising colour. Decanted for two hours. A deep and bright golden colour. An astonishing appearance for such an old wine. Elegant and open sweet nose with a hint of earth and ripe raisins. Clean, sound and ripe. Very much alive, rich, fat and intense with good botrytis fruit. Smooth, gentle and long finish. Will hold, but will not become any better. Most enjoyable now.

1948   Château Latour *(Pauillac)*   *94p*

2003/2010 x4 • D 1 h / G 2 h

This vintage is something of a paradox. The weather conditions in July and August had not been good and it was generally felt that the grapes had not received enough sunshine. The vineyard had also suffered from serious attacks of grape worms. The harvest, which began on September 27th, was of average volume. How-ever, its quality proved to be an excellent surprise.

These two rare bottles came all the way from New York to Helsinki a few years ago. Both were in good condition, and levels were high-shoulder. Decanted one hour. Dark brick red colour with a browning rim. Rich and open bouquet. On the palate the wine still boasts aggressive tannins, with an almost fleshy structure. Good intensity of ripe, sweet fruits. A convincing finale, substantial tannins still holding firm, great length pooled with class and freshness. A surprisingly satisfactory wine with lots of life ahead.

2000   Incognito Sine Qua Non *(California)*   *94p*

2007/2025 x2 • D 3 h / G 2 h

This Sine Qua Non has the capability to be a great wine, but it needs some more time. The 2000 Incognito a blend of 95 percent Grenache and 5 percent Syrah has a wonderful artistic label. Only 263 cases were made.

Decanted three hours. Attractive but rather infantile, dark and deep purple colour. Surprisingly mature nose with toffee, flower, liquorice, pepper, earth, and exotic dark fruit flavours. Ripe fruit and richness are its greatest assets. The tannins are still very firm but do not get in the way of enjoyment. A big, rich and fleshy wine with a long and perhaps somewhat too intoxicating ending. Begin to drink it now and enjoy over the next ten years.

1948   Château Léoville Barton *(Saint-Julien)*   *94p*

2002/2020 x2 • D 45 min / G 1 h

A good-looking Calvet-bottled magnum. Level was top-shoulder. Decanted 45 minutes. A deep ruby, healthy colour. Sound and open nose. A typical Saint-Julien profile of ripe fruits, tobacco, cedar, and herb flavours. Muscular body and a good concentration of mature tannin and fruit. Long, powerful ending showing lovely intensity, depth and balance. Definitely fully mature, for drinking over the next 5-10 years.

Bodegas Ysios

1945   Ruchottes-Chambertin Thomas Bassot *(Côte de Nuits)*   94p
2000/now x2 • D 1 h / G 2 h

This bottle came from a Christie's London auction. Excellent neck level. Impressive dark colour, good depth. At first a bit tight, with a vegetal nose. Later, after one hour, it was a surprisingly fresh, open and fruity Pinot Noir. Beautiful structure. Lively, full, yet soft and velvety on the palate. Quite feminine and elegant for a Chambertin. A big, fabulous bottle of great wine. Most pleasing.

1945   Château Beychevelle *(Saint-Julien)*   94p
2001/2010 x4 • D 1 h / G 2 h

Château-bottled. The level was almost by the neck. Decanted one hour. A dark, opaque red colour fading gradually to a teak coloured rim. Rich and complex on the nose with a grand depth and aromas of spice, vegetal nuances, cassis, and old oak. Full-flavoured, medium to full-bodied and well balanced. An elegant but commanding wine with flavours of sweet fruit, cedar, coffee, spicy old oak, and undertones of herbs. A silky texture, splendid concentration and a long, well balanced finish. The wine has been fully mature for over three decades already, but will still last another decade.

1974   Insignia Joseph Phelps *(Napa Valley)*   94p
2000/2010 x1 • D 1 h / G 30 min

Excellent-looking bottle. Level was by the neck. Decanted one hour before tasting. Healthy, bright colour without any signs of age. A lovely, ripe prune and spice nose. Exotic fruits and some wider scents appeared later. A rich wine with excellent complexity and concentration of fruit. Beautiful texture on the palate, which was mouth filling and almost creamy. Nice tannic backbone. A long and lingering aftertaste. What a presence - ready now but will drink well for five to ten years.

1994   Château Valandraud *(St.Emilion)*   94p
2007/2015 x3 • D 3 h / G 2 h

Château Valandraud is the achievement of hard work from a couple with a passion for wine, Jean-Luc Thunevin and his wife Murielle Andraud. Having become highly successful wine merchants in the Saint-Emilion area, their burning ambition was to own their own vineyard and make their own wine. Little by little, they bought up several parcels of vines. The name of the growth is both geographical (Val for Vale of Fongaban) and sentimental (Andraud being Murielle's last name). That was how Château Valandraud came to be. Jean-Luc Thunevin decides the harvest date once the grapes have reached the optimal maturity. For the winemaking, he adopted Burgundy's technique of punching down the cap in the fermenting vat (pigeage) and stirring the lees in the oak barrel, in order to get the maximum extraction from his grapes. He does no filtration, just racking barrel to barrel every three months. There were only 8,998 bottles produced in 1994.

Decanted three hours. The 1994 Valandraud was a skillful effort from this difficult vintage. A good, deep and bright ruby colour. Excellent nose, sound and open with ripe black cherry, vanilla and cedar aromas. Well balanced and complex on the palate with roasted coffee, chocolate, earth, and sweet tannin flavours all abundant. The intensity of fruit was excellent. Still quite a hard and tough wine. The finish was long and leathery with a nice dryness and rich, earthy, new oak flavours. Needs time, consume this over next 10 to 15 years.

1961 Château Léoville-Las Cases *(Saint-Julien)* 94p
2007/2010 x21 • D 1 h / G 1.5 h

The outside of the bottle was somewhat dilapidated, no capsule and only bits and pieces of the label remaining. Otherwise it had a bright looking colour and the level was high-shoulder. Decanted one hour. Dark, deep colour. Open, a bit hard and spicy on the nose. This wine is still a charmer with well-expressed fruit and a marvellous clarity throughout. A warm, big wine without being too powerful. Very well designed tannic structure and certain offensiveness on the finish. A classic old, powerful Claret!

1947 Château Grand-Puy-Lacoste *(Pauillac)* 94p
2003/2010 x3 • D 1 h / G 30 min

Négociant-bottling. In good condition with top-shoulder level. Decanted 45 minutes. It exhibited a dark, opaque garnet colour. This beauty continues to reveal the fragrance and elegance that one expects from wines of the 1947 vintage. A fragrant, complex bouquet of cedar, herbs, vanillin, tobacco, and coffee is followed by a soft, gentle, well-balanced, and complex palate with sweet layers of fruit. Very supple with a finely tuned concentration of fruit and firm but silky tannin, and a long, rich finish. The 1947 Grand-Puy-Lacoste is still charming and should be drunk now.

1986 Château Cos d'Estournel *(Saint-Estèphe)* 94p
2005/2020 x3 • D 2 h / G 2 h

The year 1986 really beat all previous records. July and August were warm and extremely dry. It was not until September 23rd when the sky opened and the downpour caused damage in the areas of Bordeaux, Libourne and Graves in particular. The rain only briefly touched the northern Médoc area. The problem with the vintage was the quality of the Merlot grapes because their taste was diluted, partly by the exceedingly large harvest and partly by the rain. The vineyards that had the patience to wait for the ripening of the Cabernet Sauvignon were rewarded. The weather continued to be good and dry, and the harvesting could be carried out without interruption in ideal conditions.

Fine bottle with perfect level. Decanted two hours. Moderately intense, cherry red colour. Developing nose with earthiness, leather, dried herbs, and hints of volatile balsamic aromas. A rich medium-bodied wine with markedly ripe tannins, very balanced acidity combining harmoniously with the ripe fruitiness of plums and smokiness from new oak. The cedar and tobacco leaf flavours are standing out. Long lingering finish with ripe intense fruitiness and minerality. Drinking perfectly now but can still age another 5-7 years.

1976 *Scharzhofberger Riesling Auslese Egon Müller* 94p
(Mosel-Saar-Ruwer)
2006/now x2 • D 30 min / G 1 h

The bottle came directly from Egon Müller's cellar. Perfect condition and decanted 30 minutes. The colour has now turned to almost deep amber but still shows all of the concentration, intensity and elegance that it did in its youth. There is now some maturity, spicy-honeyed botrytis and dried fruit aromas on the nose with a generous mineral sensation in the long finish. A complex mix of minerals and smokiness with an excellent balance. The velvety mouth-feel is charming. Well balanced and enjoyable.

1983 *Châteauneuf-du-Pape Château de Beaucastel* (Rhône) 94p
2005/2015 x3 • D 2 h / G 2 h

The 1983 was a rather good vintage at Château Beaucastel. Normal winter and spring. Bud break occurred early April with cold and rain following in May. Flowering started on the 8th of June. Warm but rainy July and September. The harvest started on the 12th of September and proceeded under ideal climatic conditions until the 6th of October. A small crop, only 13,000 cases were released.

The bottle was in top condition. Level by the neck. Decanted two hours. Dark, concentrated colour. Complex nose, just starting to open up. Lovely blackberry, spice and smoke aroma on the nose. Excellent balance and lovely intensity. Quite full and long, not as hard as expected. Approaching its peak, but there is no hurry. Elegant and charming with good length.

1945 *Château Montrose* (Saint-Estèphe) 94p
2003/2015 x3 • D 1.5 h / G 1 h

The bottle was in excellent condition. Château-bottled with top-shoulder level. Decanted one hour and twenty minutes. Dark, but bright ruby colour with some fading at the rim. Lovely, well developed and perfumed nose of ripe cassis, soft plum and minerals with some spicy, menthol notes. Spicy, full-bodied and dense with a rounded texture. Youthful for its age and vigorous. Well-balanced, long and soft aftertaste. Amazingly, it still tasted like if it was less than twenty years old. A classy wine that is drinking well now but will keep going for another decade.

2005   *Riesling Tradition Schloss Gobelsburg* (Kamptal)   *94p*
2006/2015 x6 • D 1 h / G 2 h

A medium-intense, straw yellow colour. Rich, deep and dense spicy nose with ripe peachy fruitiness and flowers. Dry, crisp acidity and broad oily texture highlighted by ripe peachy and waxy flavours. Long mineral finish. This unique-style wine made by the ancient oxidative methods with natural yeasts of Kamptal, shows great complexity and persistent leanness combined with wonderful intensity. True treasured experience to be uncorked after a few decades.

2000   *Château Margaux* (Margaux)   *94p*
2004/2050 x4 • D 8 h / G 5 h

On this exquisite super-vintage, only 40 percent of the Château Margaux crop was used to this Grand Vin. It was made from superbly ripe Cabernet Sauvignon complemented by only 10 percent Merlot. The appearance of the wine is a bright, moderately intense, ruby red. An attractive and complex nose shows delicate black-currant and raspberry aromas combined with violets After a few minutes the nose gains more toasty aromas with spices, roasted coffee and chocolate. On the palate the wine behaves aristocratically. Very sophisti-cated, medium-bodied structure, with marked acidity and minerality. Tannins are very firm but opulent and persistent. Wine shows classic Margaux features being elegant yet restrained. Due to this perfect vintage the fruit is extremely intense giving such tremendous potential for ageing that it could be paralleled to the 1900 Margaux. If it behaves as this legendary vintage, it will keep easily for another 50 years and more.

1929   *Le Chambertin Louis Jadot* (Côte de Nuits)   *94p*
2004/now x2 • D 1 h / G 1 h

The bottle was in fine condition and ullage was only 3 cm. Decanted for one hour. Deep colour, already mature at the rim. Immensely aromatic, wild meaty bouquet that reached all corners of the nose. Intensive and rich on the palate. Delicate flavours of coffee, truffles and violets. Not a very robust or multi-dimen-sional wine but has a lovely sweetness of soft tannins and fruit at the end. A very satisfactory Burgundy from this ordinary vintage.

1981   *Grange Penfolds* (South Australia)   *94p*
2004/2010 x4 • D 2 h / G 3 h

This very hot and dry vintage produced really concentrated wine. The blend was 89 percent Shiraz and 11 percent Cabernet Sauvignon. Decanted two hours. Dark, almost opaque black to the edge of the rim. Very closed at first. After two hours it opened with delicious concentration of black fruit and a lot of jammy berry, eucalyptus and peppery aromas. On the palate it was powerful yet stylish with plenty of depth. A long, rich, and spicy finish. We have high hopes that this 1981 will ultimately be almost as good as 1976.

1953 La Tâche Domaine de la Romanée-Conti (Côte de Nuits)   94p
2006/2015 x2 • D 1 h / G 3 h

This bottle was in a good condition and the level had dropped only 4 cm. The bottle itself was purchased at Christie´s in London. The colour was a well developed orange-brown, though it was slightly pale. An aromatic, very ripe Pinot Noir bouquet with some roasted and woody notes. Quite a strongly spiced, rich nature, full of vitality. Very good sense of fruit and balance. The flavour and bouquet lasted for several hours without losing anything. A wine, which still has several years ahead of it. A pleasant but not a never-to-be-forgotten experience.

1929 Dom Pérignon Moët & Chandon (Champagne)   94p
2006/now x3 • D 5 min / G 20 min

Wonderful bottle with fine level. Decanted only five minutes. Good, bright, slightly golden colour. Very fresh and open nose with lovely fruit and a gentle black truffle and coffee aroma. Ashtonishingly lively and energetic, the bubbles were almost dancing on the tongue. The fine mousse persists in the mouth with creamy and ripe, rich fruit nuances. All in all, this is an intense, powerful wine with plenty of character. Very long and fine indeed.

1945 Château Gruaud-Larose (Saint-Julien)   94p
2001/2015 x15 • D 1.5 h / G 2 h

Old-looking château-bottled bottle, with top-shoulder level. Decanted two hours. Full, mature colour. Rich, but less vigorous on the nose than the earlier tasted Harvey's bottling. Similar palate - ripe, sweet and full. A big, robust giant-of-a-Bordeaux - true to the vintage. Soft and long, fat aftertaste. Still very fresh and alive. Everything is in its place here.

1978 Châteauneuf-du-Pape Château Rayas (Rhône)   94p
2001/2020 x2 • D 1.5 h / G 3 h

The bottle was in good condition and level was by the neck. Decanted 1.5 hours. Intense, dark and deep colour to the rim. An open and clean, fresh peppery nose with hints of exotic fruit, balsam wood and truffle aromas. Thick, unctuously textured and pure wine. Still powerful and tannic, and has a lot of character and complexity. This is a Châteauneuf-du-Pape for those wanting immediate gratification. Very fresh and meaty wine. A powerfully spicy and rewarding finish. This is a very opulent example of Rayas.

518

1992   Clos du Mesnil Champagne Krug *(Champagne)*   *94p*

2006/2020 x4 • D 25 min / G 50 min

Deep, developing golden colour with elegant and lively small-sized bubbles. Rich, pronounced and open nose: cream, coconut, apples, and butter. A touch of wood and spiciness. Smoky minerality brings complexity on the palate. Oriental spices and honey. Sharp refreshing acidity and a focused linear structure. Highly youthful still and requires a decade to show its entire glory and finesse.

1927   Vintage Port Dow's *(Portugal)*   *94p*

2003/2015 x3 • D 2 h / G 5 h

Fine looking bottle. Decanted two hours. Lot of sediment. Medium-deep dark ruby colour. An elegant, spicy, complex nose. A very full and intense wine. Generous mouthful of wild berry, smoke, black cherry, and dried fruit flavours and aromas. Quite vigorous, but it has soft fruit there. Still very much alive and has a creamy, warm ending. Very good.

1992   Cabernet Sauvignon Herb Lamb Vineyard Colgin *(Napa Valley)* *94p*

2004/2015x2 • D 2 h / G 2 h

Superb-looking bottle. Level was by the neck. Decanted three hours. A very intense, deep, dark red colour. The rich complex nose holds a bouquet of blackcurrant and vanilla, spices and smoke with intense, dark fruit aromas. This beauty is full-bodied on the palate with muscular, slightly hard tannins, excellent purity with ripe intense dark fruitiness and moderate acidity. Cedar and vanilla-like oak aromas are adding complexity to the palate. Rich to the long, supple finish. Still young, but a very concentrated and already drinkable wine.

1979   R.D. Bollinger *(Champagne)*   *94p*

2007/2015 x6 • D 10 min / G 50 min

A cold winter and a cool, damp springtime delayed bud break. June's great weather contributed to successful flowering. The warm, and at times stormy, weather was able to produce a high quality crop. The harvest was quite late and alcohol levels remained modest at 9 degrees potential alcohol.

This late-disgorged Bollinger is well into the process of maturation. Fine, lively, full of toast and fruit. The mouth-feel is silky with harmonious small and soft bubbles. Medium-bodied, long and elegant wine. Very good from now until 2015.

1926   Château Latour *(Pauillac)*   *94p*

2003/now x2 • D 15 min / G 30 min

Healthy looking château-bottled bottle. The level was top-shoulder. Decanted 15 minutes. Deep, intense ruby colour with tawny tints. Prominent, intense nose full of rich and ripe, sweet, dark fruit aromas, blackcurrants, roasted nuances, and delicate herb tones. Solid and intense full-bodied palate, which is notably balanced between high acidity, soft tannins and ripe fruit. Long, lavish and meaty finish with mint and fresh rosemary flavours along with good acidity. Decant and drink right away!

1935 Viña Real Gran Reserva C.V.N.E. *(Rioja)*   94p

2004/2010 x4 • D 1 h / G 1 h

This 1935 was the last - and surprisingly the best - bottle for us at a vertical tasting of Viña Real. We had more than twenty vintages to go through with the friendly and openhearted winemaker, Jesús Madrazo Mateo. It was an impressive line up of wines that proved that the great reputation of C.V.N.E. was well deserved. The overall quality was impressive, and the best vintages were 1949, 1962 and this harmonious 1935. All the bottles came directly from Bodegas and were in mint condition. Decanted one hour. Beautiful, dark, a bit old-looking colour. Sound, full, fragrant, and distinctly floral bouquet. Very rich and powerful. Warm and smooth but not without acidity. It was a harmonious and round wine. Lasting, gentle finish on the tongue. We had a great time with this one!

1979 Dom Ruinart Rosé Ruinart *(Champagne)*   94p

2007/2010 x5 • D 10 min / G 30 min

Deep, developed, orange-hued colour. Delicate small-sized bubbles lasted long in the glass. Elegant nose of ripe red berries, rich toastiness and earthy spicy notes. The wide-open nose with its layers of emerging aromas is consistent with the harmonious palate: great minerality, lively firming acidity and adequate fruitiness. Silky smooth and vinous texture. Persistent finish. At peak today, but will keep for a number of years without great degradation.

1989 Pinot Gris Sélection de Grains Nobles Josmeyer *(Alsace)*   94p

2006/2020 x3 • D 15 min / G 1 h

The super warm vintage in Alsace generated the largest crop of late harvest wines of all time. Scattered September rain created circumstances for botrytis to evolve over the highly concentrated grapes. Truly one the best vintages ever in Alsace - if not the best!

Bright, intense golden colour. Huge complexity in the developing nose. Very intense with raisin, honey, burnt sugar, and hints of Crème Brûlée nuances. Absolutely a luscious wine with impeccable concentration. Moderate acidity stands out as surprisingly crisp and fresh! Fine botrytis flavours of apricot marmalade and honeyed overtones are very intense. Together with high level of alcohol the wine is in beautiful balance. The wine tastes much sweeter than it actually is with its 90 g/l residual sugar.

1973 Unico Bodegas Vega Sicilia *(Ribera del Duero)* 94p
2003/2020 x3 • D 2 h / G 1.5 h

Fine looking magnum with skilfully painted label. Level was by the neck. Decanted two hours. Bright garnet colour. Intense, rich and gamey nose with powerful aromas of chocolate and tar. A dry medium-bodied wine with mellow acidity, intense fruitiness with ripe cassis notes and big meaty tannins. A surprisingly youthful wine with great complexity. Very pleasant now.

1974 Barbaresco Angelo Gaja *(Piedmont)* 94p
2007/now x3 • D 30 min / G 1 h

This lucky bottle was in prestige condition. Decanted one hour. A paler and lighter colour than we expected, but the bouquet was very intense, complex, spicy, and sound. Instead of being a big Barbaresco, this was really an elegant and soft wine with many layers of sweet fruit and tannins covered by richness and extract. Well-balanced and not nearly as hard and robust as the 1967 vintage. It has a good length and a wonderful aftertaste - exhilarating to drink.

1998 Dom Pérignon Moët & Chandon *(Champagne)* 94p
2007/2025 x9 • D 20 min / G 50 min

Bright, moderately pale, straw yellow colour with green tints and vivid small bubbles. The lovely familiar nose of Dom Pérignon develops in this vintage towards a medium-intense combination of seductively toasty, roasted coffee, cream, and smoky mineral aromas. The crisp medium-bodied taste shows a moderate intensity and an aggressive mousse. Toasty and mineral flavours highlight the balanced, lingering lemony finish. Medium-intense texture suggest this wine reaches its peak sooner rather than later. The wine benefits from a couple of more years in the bottle and will peak in 5 to 10 years.

2000 Opitz One Willi Opitz *(Burgenland)* 94p
2006/2015 • D - / G 30 min

The modern world's most peculiar sweet wine made of red grapes. The awarded sweet wine maker Willi Opitz from Illmitz Neusiedlersee, known for providing wines for McLaren Formula One team, created this special wine originally to US President Clinton. It is still sold under the name of Mr President on the US market. The wine is 100% Zweigelt with residual sugar of 180 g/l. The sweetness is gained by drying the grapes on reef mats outside for five months.

Bright, medium intense red colour. Very intense and rich wild raspberry nose with honeyed overtones, flowers and some spices. Luscious taste with lovely crispness and silky texture. Very intense raspberry flavour with a hint of cherry. Moderately long lingering finish. A super seductive wine, drinking perfectly now.

1970 Unico Bodegas Vega Sicilia (Ribera del Duero)   94p
2002/2020 x4 • D 3 h / G 2 h

This handsome magnum was purchased in Spain a few years ago. The bottle looked like new, and the level was by the neck. Good, bright and deep colour, no signs of maturation. It has a very "Unico" personality, with an original, sweet fruit, truffles and American oak bouquet. A very concentrated, powerful and rich palate with a long and tannic aftertaste.

   In general, Unicos need a lot of air to open, both after decanting and in the glass. We decanted this magnum three hours before tasting, but afterwards we thought it had not been enough. After five long hours it opened fully and became very velvety in the mouth. A classic wine that can still age many decades.

1996 Belle Epoque Rosé Perrier-Jouët (Champagne)   94p
2006/2015 x2 • D 10 min / G 20 min

An exquisite bottle. Decanted ten minutes. Light salmon-pink colour. Small bubbles, which rise in a persistent, steady stream. The nose is very fresh and rich, with fine raspberry fruit and bready, nutty notes beneath. A full-bodied, fat and structured wine. On the palate the mousse is polished and creamy, but the wine retains its fresh and elusive character. There is a lovely balance and a smooth texture with a creamy, lightly toasted flavour in the entrancing finish. A finely tuned Rosé.

1975 Vintage Champagne Krug (Champagne)   94p
2006/2015 x5 • D 15 min / G 40 min

An attractive, excellent looking magnum. Decanted 15 minutes. Dark, golden colour. Lovely hazelnut and biscuit aromas. Very full in the mouth with a lovely, wide mousse. Lots of minerals and apples on the palate. A well-balanced wine with intense structure and marvellous complexity. Very delicious now.

1964 Pommard Premier Cru Camille Giroud (Côte de Beaune)   94p
2002/now x3 • D 30 min / G 2 h

Truly unique wine that stands out from the classic Burgundy style. Even Camille Giroud's former owners considered this wine as a black sheep of the family for not sharing the typicity of the great Burgundy. Peculiar enough, it shares amazingly parallel characters to Pomerol showing extensively complex style and firm tannins - absolutely no Pinot Noir characters whatsoever. The vintage could be one reason. Like often experienced the vintages with extremely cold winter have been followed by a hot summer. After the snowiest and hardest winter in two decades the summer turned out to be hot and dry yielding very concentrated grapes with thick skins. While sunny weather continued the beneficial scattered rain arrived in September and the grapes reached optimum ripeness. The high concentration in grapes gained extra edginess and richness from the iron rich soils of Pommard. When these factors are combined with very traditional vinification processes of Camille Giroud, the result is easily something one might not expect being Burgundy. This wine was always tasted blind among the mature Burgundies and every time it was considered being the joker of the flight - and all of the times among the top three!

Very intense, garnet colour with orange rim. Pronounced and complex toasty nose with mocha, chocolate and black fruits, cherries and plums with hints of orange peel. Full-bodied, meaty mouth-feel with firm tannic structure and intense ripe dark fruitiness with plums, cherries and brambles. Rich and tasty wine with long mineral finish wrapped with lovely mocha nuances. Such a supple and opulent wine, giving sheer pleasure drinking now, so no use storing it any longer. It will keep well though another ten years expectedly.

1970   *Hermitage La Chapelle Paul Jaboulet Aîné* (Rhône)   94p
2001/2010 x9 • D 45 min / G 45 min

A fine bottle. Decanted only 15 minutes. Quite a weak colour and a little tight on the nose. We decanted it too briefly, but happily it opened up after 45 minutes. Then it was ripe, fresh, and velvety on the nose. Still some tannins left that are not as refined as in the best of recent vintages like 1961 and 1966. Good backbone and intensity though, and no lack of fruit. Slightly robust with a harshness at the end.

1911   *Château Latour* (Pauillac)   94p
2007/now x2 • D 30 min /G 45 min

A hot summer and a drought that continued until late in the fall produced many superb, though at times quite harsh, wines in Bordeaux. Latour has been regarded as an exceptionally soft and calm wine, at least compared to the other first growth wines. Nonetheless, at least the wine we now got to taste had kept its backbone and structure well, and it was still a gentle and sophisticated wine. Decanted 30 minutes. This was our second Latour from this rare vintage, and it had improved after the first experience. As a Latour it was still surprisingly light and delicate, if tasted blind we would have thought the wine's origin to be Pomerol.

As the previous bottle already started to lose some of its fine qualities after 30 minutes from decanting, this one just started to breath. It has a good balance and a full, opulent and vivid taste. Lovely smooth fruit on top of a tannic grip. This time it was complex and thriving enough to provide real interest and quality. As has been said many times before: there are no good wines, only good bottles

1929   *Niersteiner Riesling Hermannshof* (Germany)   94p
2003/2010 x4 • D 30 min / G 50 min

Excellent bottle. Recorked in 1998. Level was by the neck. Quite a deep, green tinged golden colour. An open and clean bouquet with peach, pear and delicate mineral notes. Delicious weight on the palate with some residual sweetness. A very pure wine with pear-drop flavours, prominent acidity and an overall crisp character. Well balanced and has plenty of life. Quite a long and dry finish, with some flowery nuances peeking through. A lovely, old but youthful Riesling.

1969 *Cordon Rouge G.H. Mumm* (Champagne) 94p
2003/2010 x2 • D 5 min / G 20 min

Very youthful colour. Round and fresh nose of peaches and raspberry. High acidity, delicately lightweight but intense palate. Very well balanced. Much better and more alive than expected. A lovely bottle. Very good value for the price. A highly recommendable old champagne!

1997 *Madrona Ranch Cabernet Sauvignon Abreu* (Napa Valley) 94p
2002/2020 x3 • D 2 h / G 3+ h

One of the rarest fine wines in Napa Valley, of which only 400 cases are produced. The owner David Abreu established the winery in 1986 and the first vintage sold under Abreu brand was 1991. The quality of Madrona Ranch Cabernet Sauvignon is so highly esteemed that the many of the legendary wineries in Napa purchase the grapes from David Abreu. His clients have been Araujo, Bryant, Colgin, Harlan, Spottswoode, Viader, Neyers and Turley. This wine is 95 percent Cabernet Sauvignon with 5 percent of Cabernet Franc. The wine is aged two years in 100 percent Taransaud's new oak. No filtration or fining has been completed. To get a hold of this wine you need to sign to put your name on a waiting list.

Deep, intense, purple colour with high viscosity. Youthful and intense nose shows extensive crème de cassis notes with spicy and toasty new oak. Still little closed although hints of meaty roast aromas are indicating the complexity of the wine. Extremely concentrated on the palate. Full-bodied wine with moderate acidity and refined big tannins that are giving magnificent backbone to the rich and ripe dark fruitiness and spicy oakiness. The texture is rich and peculiarly edgy making this wine unique in style. The extremely long aftertaste charms with chocolate, tobacco and crème de cassis flavours. It is tempting to enjoy the wine now because of its edginess that challenges the taster's palate but it will certainly hold and evolve for a decade or even two, offering more aromatic nuances and tamed character for wine lovers preferring smoothness.

1955 *Clos-de-la-Roche Charles Vienot* (Côte de Nuits) 94p
2005/now x3 • D 45 min / G 30 min

A good-looking bottle, fine neck level. Mature, clean deep red colour with a wide orange rim. Ripe, smoky, elegant, and complex nose. There is much life and energy here - this has impressive depth and a lot of masculine features. Unexpectedly full, intense and powerful on the palate. This is a very satisfying experience - top quality. Great spicy Pinot Noir aftertaste. No rush!

1997 *Romanée-Conti Domaine de la Romanée-Conti* (Côte de Nuits) 94p
2006/2020 x3 • D 3 h / G 3 h

The small harvest after very hot weather conditions guaranteed very intense, ruby colour and opulent, rich and spicy nose with complex aromas of violets, ripe cherries and chocolate. Crisp, harmonious medium-bodied palate with very refined tannins and moderately intense red fruit are enhanced with mineral, spicy and toasty finish. Very long velvety aftertaste. A total of 4,814 bottles made.

1996 *Clos des Goisses Philipponnat* (Champagne) 94p

2006/2025 x8 • D 1 h / G 2 h

A big wine from the best vintage of the nineties in Champagne. This was a very ripe, but also very acidic vintage. The base wine of Clos de Goisses had already 12 percent alcohol and a pH below 3 before the sugar for second fermentation was added. In appearance the wine shines with a golden yellow colour accompanied by vigorous, fine bubbles. The nose is very yeasty with apricot tones and almonds. Full-bodied wine for Champagne. The taste is very crisp and intensively fruity with fresh rich mousse on the palate. Elegant lingering mineral finish. Has great future potential!

1958 *Chambertin Armand Rousseau* (Côte de Nuits) 94p

2006/2010 x3 • D 15 min / G 30 min

Fine looking double-magnum. Decanted 15 minutes. Clear, moderately intense golden yellow colour with fine and still surprisingly energetic bubbles. The nose is captivating. Rich and toasty with roasted coffee, butterscotch and hazelnuts. Dry and opulent palate still shows a vivid acidity and lovely creamy mousse with rich toasty flavours of cacao, hazelnuts and coffee. A delightful wine that is incredibly youthful still.

1997 *Coteaux du Layon 'Anthologie' Pierre Delesvaux* (Loire) 94p

2001/2040 x2 • D 45 min / G 3+ h

A superb vintage in Loire for this small domaine. They produced many fantastic botrytised wines, however this wine shines as the best. Clear, bright, golden amber colour with rich viscosity. Pronounced and dense nose with great amount of complex aromas - honey, dried fruits, peaches, prunes, figs, spices, nutmeg, and fresh oysters! Lusciously sweet, crisp acidity and honeyed fruitiness, preserved peaches and plums. Great length in the lingering finish. A gastronomic wine with an almost eternal future potential.

1973 *Dom Pérignon Moët & Chandon* (Champagne) 94p

2006/2020 x8 • D 10 min / G 40 min

A moderately good vintage with a hot and dry summer but a very wet September. A few premium champagne producers still succeeded in making wonderful wines. Dom Pérignon was one of them.

Bright, golden colour with attractive, playful, small bubbles. The pronounced nose is broad and very toasty with chocolate and smoky mineral tones. Quite dry, medium level of acidity and very rich mousse. Fresh and elegant toastiness with good fruitiness and hints of yeasty aromas. The finish is delicate and medium long. Overall the wine was very humble in style and reflecting the innocence of its pure character.

1967 Kiedricher Gräfenberg Riesling Auslese Robert Weil 94p
(Rheingau)
2007/2010 x4 • D 1 h / G 2 h

The bottle was in an unequalled condition, and the level was 1 cm. Decanted 1 hour. A very dark, bright golden colour. Sound, clean and fresh bouquet full of nuts, honey and raisin flavours. Very good balance and multidimensional aroma profile. A very fresh, elegant and smooth, lingering wine. Not as mature as the previous bottle but otherwise quite alike, sweet, almost beerenauslese in style, with good acidity. Top quality wine with a long, fruity and honeyed aftertaste - still a very intense and aristocratic experience.

1951 Clos des Goisses Philipponnat (Champagne) 94p
2006/2015 x2 • D 30 min / G 1 h

For a weak vintage Clos de Goisses shows very well, thanks to its unique exposure. This wine was disgorged in 2000. Drinking from a Magnum bottle the wine had reserved itself better than in a regular bottle. Clear, golden colour with refined bubbles. Rich butterscotch nose with mineral and nutty tones. Dry, moderately crisp taste is deliciously mineral with a broad range of flavours, such as rose petals, white chocolate, vanilla, and coco butter. Elegant finish, still very fresh. Probably the best Champagne of this vintage.

1900 Cuvée Nicolas Rolin Louis Jadot (Côte de Beaune) 94p
2004/now x2 • D 30 min / G 1 h

Superior looking bottle. Level was only 3cm. Decanted 30 minutes. Fully mature, bright colour. Sound and open nose with bitter chocolate and cherry flavours. No hard edges. Some volatile acidity, but otherwise very sweet, full and intense. Brilliantly balanced. Very fine grip and superb length. Lovely wine.

1966 Vintage Heidsieck & Monopole (Champagne) 94p
2004/2010 x5 • D 10 min / G 10 min

Fantastically deep and full, fruity nose. Wonderfully creamy fruit and a lot of seductive sweetness on both the nose and aftertaste. Half an hour after decanting the wine fully opened up and generated even greater complexities and flavours. An elegant and vigorous champagne!

1962 Château Haut-Brion Blanc (Graves) 94p
2004/2010 x6 • D 1.5 h / G 3 h

Haut-Brion Blanc is for us the white wine of the vintage. We have had the opportunity to taste it several times, and it has never let us down. Always a real charmer - elegant and classic.

This one had a good lower-neck level and it was decanted one and a half hours before tasting. It had a superb, fresh nose of honeyed fruits and toasty oak. Massively rich and intense wine with excellent complexity and balance. While it did not possess the weight and body of blockbuster vintages such as the 1945 and 1959, it was very impressive in its own charming, feminine way. Velvety and elegant with a texture more like old grand cru Montrachet than a severe white dry Graves. Got better and better in the glass. A very exiting wine with an everlasting finish.

1955   *Vintage Pol Roger* (Champagne)   94p

2003/now x3 D 10 min / G 20 min

These two bottles' condition was A1, and they let out a promising sigh when opened. A beautiful, golden yellow bearing to which small, quickly evaporating bubbles gave youthfulness and vitality. A deep, well balanced, rich, and tightly creamy flavour which seemed to last forever. Compared to the brilliant 1959 this maybe had a bit of modesty to it and as a whole it did not have the same power. Still an elegant and beautifully charming wine.

1964   *Brunello di Montalcino Riserva Biondi-Santi* (Tuscany)   94p

2007/2015 x8 • D 1 h / G 2 h

All the bottles were in perfect condition. Decanted for one hour. Beautiful crystal clear bright red, orange hued colour. Opulent and pronounced nose of green coffee beans, toasty, ripe red fruits, wood tones of teak and cedar. The dry, moderate acidity and round mellow tannins with very intense plummy fruitiness form a nervy balance. Long elegant finish. The wine really pleases, having peaked only just recently. It will probably keep another decade still before declining.

1962   *Colheita Niepoorl* (Portugal)   94p

2004/2015 x2 • D 3 h / G 5 h

In 1962 the weather was good but chilly for flowering. May was fine, dry and cool. Then June and July were fine and hot with an occasional thunderstorm. August was once again hot and without rain. This weather continued into early September with the rain arriving at the end of the month.

This Colheita spent 40 years in the pipes. The bottle was like new. Decanted two hours. Bright, moderately pale, tawny red colour. A very fresh and youthful medium-intense, lean nose with chocolate, orange peels and caramel notes. Sweet, beautiful concentration of acidity, soft tannins and very intense plummy fruitiness. Nutty, long and refined finish. A lively wine with dynamic appeal.

1966   *Chambertin Armand Rousseau* (Côte de Nuits)   94p

2000/2010 x3 • D 1 h / G 1 h

A fine bottle with 2cm level. Decanted one hour. Full, vigorous colour. Pure, clean and soft toffee-caramel nose. Lovely, sweet fruit. Got better and better in the glass. Round, mellow and spicy on the palate. Very harmonious. Very good but not the greatest Rousseau from the 60's. We prefer the 1969 and 1964 to this one, but it still is a very enjoyable and pleasant 1966 Chambertin.

NUMBER 551.
NUMBER 552.
NUMBER 553.
NUMBER 554.

1966 Château Latour *(Pauillac)* 94p

2006/2015 x25 • D 1.5 h / G 2 h

This bottle of Latour 1966 was in magnificent condition with base neck level. Decanted for one and a half hours before tasting. Very deep, dark colour. Distinguished, intense and youthful nose. A very classic Latour. Super-concentrated, full and vigorous wine. Very seductive attack, but in the middle it was a bit soft, dry and fairly acidic with sweet tannin and fruit. Well-balanced with long, chocolaty and truffle-flavoured finish. Ready and mouth-watering now, but it will not get any better with age.

1985 Le Chambertin Clos St. Jacques Louis Jadot *(Côte de Nuits)* 94p

2002/2020 x2 • D 1 h / G 2.5 h

This vintage is best recalled not only for its extremely cold winter in Burgundy with temperatures below -25 °C, but also for the superb weather conditions throughout the rest of the year that generated one the greatest vintages in Burgundy. This wine is a great expression of this wonderful vintage.

Excellent appearance. Level was 2 cm below the cork. Decanted one hour. Clear, bright, beautiful brick red colour with an orange rim. The nose is very complex, opulent, developed, and intensive with sweet root vegetable aromas, tints of café latte and pralines. The medium-bodied palate has a fresh acidity, refined firm tannins, moderate fruit intensity and delicate fragrant aromas with vegetal traces. The lingering finish shows beautiful finesse.

1986 Châteauneuf-du-Pape Château de Beaucastel *(Rhône)* 94p

2001/2015 x2 • D 2 h / G 2 h

The warm and dry summer turned into a miserable rainy September, delaying the harvest to mid-October. Perrin succeeded well this year thanks to the old vines and low yields. This wine has bright and clear, dark cherry red colour with tawny tints. Very rich with farmyard and animal aromas, ripe dark berries and sweet leathery scents. Full-bodied wine, vivid acidity, youthful, rich and ripe tannins, medium-intense sweet fruit character and long opulent finish.

1982 Château Calon-Ségur *(Saint-Estèphe)* 94p

2006/2025 x5 • D 2 h / G 2 h

A rather dark, brick-red colour. Very refined classical nose with currants. The elegant, medium-bodied taste combines medium-firm acids, fine ripe tannins and intensive fruitiness. A velvety, round mouth-feel; long aftertaste accompanied by firm tannins. An absolutely fine wine that will become greater with the coming years.

1949 Dom Pérignon Moët & Chandon *(Champagne)* 94p

2005/now x5 • D 10 min / G 1 h

Bottle looked like new. Decanted 10 minutes. Light yellow, bright colour, slightly darker than the 1955. Very fresh, rich, nutty, ample, and creamy nose. Complex and delicious. Fantastically feminine and sensitive but firm and full of energy at the same time. Fascinating mature champagne with great finesse. Extensive and elegant aftertaste.

1921 Clos-de-Vougeot Regnier *(Côte de Nuits)* 94p

2001/now x1 • D 1 h / G 1 h

This good-looking Clos de Vougeot had 4 cm ullage. Decanted one hour before dinner. Mature, orange-red colour, but much younger-looking than its age would suggest. Open, spicy, fruity, and very complex, elegant bouquet. Velvety, round and energetic fresh fruit palate with very soft, almost shadowy tannins on the palate. Long, gentle aftertaste. Our guests were very impressed.

Even though the taste was exceptional, the greatest thing about this wine was its amazingly complex, elegant and sensitive bouquet. A tribute to this great vineyard!

1959 Amarone della Valpolicella Bertani *(Veneto)* 94p

2002/2015 x2 • D 2 h / G 1 h

This 1959 was from the rare 1987 bottling. It was naturally in excellent condition. Decanted for two hours before tasting. More or less black, deep ruby-garnet and youthful looking colour. Intense, sound and woody bouquet with a hint of ripe fruit and vanilla flavours. A very big and heavy wine, almost too huge and intense. Well-balanced with a very pleasant, lingering, endless chocolaty finish. Very enjoyable now, but will probably last forever! A fascinating experience.

1959 Vouvray Le Haut Moelleux, Huet *(Loire)* 94p

2005/2010 x2 • D 1 h / G 1 h

Both bottles were in decent condition with by-the-neck levels. Decanted 30 minutes. Superb vintage in Vouvray as in many other Loire regions, the best since 1947. Clear, very intense golden amber colour. Intense, rich and complex nose, which constantly developed in the glass. Perfumery and floral nose with apples changing soon to earthy and vegetal, foie gras notes. Finally the wine turns into a fascinating bouquet of developed aromas such as tar, bacon and manure, reminiscent of red wine. The medium-sweet taste has a balancing crisp acidity adjusted with rich and ripe fruit with red berries, caramel and touches of mushroom flavours. Long lingering aftertaste with a mineral grip in the finish. A very peculiar and harmonious wine with great personality.

NUMBER 559.

NUMBER 560.

NUMBER 561.

NUMBER 562.

The guardian sphinx of
Château Mouton-Rothschild

1997 Bonnezeaux Cuvée Zenith René Renou *(Loire)*   94p
2005/2015 x3 • D 1 h / G 2 h

Nice looking bottle. Decanted one hour. Bright golden colour. Fresh, delicate and perfumed bouquet with aromas of lemon and some creamy, honeyed notes. Full-bodied with intense, sweet grapefruit, spiced apple and gently toasted oak flavours, firm tannins and good balance. Rounded and balanced with an extended, honeyed, cinnamon finish. Very youthful and vigorous.

1959 CS Buena Vista Haraszthy Cellars *(Napa Valley)*   94p
2004/now x5 • D 1 h / G 1 h

This 1959 Cabernet Sauvignon was a very noble and exquisite wine indeed, even though the year in California was not particularly good. The bottle was in perfect condition. Very smooth and supple, the cedar flavour and soft tannins kick in with an attractive spicy currant and plum edge. Holding up well in the glass. Still a marvellous wine with great persistence and depth of flavour on the finish, but a bit past its peak! An uncommon and wonderful experience!

1957 Crown Estate Tokaji Essencia *(Tokaj)*   94p
2004/now x3 • D 3 h / G 2 h

The Crown Estates of Hungary own 80ha of some of the greatest vineyards in the region, mostly located at three of the top sites. The jewel in the Crown is the former Royal Szarvas 'First Great Growth' vineyard, the most praised site in the entire region. Essencia is the most precious liquid obtained from Aszú grapes. The berries are picked individually from the bunch and are stored in wooden casks, with a false bottom made of loose-fitting slats. 'Essence' or juice, pressed out by the weight of the grapes, is collected and then matured in Gönci casks or demi-johns. With such a high sugar content, Tokaji Essencia ferments very slowly to about 3-4% alcohol and is a great rarity - a phenomenal nectar rather than a true wine. Due to its intensity it will mature for decades in cask and bottle before it reaches its peek.

A fine bottle. Decanted two hours before tasting. Deep, golden colour. Rich, sweet and intense raisin-like nose. Quite mature, thick, full, and very gentle. Low alcohol, elegant and easy to drink. Lovely fruit/acidity balance. Lingering and honeyed aftertaste. Beautiful to drink.

1958 Gran Reserva 890 La Rioja Alta *(Rioja)*   94p
2005/2010 x6 • D 30 min / G 1 h

The year 1958 was excellent in Rioja with very little rain and loads of sunshine. The bottle was in brand new condition, level by the neck. Decanted 30 minutes. Leather-like, mature and vigorous colour. Lively fruity aromas with some vanilla on the nose. Full and intense wine, not much taste of tannins or oak remain. Slightly acidic but still well balanced. Very persuasive and velvety aftertaste. One of the utmost old Riojas we have ever tasted - an enjoyable surprise!

1989 Châteauneuf-du-Pape Hommage à Jacques Perrin 94p
Château de Beaucastel (Rhône)
2005/2020 x3 • D 2 h / G 2.5 h

A top year all over Rhône with a huge concentration. This great Hommage à Jacques Perrin is no exception. A clear, medium-intense cherry red colour with an orange hue. A rich, warm and developed ripe nose with sweaty, farmyard and animal aromas accompanied by sweet fruity notes and cooked vegetables. The full-bodied wine shows big tannins and a moderate level of acidity balanced with sweet, vegetal fruit flavours and a long warming finish.

1970 Martha´s Vineyard Cabernet Sauvingon Heitz (Napa Valley) 94p
2000/2010 x2 • D 30 min / G 1 h

Fine looking bottles with top-shoulder levels or higher. Decanted 30 minutes. This is a profound, vigorously resonating wine with a dark, deep colour. The nose is very open and sound with chocolate, truffles and sweet Cabernet aromas. The tannins are virtually invisible, dense and velvet like. On the palate this medium-full Martha's Vineyard wine is well balanced with a wonderful flavour length and a firm structure. This is a delightfully well-made wine, which beautifully expresses the soul of this special vineyard.

1952 Barolo Riserva Borgogno (Piedmont) 94p
2003/2015 x4 • D 1.5 h / G 3 h

A very good year in Piedmont. A bright, polished tawny red colour. A really evolved nose with plenty of aromas such as tar, chocolate, butterscotch, smokiness, and horse manure. A medium-bodied palate showing a moderately high level of acidity. Tannins are austere in style but the intense fruitiness of cherries, figs, dates and glycerol-like texture balances them well. A long robust finish with the tannins dominating slightly.

1979 Chablis Premier Cru Montmains Camille Giroud (Chablis) 94p
2001/now x3 • D 10 min / G 1.5 h

Maison Camille Giroud has produced only one barrel of Chablis ever and that was this premier cru of the 1979 vintage, which was only released to the market in 2000. This was still the time before the new ownership. The Giroud brothers were ageing all their wines for tremendously long times, sometimes even without any clear strategy when to release them.

This wine showed the amazing longevity that all their wines carry, regardless of the vintage. Golden bright, medium-intense colour. Very lean, intense and expressive nose with minerals, butterscotch and vanilla flavours reminiscent of good sake. The light-bodied palate was dry and lemony with refreshing minerality. The oily texture was balanced well with a moderately high level of acidity. The long finish is less crisp but generous.

1898 Château Haut-Brion *(Graves)* 94p

2006/2015 x3 • D 30 min / G 15 min

A very tannic vintage requiring long bottle ageing to soften the wines. Who could have imagined a century ago that it could take up to 100 years to get the wines' tannins in balance? Well, it has taken at least that length of time with this particular bottle.

Medium intense, tawny red colour with some haziness. Opulent, intense and complex nose full of ripe blackcurrants and root vegetables. The taste is medium-bodied with crisp acidity, ripe stalky tannins and sweet fruitiness. The very long aftertaste shows sweetness and soy flavours. Very opulent wine with a decadent and even vulgar style. An amazingly evolved wine that is still very enjoyable and possesses even potential for further ageing!

1926 Château Léoville-Las Cases *(Saint-Julien)* 94p

2004/2015 x2 • D 30 min / G 1.5 h

The very warm growing season in 1926 produced a small crop of rich wines in Léoville Las Cases estate. Fine looking bottle with top-shoulder level. Moderately intense, clear, tawny colour with red tints. Intense developed nose with milk chocolate and toasty aromas. Medium-bodied fleshy wine with good acidic structure and ripe supporting tannins. Rich and ripe sweet fruit flavours with good concentration. An opulent wine with a fleshy finish.

1998 Château Latour *(Pauillac)* 94p

2006/2025 x4 • D 3 h / G 4 h

A rollercoaster year with frequently altering weather conditions starting with a mild, sunny spring and turning into a wet, cool summer, then a scorching hot August with 39 ºC and a stormy, rainy harvest. Although many producers were struggling to get their Cabernets' tannins to ripen fully, Latour turned out well, thanks to its unique terroir. Clear, opaque, intense ruby purple colour. Refined intense aromas of ripe blackcurrants, almonds, smoke, and spices. Full-bodied elegant taste with juicy tannins, delicate but intense dark fruit with savoury spiciness. Lovely refreshing acidity combines very well with the tannins and fruit forming a lingering, long finish and fleshy aftertaste.

1916 Domaine de Chevalier Rouge *(Graves)* 94p

2005/2010 x2 • D 1 h / G 1 h

This excellent-looking magnum came directly from Domaine. By the neck level and decanted for one hour. This wine has a very youthful, deep colour. Attractive perfume on the nose, with a changing array of smoky, cedar, blackberry, and roasted nut aromas. Very sound and open. A dense palate, not as open or lively as the nose might suggest. This has a good balance, and quite a lot of complexity. There is elegance and grace. Vigorous, long but a bit too dry finish for our taste, although an excellent Domaine de Chevalier.

1987 *Montrachet Domaine de la Romanée-Conti* (Côte de Beaune) 94p
2006/2015 x3 • D 1 h / G 1.5 h

This wine proves wrong the general lack of appreciation for 1987s. The vintage is able to show some very appealing features in DRC's hands. Golden yellow colour with rich complex nose of apricots, smokiness, spices, mineral, and honeyed overtones. Very mineral, fresh, medium-bodied palate with an intense, sweet, honeyed, glycerol texture. Buttery and apricot flavours also found in the little phenolic finish. Only 2,015 bottles made. Very good now.

1955 *Château Cheval Blanc* (St.Emilion) 94p
2005/2020 x15 • D 1 / G 3 h

Good château-bottling with by the neck level. Very deep, clear red colour. Intensive complex nose with some development. Fresh mint, dark chocolate, cassis and roasted coffee beans. Full-bodied taste with vividly pronounced acidity, meaty rich and ripe tannins and intense fruit of blackcurrants. Tremendously long finish with a robust and muscular edge. Very youthful and energetic wine that will last well over ten years from now.

1994 *Vin Santo Avignonesi* (Tuscany) 94p
2005/2015 x4 • D 1 h / G 1 h

Fine 375 ml bottle. Decanted two hours. Very deep golden colour. On the nose almonds and caramel. On the palate complex and balanced with hints of ripe melon, honey, caramel, and dried fruits aromas. This is full bodied and sweet but with good balancing crisp acidity. Young, gorgeously ful and creamy, loaded with caramel and a mouth-watering long finish.

1971 *Chambertin Camille Giroud* (Côte de Nuits) 94p
2001/2020 x2 • D 1.5 h / G 2.5 h

This is a vintage of big red Burgundys - more power, less elegance. So is the case with this wine. Surprisingly intense brick red colour with orange tints. Pronounced, dense and rustic nose with opulent fruit, sweaty horse saddle, roasted coffee, and rowanberries. Vigorous medium-bodied wine with fresh acidity, dense red fruit flavour of cherries and cranberries and supple tannins. Good length with youthful character. Delightful wine!

1994 *Vintage Port Graham's* (Portugal) 94p
2003/2040 x4 • D 4 h / G 4 h

Opaque ruby purple colour. Extremely dense, complex and rich nose with liquorice, orange blossom, violets, medicinal notes, roasted coffee, and nutty aromas. A sweet, full-bodied wine with intense dark fruit flavours with big ripe tannins and a warming long length. Anise, orange blossoms, violets, brambles, nuts, and medicinal notes all well pronounced in flavours. Beautifully balanced rich port with fragrant style, even to drink now.

NUMBER 575.

NUMBER 576.

NUMBER 577.

NUMBER 578.

NUMBER 579.

1997 Vin Santo Isole e Olena (Tuscany) 94p

2003/2020 x4 • D 10 min / G 2 h

Absolutely one of the loveliest modern Vin Santos ever made. Such an intense amber colour with enormous viscosity. A very rich, dense, sweet, honeyed wine with nutty aromas and loads of sweet spices. Lusciously sweet, moderately high acidity and intense fruit with an oxidative and nutty style make this elegant, full-bodied wine very appealing. The immense length is utterly charming. High alcohol level of 18% is well integrated and the dense oily texture is so thick. Amazing young wine!

1971 La Tâche Domaine de la Romanée-Conti (Côte de Nuits) 94p

2007/2020 x7 • D 1.5 h / G 2 h

Fine looking bottle with excellent level. Bright, moderately intense cherry red colour. The very youthful nose is rich and delicate full of ripe red berries, mainly cherries, and floral aromas. Dry, high-acidity and firm wine with very intense fruitiness. Long mineral red fruit finish. This La Tâche seems to be at its perfect stage right now with enough complexity and a supple balanced structure. Can easily keep for another 10 to 15 years more.

2003 Montrachet Domaine de la Romanée-Conti (Côte de Beaune) 94p

2007/2020 x3 • D 2 h / G 3 h

An extremely ripe vintage. The harvest was the earliest in twenty years. Bright, straw yellow colour. Pronounced, refined toasty nose with hints of vanilla, spices, butter, minerals, and ripe tropical fruits, such as pineapple. Dry, medium-bodied wine with moderate acidity and a viscous texture of buttery flavour. The toasty vanilla aromas marry well with the ripe and intensive tropical fruits. A pronounced minerality refreshes the palate delightfully. Long, mineral and toasty finish. Total production for this year was 2,871 bottles.

1955 Château d'Yquem (Sauternes) 94p

2004/2020 x3 • D 2 h / G 2 h

For us, the Château d'Yquem is one of the most consistent wine producers in the world. It is the combination of continuity, thrive for excellence and the unique micro-climate that are the key quality factors that many would like to duplicate, but few can achieve. Another key factor is the uncompromisingly low yields produced - only 9 hectolitres per ha - the equivalent of one glass of wine per vine. It hardly ever makes a faint wine and this glorious 1955 gives us a great reason to believe that.

Good-looking château bottling. Fully mature, but still very youthful and fresh. It has a deep golden, slightly brownish colour. Lovely honeyed nose. This is a well-designed, rich and very ripe Yquem, and not too sweet. Very good acidity and balance. This wine should be drunk alone as a desert, or with fresh foie gras. Not the most concentrated and richest Yquem, but a profound drink now and in the near future.

1949 Nuits-St-Georges 'Les St. Georges' Henri Gouges 94p
(Côte de Nuits)
2004/2015 x3 • D / G 1.5 h

A brilliant vintage highlighted by this brilliant wine from Henri Gouges, one of the first domaine bottlers in Burgundy. Bright, clear cherry red colour with an orange hue. Appealingly open, complex and developed, concentrated fragrant nose with intense red berry aromas and flowers. Dry, medium-bodied palate with crisp delicate acidity and very supportive ripe tannins. Sweet intensive fruit with roasted pine nut aroma are highlighted in the long finish. Lovely wine with balance and harmony.

1986 Grange Penfolds (South Australia) 94p
2003/2020 x9 • D 2 h / G 2 h

Fine looking bottle. Level by the neck. Decanted two hours. Deep, intense garnet colour with tawny tints. Pronounced, intense nose full of rich and ripe, sweet dark fruit aromas, blackcurrants, mint, spices, and vanilla. A firm and intense full-bodied palate which is impressively balanced between a moderate level of acidity, fleshy tannins and ripe fruit with grilled root vegetable and herbaceous aromas. Long, opulent and meaty finish with mint and fresh basil flavours along with unique concentration.

1983 Château Palmer (Margaux) 94p
2007/2015 x9 • D 3 h / G 2 h

After the cold, damp weather in the first five months of the year, June was warm and dry and the flowering took place under excellent conditions. A heat wave in July was followed by warm, damp weather in August that unfortunately encouraged the spread of disease. Thankfully, September was dry and hot, allowing the grapes to ripen slowly and evenly. After a string of hot, sunny days at the end of the month and into early October, the sugar levels were similar if not superior to those in 1982.

A medium-intense, tawny red colour. Complex developed aromas of farmyard, mocha, tobacco, cedar, and blackcurrants. Medium-bodied palate with stalky tannins, fleshy ripe dark fruit and spicy, toasty cigar aromas with vegetal nuances of canned bamboo shoots. An opulent wine with a long, persistent, lean finish with chewy tannins.

1937 Château Pétrus (Pomerol) 94p
2003/2020 x4 • D 1 h / G 1 h

A fine looking bottle, Château-bottled with the level by the neck. Decanted one hour. Moderately intense marrow red colour. Pronounced nose with rich ripe dark fruit with smokey, cedary and toasty aromas. A very ripe and rich style with a fleshy full-bodied mouth-feel. Mineral and stalky tannins compliment ripe and intense fruitiness. More robust than elegant in style but very appealing. Still very drinkable and good.

1999 Monte Bello Ridge *(Santa Cruz Mountains)* 94p
2007/2020 x3 • D 3 h / G 3 h

This outstanding vintage in California was also the first vintage in Montebello that Petit Verdot was included. A clear, medium-intense extracted ruby colour. Deep and intense aromas of ink, ripe black currants, cedar, sweet rum, coco, warming spices, and toastiness. Dry, moderately high acidity with firm persistent tannins and medium-bodied structure form a backbone to the wine. Intense fruit of blackcurrants balances the texture. Sweet spices and a touch of green aromas stand out in the moderately long finish. A concentrated and powerful wine with an attractive elegance and in a very good phase at the moment.

1997 Montrachet Domaine Ramonet *(Côte de Beaune)* 94p
2006/2025 x6 • D 1 h / G 3 h

Bright, yellow green colour with medium intensity. Opulent, ripe tropical fruit aromas with sweet and spicy tones. Peppermint, coffee and toasty aromas. Dry, medium-bodied, intense and very mineral palate with crisp acidity, fresh ripe yellow fruits, roasted coffee, and mint. Long buttery finish. A rich and complex wine with a delightful opulence.

1988 Romanée St Vivant Domaine de la Romanée-Conti 94p
(Côte de Nuits) 2007/2015 x3 • D 1 h / G 2 h

Bright, cherry red colour with an orange rim. Very complex nose with the wine evolving in the glass enormously. Starting from fragrant red fruit aromas with floral elegance, changing into smoky, gamey aromas after a while. Half an hour later the nose reveals very fragrant floral aromas with strawberries and raspberries. A light-bodied palate with crisp acidity, elegant, ripe tannins and an intense fruitiness of ripe cherries, wild strawberries and raspberries, all in great balance with a mineral twist and a long elegant finish.

1975 Château Trotanoy *(Pomerol)* 94p
2007/2015 x15 • D 2 h / G 2 h

The bottle was in A1 condition. Decanted 45 minutes. Good, healthy, dark red colour with the barest tinge of tawny to it. A really fine nose, displaying some almonds, oriental spices and coconut. An adequate impact on the palate, showing a very rounded structure with a backbone of fine tannins. Decent acidity but it lacks a little intensity and grip. The previous time we tasted this wine, we thought it was drying out badly, which shows how noticeably bottle variation can affect your opinion of a wine. This time it is ripe, intense and vigorous, exactly as fine as it should be.

NUMBER 588. NUMBER 589. NUMBER 590. NUMBER 591.

1996 *Musigny Domaine Leroy* (Côte de Nuits) 94p

2006/2030 x2 • D 2 h / G 3 h

A moderately intense, ruby colour. Very intense, youthful nose with touches of evolved, gamey characteristics. Mainly ripe wild strawberries, violets, liquorice, smoke, and spices. Medium-bodied crisp palate with very elegant, persistent tannins and an intense fruitiness with blueberries, raspberries and wild strawberries. Mineral long, lingering finish. Delicate and delightful wine with great potential.

1978 *Volnay Premier Cru Les Frémiets Camille Giroud* 94p
(Côte de Beaune) 2001/2015 x3 • D 1 h / G 2 h

The best year of the decade allowed Camille Giroud to produce this rich wine. Bright, cherry red colour with an orange hue. Opulent and sweet, jammy red fruit aromas of cherries and brambles. Full-bodied, elegant, refined tannins combine well with delicate crisp acidity and rich, ripe, sweet red fruit aromas. Nutty tones in the silky finish.

1998 *Opus One Mondavi & Mouton-Rothschild* (Napa Valley) 94p

2002/2020 x7 • D 1 h / G 2.5 h

Already slowed down by winter flooding caused by El Niño, the growing season of 1998 was the coolest Opus One had seen since 1991. With foggy mornings and moderate temperatures recorded during the summer, the weather extended into late October, promoting slow ripening and a very long hang time for Opus One's grapes. The excellent weather in September and October made for an orderly harvest of the five classic Bordeaux varietals. The blend has 91 percent Cabernet Sauvignon, 7 percent Cabernet Franc and 1 percent each of Merlot, Malbec and Petit Verdot.

Deep, intense ruby colour. Energetic, fresh nose, full of ripe cassis and dark fruits, cedar and chocolate aromas. A full-bodied wine with balanced acidity, refined meaty tannins and rich, intense and almost jammy fruit of cassis. Although a big wine, it is at the moment beautifully balanced with a harmonious long finish. Still very youthful, of course.

1998 *Barbera d'Asti Quarum* (Piedmont) 94p

2001/2010 x 2 • D 45 min / G 1.5 h

This is the result when the world's five best Barbera producers combine their skills - a real masterpiece and tribute to the vibrant Barbera variety. Maybe because of Quarum being a new project from 1997, the producers - Berta, Braida, Coppo, Prunotto and Vietti managed to create a better wine from this difficult but good year compared to their debut super-vintage of 1997.

A dark, moderately intense violet colour. The seductive and opulent nose is feminine serving plums, roasted coffee beans and perfumed aromas of violets. The palate is surprisingly rich whilst fresh with vivid acidity and firm, supple tannins. A ripe and intense cherry taste combined with lovely toasty and spicy flavours of new oak. The long, lingering aftertaste leaves a really fleshy taste. A wine for immediate pleasure, will not benefit from longer ageing.

1997 *Riesling Smaragd Dürnsteiner Kellerberg FX Pichler* 94p
(Wachau)
2007/2015 x2 • D 1 h / G 2 h

Franz Xaver Pichler, also known as the pope of Wachau, makes his wine in large wooden vats with natural yeasts, ageing for half a year.

This wine has a bright, moderately pale, green-yellow colour. The very opulent nose shows loads of ripe peaches, tropical fruits, mango, honeysuckle, and a refined spicy nose of nutmeg. Plenty of ripe fruit makes the wine appear semi-dry, despite its dry nature. The oily texture together with a mineral rich finish shows tremendous power that can handle a very long ageing, at least for more 10 years.

1955 *Château Lafleur (Pomerol)* 94p
2004/2010 x4 • D 1 h / G 2 h

For many people, Lafleur is the only other wine in Pomerol that has both the excellence and capability of Château Pétrus. There are only 4.5 ha of vines, planted as 60 percent Merlot and 40 percent Cabernet Franc, with an average of 35 years of age.

Good appearance, château-bottled and the level was high-shoulder. Very dark and exciting colour. Complex, delicate nose with aromas of tobacco and smoky meat. Full, round, and clean fruit on the palate. Lots of depth and elegance here, but somehow it did not have the delicate richness and weight of the Petrus 1955. Otherwise a first-rate and exotic wine.

1986 *Martha's Vineyard Cabernet Sauvignon Heitz (Napa Valley)* 94p
2004/2010 x3 • D 1 h / G 1 h

A fine bottle. Decanted one hour. Deep, youthful colour. Slightly leathery, eucalyptus, mint, and oak nose. Not very intense or complex, but beautifully integrated ripe tannins, along with the exotic fruit and velvety-bodied texture carries this wine nicely to the finish. A pleasure to drink now.

1947 *Château Margaux (Margaux)* 94p
2007/2015 x13 • D 30 min / G 1 h

Bottle in good condition with top-shoulder level. Decanted 30 minutes. Quite light, red/brown colour. Open and sound nose with an abundance of sweet raspberry and wild berry aromas and flavours, all with an appealing cedar overlay. This quite light bodied and not very tannic wine opens beautifully in the glass. Not the

NUMBER 596.

NUMBER 597.

NUMBER 598.

599

NUMBER 599.

Château d'Ampuis
Philippe Guigal

biggest or the most intense of Margaux, but has lots of finesse and lovely balance. On the palate an elegant sweetness of alcohol and ripe fruit. This is a wonderful, kind-hearted Margaux.

1953 *Unico Bodegas Vega Sicilia* (Ribera del Duero)   94p
2006/now x8 • D 2 h / G 2 h

In our opinion this is one of the best Unicos of the 1950's. When we last had the opportunity to taste this almost majestic wine at a tasting arranged by Decanter in London, the half century that this wine has lived through had started to show.

The colour was quite brown even for its age, but there was still a noble purple-red shimmer peeking through. The scent was typical of the Unico elegance, full of berries with a breath of eucalyptus and herbs - promisingly intensive and clear. Very well balanced, fruity and fresh. The aftertaste was maybe somewhat short and dryish. The first time we tasted this wine was at the winery in the early 90's. The experience then approached perfection. Though the bottles now being tasted also came straight from the producer's cellars, we could not help but recall longingly those moments from over ten years ago. Now this wonderful wine is losing its peak condition, in a very harmonious and beautiful way. Still a very attractive wine!

1950 *Château Haut-Brion* (Graves)   94p
2002/2015 x3 • D 2 h / G 1 h

In 1950 Haut-Brion made first-rate wine. The bottle was in good condition with high-shoulder level. Decanted two hours. Dark, healthy colour. Wide and open nose with cedar, smoke and black berries. Very full and complex wine with good balance. At first it was a bit too tight and unwilling, but after one and a half hours, it opened up completely and developed opulence and exquisite fruit flavours. Good and fine ending with velvety texture and viscosity. Will not improve, but will last.

1949 *Château Rieussec* (Sauternes)   94p
2000/2015 x4 • D 1 h / G 3 h

Bottle was without label, otherwise in excellent condition. Decanted 45 minutes. A noble, deep, golden colour. A fresh, slightly sweet, honeyed and vanilla flavoured nose. A full, rich, multi-dimensional wine, which is still very youthful and luscious. Good depth and balance. The follow-through is brilliant.

1959 *Château Lynch-Bages* (Pauillac)   94p
2004/2015 x3 • D 1 h / G 1 h

Good looking négociant-bottled wine. Level was by the neck. Decanted 45 minutes. Fully mature, but still youthful looking and fresh wine. It has a deep dark ruby colour, but with a touch more maturity than the 1961. Lovely complex nose of minerals, roasted herbs, acacia flowers and red and black fruits. This is a well-made, full and ripe Lynch-Bages. Very good acidity and balance. A bit tight and dry aftertaste. Not the most concentrated and richest Lynch-Bages, but most enjoyable drink now and tomorrow.

1949 Château Léoville Barton *(Saint-Julien)* 94p

2007/2010 x4 • D 45 min / G 1 h

Bottle in good condition. Decanted 45 minutes. Very full, deep vigorous colour. Profound and sound nose, perhaps a little old fashioned, in a good way. Very rich and fat wine. Splendid combination of fruit and concentration. Long, classy and harmonious. Very good indeed, if not great. Now fading a little, so drink up.

1900 Château Lafite-Rothschild *(Pauillac)* 94p

2007/now x2 • D 1 h / G 1 h

Négociant-bottled Lafite with mid-shoulder level. Capsule and cork were in good condition. Decanted 30 minutes. This 1900 Lafite was a few decades past its peak, however, still very enjoyable. Good, clear colour. On the nose this fine bottle blended spicy, delicious plum, sweet cherry aromas and meaty undertones. Not very intense or powerful, but has a delicate, elegant structure and refined, mature fruit flavours. The finish was smooth and exceptionally long. Very classic and comfortable to drink.

1943 Barolo Monfortino Riserva Giacomo Conterno *(Piedmont)* 94p

2003/2010 x2 • D 1 h / G 1 h

Fine looking bottle. Level was by the neck. Decanted one hour. The colour is deep and intense. The nose displayed complex aromas. The palate was wonderfully intense: full of fruits, very structured, keenly concentrated, and well-balanced. The tannins are soft and the finish is fresh and long. A splendid wine which still has some future left.

1983 Musigny Vieilles Vignes Comte Georges de Vogüé 94p
(Côte de Nuits) **2004/2020 x1 • D 1 h / G 1 h**

A developing medium-deep brick red colour. The nose is loaded with primary fruitiness, dark cherries and cherry confectionary as well as fresh raspberries. Some volatile notes. The youthfulness continues on the palate, intense and clean fruitiness with perfumery elegance. A long lasting wine that shows very well today but will keep for a decade or two more.

1949 Château Margaux *(Margaux)* 94p

2006/2015 x9 • D 1 h / G 2 h

We have tasted this wine several times and it has always been very delicious and enjoyable. Last time we sensed a touch of eucalyptus, earthy, and sweet strawberry aromas on the nose. Due to its surprising power and firmness, it is almost Pauillac in style. Sweet and intense fruit. A full-bodied palate with lovely soft tannins and a long, elegant finish. Acidity is starting to show now, so it is time to drink the wine soon.

1958   Barolo Pio Cesare *(Piedmont)*   94p

2005/2010 x3 • D 1 h / G 1 h

This fully matured Pio Cesare Barolo 1958 had a beautiful, simple black label, and it was in good general condition. Decanted one hour. A dark and deep colour with an orange-mahogany tint on the rim. Quite a straightforward and powerful nose at first. But after one hour, it became more deep and complex with a hint of truffle, mushroom and black fruit flavours. A beautiful texture on the palate, full and mouth-filling. A delicious taste combined with some flavours of black, sweet fruits and spicy tannins, there was also a slight acidic sharpness lifting the palate, but yet again the ending was wonderfully soft, hot and long. The wine has held extremely well. Old Barolos do not get much better than this!

1971   Tignanello Antinori *(Tuscany)*   94p

2007/now x3 • D 1 h / G 1 h

In 1971 Tignanello became the second "Super-Tuscan" wine after the winemaker decided to alter the blend, lessening the amount of white grapes in violation of the Chianti rules. Tignanello 1971, released in 1974, set the stage for an Italian wine revolution and brought the international spotlight to Tuscany with other Cabernet Sauvignon infused-blends including Sassicaia, Ornellaia and Solaia.

Tignanello is produced exclusively from the Tignanello vineyard, 47 ha at Antinori's Santa Cristina Estate. It was the first Sangiovese to be aged in small oak barrels, the first Tuscan red wine in modern times to use a non-traditional grape variety, Cabernet, in the blend, and among the first red wines made in Chianti with no white grapes. Tignanello, originally a Chianti Classico Riserva labeled Vigneto Tignanello, was first vinified as a single vineyard wine in the 1970 vintage, when it contained 20 percent Canaiolo and 5 percent Trebbiano and Malvasia, aged in a small oak cooperage. With the 1971 vintage the wine became a Vino da Tavola della Toscana and was named Tignanello after the vineyard from which it originates. From this vintage onwards, Tignanello stopped adhering to the rules laid down by Chianti Classico Disciplinare, and with the 1975 vintage, white grapes were totally eliminated. No Tignanello was produced during 1972-1974.

A dusty, old looking bottle. Bought from Milan. Level by the neck. Decanted 30 minutes. Quite a dark, healthy colour. An open, spicy Cabernet nose with vanilla, cassis and black fruit aromas. Very fruity. Surprisingly youthful and vigorous. A much better bottle than the previous ones, not nearly as dry. Lots of depth and a good acidity. Delicate, not very powerful or rich, but has class and elegance. Slight sharpness at the finish, but very enjoyable overall. It was a very brave choice for Tignanello to make back then, but certainly worth the risk. A lovely wine!

1979   Barolo Granbussia Riserva Aldo Conterno *(Piedmont)*   94p

2006/now x2 • D 1 h / G 1 h

This is the best Barolo we have tasted from this fine year, which had a cold snowy winter, a late spring and a hot and dry summer. The bottle was in A1 condition. Decanted 30 minutes. A very good, bright deep colour. Some orange at the rim. A strong, spicy and fruity nose. Full and quite tannic with low acidity but good, rich fruit. Well balanced. Fairly long. A rather masculine wine, it even has some soft spots.

1990 *Solaia Antinori* (Tuscany)   *94p*

2006/2015 x8 • D 1 h / G 1 h

A deep, intense, violet colour showing some development. Pronounced nose of ripe dark berries: cassis, blueberry, blackberry, spiciness, pencil shavings, and hints of horse stable and tar. The full-bodied palate shows balancing acidity along with intense and rich fruitiness and refined ripe tannic structure. Intense flavours of dark berries, cherries, spices, liquorice, and anise show great complexity while escorting the long lingering finish. Reaching its peak but will keep well until 2015.

1900 *Château La Mission-Haut-Brion* (Graves)   *94p*

2003/now • D 30 min / G 1 h

The label is badly bin-soiled, illegible and, although the cork and capsule are embossed, the vintage on these is also illegible. This was identified as the 1900 vintage from the old cellar book.

A fantastic old wine. Level was top-shoulder. A dark red with an amber edge. Complex aromas of blackberry, mint and chocolate. Full-bodied and extremely well bound, with smooth tannins and a long, gentle aftertaste. Beautiful and harmonious.

1996 *Barolo Le Vigne Luciano Sandrone* (Piedmont)   *94p*

2007/2020 x3 • D 1 h / G 1 h

A medium deep developing brick red colour. The layered nose is full of interesting nuances: violets, tar, roasted aromas, sour cherries, and herbs. The wine changes constantly in the glass bringing out new aromas over time. Lasted well in the glass. Silky texture, ripe firm tannins and refreshingly high firming acidity. An appetising and refreshing wine that is in a great phase of its life span. However, no rush to drink up. Highly recommendable.

1990 *Grande Cuvée Billecart-Salmon* (Champagne)   *94p*

2004/2030 x4 • D 1 h / G 1 h

Superbly well-made wine from this great fruity and structured vintage. A refined and minerally nose packed with delicate fruitiness. Toasty bread aromas, cream, toffee, and gunflint notes. Caramelised sugar and yeasty notes overwhelm the palate. Tightly knit structure of crisp acidity and elegant fruitiness. A silky texture and well-integrated bubbles. Very youthful but enjoyable. This wine will develop and bloom over the next ten years.

1997 *Montrachet Domaine de la Romanée-Conti* (Côte de Beaune)   *94p*

2004/2020 x3 • D 30 min / G 1.5 h

Very hot summer and good weather during the harvest guaranteed a third good year in a row for white Burgundy. Due to the heat, wines express more exotic fruitiness and less acidity compared to 1996 for instance. Such is the case with this wine. A bright, moderately pale yellow colour. The wonderfully intense and complex nose reveals ripe pineapples, butter, toastiness, and spices. The very refined medium-bodied palate shows gentle acidity with rich minerality to balance the broad oily texture and exotic fruitiness. The alcohol level of 14 percent is very well integrated with the spicy oakiness. Good concentration and long finish. Drinking up perfectly already now. 2,644 bottles produced.

1996 R.D. Bollinger *(Champagne)* 94p

2006/2025x3 • D 30 min / G 1 h

Champagne Bollinger launched the R.D. concept (Recemment Degorgé) with the 1952 vintage in 1961. The blend is similar to the Grande Année but the wine is cellared for 8 to 25 years before launch. The other peculiarity of the R.D. is its Extra Brut nature with a maximum of 5 g/l dosage. It is always a lively and truly unique wine. The 1996 was launched fairly young and therefore the difference to the regular Grande Année is not great but still significant.

A moderately intense yellow colour with a rich pearl necklace of refined bubbles. Typical refined oxidative style combined with delicate Asian spiciness, lemon and exotic fruits. An open, extremely vivid and intense wine with lovely mousse. This wine seems to have no best before date since its lovely crisp acidity generates backbone for long-term ageing.

1983 Barca Velha Ferreira *(Portugal)* 94p

2007/now x4 • D 1 h / G 1 h

Top vintage for Barca Velha. Developed, clear, moderately intense tawny colour. The very complex medium-intense nose offers an extensive range of charming aromas. Ripe plums and violet aromas with figs and damsons enriched by leathery animal aromas with nuts, dark chocolate and a touch of tar. A fleshy full-bodied palate with tightly-knit fruitiness with firm, ripe, velvety tannins and great length. It is amazing how charming, youthful and intense this traditional and oxidatively vinified wine can be. Drinking perfectly now but it still has potential to age a few more years.

1976 Romanée-Conti Domaine de la Romanée-Conti *(Côte de Nuits)* 94p

2006/2020x1 • D 1 h / G 2 h

Fine looking bottle. Level was 2 cm. Decanted 1.5 hours. A maturing garnet colour. A restrained nose of cherries, earthy notes and spicy mushroom nuances. Some sweet appearing chocolate notes on the palate. A medium-bodied lively wine with silky texture, low ripe tannin and balanced high acidity. Not one of the most impressive Romanée-Contis, but the elegance and harmony of this wine are able to charm. Drinking very well today, however, the balance is enough to carry the wine for another decade or two.

1979 Opus One Mondavi & Mouton-Rothschild *(Napa Valley)* 94p

2007/2010 x3 • D 30 min / G 1 h

Opus One was founded by Baron Philippe de Rothschild, the famous proprietor of Château Mouton-Rothschild, and the well-known Napa Valley vintner Robert Mondavi. By combining the winemaking traditions and innovations of both families, their singular goal was to create an inimitable wine in the heart of the Napa Valley.

NUMBER 617.

NUMBER 618.

NUMBER 619.

NUMBER 620.

Mouton-Rothschild's winemaker, Lucien Sionneau, and Timothy Mondavi made the partnership's first vintage at the Robert Mondavi Winery in 1979. This first Opus One was made and aged in barrels at the Robert Mondavi Winery until the fall of 1991, when the winery celebrated its grand opening and first harvest in the new facility.

The 1979 had a seemingly perfect growing season from bud break to the beginning of harvest, but it was challenged by rain in September. Early harvesting yielded clean, well-balanced fruit and a wine of resilience and finesse. Blended from 80 percent Cabernet Sauvignon, 16 percent Cabernet Franc, 4 percent Merlot and aged for 24 months in new French oak barrels.

A fine looking bottle with by the neck level. Decanted 30 minutes. A very bright, dark ruby colour with little browning. An ntense and sound nose, with a touch of cedar, tobacco, dark chocolate, and blackcurrant aromas. Still surprisingly youthful, luscious and mouth-filling, with a medium-full body and good balance. Already a bit too dry and not as complex as one would wish, but it has a long and tasty ending. An excellent first vintage with a few more years to go.

1999   *Vieilles Vignes Françaises Bollinger* (Champagne)   94p
2006/2020 x3 • D 30 min / G 1 h

Until the phylloxera ravages of the late 19th century, all vineyards of the Champagne region were cultivated using the layered provigneage method. Three tiny plots of Bollinger's vineyards resisted phylloxera for reasons unknown, and are being cultivated using the laborious ancient method. The yield on those Pinot Noir parcels is 40 to 50 percent lower than usual, amounting to 300 percent higher costs. It was an English author Cyril Ray (he wrote Bollinger's history), who came up with the idea for the Vieilles Vignes Françaises. He persuaded Madame Bollinger in 1969 to bottle the VVF separately. The product was first launched onto the market in 1974, and became an instant success and a collector's item.

The wine used to originate from two parcels in Aÿ and one in Bouzy. The Bouzy plot lost its battle against phylloxera in 2004, making VVF a monocru wine. The total vineyard size is now 0,36 ha. Minuscule in volume and profitability, VVF remains very important to Bollinger due to its role as the "living museum of Champagne". The 1999 was an outstanding vintage throughout the region. Therefore it is no surprise that the Vieilles Vignes Francaises offer an exceptionally fine experience.

A light steely yellow colour, rich in fine bubbles. A concentrated and complex nose with spices, crepes and apples. Very dense, powerful and rich on palate with appealing roundness. The crisp acidity is well hidden into dense structure, suggesting the wine to be consumed with food rather than as on its own. For its young age surprisingly open and enjoyable, but will not hit its peak until ten years from now.

1994   *Barolo Monfortino Riserva Giacomo Conterno* (Piedmont)   94p
2004/2020 x2 • D 2 h / G 3 h

Decanted two hours. Dark, deep colour. This Monfortino had a stunning nose with aromas of red currant, liquorice, cherries, and black fruits. Very ripe and full-bodied with a powerful but tight palate. Good concentration and balance. The finish was long and leathery with pleasant dryness and rich, earthy flavours. This is delicious enough to drink now but it needs another ten years to reach its peak.

1926   Château Mouton-Rothschild *(Pauillac)*   *94p*
2003/2010 x4 • D 1 h / G 30 min

After having pioneered château bottling in 1924, Baron Philippe de Rothschild commissioned architect Charles Sicils in 1926 to build the 100-meter long barrel hall known as the Grand Chai. This first year cellar, which is still in use today, measuring approximately 100 by 25 meters, regulates the temperature between 12° and 14°. 1926 was a successful, small volume year for Mouton.

A good-looking magnum with top-shoulder level. In the past we have tasted Mouton 1926 twice from a normal bottle, and both bottles were quite tired and did not reveal all of their qualities anymore. The variation between the different bottle formats grows greater as the decades go by, and some vintages that appear relatively tired in a bottle can be much more alive and fresh in a magnum. This Mouton 1926 magnum proved that point well.

Decanted two hours before tasting. Very good, dark and bright colour. Wonderful, classic old Cabernet nose with the touch of sweet black fruits, herbs and cedar. Full-bodied and powerful but in a gentle way. Excellent depth and ripeness with good balance. Long and smooth finish. Otherwise an excellent wine, but it dried out in the glass too fast, becoming more marked by acidity and hard tannin after 30 minutes. Anyway, a truly respectable example of this wine.

1967   Brunello di Montalcino Riserva, Il Poggione *(Tuscany)*   *94p*
2007/2020 x3 • D 30 min / G 1 h

The bottle was like new. Decanted 15 minutes, some sediment. Light, weak colour typical for an old Brunello. Sweet fruit, complex and spicy nose. Still holding very well. Quite long on the palate, good grip, straightforward and well balanced. One of the best Brunellos from 1967.

1959   Château Pichon Longueville Comtesse de Lalande *(Pauillac)*   *94p*
2006/2010 x 12 • D 1 h / G 1 h

A fine looking négociant-bottling with by the neck level. Decanted 45 minutes. The colour is very deep and dark with ruby highlights. The bouquet has the spiciness of really ripe Cabernet Sauvignon, and a hint of exotic fruit. A very long, fresh aftertaste gives an added dimension. This is a subtle wine, but one with the sort of perfect balance and aftertaste that one wishes for every wine. A really great vintage at Pichon.

1888   Clos-de-Vougeot Louis Jadot *(Côte de Nuits)*   93p
2004/now x4 • D 45 min / G 1 h

Superb looking bottle, covered in dust and mud. Has outstanding by-the-neck level. Decanted 45 minutes. Quite deep, bright and pure, brownish red colour. Open and sound nose with glamorous, sweet fruit, chocolate, caramel, and old leather aromas. A gentle and charming wine with lots of its fundamental power and backbone left. On the palate gentle, sweet, with nice acidity. Rich and quite firm, and has good balance and complexity. A bit modest, dry and short aftertaste. An ancient wine from a great terroir.

1929   Château Mouton-Rothschild *(Pauillac)*   93p
2003/2010 x4 • D 1 h / G 1 h

A kind and warm wine from this superb vintage. An excellent looking bottle with good label and top-shoulder level. Decanted 45 minutes. Deep, clear, browning colour. A rich nose of ripe dark berries, cedar and exotic spices with mineral tones. Pleasant yet still powerful enough with some acidity and sweet fruit left. Well balanced but also a bit one-dimensional. A long and giving finish. Very interesting now and in good circumstances will still keep for a few more years.

1969   Grüner Veltliner Spätlese Schloss Gobelsburg *(Kamptal)*   93p
2007/now x3 • D 30 min / G 1 h

The 1969 vintage Schloss Gobelsburg is an epitome of traditional style winemaking. No settling, fermentation in wood casks of local oak or acacia wood, and several rackings with an oxidative effect. They have replicated that process today with their Tradition series Grüner Veltliners and Rieslings. We opened these two bottles, which were in excellent condition with only three centimetres ullage. This fairly pale, clear yellow coloured wine has more character and complexity than many upper class Montrachets. It had a great balance and structure. There was great charm and depth in the smooth yet fresh aftertaste. A surprisingly youthful and imposing wine and great proof of aging capacity of Grüner Veltliner.

1898   La Romanée Louis Jadot *(Côte de Nuits)*   93p
2005/now x1 • D 30 min / G 1 h

Estate bottled. Fill level 3 cm. A fairly intensive, slightly cloudy cherry red colour. A very delicious cherry nose with hints of violet and intensive fruit. Decayed meaty aromas create additional fragrance dimensions. The vividly acidic, fairly full taste is complemented by an intensive, silky mouth-feel. The abundant taste is complemented by fairly high alcohol and slight volatility. Sweet nuances of boiled root vegetables in the aftertaste. An incredibly vivid Burgundy with a lot of personality and a great expression of classic, refined Pinot Noir properties. Will not develop positively any more, but will keep for a few more years.

1985 Château Mouton-Rothschild *(Pauillac)* 93p
2007/2015 x11 • D 1.5 h /G 2 h

This Paul Delvaux Mouton had a lovely depth of colour. A very good, ripe, toasty, mature, and intense cedar nose. Still quite a tannic, masculine but fruity wine. Pretty forward in style, but a very good complexity and a solid backbone. It does not possess the perfume of Lafite-Rothschild or the power of Latour, nevertheless, this is a very attractive Pauillac. An excellent bottle. Ready, will last well into the next decade, but will not improve much.

1899 Château Cos d'Estournel *(Saint-Estèphe)* 93p
2004/now x3 • D 15 min / G 45 min

Christie's bottle. A clear, medium-intense tawny brown colour. A pronounced complex and developed nose that is rich, leathery, chocolaty, with marzipan and bell pepper aromas. A balancing acidity and juicy texture, with softened yet persistent tannins, give backbone to this moderately long, medium-bodied wine. The fruit intensity is moderately low but on an acceptable level for a wine of such a noble age.

1953 Château Latour *(Pauillac)* 93p
2006/2010 x7 • D 1 h / G 1 h

The 1953 Latour has never been one of our favourite vintages. Many wine connoisseurs have talked about it in superlatives. In those days, when the wine was delivering such enormous enjoyment, they were not yet aware of fine wines, we are sorry to say. Now this wine has passed its peak, but it is still worthy of some interest. Our last tasting notes were: A very good, promising colour, deeper than in the 1952. A fresh mint, cedar and smoke nose. The palate was sweet and rich with distinct fruit and flavour. Great balance but to us it showed some signs of breaking down. This Latour must have been an extremely gentle, yet so powerful and splendid wine during the 80`s. Though maybe not as powerful now, it still has a kind, harmonious and warm nature. A good bottle rates easily over 90 points. Tasted seven times.

1982 Dom Pérignon Moët & Chandon *(Champagne)* 93p
2007/2020 x16 • D 15 min / G 1 h

Dom Pérignon is reputedly a wine that requires time to show its greatness. This 1982 was a great example of this and the potential of Dom Pérignon. This ripe however firm structured vintage produced a spectacular DP, which is only starting to open up. Developed crystal clear golden colour. Developing, creamy and tropical nose of nuts, honey and creamy toastiness. Ripe pronounced palate with tightly knit fruitiness and charming minerality. Stylishly steely and linear acidity promising a great future. Creamy and silky texture with great length and finesse. All the pieces are there for this great Dom Pérignon. Give it a decade more and it will excel.

1899 *Château Lafite-Rothschild* (Pauillac) 93p

2005/now x2 • D 20 min / G 1 h

A good looking half-bottle. Bottled by Nicholas. Decanted twenty minutes. Fill level top shoulder. A little cloudy, medium-deep, cherry colour. Slightly closed nose - cherries, earth, horse. Fairly light and acidic structure gives the wine elegance with medium-tannins giving firmness. The taste, however, lacks intensity and fruit. Slightly short, incomplete and bony, sweet aftertaste. This wine has seen better days, but still provides an enjoyable experience.

1950 *Château Mouton-Rothschild* (Pauillac) 93p

2006/2015 x4 • D 1 h / G 2 h

Another perfect looking bottle. The level was by the neck. Decanted for only 30 minutes. A bright, ruby red colour with relatively little sign of development. At the start the nose was a bit blocked, but after 30 minutes it opened with an intense bouquet of blackcurrant, other black fruits and hints of vanilla sweetness. Round and neat, but maybe not as fleshy and loaded as we remembered. A little too light and short in the aftertaste. Somewhat lighter and drier than the other two 1950s we had tasted last year. However, it is always a lovely and pleasant experience!

1957 *Barca Velha Ferreira* (Portugal) 93p

2006/2015 x3 • D 1 h / G 1 h

Fine old-looking bottle. The level was by the neck. Decanted 45 minutes. Very dark and mature colour. Sound, fragrant, earth and black currant bouquet. Surprisingly fresh and youthful on the palate and has a much better balance and fruit than the younger 1964 or 1966 Barca Velhas. Even though many comment that that Barca Velha tastes Bordeaux-like, we do not see it that way. It has its own style and taste that falls somewhere between new-style Douro wines and Vega Sicilia. Well, that is just one opinion. Very tasteful and full yet rustic. Slightly tannic texture and ripe mature fruitiness and vigorous acidity. Marvellous balance of power and finesse. Very enjoyable now, but not for too long.

1928 *Imperial Gran Reserva C.V.N.E.* (Rioja) 93p

2004/2010 x1 • D 1 h / G 1 h

This elegant 1928 Imperial came directly from the Bodega's antiquated cellars, and was in first-rate condition. Decanted 45 minutes before tasting. A good, dark and healthy red colour. At first the bouquet was a bit unclean and unrefined, but after 30 minutes in the glass it turned out far better than we initially thought it ever would - a fresh, graceful bouquet of sweet, toasty, gentle woody bouquet mixed with ripe black cherries and olive aromas. On the palate it was a bit dry and fruitless (but not entirely) with very low acidity, whilst simultaneously having a very good balance and intense mouth-feel with extremely soft and gentle tannins. A lovely and fragile wine with an extensive and silky aftertaste. We cherished it.

1945 *Château de Rayne-Vigneau Crème de Tête* (Sauternes) 93p
2003/2010 x3 • D 15 min / G 1 h

One of the four premier crus in Bommes. This wonderful estate is not only known for its wines but also for the treasure stones – such as white sapphire, onyx, quartz, and agates - in its vineyard. The vintage 1945 was outstanding in the Sauternes region. Very limited yield due to severe spring frosts and hail storms. The summer was very dry reducing the size of the berries. The crop ripened very early and produced highly concentrated grapes.

Bright golden amber colour. Intense, waxy nose with dried fruits, apricots, orange peel, vanilla, and spices. Medium sweet, oily texture with moderately high acidity and intense dried fruit flavours of apricot enhanced with spices and honey. Long intense mineral finish is well balanced with high viscosity and honeyed overtones.

1970 *R.D. Bollinger* (Champagne) 93p
2007/now x3 • D 20 min /G 1 h

A golden-yellow colour with modest amounts of small bubbles. A very complex and rich nose with strong yeasty aromas. A lovely Bollinger style wine with ripe apples notes combines well with the smoky aromas. A dry and crisp wine with delicate mousse and very edgy acidity. Great depth of flavours thanks to long ageing "sur lie". A lingering long, spicy, smoky, and lemony mineral finish. Drinking superbly now but will keep easily over a decade still.

1945 *Château Cos d'Estournel* (Saint-Estèphe) 93p
2000/2010 x4 • D 1 h / G 1 h

A fine looking Magnum. Level was by the neck. Decanted one hour. A medium-full, surprisingly mature colour for a magnum. Ripe, quite spicy but not too vigorous a nose. Medium to full-bodied, classy, lush and ripe on the palate. Not biting or overly tannic though. This has a lot of depth and it is still very vibrant.

1926 *Château La Mission-Haut-Brion* (Graves) 93p
2000/now x2 • D 1 h /G 1 h

Château-bottled. Level was top-shoulder, otherwise in good shape. Decanted one hour before tasting. Very deep, dark and brown colour. Generous nose with some moist undertones. Surprisingly sweet attack of fruit in the mouth. Full and very intense. Good structure and balance. Splendid bottle. Has held extremely well - a big-hearted surprise!

1921   Château Haut-Brion *(Graves)*   93p

2000/now x2 • D 1 h / G 1 h

1921 was an extremely hot and difficult year for the winemakers in Bordeaux. Generally the reds were good, with St. Emilion and Pomerol making some impressive results. The small crop was harvested very early, but unfortunately the very hot weather during the harvest prevented an all-around success. The wines often had excessive acidity and volatile notes. With hard work the great winemakers made exceptional wines like this Haut-Brion.

The bottle was in a good condition, ullage was top-shoulder. Bought from Christie's London and decanted one hour before tasting. A very deep, mature colour, but still much younger looking than its age would indicate. A complex and open nose of earth and truffles. Rich, round and full - quite similar to 1926, which has a bit more complexity and fullness. Great length and aftertaste. At its peak now and needs drinking. Most enjoyable!

1958   Barolo Monfortino Riserva Giacomo Conterno *(Piedmont)*   93p

2003/now x2 • D 1 h / G 1 h

This sleeping beauty came direct from Conterno's cellars, therefore it was in perfect condition. Decanted two hours before tasting. Surprisingly youthful looking, bright red developing colour. Full, rich, complex, and quite intense nose. Ripe and full, but getting a little bitter and sharp. Well balanced and plenty of depth. A bit old-fashioned but in a positive way. It shows the superb quality of the wines that Conterno produced in those golden days. Warm and round aftertaste.

1966   Vintage Champagne Louis Roederer *(Champagne)*   93p

2004/2010 x2 • D 15 min / G 30 min

Developed deep yellow colour with lovely gentle effervescence remaining. Fine and lively nose of dried fruits and elegant creaminess. Gentle mousse on the palate, with great purity and a sweet ripe fruit impression at the finish. Noticeably more acidic than the Heidsieck 1966. A dry, refined and stylish wine, giving a very good example of the 1966.

1948   Château Pétrus *(Pomerol)*   93p

2006/2015 x5 • D 1 h / G 1 h

This is one of the rarest Pétrus vintages on the market. Belgian-bottled with the château-label, level was top-shoulder! The cork came out in one piece, but there was no information on it. Decanted one hour. Dark, mature and healthy colour. Full, voluptuous, spicy, and rich on the nose. At first it was a bit dull, hard and tannic on the palate. After one and a half hours it softened and woke up. Round, full and still quite a powerful wine with pleasant depth and balance. This is a fairly notorious wine - it's big and powerful and at the same time somehow modest and tight for a Pétrus. A peculiar but pleasurable experience! This is now as good as it is ever going to be, but will still last for another five to ten years. Tasted five times with very dissimilar notes!

NUMBER 642.
NUMBER 643.
NUMBER 644.
NUMBER 645.

1964 Hermitage La Chapelle Paul Jaboulet Aîné *(Rhône)* 93p
2007/2015 x2 •D 1 h / G 1 h

Excellent bottle. Decanted one and a half hours. Impressive dark colour. Full-bodied and wonderful in its complexity. This lovely La Chapelle continues to demonstrate rich, thick, elegant aromas and flavours that range from blackberries, ripe plums and chocolate to leather. Sound, chunky and long. A good effort, but not nearly as good as the impressive 1961, or soon to be great 1990. Ready now, but will last for at least one more decade.

1981 Zinfandel Swan *(Sonoma)* 93p
2004/2010 x2 • D 45 min / G 1 h

An attractive, stylish and developing nose of spicy blackberry and farmyard notes. Expressive palate of firm ripe tannin, still with a good grip to it. The palate has a very good intensity of fruit for a mature wine like this. High but balanced alcohol and moderate acidity. A big and mature Zinfandel.

1968 Sassicaia Tenuta San Guido *(Tuscany)* 93p
2006/now x3 • D 1 h / G 1 h

This Sassicaia 1968 was one of those 3,000 bottles that were released to the market in the early 1970s. It was in excellent condition and the level was by the neck. Made with 100 percent Cabernet Sauvignon. A very deep, dark and healthy colour. Open, harmonious and sound nose with a scent of truffles, blackberries and vanilla. Not as massive and intense a wine as 1978 and 1979, but it was well balanced and had a lovely sweet, mature fruit and some soft, rounded tannins left. A medium-weight wine with a good, firm, masculine structure. A bit dry and acidic with a short aftertaste.

Nevertheless, it is still very easy to understand why this historical wine is responsible for launching the Super-Tuscan movement and it remains as one of the most hunted wines in the world.

1922 Vintage Port Croft *(Portugal)* 93p
2004/2010 x3 • D 3 h / G 2 h

Decanted three hour before tasting. An outstanding looking bottle. A pleasant nose with rich dark fruits, toffee and caramel. Good initial attack, ripe and smooth. A bit of a burn on the palate, but it keeps coming back with a very long finish accompanied by lingering complexities, tannins fully resolved. Unexpectedly enjoyable and well balanced considering the weak reputation of the vintage.

1926   Chambertin Joseph Drouhin *(Côte de Nuits)*   93p
2006/now x4 • D 30 min / G 1 h

Very peculiar and old-looking bottle with a fine label and only 3 cm ullage. Decanted 15 minutes before tasting. Quite a lot of sediment. It still has a dark, but quite evolved colour. Sound, open, soft, and mature, vibrant nose that was backed by sweet fruit and dark raspberry scents. On the palate, medium-full, round, a bit dry with velvety tannins and a decent length. A pleasurable and intense wine. A long and clean finish. Some tannin still left, but has been at its peak already for several decades.

1962   Château Mouton-Rothschild *(Pauillac)*   93p
2006/2015 x7 • D 1 h / G 2 h

In Bordeaux this was a first-class year that has never achieved the reputation it deserves because it has always lived in the shadow of 1961. The wines became rich and complex and they were slow to come around. The Mouton-Rothschild 1962 also came around fairly late. It was in the mid-1980s when we tasted it for the first time, and then it was quite difficult and considered a "green" wine. But during the last twenty years it has developed a lot.

Top-shoulder, decanted for one hour. Very deep, almost black colour. Wide and healthy nose. The palate is now stylish, almost sensual, with attractive, ripe fruit flavours. Reasonably long and smooth finish. Those who have had the patience and trust to let this wine age in peace are now grandly rewarded

1981   Estate Chardonnay Reserve Chalone *(California)*   93p
2000/2010 x1 • D 30 min / G 1 h

A fine bottle with light and bright, yellow colour. Decanted 30 minutes. A fresh and rich nose full of vanilla, smoke, butter, and baked white fruits. Delicious, fat and rich. It was a mouth-filling Chardonnay, still lush and full of decadent, sweet fruit flavours despite its age. A very meaty character. Adequate acidity and a lingering, but crispy ending.

1998   Black Sock Magpie Estate *(Barossa Valley)*   93p
2002/2015 x3 • D 1 h / G 3 h

One of the adorable rarities from Australia. Only 1,800 bottles made. 60-year-old Shiraz vines provide 80 percent of the blend. The rest comes from the 80-year-old Mourvedre vines. The wine has been matured for 2.5 years in 55 percent new French and American oak. An extracted, opaque, purple colour with ruby tints. The powerful spicy nose is rich and full of ripe dark fruits, mulberries, blueberries, and wild strawberries with chocolate, butterscotch, cinnamon, clove, and vanilla tones. The full-bodied, explosive palate is robust and full of ripe, almost jammy dark fruitiness. Massive, edgy but softening tannins. Highly warming alcohol that shows great integration into the beefy taste. A long finish highlights the sweet spices, bitter almonds and preserved cherries flavours. A big wine that reminds us very much of top quality Amarone. Not a wine for long term ageing but drinking greatly now.

Chevalier-Montrachet

1964 Clos-de-Tart Mommessin *(Côte de Nuits)* 93p

2000/now x4 • D 1 h / G 1 h

Clos-de-Tart is one of the most ancient vineyards of Burgundy. It has had only three owners since the Middle Ages. The 7.22 ha walled vineyard belonged to the nuns of Tart from 1141 until the French Revolution. It then passed on to the famous Marey-Monge family and from 1932 it has been a monopole of Mommessin of Macou. Good-looking bottle, ullage 2cm. Decanted 30 minutes before tasting. Fair amount of sediment. It has a light, quite developed colour. Forthcoming, open, soft, and mature nose. Full, round, lively fruit with velvety tannins and good length. Delicate and complex wine. Long and clean finish. Will not improve, but no rush. At its peak, but should hold there for at least three to five years.

1997 Lapsus Abadia Retuerta *(Sardon del Duero)* 93p

2002/2020 x5 • D 1 h / G 2.5 h

A clear, opaque, ruby colour. Pronounced, intense nose of smoke, tar, bacon, spices, cardamom, leather, and ripe brambles. Moderately high acidity and rich firm tannins are dominating the palate while the intense, ripe, dark fruitiness lays underneath. Well-integrated high alcohol extends the length of the after-taste in the spicy finish.

1863 Madeira Bual Barbeito *(Portugal)* 93p

2005/2040 x3 • D 30 min / G 2 h

Clear, medium-intense, tawny brown colour. Intense, rich dark chocolate nose with almonds and teak aromas. Medium-sweet wine. Crisp acidity balances the oily texture of this medium-bodied wine with salty mineral taste. A powerful taste of almonds, dried figs, dates, apple, and orange peel. Long warming finish. It is a rare treat to enjoy a glass of Barbeito's Madeira from such a good old vintage as this.

1970 Gran Coronas Black Label Torres *(Penedès)* 93p

2004/now x3 • D 1 h /G 1 h

In the summer of 2006 when Mr Nuikki acted as an auctioneer in a charity wine auction, one of the wines that awakened the most interest was the Torres Gran Coronas Black Label 1970 magnum, a wine that Miguel Torres himself had brought with him and donated to the auction. Mas La Plana has been the single vineyard flagship wine of Torres for nearly 35 years. Originally labeled as Torres Gran Coronas, the name "Mas La Plana" was added to the label in the early 1990s. This first vintage of Gran Coronas, the 1970, triumphed over some of the most famous wines in the world, including Château Latour 1970 and Château La Mission Haut-Brion 1961, and was voted top in the Cabernet class in the Paris Wine Olympics in 1979. This success has since then been repeated on several other occasions.

Since our previous experiences of this "Olympic champion" had been most pleasant, we asked a friend to bid on this magnum for us. However, its price quickly rose above our price limit and so this historical wine found its happy new owner elsewhere. After returning home from the auction we opened, for our consolation, the last bottle of Gran Coronas 1970 from Mr Nuikki's cellar, and our notes were then:

The bottle was like brand new. Level was by the neck, decanted for one hour. A very dark colour, almost as dark as its distinctive black label. Quite closed and tight bouquet at first, but after one more hour of airing it opened beautifully with wonderful flavours of cranberries, leather, truffles, and vanilla. A big and sweet wine with smooth but substantial tannins. Full and elegant, almost creamy, but the fruit was starting to dry out and the acid became slowly more prominent. Long and complex aftertaste. This has been a magnificent and fresh wine during the 80s and early 90s, but now, while it is still a good wine, it needs to be consumed!

1997 *Barolo Cannubi Boschis Luciano Sandrone* (Piedmont) *93p*
2002/2030 x4 • D 2 h / G 1.5 h

Bright, cherry red colour with orange tints. The seductive nose reveals butterscotch, strawberry jam, floral notes such as orange blossom and white chocolate aromas. Full-bodied wine, crisp acidity and substantial stalky tannins. Moderately intense, ripe, red fruit palate with high alcohol. The warming finish makes this wine feel a bit robust in style, although very appealing. Still very young.

NUMBER 658.

1949 *Château Pape-Clément* (Graves) *93p*
2004/now x3 • D 1 h / G 1 h

Unlabelled, otherwise good looking château-bottled Pape-Clément. Level by the neck. Decanted one hour before tasting. Excellent Graves. Although Pape-Clément is more drinkable at an earlier age than many other Bordeaux, it can easily last as well as the best of them. This 1949 is one of the best examples of this. During the 1940s almost the entire vineyard was replanted, and many other renovations were made at the property. With this magnificent 1949, we get the first impression of the celebrated future, which actually started with the 1953 vintage.

Medium-dark, bright and youthful colour. Wide-open bouquet of minerals, black fruits and a hint of tobacco - a very appealing combination. Mature, soft and lovely wine. Very much like the 1947 vintage, but with extra complexity and length. A bit modest but long aftertaste. Most enjoyable. Should hold easily for five more years. Tasted three times with comparable notes.

NUMBER 659.

1992 *Vieilles Vignes Françaises Bollinger* (Champagne) *93p*
2007/2020 x6 • D 30 min / G 2 h

Clear, bright, lemony colour with fine energetic bubbles. Clean, very intense youthful nose of Granny Smith apple aromas and spices, mainly cinnamon. Dry, crisp acidity, medium-bodied style. Intense fruitiness of ripe green apples and a zesty lemony finish with rich minerality. A very muscular but smooth Champagne that brings great pleasure.

NUMBER 660.

2001 Chablis Premier Cru Montée de Tonnerre Raveneau *(Chablis)* 93p

2006/2015 x3 • D 1 h / G 1 h

This vintage was a challenge in the vineyards of Chablis due to significant botrytis problems. This can be sensed as honeyed and waxy overtones in the wine's rich nose. Very ripe fruit, pineapples and apricots. The dry medium-bodied palate is complex and rich with a less acidic style. A broad texture on the palate reflects nutty and spicy notes with waxy and sweet candy tones. An opulent lingering finish.

1998 Shiraz Roennfeldt Road Greenock Creek *(Barossa Valley)* 93p

2005/2025 x8 • D 3 h / G 2 h

The scattered dry-grown Greenock Creek vineyards, located near Seppeltsfield, lie on varying soils ranging from red loamy to alluvial soils, bordering on clay soils in a pocket undulation cut by a dry creek bed. The Roennfeldt Road Shiraz, which draws fruit from vines planted in the 1950s, is vinified in open sunk slate fermenters and regularly plunged over. The free-run wine and pressings are kept entirely separate to increase blending options. The wine is drained and pressed in Hypac basket presses and transferred into new American oak hogsheads where it spends 36 months.

Decanted one hour. The nose is still quite tight, with the warmth of alcohol and fruit dominating. On the palate, very opulent and concentrated, with blackberry and currant flavours with hints of cedar. Balanced, but with a slight overdose of tannin. Drinking courteously now, but it is better to let it sit for a few years more. This will mould into a beautiful Shiraz!

2000 Montrachet Domaine de la Romanée-Conti *(Côte de Beaune)* 93p

2007/2015 x3 • D 1 h / G 1 h

2000 was not a great vintage in Burgundy. Once again the greatest Chardonnay parcel in Burgundy in the hands of a magnificent producer is able to yield another wonderful wine. The secret with this wine was the late-picking of the grapes. The harvest actually took place after Pinot Noir! The yield was just below 40 hl/ha and the total production was 3,541 bottles this year.

Deep shining yellow colour with intense smoky and buttery nose. Delicious aromas of ripe fruits, pineapple, white peaches, and lemon. Very crisp on the palate with broad oily texture and rich toasty flavours. Ripe fruitiness balances the still dominant oak. A lingering mineral finish with a strong oaky touch. Appealing already now but it will certainly improve in the years, if not the decade, to come!

1959 Grange Penfolds *(South Australia)* 93p

2006/2015 x2 • D 1 h / G 1 h

Last of the three 'hidden' Granges made by Max Schubert in defiance of a company order to cease production. The wine was released commercially after the ban was lifted. New oak was not used in these three vintages. Bottles were labelled with Bin numbers 46, 49 and 95. 1959 is a blend of 94 percent Shiraz and

6 percent Cabernet Sauvignon.

A superb looking bottle, level was by the neck. Decanted two hours. Very clear, dark, almost black colour. Beautiful, sweetly fruity, mushroomy nose. Round, soft, but not as elegant and rich as the 1961. Earthy, a bit austere with an agreeable length. Slightly tannic. At its absolute peak now. A serious wine, yet it lacks that magical strength and sumptuousness Grange generally has.

1970 Château Cheval Blanc (St.Emilion) 93p

2007/2020 x18 • D 1 h / G 1.5 h

A clear, medium-intense tawny colour. A ripe and seductively open nose of mocha, chocolate, cigars, and spiciness. Medium-bodied elegant character with delicate lingering acidity, ripe supple tannins and herbaceous blackcurrant finish. Pure elegance.

1947 Château Léoville-Las Cases (Saint-Julien) 93p

2003/2015 x12 • D 30 min / G 2 h

Fine looking château-bottling. Level was top-shoulder. A clear, slightly cloudy, medium-intense dark red colour with a tawny rim. The clean moderately intense nose speaks for development: rich and ripe vegetal character with bell pepper. There is a balanced taste of ripe, persistent and big tannins with a lovely mellow acidity and elegant fruit intensity of blackcurrants. A subtle and long finish.

1999 Gewurtraminer Heimbourg Zind-Humbrecht (Alsace) 93p

2003/2010 • D 1 h / G 1 h

Excellent appereance. Decanted one hour. A bright intense golden yellow colour. The wine moved extraordinarily viscously in the glass. A honeyed and complex nose with less perfume than in other Zind-Humbrecht's Gewurztraminers. The medium-sweet palate is enriched with a refined, moderate acidity and a mineral mouth-feel. The ripe tropical fruitiness with a touch of green fruits forms a unique taste to the long finish of the wine. The high alcohol level is married delightfully with the wine's rich structure. The aftertaste is extremely seductive.

1987 Unico Bodegas Vega Sicilia (Ribera del Duero) 93p

2005/2015 x9 • D 1 h / G 1 h

The year 1987 was a challenge in the Ribera del Duero. A wet winter and occasional rain during the entire growing season, including harvest time, made this vintage a risky business. Vega Sicilia managed remarkably well by being able to produce 80,000 bottles of Unico, taking into account that the range of Unicos produced can vary from 0 to 100,000 bottles based on the year. This vintage of Unico drinks fairly young, and they have, despite the challenging conditions, been able to produce a charming and harmonious wine.

A fairly youthful, deep, dark red colour. The nose is pronounced with meat, smoke and tobacco aromatics. The palate reveals farmyard tones and fresh ripe raspberries. The refreshing acidity combines well with the wine's balanced alcohol. The exceptionally long, persistent finish lifts this wine into the super-premium category. Starting to drink well now but it will benefit from 10 years of additional bottle maturation.

NUMBER 669.

1949 Georges de Latour Beaulieu Vineyard (Napa Valley) 93p
2003/now x2 • D 30 min / G 1 h

In 1938, André Tchelistcheff, a winemaker born in Russia and educated in France, came to Beaulieu. He stayed and worked there successfully as a winemaker for 35 years. During these years he became the 'father' of Napa Valley winemakers of the time. George de Latour died in 1940, and a wine - that led the estate to world fame - was produced in his honour in 1941; BV George de Latour Private Reserve.

There was a malicious frost in 1949, which cut the crop size in half. The best Cabernets were well structured and age-worthy. Decanted 30 minutes. Very deep, mature and healthy colour. Sound, long chocolaty nose. Quite good depth, complexity and persistent aftertaste. The wine has held remarkably well. One of the oldest California Cabernets we have tasted.

NUMBER 670.

1953 Château Calon-Ségur (Saint-Estèphe) 93p
2006/2015 x2 • D 45 min / G 1 h

Bottled by Barrière Frères. Clear, medium-intense tawny colour. A moderately intense, rich, evolved nose of animal aromas, roasted coffee, chocolate, liquorice, and ripe blackcurrant aromas with tobacco. Rich medium-bodied taste with moderately high acidity, elegant tannins and a very long finish. An elegant, delicate wine.

NUMBER 671.

2002 Corton-Charlemagne Bonneau du Martray (Côte de Beaune) 93p
2006/2020 x3 • D 2 h / G 2 h

Pale, straw yellow colour. An intense, rich, yeasty, and buttery nose with lemon zest. Crisp acidity, mouth-filling minerals and elegant, fresh fruitiness combine well with new oak and the spiciness given by it. Very refined and balanced wine, which is not yet giving its best. It needs at least five more years to open up fully.

NUMBER 672.

1997 Coteaux du Layon SGN Aprés Minuit Domaine de la Coeur d'Ardenay (Loire) 93p
2001/2030 x3 • D 1 h / G 2 h

The best vintage of the decade since 1990. This great botrytised wine, made by Patrick Baudoin, glitters in the glass with its bright, golden-yellow colour. The pronounced and intense nose is intriguingly complex, consisting of dried fruits, flowers, honey, spices, apricot marmalade, and cooked white asparagus. The lusciously sweet and intense taste is well balanced with the crisp acidity. A very concentrated wine with a syrupy texture. Honey and rhubarb compote flavours are present in the nearly never-ending finish. This will be an even more fascinating wine to taste ten to fifteen years from now.

1962   Dom Pérignon Moët & Chandon (Champagne)   93p

2005/2010 x8 • D 1 h / G 1 h

A really joyful wine which is still unexpectedly fresh and youthful. A pale yellow colour with playful, small bubbles. Intense, fresh nose with a layered toastiness common to Dom Pérignon. The crisp acidity with fresh and rich mousse forms an energetic mouth-feel with ripe yellow fruit flavours, hints of roasted coffee and creaminess. Long lemony fresh finish. A delightful Dom Pérignon to enjoy now!

NUMBER 673.

1989   Château Lafite-Rothschild (Pauillac)   93p

2007/2020 x11 • D 2 h / G 1.5 h

No winemaker had seen such an early harvest at Lafite: the earliest since 1893. Beginning at the end of August, the grapes were ripe and extraordinarily sweet. While early maturity doesn't always lead to fine wines, we still bet heavily on the excellence of this vintage, and the wines that it produced are truly delicious. Médoc produced deeply coloured wines that are rich and light, similar to the 1982 vintage.

A fine bottle with by the neck level. Decanted two hours. Clear, promising, deep tawny colour. Very intense, developing and complex aromas of yoghurt, milk chocolate and intense dark and red berries with bell pepper. A concentrated taste with a ripe, almost jammy fruitiness. The moderately high acidity balances the ripe fruit and firm, big tannins. A long finish with an attractive concentration and finesse. Very good future potential!

NUMBER 674.

1990   Château Palmer (Margaux)   93p

2000/2020 x8 • D 2 h / G 2 h

An exceptional year at Château Palmer, completing the trio of great vintages 1988, 1989 and 1990. Throughout the year, the weather was fine and warm, resulting in high sugar levels and relatively low acidity. The wines are concentrated and characterised by ripe fruit flavours and supple tannins. A moderately deep, ruby red colour with a tawny hue. A pronounced spicy nose with cedar, tobacco and soy aromas. Ripe blackcurrants together with floral mocha tones. The medium-bodied palate contains lively acidity, firm, refined tannins and intense, jammy dark fruit aromas. An elegant wine with a long finish.

NUMBER 675.

1998 Black Sears Vineyard Zinfandel Turley *(California)* 93p
2001/2015 x4 • D 1 h / G 1 h

Turley only made around 400 cases of this wine. The over 80-year-old vines on the Black Sears Vineyard in the Howell Mountain district enjoy the cool condition of this Napa Valley AVA district.

A very dark mahogany red colour with brown tints. A really upfront, spicy nose with white pepper, smokiness and fried bacon. Full-bodied opulent taste with refined powerful tannins, very ripe but not jammy dark fruits, white pepper, and fleshy wine with smoky aromas remind us very much of the rustic Rhône style. A long finish with surprisingly well-integrated high alcohol content (15,7%) extends the length of the flavourful aftertaste.

1952 Vin Santo Fattorio Montaquari *(Tuscany)* 93p
2003/2015 x1 • D 1 h / G 1 h

An old-looking bottle, mid-shoulder fill and a slightly scruffed label. Decanted for one hour. A dark and deep, vigorous looking colour. An excellent, wide-open nose with suggestions of raisins, dried fruit and herbs. Good acidity and fine balance. Not as sweet as we expected, but it has a gentle sweetness and a noticeable coal left. This was a round and smooth wine with a mellow, refined and dry finish. Unquestionably ready, but well structured and should hold well for another 10 years. What an inspiring way to end any unforgettable evening.

1968 Cabernet Sauvignon Private Reserve Robert Mondavi 93p
(Napa Valley) **2003/2010 x3 • D 1 h / G 1 h**

Robert Mondavi is one of the most influential people in the history of the Californian wine industry. In 1943 he started as a wine maker's apprentice at Charles Krug's estate. During the next two decades Robert, together with his brother Peter and his father Cesare Mondavi, turned Krug into a prominent wine producer in Napa Valley. In 1966 Robert Mondavi founded his own estate in Oakville, California. The Robert Mondavi Winery, now a public corporation, has grown into America's largest producer of premium wines. These bottles are from the fascinating early days of the later-to-be wine giant. The bottles came from the Chicago Wine Company a few years ago. They were all in excellent condition.

Decanted one hour. Very dark, almost black colour. Lovely spicy, mint and cedar nose - typical California Cabernet aroma profile. Elegant, good flavours but not as structured or complex a wine as we expected. Good balance and quite a long, satisfying aftertaste. Still has some future left.

1999 Tokaji Aszú 6 puttonyos István Szepsy *(Tokaj)* 93p
2005/2040 x2 • D 1 h / G 3 h

István Szepsy is considered the king of sweet Tokaji makers due to the reputation gained from his extraordinary sweet concentrated wines. Only about 8,000 bottles of this wine were produced.

NUMBER 676.

NUMBER 677.

NUMBER 678.

NUMBER 679.

The clear, intense and golden coloured wine has an incredibly intense spicy nose with apricot, marmalade and botrytis. The 1999 vintage is known for its big acidic structure, and this Tokaji makes no exception. Crisp acidity cuts the delicately oily, lusciously sweet, velvety texture. Honeyed overtones with a touch of jasmine and ginger. Very intense fruitiness and rich botrytis flavours combine with a moderate level of alcohol, all adding extra dimensions to this immortal wine.

NUMBER 680.

1997 *Richebourg Domaine de la Romanée-Conti* (Côte de Nuits)   93p
2002/2020 x3 • D 2 h / G 2 h

Another good year for Vosne-Romanée but a hot September ripened the grapes very early, leading to the earliest harvest on Richebourg for over a decade.

Intense dark ruby colour. Very powerful nose with ripe raspberry aromas combined with smoky, tar-like and violet tones. A beautiful balance with high acidity, intense red fruitiness and moderately rich and persistent tannins. Ripe red berries combined with perfumed and liquorice flavours. Very masculine in structure but with elegance and great length. Closing down now and opening for its second life in five year's time.

NUMBER 681.

1969 *Romanée-St.Vivant Domaine Marey-Monge* (Côte de Nuits)   93p
2003/now x2 • D 1 h / G 2 h

Beginning in 1966, DRC managed the holdings by the Marey-Monge family and ultimately purchased them in 1988. This bottle came from the USA. Ullage was 4cm and the bottle looked much older than it should. The colour of old tiles. Marvellous, explosive nose. Perfect maturity on the palate - there were all the "feminine" qualities of Romanée-St.Vivant - intense, violet perfume with rich and full structure. A good length and balance. Simply a great drink.

NUMBER 682.

1997 *Brunello di Montalcino Pertimali* (Tuscany)   93p
2002/2015 x4 • D 2 h / G 2 h

Bright, intense, ruby colour. The powerful nose charms with plenty of dark berries, blackberries and brambles complimented by meaty complexity. Lovely crisp acidity, firm powdery tannins and red fruit of strawberries, raspberries and hints of herbaciousness, all in beautiful balance. A long youthful taste with a nice twist of spices in the elegant aftertaste. A very classy wine from this small 7 ha premium Brunello estate of Pertimali, run by the Sassetti family.

NUMBER 683.

1990 *Domaine de Trévallon* (Rhône)   93p
2007/2015 x3 • D 1 h / G 1 h

This wine is like mixing the best out of the left bank of Bordeaux and the northern Rhône. The equal blend of Cabernet Sauvignon and Syrah results in a dark, intense, brick red colour. Pronounced nose of ripe blackcurrants, capsicum, and vegetal tones combined with leather, tar and a cigar box. Full-bodied with firm tannins and moderate acidity enhanced by green vegetal tones. A long savoury and fleshy finish.

1996 *Martha's Vineyard Cabernet Sauvignon Heitz* (Napa Valley) 93p
2002/2015 x3 • D 3 h / G 2 h

Deep, ruby colour. The rich but elegant etheral nose shares aromas of blackcurrant leaves, blackberries, mint, eucalyptus, dark chocolate, and cinnamon. A very intense, ripe and fresh fruitiness together with subtle tannins give this full-bodied wine a very mouth-filling concentrated taste that lasts a long time. Lovely elegance, ready to drink now!

NUMBER 684.

1928 *Château L'Evangile* (Pomerol) 93p
2005/2010 x3 • D 30 min / G 1 h

A good looking half-bottle. Bottled by Nicholas. Top shoulder level. Decanted twenty minutes.
A deep, not very bright colour, rather old looking. Dark brown at the rim. Wonderfully clean, fruity and quite rich on the nose. Thick, sweet and well balanced on the palate. Good freshness but some astringency at the end. Not as concentrated or as complex as the Pétrus 1928 but nevertheless a lovely wine with a soft, medium-long finish. The Château Pétrus is more vigorous and intense but L'Evangile is more elegant.

NUMBER 685.

1966 *Vintage Champagne Krug* (Champagne) 93p
2002/2015 x3 • D 1 h / G 1 h

Fine looking bottle. Decanted only 15 minutes. Bright, dark yellow colour with really tiny, energetic bubbles. The powerful mineral nose shows ripe apples and citrus with hints of toastiness, gunflint and ashes. Dry, very crisp acidity balanced with ripe apple fruit and fresh mousse. The long persistent finish loosens up a bit in the end giving the wine suppleness and the wine-lover a moment to breathe. Still a huge wine with very persistent and lean style - a true Krugist's choice.

NUMBER 686.

1998 *Masseto Tenuta dell'Ornellaia* (Tuscany) 93p
2007/2015 x6 • D 3 h / G 3 h

Moderately intense ruby colour. Open, complex and developing nose with raw coffee, cedar and earthy aromas combined with ripe blackberry notes. A full-bodied extracted taste with refined ripe tannins, very intense, ripe dark fruit and a well balanced, pronounced oak character that stands up with vanilla flavours. The long finish is highlighted by alcohol and glycerin with liquorice flavours in the aftertaste.

NUMBER 687.

1971   *Cristal Roederer* (Champagne)   93p

2006/2010 x4 • D 15 min / G 30 min

The year was characterised by uneven weather conditions throughout the growing season. Storms in late July and disastrous hail in August limited the yield. Continuous hot weather in September further contributed to the tiny average crop of 5,100 kg/ha. But in most cases the quality was exceptionally high despite some wines that suffered from medium-low acidity. There is nothing wrong with Cristal's acidity, however.

Developed deep golden colour and lively small-sized bubbles in the glass. The nose is intensely fruity and impeccably stylish: toast, honey, apple, and caramelised sugar and some spiciness. Full mouth-feel with smooth silky texture and lively elegant mousse. Great example of Cristal that is at its peak, but will keep there for at least five more years.

1952   *Colheita Niepoort* (Portugal)   93p

2002/2020 x4 • D 2 h / G 4 h

This was not a classic year for the region, although some very good wines were produced. The dry weather continued through April until May, at which point the rain came to stay until the second half of June. Harvesting began on the 25th of September under ideal conditions.

The light tinges of ruby in the heart of this wine largely represent a well-evolved colour. The lean, opulent and very developed nose is full of tertiary aromas - manure and blue cheese. Ripe, plummy aromas stand out. As the wine opens in the glass, along comes burnt sugar and smoky notes. Sweet, vivid acidity and a high level of alcohol form a structure to this flavourful wine of dried fruits, flowers, chocolate, and nuts. An absolutely charming wine.

1995   *Clos Saint Hilaire Billecart-Salmon* (Champagne)   93p

2005/2030 x3 • D 1 h / G 1 h

This is the first vintage of Billecart-Salmon's top of the line single vineyard wine. In 1818 spouses Nicolas François Billecart and Elisabeth Salmon founded their champagne house is Mareuil-sur-Aÿ, where the Billecart family had been established since the 17th century. The one ha parcel, where the Clos Saint Hilaire wine originates, has always belonged to the family. It was named after the patron saint of Mareuil-sur-Aÿ and planted with Pinot Noir in 1964. Prior to 1995, it was used to make red Coteaux Champenois.

The Clos Saint Hilaire parcel is located right next to the wine cellar, and was used as a family garden before being planted with vines. The original massal selection vine stocks are maintained to produce a limited 50 hl/ha crop. The terroir in the plot is provided by the sum of small details such as higher temperature inside the village giving frost protection and higher ripeness, with a potential alcohol level of 10.5%. Billecart-Salmon aims to maintain all possible aromatics in the wine by minimum filtration. Terroir characteristics are respected by 0 to 4 g/l dosage.

A deep golden-hued colour. Super-fine bubbles in the glass. Rich, creamy and developed nose of apples and smokiness. Outstanding acidity is combined with a firm Pinot Noir structure. Silky mouth-feel with cigar and tobacco in the finish. Masculine and multilayered style with great aging capacity.

1994 *Vintage Port Taylor Fladgate* *(Portugal)* *93p*

2007/2050 x5 • D 4 h / G 4 h

Opaque, purple colour with very pronounced and intense nose of medicinal tones, anise, violets, liquorice, dark fruits, blackberries, and spices. Full-bodied, moderate acidity and big stalky tannins are dominating this youngster. A very intense, ripe, jammy dark fruitiness and violet flavours are accompanied with loads of spices, liquorice, smoky, and tarry flavours. The high level of alcohol is very well integrated into the wine, prolonging the youthful aftertaste.

1945 *Brunello di Montalcino Riserva Biondi-Santi* *(Tuscany)* *93p*

2007/now x2 • D 15 min / G 1 h

A moderately pale and surprisingly yellow toned colour for red wine. Delicate, moderately intense, reserved nose with smoky, toasty and sweet dried fruits aromas. The racy acidity with a voluminous alcohol mouth-feel actually forms the spine of the wine. Moderate fruit intensity in absence of tannins. Still everything is in balance. Not a great length but an astonishing red wine. Although extremely developed, the wine seems to still be alive. A true vini di meditazione.

1997 *Duck Muck Shiraz Wild Duck Creek* *(Victoria- Heathcote)* *93p*

2005/2015 x4 • D 4 h / G 3 h

Wild Duck Creek Estate, located in the voluptuous countryside around Heathcote, was established in 1980. At the age of 18 David Anderson bought his first block of land after receiving his first pay packet and getting a bank loan. The Wild Duck Creek Estate comprises of nine acres of vineyard located on mudstone and shale, interspersed with quartz, 'classic broken up gold country'. Fruit is also sourced from another seven vineyards in the area, planted on varying soils, including Heathcote's red loams.

The Duck Muck Shiraz (about 200 cases produced) is made only in exceptional vintages. The vines are vertically shoot positioned and are grown on a protected eastern aspect to take advantage of the morning sun. The harvest can take place over a six to eight week period, every vine triaged for optimum ripeness and flavour development. The fruit comes in with naturally high acids and a staggeringly high 17+ degrees Baumé. The wines are vinified in a jumble of different-sized open fermenters and they are regularly hand plunged. At dryness, the wines are drained and pressed in a homemade hydraulic press and then transferred into 100 percent new French and American oak. Interestingly, and almost impossibly, some of Anderson's wines are made without any sulphur addition whatsoever.

Lovely label. Decanted three hours. An opaque black colour fading to a deep purple. Heavy blackcurrant nose with cream, some oak and vanilla, lots of alcohol. Very full-bodied, thick, velvety texture with flavours of jammy fruit, savoury salty and mint nuances. Good balance with firm tannins and crisp acids. Lengthy finish with flavours of dark chocolate and smoked oak coming through. Not the most drinkable wine yet, but certainly interesting and worthy of cellaring.

1990 *Grande Année Bollinger* (Champagne)   93p
2004/2025x3 • D 1 h / G 1 h

The year was in many ways comparable to 1989. There was an early bud break followed by vast spring frosts on the 5th and 19th of April that affected 45 percent of the total surface area. The secondary buds were able to recover much of the loss and the Indian summer authorised two harvests: the first starting on the 11th of September, the second, five weeks later, on the 18th of October. The quality and quantity both excelled. Bollinger compares their 1990 to the 1928.

Developing a deep, shiny colour. The nose is very expressive of oxidising apples, fruitcake and some mushroom and earthy tones. Complex and layered, this wine joins together power and persistence. Highlighted acidity and very ripe pronounced fruitiness. A great champagne from a top vintage.

1989 *Château Calon-Ségur* (Saint-Estèphe)   93p
2007/2030 x12 • D 2 h / G 2 h

A rather deep, cherry-red colour. Medium-strong, elegantly full nose with blackcurrants, rose petals and smoke. A very intensive, juicy and fruity, moderately full taste enhanced by lively acids and ripe, elegant tannins. Refined, long and vivid aftertaste. A distinct style shift towards more fullness, when compared to the 1986 vintage. The youth of the wine is hinted at by the lack of tertiary bouquet aromas.

1990 *Châteauneuf-du-Pape Réserve des Celestins Henri Bonneau* 93p
(Rhône)   2006/2020 x 3 • D 2 h / G 1.5 h

Dark, moderately intense, red colour. Magnificently complex and profoundly intense nose with fragrances of ripe blackberries, spice, white pepper, and coffee. Medium-bodied on the palate, serving a sweet ripe fruitiness combined beautifully with big ripe tannins. Sensible acidity with volatile flavours adds complexity to the quite long aftertaste. All flavours are very concentrated whilst the wine is still surprisingly vibrant and young at heart for its age.

1992 *Sassicaia Tenuta San Guido* (Tuscany)   93p
2005/2010x5 • D 1 h / G 2 h

1992 is not one of the most successful Tuscan vintages, but this Sassicaia's charm lies in its harmony and elegance. A great example of an off-vintage that is very attractive for mid-term drinking. A deep developing ruby red colour. The lifted nose is filled with blackcurrant, tar and game aromas, spiced up with bell pepper and tobacco nuances. The mouth-feel is silky, rich and elegant. The refreshing appetising acidity and firm yet high tannin support each other well. A multidimensional, attractively elegant and refreshing wine. Very enjoyable today and will not benefit much from further bottle maturation.

1996 *Almaviva* (Maipo Valley - Chile) 93p

Almaviva 1996 is made from a blend of three classic Bordeaux grape varieties - Cabernet Sauvignon, which dominates, Cabernet Franc and Carmenère. Almaviva is the result of a felicitous encounter between two cultures. Chile offers its soil, its climate and its vines, while France contributes with winemaking skills and traditions. The name Almaviva, though it has a Hispanic ring to it, nevertheless belongs to classical French literature: Count Almaviva is the hero of The Marriage of Figaro, the famous play by Beaumarchais (1732-1799), later turned into an opera by the genius of Mozart. The label, meanwhile, pays homage to Chile's ancestral history, with three reproductions of a stylised design, which symbolised the vision of the earth and the cosmos in the Mapuche civilisation.

The design appeared on the "kultrun", a ritual drum used by the Mapuche. Hand-in-hand, two great traditions thus combine to offer the whole world a promise of pleasure and excellence.

Decanted 30 minutes. The dark ruby-coloured 1996 Almaviva exhibited aromas of cedar, blackberries and tobacco. Full-bodied and elegant, but at first quite closed. Gradually the silkiness and multi-layered structure of the wine emerges, dominating the end of the tasting. The finish was very long and loaded with ripe, round tannins. Very good already, hard to say yet if it is going to be any better in a few years.

1953 *Vintage Bollinger* (Champagne) 93p

Very good-looking Double Magnum. Decanted only 15 minutes. Vibrant, bright golden colour. A few bubbles were still around. Fat, toasty nose of baked apples. Full-bodied with rounded sweet, ripe fruit, creamy acidity and a long, powerful ending. Lots of layers in a lovely balance.

1997 *Cabernet Sauvignon Howell Mountain Dunn Vineyards* 93p
(Napa Valley)

This ought to be one of the most massive Napa Cabernets with huge concentration and purity. Randy Dunn created the wine first time in 1979 and has obtained this unique standard. This vintage yielded only in total 3,454 cases.

Thick, opaque, ruby colour with enormous viscosity. Big and powerful, spicy and surprisingly vegetal nose with nutmeg and oriental spices. The full-bodied palate surprises again with moderately high acidity. Big chewy tannins are forming a solid backbone for intense dark fruitiness. Spices, liquorice, nutmeg, and cacao with bitter chocolate flavours are all well pronounced mineral finish. Big wine with no flabbiness thanks to delightful minerality. Drinking well now but will still keep for decades.

CHATEAV
SMITH HAVT LAFITTE

Château Smith Haut-Lafitte

1961   *Château Grand-Puy-Lacoste* (Pauillac)   *93p*

2005/2015 x4 • **D 1 h / G 2 h**

The bottles were like brand new. Deep, youthful and bright colour. Cedary, spicy and fruity nose. Very ripe, full and intense. Perfectly approachable now, it even felt fairly youthful. Very thick and well-balanced. Still quite tannic and powerful. One of the best wines on this 1961 tasting, only Palmer was richer and more elegant. The vintage does not come much better than this! A very good wine.

1970   *Château Ducru-Beaucaillou* (Saint-Julien)   *93p*

2004/2010 x38 • **D 1 h / G 1 h**

This very big harvest had the advantage of excellent weather conditions throughout the whole summer, right up to the end. After a fairly mild winter, growth started towards the end of March, but the vegetation was immediately and adversely affected by frosts at the beginning of April. June was fine and warm and July brought hot, dry weather with only occasional rain. The hot weather in September, which continued through to harvesting, meant that the grapes were concentrated.

Excellent double-magnum. Good-looking, full, vigorous red colour. Voluptuous nose, full of developing bouquet aromas. Farmyard, spices, leather, smokiness, and exotic fruits indicate the complex richness this wine possesses. Medium-bodied taste shows surprisingly smooth tannins, ripe fruitiness, perfume and floral tones just before a refined but rustic long finish. Drinking perfectly now but will hold for several years to come.

1969   *Bonnes-Mares Domaine Dujac* (Côte de Nuits)   *93p*

2004/now x 3 • **D 1 h / G 1 h**

Ullage 3 cm, otherwise the bottle was as good as new. Medium-deep colour. Rich and broad nose of menthol. Very smooth, round and full wine. This has a good concentration with sweet, attractive fruitiness. Fine balance. A generous, well made wine. Will not improve, but no hurry.

1958   *Reserva Marqués de Riscal* (Rioja)   *93p*

2007/now x 8 • **D 30 min / G 1 h**

All the six bottles were in very good condition. Levels were top-shoulder or better. Decanted 30 minutes. Fully mature medium-deep brick red colour with browning on the rim. Wide open roasted, leathery, earthy, and red berry notes. Complex and evolved. The palate is charming with great harmony. Silky texture, medium tannin and lively acidity. The alcohol level is admirably balanced and fully integrated. At peak now and will no longer improve. A great example of the style and potential of the original Rioja wines.

1959   Castillo Ygay Gran Reserva, Marqués de Murrieta *(Rioja)*   93p
2005/2010 x1 • D 1 h / G 2 h

Castillo Ygay Gran Reserva Especial is a wine destined for long term cellaring. It is probably the most celebrated of wines produced in the Rioja. This 1959 is a traditional Tempranillo dominated blend, which has
spent a prolonged time in American oak casks before bottling.

Bottle looked like new. Level by the neck. Decanted one hour. This 1959 Ygay is beginning to show
some appealing bottle-aged personality. It has a good deep red colour, fading to a salmon pink al the rim
with no tawny or browning that would signify almost 50 years of aging. The nose has a strong spirit, good
weight of fruit and a dash of earthiness. In the mouth it is supple, smoothly textured with fully integrated
tannins, offering a harmonious blend of ripe blackberry and strawberry fruits with bottle-aged finesse,
typical for a good Gran Reserva. This is a really extensive wine, not too powerful, but divine and long with
some good times ahead of it.

1952   Romanée-Conti Domaine de la Romanée-Conti *(Côte de Nuits)* 93p
2007/2010 x5 • D 30 min / G 1 h

Both bottles were in good condition. Levels were 4 cm and 6 cm. Decanted 45 minutes. An almost black, thick
colour, unlike in the previous bottles. Very open and sound nose with huge chocolate, truffle, smoke, and ripe
Pinot aromas. The palate was full with good acidity. Perhaps a bit over the top already but still very genuine
and pure Romanée-Conti. There was a kind of finesse and fine balance to the mouth, with touches of smooth
tannin and ripe fruit. A bit dry and one-dimensional ending.

1990   Rauenthaler Nonnenberg Riesling Spätlese Georg Breuer   93p
(Rheingau)   2005/2020 x2 • D 45 min / G 1.5 h

This is the crown jewel of Breuer's vineyards - the 5 ha Nonnenberg vineyard in Rauenthal with southern
exposure and deep phyllite soils has been a unique privilege to the Breuer family since 1990. Intense, golden,
rich colour. Ripe, intense, honeyed peachy tones with hints of waxiness, petrol and green apples. Dry, crisp
and medium-bodied palate shows a racy acidity (total acidity 11,2 g/l) and immense minerality with lemony
flavours. An oily texture turns into a vibrant and long, lemony finish. Drinking perfectly now but will keep
easily for another 15 years.

1952   Dom Pérignon Moët & Chandon *(Champagne)*   93p
2006/now x3 • D 10 min / G 30 min

The greatest vintage of the decade along with 1959. A wonderful dry and sunny summer was followed by a
rainy August, swelling the grapes ideally, not diluting them.

Golden, moderately pale colour and refined bubbles. Pronounced toasty nose with great depth given by
yeast, delicious ripe yellow fruits and brioche flavours. Lovely mousse on the palate, crisp acidity, ripe dried

fruits, sweet spices, toasty, and smoky flavours. Broad mouth-feel with a long lasting, supple and elegant finish. Can still keep for years so there is no excuse to pop the cork today!

1961 *Vintage Pol Roger (Champagne)*   93p
2004/now x 4 • D 20 min / G 30 min

Fine-looking bottle. Decanted 30 minutes. Quite dark, mature colour - looked much older than 1959. Steady stream of fine bubbles. A rich, creamy and fruity, sound bouquet that evolved beautifully in the glass. A very fragrant and soft wine, not as generous or as big as 1959, and has a drier and shorter finish, but nevertheless a well-balanced and beautifully matured champagne with excellent acidity. A delicate and elegant cuvée.

NUMBER 709.

1961 *Special Selection Cabernet Sauvignon Louis M. Martini*   93p
(Napa Valley)   2004/2010 x3 • D 1 h / G 2 h

We once bought a few mixed cases of Martini's wines from the 1960s - Cabernets, Pinot Noirs and Rieslings. This was one of those bottles, and it was in excellent condition. Napa Valley Cabernets normally age exceptionally well and this was no different. A beautifully defined, rich, elegant, and complex wine in a firm package. Not a very powerful wine, but round, smooth and intense. This is showing the most depth and finesse of any Martini's Cabernets since the 1940s. A charming wine.

NUMBER 710.

1965 *Grange Hermitage Bin 95 Penfolds* (Australia)   93p
2001/now x3 • D 30 min / G 20 min

The 1965 Grange won the coveted Jimmy Watson Trophy, awarded to the best one-year-old red at the Melbourne Wine Show in 1966. It also won two more gold and six other medals between 1966 and 1973. This 1965 Grange is a blend of 95 percent Shiraz and 5 percent Cabernet Sauvignon.

Excellent condition and level was by the neck. Decanted for one hour. An evolved colour with an orange trim. Fresh and exotic, sweet fruit on the nose. But the taste was unexpectedly one-dimensional and boring. We probably decanted it for too long and then it became simply too alcoholic, hot and an unkind wine with a nasty, sharp aftertaste.

The second bottle was decanted only 15 minutes before tasting and was happily much more alive and had better fruit and structure than the first one. Unfortunately this also started to fade very rapidly in the glass. But those first 30 minutes were splendid: it displayed lovely ripe and vigorous fruit with soft and gentle tannins. Great balance and good depth. This was not one of those muscular Granges, which they all seem to be today. 1965 was a surprisingly elegant and sweet wine, but for no more than the first 30 minutes. Drink up – fast!

NUMBER 711.

1955   Vintage Champagne Louis Roederer (Champagne)   93p

2003/now x4 • D 20 min / G 1 h

Fine bottles with tight capsules and good levels. Decanted ten minutes. Excellent, bright yellow colour. Nose was quite closed at first, but after 30 minutes it opened well with honey, white chocolate and nutty aromas. A very classy, well-balanced, long and sensual Roederer. Intense structure with its long taste and vigorous personality. It was still fresh and had a few bubbles left to prove it. Very good now.

1870   Château Latour (Pauillac)   93p

2007/now x4 • D 30 min / G 1 h

The 1870 was one of the very last, old, grand vintages before the destruction brought about by phylloxera. Mildew attacked Latour´s vineyards from 1879 to 1887 and, together with phylloxera, ruined almost the entire vineyard. It was not until 1920 that the whole Latour vineyard was replanted with American rootstock. A fine-looking, beautiful old bottle. Not recorked. Level was mid-shoulder. Decanted 15 minutes.

   Good mature, clean and bright colour. Sound and open nose with chocolate, truffles, mint, cedar, and ripe fruit aromas - very promising. Rich and long, surprisingly youthful for its age. Some traces of oxidation. Still very much alive, but on its way out faster than we were hoping. A rare, old-style, big and fruity Latour, which still has depth and power left. The previous bottles that we have tasted (one château- and one probable Whitwham-bottling) were not this good.

1995   The Dead Arm Shiraz d'Arenberg (McLaren Vale)   93p

2006/2020 x4 • D 3 h / G 2 h

Since 1912, the Osborn family have tended their 19th century vineyards, located adjacent to their d'Arenberg winery, McLaren Vale, South Australia. The first of the now famous d'Arenberg red stripe labels was released in 1959. D'Arenberg is a rustic place and in the vineyards no irrigation is used. The wine is handcrafted using the very gentle, traditional basket presses and, in the case of their reds, small batch fermenters combined with the age-old technique of foot-treading. The hands-on and feet-on approach to winemaking ensures d'Arenberg wines are patiently and individually nurtured, giving them unforgettable personalities.

   Bottle in A1 condition. Decanted three hours. A nose of red and black spicy fruits, but still very young. Generous structure in the mouth with smooth and racy tannins. Very long finish on the palate. Already pleasant to drink for those who love young, spicy and big wines, but its optimal maturity should be reached around 2015.

1968 Barolo Giuseppe Mascarello (Piedmont)   93p

2000/now x2 • D 30 min / G 1 h

Ullages 3 cm, all the bottles were in pristine condition. Dark, almost black, deep colour. Full, open nose. A rich, tannic and voluptuous wine. Respectable balance and length. Skilfully made. A powerful, but very silky and lingering finish. Really high-quality wine that held up very well in the glass. A fine experience.

1961   *Château Cheval Blanc* (St.Emilion)   *93p*

2007/2015 x15 • D 1 h / G 3 h

Château-bottled. Good condition with by the neck level. Decanted one hour. Moderately intense, bright brick red colour. Nose delivers lots of green aromas - blackcurrant leaves, capsicum and mint. Refined, medium-bodied palate with aristocratic, firm tannins. The marked acidity is enhanced by green aromas of the wine delicately highlighting cedar and cigar box flavours. Very concentrated in style but reserved compared to the opulent and rich 1947. This wine definitely has style, but it will never grow as big and outstanding as the 1947 or even the 1964.

1966   *Château Mouton-Rothschild* (Pauillac)   *93p*

2007/2015 x4 • D 1 h / G 1 h

The 1966 vintage is an excellent one for refined classic wines. They combine the typical features, style and quality of Bordeaux wines, making them elegant and balanced. Most of them are still in fine condition today. Many of the best wines may still mature if kept correctly, but the general principle is: drink now or sell

In 1966 Mouton made first-rate wine; dark colour, open and fine bouquet of earth and tobacco. Very full and not as light-bodied as many other wines of this sensitive vintage. Complex with a good balance. At first it was a bit too tight and dry, but after one hour it opened up completely and developed richness and beautiful fruit flavours. Good and long, but a bit awkward and a dry aftertaste. Will not improve, but will still last well. A good, skilfully made wine.

1961   *Château Cos d'Estournel* (Saint-Estèphe)   *93p*

2007/2020 x6 • D 1 h / G 2 h

It is well known that Cos's first harvests were sold in India where these wines graced the sumptuous tables of the Maharajahs and Nabobs. The famous Pagodas, which surmount Cos's cellars and their door, sent from the palace of Zanzibar, symbolize this pioneering break out into the world trade. In the days of Louis Gaspard d'Estournel, Queen Victoria and the Tsar of Russia all drank Cos, as did the Emperor Napoleon III who loved this wine so much that he had several thousands bottles sent to the Palace of the Tuileries. This universal appeal embraced intellectuals; writers as famous and varied as Stendhal, Jules Verne, Eugène Labiche or Karl Marx loved Cos.

This 1961 Cos D'Estournel was in excellent condition. Château-bottled and recorked in 1996. Good, deep red colour, no sign of age. Very open and sound nose. Big and powerful, still tannic. Rich, complex and already in good balance. Nevertheless, a bit closed and hard. A well-made wine with a good future ahead of it. Tasted six times with similar notes.

1979 Cristal Rosé Roederer (Champagne) 93p

2006/2020 x2 • D 15 min / G 1 h

Superb magnum. Decanted ten minutes. Full golden colour, only a slight pink hue. Delicate, intense and toasty nose with some perfumed tropical fruit and toffee tones. A very powerful, aromatic wine, full-bodied and mouth-filling with toasty flavours, redcurrant and strawberry fruit. Good acidity and a long fresh, finish with white chocolate and apple flavours. Very pleasant now but should develop well in the bottle.

1994 Meursault 1er Cru Charmes Comtes Lafon (Côte de Beaune) 93p

2007/2020 x3 • D 1 h/G 3 h

Deep golden-hued developing eye. Soft, buttery and an astonishingly tropical nose. A fruit driven wine with delicate new oak aromas detectable on the nose and the palate. The rich and full oily mouth-feel is refreshed by medium acidity. A powerful wine with an immortal nutty finish. A great example of a maturing Meursault at a very interesting age. This wine has the structure to age for another 5 to 10 years.

1952 Vintage Bollinger (Champagne) 93p

2006/2010 x5 • D 15 min / G 1 h

The bottle was in a good condition, decanted 15 minutes. A deep, golden colour with plenty of lively, small bubbles. Open and delicious, honeyed bouquet. Rich and more flavour than you would ever expect in champagne. The taste was more like Montrachet than champagne. A full and well-balanced wine with a lengthy, gentle finish. Showing its age, but gracefully.

1961 Château Lynch-Bages (Pauillac) 93p

2004/2015 x7 • D 1 h / G 2 h

Harmonious and elegant are the best words to describe the style of Château Lynch-Bages. Therefore it is no surprise that the outstanding 1961 vintage has taken time so well. A beautiful, deep ruby red colour with a garnet rim. The nose is stylish and layered, opening up in the glass and revealing new nuances time after time. The range of aromas spans from red berry, salted liquorice, wood, and leather all the way to earthy notes. The youthful palate is firm and harmonious. This wine is peaking now, but will have no problems hanging onto its top form for another 10 to 15 years. Very recommendable.

1961 Château Lafite-Rothschild (Pauillac) 93p

2006/2015 x32 • D 45 min / G 1 h

Fine looking magnum. Excellent by the neck level. Decanted 45 minutes. Deep, dark brick red colour. The nose is expressive and stylish, but not nearly as intense and seductive as the 1959. Fine degree of fruitiness left, dark berries, roasted aromas and spiciness. Well balanced, but not as complex and multi-layered as one might expect from this great vintage's First Growth. Fairly good combination of elegance and power. Harmonious, firm yet refreshing. Softened, fully ripe tannins. At peak today but will keep there for another decade.

1998 *Celebris Gosset* *(Champagne)* 93p

2006/2020 x4 • D 30 min / G 1 h

Champagne Gosset purchases 90 percent of its grapes from all around the region's best villages. The Celebris is made exclusively of Grand Cru grapes from eight top villages. The 1998 is made of 64 percent Chardonnay from Avize, Cramant, Le Mesnil-sur-Oger, and Chouilly. The 36 percent Pinot Noir originates in Ambonnay, Aÿ, Bouzy, and Verzenay. Gosset is not a mass producer and Celebris production volumes are minimal, between 20,000 and 50,000 bottles. 40,000 bottles were made in 1998.

Rich and concentrated nose full of lively ripe fruitiness. Charmingly classical nose full of this great medium-sized producer's typical charisma. Open and voluptuous nose with spices, cinnamon and red berries. The generous fruitiness continues on the palate. The structure is stylish and firm with velvety elegant mousse. Fascinating and mouth-filling experience that is drinking well already now but possesses aging potential for 10 to 20 years' maturation.

1962 *Vintage Champagne Krug* *(Champagne)* 93p

2001/2010 x4 • D 10 min / G 45 min

A great vintage but partly forgotten and overshadowed by the 1961 vintage. This vintage has a special meaning for many, but in Krug's perspective it yielded more than just a great vintage champagne. This year Henri Krug took the lead in the house.

Moderately pale golden yellow colour. Persistent, intense and elegant nose with great depth by autolysis characters, brioche and hints of dried apricots. Very crisp palate with vivid mousse and persistent lemony flavours with dried fruits. Wonderful yeasty character adding extra dimension and texture. A long, lingering mineral finish. Beautiful balance and harmony. Just pure enjoyment!

1964 *Château Pichon Longueville Comtesse de Lalande* *(Pauillac)* 93p

2005/2015 x8 • D 30 min / G 1.5 h

Excellent magnum. Decanted only 30 minutes. Medium-intense, brick red colour with a touch of haziness. The rich and developed nose is full of cassis, soy, leather, horse saddle, and tobacco. Vivid medium-bodied palate with a moderate level of volatility adapting well with softer tannins and ripe dark fruitiness. Such a lovely wine with a silky texture and a delicate length with a great balance.

1962 Chardonnay Stony Hill Vineyard (Napa Valley) 93p

2005/now x1 • D 30 min / G 1 h

Fine looking bottle. Level was 2 cm. Decanted twenty minutes. Bright, dark golden colour. Discreet but attractive nose of minerals, cream, apples, and oak with lots of warming alcohol. Medium to full-bodied with a lovely plump texture and mouth filling flavours of vanilla, nuts, cream, and sweet peaches. Excellent integration and balance with a good, mineral, dry finish. Surprisingly good.

1960 Gewürztraminer Lenz Moser (Austria) 93p

2006/2010 x2 • D 1 h / G 1 h

The rise of the Austrian viticulture culminates from many viewpoints on the Moser family. For instance the way to cut the vines, which is still in use all around Austria, was developed by the Moser family. This Gewürztaminer is a very good example of Moser's ability to produce long-living, high-quality wines already at a time when nobody expected it from the Austrians.

This fine-looking bottle was as newborn, and purchased directly from Moser's old cellars. Level was by the neck. Decanted one hour. Surprisingly pale and light colour but has a complex, mature and spicy nose. Almost dry. Warm, full and a very pleasing soft wine. Well balanced, yet we found it lacking finesse and depth, and a bit short finish. Before tasting we had badly overlooked this wine. Genuine, serious wine of great quality that has aged gracefully.

1953 Château La Mission-Haut-Brion (Graves) 93p

2006/2010 x8 • D 1.5 hours / G 1.5 h

This great vintage was actually almost made by a single month since superb weather conditions in August took place in Bordeaux with warmth and sunshine. Although September was rainy, it caused no real damage to the well-ripened and concentrated grapes. All the five bottles were in good condition. Château-bottlings with very high-shoulder levels. Decanted one hour. Moderately intense brick red colour. Intense floral nose with ripe cassis, leather, cedar, and spices. Medium-bodied palate with elegant tannic structure, vivid acidity and intense minerality combined with ripe dark fruitiness. Spices and floral tones are more apparent in the aftertaste, which remains deliciously long. Still a very appealing wine, no further ageing is recommended.

1955 Hermitage La Chapelle Paul Jaboulet Aîné (Rhône) 93p

2003/2010 x4 • D 1 h / G 1 h

Fine looking bottle, ullage was no more than 3 cm. Domaine-bottled. Very dark, impressive, almost black colour. Coffee and chocolate nose of older wine, but still very fresh and clean. This is a deep, rich and still tannic, solid wine. Reminded us a lot of the legendary 1961, but it was not quite as concentrated and complex. Also, a bit drier and harder at the finish. On the other hand, it has good fruit and balance - a fine endeavour.

2000 *Château Mouton-Rothschild* (Pauillac) 93p

2006/2040 x4 • D 3 h / G 2 h

What could be a more perfect start for the new millennium than the 2000 vintage, already hailed as legendary? Very good, bright and intense colour. Wonderful, classic Cabernet nose with a touch of crème de cassis, truffles and cedar. A wine of enormous constitution and overwhelming power. Aromas of very ripe raspberries, with breadcrumbs and tobacco. Excellent depth and ripeness with a good balance. A long and tannic finish. A truly respectable masterpiece of this château.

1999 *Vigna d'Alceo Castello dei Rampolla* (Tuscany) 93p

2003/2020 x4 • D 3 h / G 2.5 h

One of the best Super-Tuscan wines available. A blend of Cabernet Sauvignon and Petit Verdot is something no other Italian producer would easily do. Decanted two hours. Deep purple and ruby colour. Very inky and spicy nose full of dark fruits and cedar aromas. The full-bodied palate is dominated by racy acidity, powdery ripe, big tannins and a very intense ripe fruit of cassis and cherries. Oak is sublimely well integrated, adding loads of spicy anise, smoke and hints of tar aromas. The long lingering and intense finish reflects true harmony and sophistication, guaranteeing a great future for this wine.

1968 *Prado Enea Bodegas Muga* (Rioja) 93p

2006/2010 x4 • D 30 min / G 1 h

This beautiful 1968 looked as good as new. The level was by the neck. Decanted for only 15 minutes. A bright, ruby red colour with relatively little sign of development. At the start the nose was a bit blocked, but after 15 minutes it opened with an intense bouquet of black currant and other black fruits, with hints of vanilla and woody notes. Round and neat, fleshy and as loaded as we remembered. A light and slightly too short aftertaste. This was a lovely and pleasant experience!

1998 *Grange Penfolds* (South Australia) 93p

2006/2025 x7 • D 4 h / G 2 h

Enjoying a very good reputation, the Penfolds Grange 1998 is placed within the classic vintages. Despite being labelled as Shiraz, the 1998 has three percent Cabernet Sauvignon in it. The grapes are sourced from the Penfolds Kalimna Vineyard and other Barossa Vineyards, with proportions from Padthaway. The Magill Estate Shiraz accounts for seven percent of the blend. Warm summer and low rainfall characterised this structured and fine vintage.

Opaque, dark, near-black colour. The nose is pronounced and packed with fruit and overwhelming cassis, liquorice and menthol aromas. The palate is very full and thick with concentrated fruitiness and new oak. A blockbuster wine of firm ripe tannins, balanced acidity and warming alcohol. Voluptuous mouth-feel and a persistent finish. Needs time in the bottle for improved integration. At its peak within five years and will keep there up to 20.

1918   *Corton-Charlemagne Faiveley* (Côte de Nuits)   *93p*

2006/now x3 • D 30 min / G 20 min

The First World War ended on November 11, 1918. It cost France hugely. The country lost more than 1.3 million men, with three million more wounded. The Germans had destroyed several towns, mines and railways, and agriculture suffered. The population in Reims dropped from the pre-war 117,000 to 17,000. The price of products and services had risen fourfold since the beginning of the war. On the other hand, inflation raised the prices of agricultural products higher than their production cost, which meant that wine growers, among others, did better than before 1914.

Most Burgundy villages had made it through the war with only light damage, but there was a great deficit of skilled workers. Despite the difficult times, the rather average harvest of 1918 created a few excellent wines, such as this golden beauty.

From the outside the wine was in good condition, fill level 4 cm and bottled at the domaine. Decanted for 25 minutes, retained its best qualities for approximately 20 minutes in the glass.

Deep golden and pure colour. Attractive and open, slightly woody, but an abundantly fruity nose. A very full and masculine wine. A surprisingly multilayered and interesting experience. A touch too acidic, but otherwise a very balanced, harmonious wine. The aftertaste could not be described as short, but it was too soft and unnoticeable, perhaps too subtle for an otherwise muscular wine. A good job by peace-loving people.

1996   *Monte Bello Ridge* (Santa Cruz Mountains)   *93p*

2006/2015 x2 • D 2 h / G 2 h

The year began with two storms. March and April provided beautiful weather for vine development, but a rare May thunderstorm with winds struck just as the vines bloomed. On Monte Bello's upper and middle vineyards, Cabernet Sauvignon and Merlot yields were reduced by a third; on the lower vineyards even more. The hot summer and small crop accelerated ripening and Monte Bello was harvested two weeks before normal.

Aged almost entirely in new American oak, the 1996 is a remarkably balanced, silky and structured wine. Developed Cabernet nose of farmyard and vegetal notes, as well as cassis. Nuanced and layered, this wine succeeds in being thick and elegant at the same time. Very balanced alcohol and ripe structured tannin. A masterpiece of style.

1897   *Pinot Noir Inglenook* (Napa Valley)   *93p*

2005/now x3 • D 30 min / G 1 h

By 1890 Inglenook had become a shining example for all Californian wineries. Around that time the Napa Valley wine industry gained extra support through Europe's misfortune. The period between 1880 and 1896, when the phylloxera was ravaging the vineyards of Europe, was the high point for all Napa Valley Wineries.

When Captain Niebaum, the founder of the Inglenook Estate, died in 1908, he was one of America's wealthiest men. His story, of a non-English speaking Finnish cabin-boy who became one of the wealthiest men in America, and who eventually spoke seven languages, is one of those pioneer stories that created the myth of "the American dream". This American dream continued in 1975 when the world famous film director Francis Ford Coppola purchased Inglenook and continued successfully the making of high quality wines.

This old, fine looking Pinot Noir was discovered recently from an old cellar in Austria. We have no idea how it got there. The level was good, three centimetres below the cork, and the label was still readable. Decanted for 15 minutes. Quite a dark, deep red colour. Sound and open, quite sweet, clean chocolate nose with a touch of earth, truffles and leather. Fuller and more intense than the previous bottle. A very good bottle. Has some good fruit and acidity left. Still very drinkable, a well-made wine.

1960   Château Musar *(Lebanon)*   93p
2003/2010 x3 • D 1 h / G 1 h

The 1960 was the first vintage made with new philosophy brought by Serge Hochar to the winemaking process at Musar: no additives, no fining, no treatment, and no filtration applied to the wines.

This forty-year-old bottle looked like new, and had excellent by-the-neck level. A very dark and deep, mature-looking appearance. A sound and clean bouquet with wonderful scented flavours of chocolate, vanilla and strawberry fruit. A surprisingly full-bodied and complex wine. Still very sweet on the palate with soft, melted tannins. This Musar has a long and lingering, smooth aftertaste. This one was a lot more enhanced and youthful individual than the previous two bottles we had tasted. The old saying "there are no great wines, only great bottles" rings true again! For us Château Musar is the best wine of the difficult 1960 vintage.

1945   Château Lafite-Rothschild *(Pauillac)*   93p
2007/2015 x11 • D 1 h / G 1 h

Lafite has the lightest colour of the 1945's Premier Crus, now quite tawny. This was a top-shoulder bottle, and the colour was promising - clear and bright! New capsule - probably recorked at the Château. Very sound, ripe, concentrated, mellow nose, quite full and vigorous, promising some classic fruit and complexity, but on the palate a bit too thin, light, and moderate - lacking some fruitiness and follow-through. Nevertheless, this is a mellow and sophisticated wine. Needs good decanting and attention to be really appreciated.

1978   Barbaresco Costa Russi Angelo Gaja *(Piedmont)*   93p
2004/2010 x2 • D 30 min / G 1 h

Great vintage for Barbaresco and Barolo. Average winter, cool and wet spring. The hot and dry season started in mid-June and lasted through the harvest. Natural selection and a warm autumn destined a very small crop with high tannin and alcohol levels.

The eleven-acre Costa Russi vineyard was acquired by the Gaja family in 1950. A "costa" is the side of a hill that faces the sun. "Russi" is the name of the former owners of this vineyard. The first vintage of Costa Russi single-vineyard Barbaresco to be vinified separately was 1978 (released in 1981).

A fine bottle. Decanted 30 minutes. Open, sound and mature nose with aromas of leather and cocoa dominating. On the palate the wine shows generous amounts of dark, ripe fruit and soft tannins. Rich but lacking an element of real charm and was not as well balanced as expected. Not too short or cruel but it did not hold up well in the glass. Still a very good but not great wine.

1942 Unico Bodegas Vega Sicilia *(Ribera del Duero)* 93p
2003/2010 x4 • D 1 h / G 1 h

Fine looking bottle with good level. Decanted one hour. Superlatively aromatic, meaty bouquet - almost like an old Burgundy. It has a very complex, solid and firm structure. So fresh and youthful, but not as concentrated and generous as the 1953. A very fine effort, but not enough to be great!

1955 Chambertin Clos-de-Bèze Jules Belin *(Côte de Nuits)* 93p
2004/now x11 • D 1 h / G 1 h

Level 4 cm. Decanted 45 minutes. Mature, healthy colour. Very ripe nose. Ample, plummy and full of fruit. This is very seductive. Round and opulent and with a very good grip and balance. A sweet and tender aftertaste. Very good at best.

1967 Romanée-Conti Domaine de la Romanée-Conti *(Côte de Nuits)* 93p
2004/2010 x2 • D 45 min /G 30 min

This 1967 was in very good condition - ullage was only 1 cm. Smoky, rich and wide nose - opened up beautifully. Great chocolaty, spicy extract. Quite a good balance but not as complex or masculine as one would hope. Light and "too easy" to drink. Within 45 minutes this wine dried out. It will not get any better and needs to be drunk up. Pleasant experience, nevertheless.

1962 Château Latour *(Pauillac)* 93p
2002/2015 x3 • D 1 h / G 1 h

A good-looking bottle, top shoulder and a very promising deep, dark colour. Quite a powerful and fruity bouquet. This is attractive, sound and nicely balanced. The palate opened well with a gentle touch of mint and chocolate, finishing with soft tannins and charm. The Latour, which is usually such a slow developer, is less tight and coarse than many wines of this vintage. Tasted three times with similar notes.

NUMBER 741. NUMBER 742. NUMBER 743. NUMBER 744.

1996   Dom Pérignon Moët & Chandon *(Champagne)*   93p
2007/now x7 • D 15 min / G 1 h

This equal blend of Chardonnay and Pinot Noir is an epitome of purity and intensity. A refined nose of white fruits and a touch of smoky minerality. Still a somewhat closed and youthful wine, masking a great deal of the complexity. Well-integrated smooth bubbles and searing acidity refresh the wine beautifully. This vintage is practically immortal, so hold on to this Dom Pérignon as long as your patience lasts.

1970   Tignanello Antinori *(Tuscany)*   93p
2006/now x2 • D 1 h / G 3 h

The bottle was in a decent condition with base neck level. Decanted for one hour. A very deep, brown colour - like an old Barolo. Not a very wide nose, rather restrained and flat, and it stayed like that. Also blocked on the palate, all the flavour was hidden. It took almost two hours for them to become noticeable, but it was worth the wait. No attack, but then it had some sweet fruit, alongside the soft tannin and enough acidity to keep the wine alive. After three hours it became more and more seductive. Lovely, rich taste packed with sweet fruit, coffee and chocolaty flavours with a bit short but sweet finish. This wine truly needed a few hours to be something special, as in real life, it took some years before Tignanello found that ideal blend and structure which put them on the top of the Tuscan wine map permanently. A very promising start!

1995   Salon *(Champagne)*   93p
2005/2020 x12 • D 30 min / G 1 h

Salon is considered to be the first marketer of true terroir champagne in 1911. It is a monocru, mono-cepage Chardonnay from Le Mesnil. Its razor-sharp style at youth is a result of its non-maloed nature and top quality Le Mesnil grapes. Therefore, it is a very difficult wine to judge before the metamorphosis of Chardonnay into its creamy, broad and nutty form has taken place. The points for this 1995 will undoubtedly rise within the next ten years. A vin de grade.

Rich and ripe fruity nose with floral tones, wax and toast aromas. The fresh yet vinous palate is smoky and mineral. Fruit intensity could be still a touch higher. An elegant and mineral Chardonnay that is still extremely youthful. Mousse was slightly aggressive on the palate, but the wine opened up and improved significantly in the glass. There is great potential and the wine needs at least 10 more years until it is starting to reveal all its charm.

1961   Ygrec Y, Château d'Yquem *(Bordeaux)*   93p
2004/2010 x2 • D 2 h / G 2 h

We believe, "Y" is a high quality, out of the ordinary, dry white wine with great ageing potential – up to 100 years. This 1961 was in perfect condition. Level was by the neck. Decanted 30 minutes. Medium-gold, fine and fresh colour. A round vanilla and sweet fruit nose. Heavy and well balanced. In the mouth the wine was still quite tight, but all the elements of good concentration, touches of botrytised fruit and a firm structure, were there. Just decant the wine a few hours before tasting and wait. Your patience will be rewarded. A very long and complex, curious and most intellectual wine.

1952 *La Tâche Domaine de la Romanée-Conti* (Côte de Nuits)   *93p*
2005/2015 x5 • D 1 h / G 1 h

Excellent appearance. Level was 3 cm below the cork. Decanted one hour. The nose is very strong, exotic fruits and spices and intensive peppery nuances. Slender fruit, the experience was somewhat modest, and did not meet the expectations of the bouquet and colour. The aftertaste was short but balanced. On the whole, it was a slight disappointment despite the bottle's flawless condition with a 3 cm ullage.

1975 *Grüner Veltliner Schloss Gobelsburg* (Kamptal)   *93p*
2007/2010 x2 • D 1 h / G 1 h

This wine came from the cellars of Schloss Gobelsburg and was made by the Stift Zwettl cistersian monks. The dusty and mouldy bottle revealed outstanding content. The colour was a deep, straw yellow and developed. The nose was fairly pronounced with spicy, lanolin and vegetal notes. The medium-bodied wine was admirably intensely fruity, refreshed by the crisp acidity and moderate alcohol. An attractive mature Grüner Veltliner, which shows the variety's potential in retaining fruit and structure for decades. At peak now.

1961 *Château Talbot* (Saint-Julien)   *93p*
2004/2020 x6 • D 1 h / G 1 h

A great Talbot from this superb vintage. A medium-deep, brown-hued, mature colour. A sophisticated and fascinating multidimensional aroma: tobacco, roasted aromas, bell pepper, and leather. Refreshing acidity and firm and mature tannins. A medium body that could use some more weight on the mid-palate. Otherwise delicious and drinking still perfectly today.

1996 *Run Rig Torbreck* (Barossa Valley)   *93p*
2006/2015 x4 • D 2 h / G 2 h

The Torbreck Run Rig Shiraz (first vintage 1995) is sourced from 80 to 125-year-old dry grown vineyards located on the western ridge of the Barossa. Dave Powell's simple philosophy of "great wines are made in the vineyard" leads to a laissez-faire approach. Traditional winemaking techniques comprising of batch vinification in open concrete fermenters are combined with suitably offbeat ideas about the effects of ultra-violet and gravitational pull on polymerisation of tannins, fermentation speeds and Baumé levels. The tiny (3%) Viognier component and the American oak matured Shiraz pressings profoundly influence the aroma and flavour profile. The wine is matured in 40 percent new French oak for up to two and a half years. Yields were only 1.5

Domaine de Chevalier

tons of fruit per acre, and production was a minuscule 150 cases.

Decanted four hours. Rich, aromatic bouquet with aromas of roasted herbs, blackberry and smoke. Warm and inviting. The palate is terrifically complex, and solidly packed with concentrated black fruit, yet it is composed and well balanced with a powerful, long, intense finish.

1979 *Charles Heidsieck Rosé* (Champagne) 93p

2005/2010 x2 • D 1 h / G 1 h

Cold winter and May frosts characterised the early part of the 1979 growing season. In June and July the weather was very favourable and warm, ripening a healthy and unproblematic crop of good volume (11,061 kg/ha). These structured and elegant wines have matured graciously. This Charles Heidsieck Rosé was at a great age for drinking and showed very well.

A developed orange-hued colour. Wide watery rim suggests aging as well. Rich and sweet aroma profile: roasted coffee beans, caramelized sugar and red berries. Mushroom character on the palate as well. A very delicate silky mousse. A pronounced entity that is refreshed by the lively acid structure.

1875 *Chambertin Bouchard Père et Fils* (Côte de Nuits) 93p

2006/now x3 • D 30 min / G 30 min

Good-looking, very dusty bottle with only remnants of the label left. Level was 5 cm and colour was extremely promising. Decanted 30 minutes before tasting. Attractive, dark, evolved colour. No trace of oxidation. Sound and wide open bouquet with chocolaty and ripe fruit flavours. Very fresh and alive - almost too breezy. Round, soft, forward, and syrupy wine. Not much tannin but still has a good backbone. A very long and hot, sweet aftertaste, as if some chocolate liqueur was added. An unusual and curiously fascinating experience!

1982 *Cristal Rosé Roederer* (Champagne) 93p

2005/2020 x3 • D 20 min / G 1 h

Light salmon rose colour with refined bubbles. Decadent and delightful nose with strawberries, biscuit and hints of toastiness. A very crisp, light-bodied wine with a persistent and mouth-capturing mousse reflecting marked minerality and lovely brioche flavours that are enhanced by delicate strawberry aromas. Long, lingering finish.

1947 *Château Figeac* (St.Emilion) 93p

2007/2015 x17 • D 45 min /G 1 h

Bottles were in decent condition. All had very good top-shoulder levels and promising colours. Solid, mature ruby colour with a wide, bright orange rim. Lovely, open and sound nose. Not huge, but packed with very ripe, sweet, cassis fruit and dark chocolate. Attractively soft and round on the palate, with perfectly balanced tannins and a good, supporting acidity. Plenty of heat and concentration too, but lacks some complexity and weight. Very nice wine, with a generous nature and sweet, dry, medium-long finish.

1929 *Hermannshof Auslese Franz Schmitt* (Germany)   *93p*
2004/now x5 • D 30 min / G 1 h

Excellent appearance. Recorked in 1999. Decanted for 30 minutes. Clear, bright-gold colour. Fresh, sound and magnificently sweet nose with just a hint of petroleum. Almost perfect balance and structure. Round, delicate and long, spicy, flavourful aftertaste. Top quality and still in outstanding condition. It is always somehow sad to drink a wine you are never going to find again - a memorable moment.

1945 *Château Margaux* (Margaux)   *93p*
2003/2010 x3 • D 1 h / G 2 h

Fine looking bottle with top-shoulder level. The browning, deep colour looked and felt familiar. A clean, yet quite closed and faint bouquet did not yet tell much about the wine. Only after about an hour did the bouquet start to build up with depth and diverse layers. A round and elegant wine. Silky, though some slightly harsh tannins regrettably interfere on the mid-palate. Somehow we could not find the balance and harmony that Margaux is famous for. Good, but not quite the level one would expect from a magnificent 1945 first growth wine.

1995 *Cabernet Sauvignon Reserve Robert Mondavi* (Napa Valley)   *93 p*
2003/2015 x2 • D 2 h / G 1.5 h

Cool weather conditions in the Napa Valley extended the ripening time, resulting in exceptional depth of flavours. The vintage is reminiscent of 1986, 1991 and 1994, only showing a little warmer night time temperatures compared, for example, to 1994. Thus the acidity levels are not as high but the balance and complexity are very apparent in this lovely wine. The blend is 92 percent Cabernet Sauvignon, 4 percent Merlot and 4 percent Cabernet Franc.

Deep garnet colour with tawny tints. The intense and rich nose serves ripe cassis combined with developed meaty, leathery and spicy aromas. On the palate the wine is very open with a harmonious texture. Cheerful acidity balances nicely ripe and round, velvety tannins and intense, dark fruit. A very opulent, full-bodied wine maturing gracefully, but still showing a charming youthfulness. Very enjoyable at the moment but will keep for another ten years.

1943 Château Pétrus (Pomerol) 93p
2005/now x4 • D 1 h / G 1 h

A wonderful-looking, château-bottled Pétrus. Decanted 45 minutes. Top-shoulder level. Dark, good, bright colour. Quite tight and tough right after decanting - blocked and tight on the nose. But after 30 more minutes it opened and became a generous, open-handed wine. Fleshy, rich and nicely balanced, but the body was rather simple, lacking intensity and complexity. It also has quite low acidity and a long, gentle finish. While it was certainly delightful now, it is not going improve, or even last for long.

1937 Chapelle-Chambertin Domaine Leroy (Côte de Nuits) 93p
2005/2010 x3 • D 30 min / G 1 h

Very old looking bottle with 5cm level. Decanted 30 minutes. Bright and deep colour. A subtle, integrated nose - earthy, slightly vegetal with faint blackberry and apricot fruit - appealing. Full-bodied with intense flavours of black fruits, dark chocolate and gentle woody notes. Layered with a kind undercurrent of barnyard and mushrooms - not too dry and quite well balanced. Decent length. Although not a big wine, it is charming, fruity and delicious. Drink now.

1947 Echézeaux Domaine de la Romanée-Conti (Côte de Nuits) 93p
2007/2015 x3 • D 1 h / G 1 h

Wonderful, old-looking bottle with 4 cm level. Decanted one hour. Bright, developed, brick red colour. The nose is lively and roasted with the cherry aromas well preserved in this mature wine. The refreshing and vivid palate suffered from a slight volatility and tart acidity. The medium-bodied wine was softened attractively by the smooth silk-like mouth-feel. A charming, mature wine that will no longer improve but will keep for another 5 to 10 years.

1997 Gewürztraminer Sélection des Grains Nobles Rimelsberg 93p
Marc Tempé (Alsace) 2002/2015 x1 • D 1 h / G 2 h

Bright and rich yellow colour. A very rich perfume nose with floral tones of roses and honey with hints of ly- ches. Luscious palate with incredible syrupy texture, refreshed by a tropical fruitiness and apricots. Although the wine shows a moderately low acidity, it is still enough to carry it. Long, concentrated finish is delightfully fresh and balanced. Enjoy whenever you find a bottle of this heart melting wine!

1999 Château Mouton-Rothschild (Pauillac) 93p
2006/2015 x3 • D 2 h / G 2 h

Very deep, dark colour. Distinguished, intense and youthful nose. There were lots of earth and carob flavours and a touch of blackcurrant, along with secondary flavours of coffee and raisins. A very classic Mouton look.

Super-concentrated, full and vigorous wine. Well-balanced with a long, chocolaty and truffle-flavoured finish. Ready and mouth-watering now, will get better with more age. An elegant, seductive wine.

1921   *Vintage Champagne Fred Lerouix* (Champagne)   *93p*
2006/now x5 • D 10 min / G 10 min

All these five bottles were like new. Fine levels and labels. Decanted only ten minutes. Medium deep, mature golden colour. Very slight effervescence detectable. Wide open ripe honeyed and toasty nose. The nose promises a lot for the palate but fruitiness is almost on decline. Acidity keeps the wine lively and attractive. Past its peak but very enjoyable, nearly still wine from Champagne.

NUMBER 765.

1922   *Reserva Marqués de Riscal* (Rioja)   *93p*
2005/2010 x5 • D 1 h / G 1 h

An old bottle with only a few parts of the label left. Otherwise in excellent condition with top-shoulder level and a colour that raised our expectations. Decanted 30 minutes. Not a very deep colour, but bright and clear. The bouquet did not reveal itself at once. Another 30 minutes aeration in the glass opened it fully: rich bouquet of very ripe fruit, vanilla and spice aromas developed. In the mouth, the wine was extremely sensitive and light, but perfectly harmonious. The tannin was very well absorbed. Medium-long, delicate finish. Drink now.

NUMBER 766.

1876   *Geisenheimer Rothenberg Auslese Weingut Langwerth von Simmern* (Germany)   *93p*
2004/now x2 • D 15 min / G 30 min

This rare beauty was tasted at Rheingau Wine and Gourmet Festival in Hattenheim. The bottle was in perfect condition. Decanted 15 minutes. Surprisingly light, pale colour. The bouquet was quite modest and dry. On the palate, this well-matured, nicely balanced, a bit one-dimensional wine was ample with citrus fruit, white chocolate, and poached pear aromas. A little bit too dry and not very complex wine, but it had good length and a pure finish. A rare and unique tasting.

NUMBER 767.

1959   *Brut Impérial Moët & Chandon* (Champagne)   *93p*
2004/now x3 • D 20 min / G 15 min

Tasted as an aperitif a large Mouton-Rothschild dinner in Rheingau. The bottle was in excellent condition. A wonderful wine, full of life with a great, golden colour. Lively, small bubbles. A very rich, toasty and soft, elegant wine. Perhaps not as complex and classy as Dom Pérignon 1959, but very close. A bit tired and short at the finish, but otherwise almost liquid gold!

NUMBER 768.

1947   La Tâche Domaine de la Romanée-Conti *(Côte de Nuits)*   *93p*
2005/2010 x4 • D 1 h / G 1 h

Fine looking bottle. Level was 3 cm. Decanted 45 minutes. Good, bright and healthy colour. The nose was very strong, exotic and intensive with hints of exotic spices, but the palate was somewhat modest, and did not meet the expectations laid by the bouquet and colour. Still quite full-bodied, well-balanced and sweet, with high viscosity and alcohol. The aftertaste was a bit sharp, but pleasurable and long. A better bottle than the previous ones.

1999   The Dead Arm Shiraz d'Arenberg *(McLaren Vale)*   *93p*
2005/2015 x2 • D 2 h / G 3 h

1999 had a dry winter, accompanied by moderate temperatures for all months. However, there were a considerable amount of drizzly days at the time of the harvest, causing a few headaches with varieties that are sensitive to Botrytis bunch rot, i.e. Grenache. It did clear up, though, and the wines produced were all closed and slightly below average in intensity. They are looking better all the time.

Deep, almost opaque, purple colour. Very intense ripe dark fruity nose with blackcurrants and blueberries, butterscotch and spicy cedar notes. A full-bodied, refined and complex wine with velvety texture. Loads of jammy dark fruit, refined tannins and a great broad taste with vanilla and coffee tones. A touch of menthol in the long finish. An immense concentration due to the old vines and dead arm disease reduced yield.

1990   Belle Epoque Perrier-Jouët *(Champagne)*   *93p*
2004/2020 x6 • D 15 min / G 30 min

The Perrier-Jouët prestige cuvée is made to express the spirit of the Belle Epoque era with its sophisticated, rich, fruity and floral style. The blend is 50 percent Chardonnay, 45 percent Pinot Noir and 5 percent Pinot Meunier. Today 60 percent of the grape need comes from the house's own vineyards with emphasis on Cramant and Avize origins. The champagne is made customarily from cuvée only, which is fermented at approximately 18 degrees centigrade. Malo-lactic fermentation is carried out without exception. Dosage is around 8-8,5 grams emphasizing the elegant style but making it a difficult champagne to appreciate when young. The 1990 is fruity, rich, sweet, brioche like on the nose with apple aromas. Mouth-feel is creamy and elegant with the Chardonnay starting to show its wide and toasty side. Acidity is not highlighted. At the finish more mineral notes emerge and the structure becomes firmer. Quite easily approachable champagne today that is reaching its peak in five to ten years time.

1978   Tinto Pesquera Reserva Alejandro Fernández *(Ribera del Duero)*   *93p*
2007/2010 x 4 • D 30 min / G 30 min

The third vintage of Tinto Pesquera ever made. This was never released to international markets. Bottles were in perfect shape, handed directly from Bodegas by Alejandro Fernández.

Moderately intense cherry red colour with orange tints. Restrained little closed nose with leathery and nutty aromas. A lovely, delicate, medium-bodied wine on the palate with vivid acidity, powdery tannins and a satin-like texture. Very concentrated although restrained in style. Moderately long harmonious finish with mineral and nutty tones. Wine has most likely peaked around ten years ago, but has still aged gracefully and is drinking absolutely perfectly now.

1941 *Vintage Champagne Mercier* (Champagne)   93p

2005/now x2 • D 10 min / G 1 h

Eugène Mercier, the founder of this lively champagne house, was a man of amazing energy and ideas. He was only twenty years old when his ambition to bring high-quality champagne to ordinary folk began. To get the awareness of the masses, he promptly developed a highly creative advertising strategy with a series of stunning events. One of his greatest publicity stunts was a giant, twenty-ton "Cathedral of Champagne" cask. He wanted to build it from old Hungarian oak, and for this reason he travelled to Hungary to hand-pick those 150 oak trees, which would be cut down for the vat's construction. After twenty years of hard work, the vat was ready for transportation to Paris for the 1899 World Exhibition. It took eight days and nights, twenty-four oxen and eighteen horses, to transport the world's largest wine cask with 200.000 bottles capacity from Epernay to Paris. A number of city lights and building facades were damaged on route, but the publicity achieved made all the tough work worthwhile. Afterwards it was returned to Epernay, where it was used for blending until 1947.

A very good-looking bottle, almost in mint condition. Decanted for 30 minutes. A marvellous bright, golden colour with some tiny, slowly running bubbles left. Clean and fresh, delicate bouquet with hazelnut and apricot flavours, deliciously honeyed. Round and luscious, showing age and immense richness. The finish appeared to be slightly sharp, one-dimensional and short. However, it was a splendid wine with great balance, and far from average, everyday champagne. It should be drunk fairly quickly after opening. Old gentle champagne with a captivating commercial saga.

2000 *Côte-Rôtie La Mouline Guigal* (Rhône)   93p

2007/2020 x2 • D 4 h / G 3 h

"La Mouline" parcel in the Côte Blonde part of Côte-Rôtie is a significant vineyard to the Guigal family. The Côte Blonde is a limestone and chalk terroir giving a distinguished and elegant nature to its wines. La Mouline is a 1 ha parcel planted with 89 percent Syrah and 11 percent Viognier. Average age of the vines is very high and the annual output is tiny, around 5,000 bottles.

Still a very youthful wine, evident from its deep undeveloped colour and primary aromatics. Fairly closed nose of dark forest berries, elegant pepperiness and earthiness. High new oak influence is still present on both nose and the palate. A firm-textured, tight and mineral mouth-feel is appealing by being pronounced and restrained at the same time. A very elegant wine with promises of a great future due to its inherent harmony and complexity.

NUMBER 773.

NUMBER 774.

1877 Château Margaux (Margaux)   93p

1999/now x2 • D 15 min / G 30 min

Very old and dusty looking bottle. Négociant-bottled. Level was low-shoulder, but the wine still showed a healthy, promising colour. Decanted 30 minutes. A wonderful complex nose, touch of melted butter and cedar. A lovely, smooth and well balanced structure. Deliciously complex, mature and still vibrant, with spicy, mint and chocolate flavours. The finish was fairly dry and not very persistent. Otherwise a wine that is still not only alive but one offering a delicate, succulent experience. Needs careful decanting shortly before drinking.

NUMBER 775.

1990 Cabernet Sauvignon Coonawarra John Riddoch   93p
Limited Release Wynn's Coonawarra Estate 2007/2020 x4 • D 1 h / G 1 h

What is now Wynns Coonawarra Estate was founded by Scottish pioneer John Riddoch, who noticed the fertility of a small strip of red soil - terra rossa - in the far south-east of South Australia. He planted vineyards in 1891 and completed the estate's three-gabled winery in 1896. Riddoch died in 1901 and Coonawarra languished for the first half of this century. Coonawarra's revival began in 1951 when Melbourne wine merchants Samuel and David Wynn purchased Riddoch's original vineyards and winery and renamed the property Wynns Coonawarra Estate. The Wynns recognised the intrinsic qualities of Coonawarra wines - their richness and intensity of fruit character - and set out to build an independent identity in the region. They created the famous label that has made John Riddoch's winery one of Australia's best-known buildings.

Today Wynns Coonawarra Estate is the region's pre-eminent wine producer and the largest single vineyard holder with the best and longest established vineyard sites in Coonawarra. Its wines are regarded as benchmarks for the district, lauded for their consistent quality and depth of flavour. Of all the Australian wine making regions, Coonawarra - an Aboriginal word meaning 'honeysuckle' - stands alone in a number of respects. Most other Australian wine regions were established close to the major Australian cities. Coonawarra however, is an isolated region 450 km away from either Melbourne or Adelaide. In contrast to its worldwide reputation, the Coonawarra region is a relatively tiny, cigar shaped strip about 15 km long and 2 km at its widest point. Like many great wine regions of the world, Coonawarra's climate is cool and marginal. It is South Australia's southernmost wine region, only 60 km from the chilly southern ocean and cold Antarctic winds. This cool climate ensures a long ripening period that builds up the intensity of flavours slowly in the grape. The resulting wines will always be among Australia's greatest wines for their richness, intensity, depth of flavour, and excellent longevity.

Wynns Coonawarra Estate John Riddoch Cabernet Sauvignon has, over the past decade, confirmed its status as Coonawarra's benchmark Cabernet. The 1990 Cabernet continues the tradition with its rich, firm style and the capacity to develop great complexity with extended cellaring.

Decanted one hour. Opulent, ripe and multifaceted, the appealing bouquet is a vigorous blend of blueberry, mint, black coffee, dark chocolate, and earthy aromas and flavours. Full-bodied and powerful, the wine is intense and concentrated, yet smooth and vibrant. It finishes with a long, complex, detailed aftertaste that lingers. Drink from now to 2015.

NUMBER 776.

2000   Château Lynch-Bages *(Pauillac)*   *93p*

2004/2030 x9 • D 8 h / G 3.5 h

Dark, purple colour. Very sophisticated and complex nose revealing cassis, capsicum, coffee, and mint. The very same aromas, as Mouton has on the nose. An opulent, medium-bodied wine with extraordinary concentration and a chewy texture. Ripe round tannins with a mouth-watering acidity and intense dark fruitiness. The flavour shows dark chocolate and hints of anise. A very intense and long finish. An absolutely gracious wine with a long life ahead. Further bottle ageing of 10-15 years will enhance the charm of the wine.

1918   Château La Mission-Haut-Brion *(Graves)*   *93p*

2000/now x3 • D 1 h / G 1 h

We bought this 1918 La Mission for $215 in 1997, and thought it was a fair price for this surprisingly fresh and broad wine. An excellent bottle. Level was top-shoulder. Decanted one hour. A deep, dark, bright and youthful colour. A superb open bouquet with spicy fruit and truffles. At first, it tasted a bit dry and tannic, but after 30 minutes it turned into a full, round and elegant wine with high complexity of taste. Very ripe and velvety in the mouth. It ends quite hard and dry but with a warm and long aftertaste. Surprisingly attractive.

1970   Georges de Latour Beaulieu Vineyard *(Napa Valley)*   *93p*

2002/2010 x4 • D 15 min / G 45 min

This historic and legendary Napa Valley winery was established by George de Latour and his wife Fernande in 1900. The name indicates a beautiful place and it was named when Fernande saw the estate surroundings for the first time. The estate became the benchmark winery after hiring the famous winemaker André Tchelistcheff as chief winemaker after Prohibition in mid-1930s. Within next ten years the BV wines were served at all major White House functions. This 100 percent Cabernet Sauvignon wine, the benchmark California Cabernet, was made from an extraordinary small crop from a very good vintage. The crop remained small due to almost a month's heavy night frosts and the heat stress during the extremely hot summer. The wine expresses wonderfully the vintage with huge concentration.

The appearance shows very unpromising signs being excessively developed and brown in colour with plenty of sediment. The nose turns very clean and intense. Moderately intense, developed aromas of leather and tar marry well with chocolate, plums and figs. Mellow tannins, balancing acidity and surprisingly intense fruitiness with dark strawberry, plum and fig notes. A balanced and elegant wine with a long finish. Very pleasant, classy and adorable mature Cabernet from Napa.

1996   Château d'Yquem *(Sauternes)*   *93p*

2005/2030 x12 • D 3 h / G 5 h

Half-bottle. Decanted two hours. Light yellow colour. Multilayered nose with intense, perfumed, dried apricot, violets, honey aromas, and some savoury oak nuances. Very concentrated, supple palate with delicious lemon and orange peel flavours balanced nicely by savoury oak and razor-sharp acidity. It has a super-expansive mid-palate, in addition to the luxurious richness for which this great property is well known. A medium-sweet and long finish. Will develop and last for decades.

1950 *Château Gruaud-Larose* (Saint-Julien) 93p
2004/now x3 • D 1 h / G 2 h

A fine-looking bottle, the level was top-shoulder. Bottled by Cordier. Decanted one hour. A fairly deep appearance, but was showing an orange-rim maturity. Ripe, earthy, sound nose with some mushroom and truffle flavours. Seemed quite promising and opened up fully in two hours. Around this time we noted some sweetness, cedar, vanilla, and spice on the nose. Quite a big, serious wine, but almost too tannic for our taste. Very fleshy and rich with good length and a dry finish, a touch of unpleasant bitterness. This is now as good as it gets, so drink up before it dries out.

1999 *Chardonnay Three Sisters Vineyard Marcassin* (Sonoma) 93p
2005/2015 x4 • D 2 h / G 2 h

Decanted two hours. Interesting nose of citrus notes and butter. Much grander taste than the nose -lemon, tart apples and buttered popcorn. Very concentrated palate with lots of fruit and acidity, but then followed by a long robust finish. Overall, a bit tight and not very harmonious, but very promising. Should be very good with aging and integration-probably needs 3-5 years.

1896 *Colheita Quinta do Noval* (Portugal) 93p
2001/now x2 • D 1 h / G 3 h

Fine-looking bottle rarity. Level was by the neck. Decanted one hour. Bright pale tawny colour with just a hint of amber. Enveloping and warm nose with richness of plums, white chocolate, jammy cherries, all lifted by little hints of smoke and tobacco. Smooth-textured and soft-edged on the palate, with a delicious sweetness. Not very complex or multi-layered, but has beautiful harmony and drinkability. Good length and awareness. An elegant, soul-warming colheita.

1949 *Viña Real Gran Reserva C.V.N.E.* (Rioja) 93p
2007/now x9 • D 1 h / G 1 h

Bottle came directly from the bodegas. Excellent condition with by-the-neck level. Decanted 45 minutes. This 1949 Viña Real is notable for its finesse, elegance and even more notable in the graceful way it has aged. Almost 60 years old, and still a beautiful Rioja.

Deep, bright ruby colour, with small tawny orange hue. Wonderful perfumed nose of sweet fruit, vanilla and truffles. The flavours are pure, with no sense of the fruit having dried out. Velvety mouth-feel, silky smooth texture with flavours of old leather and white chocolate emerging over a firm background. Relatively low acidity, otherwise well balanced. Very soft tannins and a long, sweet, but a bit too dry aftertaste.

1949   *Scharzhof Auslese Egon Müller* (Mosel-Saar-Ruwer)   *93p*
2005/2010 x2 • D 30 min / G 1 h

Fully mature deep colour. The nose is aromatic with honey, apricot and mineral nuances. The palate brings on lemony tartness in perfect harmony with the residual sweetness. Mushroomy and earthy developed flavours bring complexity to this well-preserved wine. Full and oily, yet refreshing. At its peak but there is no hurry. This wine will keep for a number of years without declining noticeably.

1942   *Vintage Port Niepoort* (Portugal)   *93p*
2004/2010 x3 • D 3 h / G 2 h

A perfect, fully mature port. Decanted four hours before tasting. An extremely sweet, hot, wide-open nose. A full-size, powerful, spicy, and well-balanced wine. Velvety and very elegant on the palate. Good fruit and structure, and will probably last eternally. Lingering and almost too burning an aftertaste. A top quality bottle.

1961   *Châteauneuf-du-Pape Devigneau* (Rhône)   *93p*
2004/2015 x 5 • D 1 h / G 1 h

These bottles came from Belgium and were in good condition. Ullages were around two centimetres. Brilliant, dark colour. Very intense, ripe and spicy nose. Full, rich and lots of flavours of chocolate and truffles. Good fruit. A lovely and soft wine. Most enjoyable now, but will keep well past this decade. Tasted five times with similar notes.

1879   *Château Pontet-Canet* (Pauillac)   *93p*
2004/now x6 • D 30 min / G 1 h

This was the first vintage in Bordeaux afflicted by phylloxera. It was very difficult with the latest harvest on record - the end of October. Somehow Pontet-Canet managed to produce a wine that has lasted surprisingly well in to the 21st century from this irregular and overall poor vintage.

Fine-looking bottle. Clear, medium-intense cherry red colour with brown hues. A classic, elegant Pauillac nose with ripe blackcurrants, brambles, cedar, a touch of minty herbaceousness, and delicate floral aromas. The leathery, earthy nose indicates development. A medium-bodied classy wine with a moderate level of acidity and firm slightly green tannins. A savoury wine with moderate fruit intensity and a touch of oxidation in the end. In shockingly good condition still.

1964 *Vouvray Clos du Bourg Moelleux Huet* (Loire) **93p**

2002/2020 x3 • D 1 h / G 1 h

Clear, medium-intense, golden-yellow colour. An intense, complex and barely developed nose impresses with plenty of dried fruits, apricots, hints of butterscotch, flowers, and jammy strawberries. The nose is reminiscent of matured champagne. The medium-sweet taste is in great balance with the crisp acidity, rich, ripe fruit of strawberry and dried fruit flavour. A balanced, long and subtle finish.

1990 *Comte Audoin de Dampierre Réserve Familiale* (Champagne) **93p**

2004/2015 x8 • D 15 min / G 1 h

Pale yellow colour with green tints and very fine bubbles. Pronounced apple nose with brioche, vanilla and nougat. Crisp, medium-bodied wine with a delicate mousse, brioche and nutty nougat aromas with lychee flavours. Long mineral finish.

1996 *Côte-Rôtie La Turque Guigal* (Rhône) **93p**

2004/2025 x3 • D 2 h / G 2 h

Deep, purple ruby colour. Fresh and youthful nose with intense dark fruits, sweet, toasty oakiness, smoked ham, and fried bacon aromas. Very refined full-bodied palate with a high acidity and volumes of fully ripe tannins. A very fleshy wine with spicy, toasty and leathery aromas. A long, warm and elegant finish. A very supple nicely matured wine gaining further complexity in future.

1995 *Ried Pfaffenberg Steiner Riesling Beerenauslese Emmerich Knoll* (Wachau) **93p**

2001/2030 x5 • D 45 min / G 2 h

This wine is a peculiar exception in Knoll's portfolio, since this single vineyard is actually located just outside the western-most part of Wachau on the Kremstal side. An intense yellow colour with high viscosity. A rich, honeyed, apricot and lemon nose with an elegant touch of botrytis. A sweet, oily texture with crisp acidity, ripe fruitiness of apricots and honey overtones. An immensely long, lingering finish.

1984 *Insignia Joseph Phelps* (Napa Valley) **93p**

2002/2010 x4 • D 1 h / G 1 h

After a wet winter, the rest of the year was spent sunbathing in the heat. The harvest was the earliest on record. An excellent bottle with perfect level. A developed, bright, brick red colour, fine sediment. A lean and very developed nose with earthiness, meatiness and roasted coffee bean aromas. Medium-bodied palate with dried fruits, supple tannins and moderate acidity. Very savoury and ripe aftertaste with mocha flavours. A very good wine even though it is retiring.

1981   Krug Collection Champagne Krug *(Champagne)*   93p
2002/2010 x4 • D 20 min / G 1 h

This year was such a thrilling year for vine growers in Champagne. The surprisingly mild winter encouraged an early bud break followed by several frosts in April and hailstorms in May, reducing the crop to the smallest since 1978. The summer turned out to be very cold, leaving almost no hopes for producing vintage wines. It was only due to the radical change of weather in August and September that made the good quality vintage.

A moderately pale, golden colour with lovely rich bubbles. The developed nose gives a rich aroma profile of creaminess, crème brûlée, and preserved fruit notes of pears, apples and apricots. A very crisp, dry palate holds very refined and elegant mousse. The lemony and mineral taste is dominating in the persistent, vivid finish. More elegant and crisp in style than the regular 1981 vintage.

1998   Acininobili Fausto Maculan *(Veneto)*   92p
2002/2015 x 2 • D 2 h / G 1 h

Fausto Maculan can be called the king of sweet wines in Italy. Acininobili has been named the Château d'Yquem of Italy. On average, only 4,000 bottles are produced per year and it is made of a blend of botrytised Vespaiolo (85%), Tocai (10%) and Garganega (5%).

A bright, moderately intense golden colour. Very rich aromas of ripe tropical fruits, honey and apricot marmalade on the nose with hints of floral aromas, vanilla and spiciness from new oak. A luscious, medium-bodied wine with very high sugar concentration (residual sugar 205 g/l) and tropical fruits. A fresh lingering finish highlights the orange peel flavoured botrytis. A true Italian nectar rivalling the Sauternes. Can keep but an absolute pleasure to drink now.

1945   Château Mouton d'Armailhac *(Pauillac)*   92p
2004/now x4 • D 1 h / G 1 h

In 1933, Baron Philippe de Rothschild purchased a neighbouring vineyard, Château Mouton d'Armailhacq, a classified growth in 1855. It was renamed Château d'Armailhac in 1989 by Baroness Philippine. The estate came with a small wine trading company, destined to expand dramatically and become known as "Baron Philippe de Rothschild S.A.". In the 1930s, this company also began marketing a wine called Mouton Cadet.

Négociant-bottled, odd-shaped bottle. Level was mid-shoulder. Decanted for 30 minutes. Cork and capsule in tolerable condition. Dark and brown colour, not much sediment left. Healthy and surprisingly fresh on the nose. Elegant and open, typical Pauillac-bouquet, which tended to grow in amplitude and articulacy. Graceful, full-bodied and extensive wine, but very forward. Not much tannins, and slightly high acidity, but very pleasant and pleasing. Certainly a good wine, but not for much longer.

1950 Château d'Yquem (Sauternes) 92p

2007/2015 x3 • D 2 h / G 1 h

A reasonably good-looking bottle with by-the-neck level. Decanted two hours. A bright, light-gold colour. Quite closed and introverted on the nose. Medium-bodied on the palate. Fairly elegant and charming, and quite a complex and intense wine. Has some sweetness and acidity left, but a definite monochromatic style. A subtle, long finish. Good but not great.

NUMBER 797.

1848 Bual Madeira Barbeito (Portugal) 92p

2003/2030 x2 • D 2 h / G 1.5 h

Wonderful, very old-looking bottle. Good level. Decanted two hours. A clear, medium-intense tawny brown with an olive green rim. The powerful and clean nose is amazingly intense and rich full of dark chocolate, almonds and woody teak aromas. Although considered a medium-sweet wine, the palate is more medium-dry in style with racy acidity, rich oily texture, and powerful with dried fruit flavours, figs and dates, dried apple skins, orange peel, and almonds. A warming, long finish with enormous concentration. The wine has a fascinating salty taste and sensations of the fifth taste, umami.

NUMBER 798.

1957 Unico Bodegas Vega Sicilia (Ribera del Duero) 92p

2001/2010 x3 • D 1 h / G 2 h

In Ribera del Duero the weather conditions during 1957 were normal. The winter was fairly cold with average rainfall. There was an early, dry spring and a long and burning summer with only a small amount of rain. The mild and dry autumn weather continued during the harvest. At Bodegas Vega Sicilia they produced 25,500 bottles, which were commercialized in the early seventies. In 1957 they only used two varieties of grape to blend Unico: Tinto Fino (80%) and Cabernet Sauvignon (20%).

We purchased this 1957 with a 1960 vintage from Winebid Australia, and both bottles were in excellent condition, regardless of their long journey to Helsinki. The level was by the neck. Decanted two hours. A fine looking, dark and mature colour. A sound, fragrant, tobacco and leather bouquet. Fresh and youthful on the palate and has much better balance and fruit than any 1957 Bordeaux. Almost a too sturdy and hard wine, it might even need more time in the bottle. Very vigorous and high in acidity. Even so, it was an elegant and complex wine with a long and promising future ahead of it. Very enjoyable now, but might be even better after a few more years.

NUMBER 799.

1890 Château Filhot (Sauternes) 92p

2005/2010 x2 • D 45 min / G 1 h

Very old-looking bottle. Only a few parts of the label left. Level was upper mid-shoulder. Decanted 30 minutes. Dark, gold colour. Almost weak, plump nose, quite evolved. Still fresh and vigorous. Well structured with good acidity which gives it elegance and definition. Honeyed and vanilla-flavoured, gentle old vine on the palate. Drying finish, but otherwise a beautiful example of a 117 year-old Sauternes.

NUMBER 800.

1955 Grange Penfolds *(South Australia)* 92p

2002/now x3 • D 30 min / G 1 h

The 1955 is the most decorated of all the Granges, the winner of 12 trophies and 51 gold medals. It was a personal favourite of Max Schubert, partly because this was the vintage that vindicated him by winning a gold medal in the open claret class at the 1962 Sydney Wine Show. Grange 1955 spent only nine months in oak. It is a blend of 90 percent Shiraz and 10 percent Cabernet Sauvignon. The fruit was sourced from Magill and Morphett Vale, Kalimna and McLaren Vale. The winter of 1955 was mild to warm. A wet growing season (rainfall 60 percent above average) was followed by a harvest in ideal conditions.

Very good looking bottle with the original label left. Top-shoulder level. Decanted 30 minutes. Quite deep, bright, dark red colour. Open and sound nose with exotic sweet fruit, white chocolate and old leather aromas. Still a fresh, gentle and suave wine with some of its original power and backbone left. On the palate surprisingly sweet and a bit spicy. Not very rich or firm any longer, but still has a good balance and complexity. A medium-long, dry and smooth finish. A historic wine, which has lived up to its early promise.

NUMBER 801.

2000 Cepparello Isole e Olena *(Tuscany)* 92p

2007/2015 x9 • D 1 h / G 2 h

Paolo De Marchi of Isole e Olena was one of the trendsetters of modern Tuscan wine. It was in 1980 that he started production of Cepparello, a 100 percent Sangiovese from Chianti Classico labelled as Vino da Tavola. Cepparello was one of the first in this now trendy and promising style of Tuscan wine. The 2000 is a very interesting vintage in its elegance and harmony. No blockbusters but wines that will age graciously due to their balanced and fine nature.

A developing brick red colour. A roasted and charming multi-layered nose. A stylish structure of a classical vintage. The silky texture is firmed by a stylish tannin structure. A long aftertaste full of roasted and dark fruit nuances. A feminine and harmonious entity at a lovely drinking age.

NUMBER 802.

1995 La Grande Dame Veuve Clicquot *(Champagne)* 92p

2003/2020 x7 • D 20 min / G 1 h

La Grande Dame 1995 was made of grapes from eight different Grands Crus around Champagne. 62.5 percent Pinot Noir and 37.5 percent Chardonnay in a ripe vintage brought immense depth and roundness, even heaviness to the wine. Fruit-packed, voluptuous, solid, and mouth-filling. This wine was astonishingly enjoyable right from its launch. A truly Great Lady!

NUMBER 803.

1990 Châteauneuf-du-Pape Château de Beaucastel *(Rhône)* 92p

2001/2015 x4 • D 1 h / G 1 h

Beautiful, moderately pale, tawny red colour. Voluptuous nose, full of developing bouquet aromas. Farmyard, spices, leather, smokiness, and vegetal tones of bamboo shoots indicate the complex richness this wine

NUMBER 804.

possesses. Full-bodied taste shows surprisingly stalky tannins, ripe fruitiness, perfume, and floral tones just before a refined but rustic warm finish. Drinking perfectly now but will hold for several years to come.

1986   *Château Latour* (Pauillac)   92p
2003/2020 x16 • D 3 h / G 2 h

After a rainy and mild winter, May started by boosting the heat and dryness. Flowering occurred in these great conditions leading to a large crop. The development of the grapes was so wonderful that for the first time in Latour history, a general crop thinning was carried out in July in order to improve natural concentration. Just before harvest heavy rainfall caused some harm to the crop diluting the grapes slightly, together with grey rot. The picking was done in very good weather.

Dark-red, medium-intense colour. Open nose of blackcurrants, flowers and vegetal tones. Medium-bodied taste is dominated by firm tannins and mild acidity. Mineral flavours are enhanced with tobacco leaves, leathery animal aromas and ripe dark berries. Earthy, long finish and very enjoyable now but will hold for a decade.

1997   *Estate Cabernet Sauvignon Château Montelena* (Napa Valley)   92p
2002/2015 x6 • D 1 h / G 1 h

Super vintage with very concentrated wines. In Château Montelena this vintage is considered to be as perfect as it can possibly get. Dark, even, opaque ruby colour with high viscosity. Youthful, powerful and complex nose with smokiness, tobacco, cedar, liquorice, and preserved bamboo shoots. Silky structure with mellow tannins, ripe intense dark fruits and chocolate aromas. Sophisticated, long intense finish.

1990   *Grand Vin Signature Jacquesson* (Champagne)   92p
2004/2015 x8 • D 15 min / G 1 h

Jacquesson is a true grower-producer whose champagnes have been constantly improving ever since the Chiquet brothers purchased this traditional estate in 1974. The house owns 95 percent of the vineyards for its own grape needs. Preserving terroir characteristics is the objective, with lutté raisonnée methods in the vineyards, no artificial cold stabilisation, no filtration, and minimal or no dosage in the cellar. The Chiquets are interested in terroir wines and are strongly involved in developing champagne into a serious gastronomic wine. The fruity, powerful and structured 1990 vintage was very successful at Jacquesson:

A developed deep golden colour. Low effervescence both in the glass and on the palate. A pronounced nose of apples, sherry and old wood. A full-bodied, rich and powerful wine that is even surprisingly developed for its age. Great age for enjoyment but will continue to develop positively.

1997 *Coeur de Cuvée Vilmart* (Champagne) 92p
2007/2015 x6 • D 15 min / G 1.5 h

A good vintage in Champagne if not a great one. The flowering was uneven due to a late frost in May and was followed by poor weather in July. The rot caused problems in summer but luckily glorious August saved the crop and made the vintage. Vilmart is a small size family winery established in 1890. The total production is around 80,000 bottles and the Champs family has focused producing all their wines from 11 hectares of premier cru vineyards bio-dynamically. This Coeur de Cuvée represents their flagship cuvee, which is made from the purest quality juice (800-1,500 litres) pressed from the first pressing of 2,050 litres. The blend is made from 40-years-old vines of Chardonnay (80%) and 20-year-old Pinot Noir vines (20%) deriving from the two best vineyards of the house. The Champs use also new oak in vinification during the first fermentation.

Moderately pale, straw yellow colour with vivid small bubbles. Pronounced ripe apple and apricot nose with good depth of yeasty characters, brioche and refined toastiness. Dry and crisp creamy taste with delightful elegance and depth. Buttery, biscuit and brioche flavours with a refreshing twist of minerals and lemon. Long lingering finish shows ripe apricots and apples with lovely spiciness at the end. Very rich and opulent Champagne with delicious personality and potential for another ten years of ageing.

2000 *Barolo La Serra Roberto Voerzio* (Piedmont) 92p
2005/2020 x2 • D 2 h / G 2 h

Roberto Voerzio is regarded by many of the leading wine critics as a new master of Barolo. He inherited his holdings from his father Gianni, who bottled wines under his own name until the early 1980s. Roberto is famous for his fanatical insistence on vineyard selection and very low yields. He owns three separate plots of Barolo vines in La Morra, in the vineyards of Brunate, La Serra and Cerequio.

Excellent bottle. Decanted two hours. Fine, deep purple colour. Very seductive on the nose with flavours of spice, plums, blackberries, and tobacco. Medium- to full-bodied with silky tannins and super-concentrated, ripe fruit. Excellent balance between tannins, acids, fruit, and wood make this a good candidate for further aging. Very good now, but it will definitely be even better in ten year's time. A very promising Barolo. Only 440 cases made.

1949 *Cabernet Sauvignon Charles Krug* (Napa Valley) 92p
2003/now x2 • D 30 min / G 1 h

The Charles Krug Winery is one of the oldest vineyards in California. It was founded by a Russian immigrant Charles Krug in 1861. He started from scratch and built a successful wine enterprise which covered 123 hectares at its peak. Two years after his death in 1894, the phylloxera that had already been a strain on the whole wine world finally found its way to his estate and destroyed the vines totally. Shortage of new vines and the new prohibition forced the estate to give up cultivation, and soon it was re-possessed by the banks. Italian born Cesare Mondavi purchased Charles Krug's winery in 1943 and modernised its wine production methods radically. The estate was a pioneer in the Californian wine industry.

This 1949 came from the New York auction house. Condition was excellent and level was high-shoulder. We cannot stop marvelling at the condition of these old Californian Cabernets, which seem to age exceptionally well. Very impressive, dark, bright colour to rim, an even more brilliant colour than the famous 1958. Lovely concentrated red fruit, dusty minerals and butter to nose. Quite complex, well balanced and thick yet lively. Big, even beefy and some soft tannin left. Has held very well, but does not improve.

NUMBER 811.

1949   Château Pavie *(St.Emilion)* 92p
2006/2010 x8 • D 45 min / G 1 h

Négociant-bottled (Philippe Raymond), good condition and level was by the neck. Very fine, dark and healthy colour. Decanted for one hour. Ripe, classic, rich, warm, and concentrated nose. Very full, but less tannic and dense than 1945 Pavie. Still a reasonably fresh, round and gentle old wine, showing some oxidation, but not too much. Chocolate and exotic old fruit flavoured. Still very positive and vigorous at the end.

NUMBER 812.

1948   Château Mouton-Rothschild *(Pauillac)* 92p
2007/2015 x2 • D 30 min / G 1 h

Brilliant level and appearance. Fully mature and healthy, dark colour. Decanted only 15 minutes before dinner, but already had a quite open and robust bouquet. Surprisingly rich and stylish wine with good complexity. Very full, cedary and fruity wine. Extensive and sweet aftertaste. We enjoyed the wine very much. Ready and will not improve. A satisfying surprise!

NUMBER 813.

1927   Vintage Port Sandeman *(Portugal)* 92p
2001/now x4 • D 2 h / G 2 h

Fine looking bottle. Decanted three hours. Dark colour with just a hint of amber. Deep bouquet with enveloping flavours. Intense and most attractive. Full-bodied and well balanced with sweet and gentle finish. Will still keep for many years.

NUMBER 814.

1999   Aalto Bodegas Aalto *(Ribera del Duero)* 92p
2002/2010 x3 • D 1 h / G 2 h

This can be called the first ultra-modern bodega in Ribera del Duero. And this was the first vintage ever made of this wine. After being a wine maker in Vega Sicilia for 29 years, Mariano Garcia decided to create a new super-wine together with Javier Zaccagnini. This deep purple coloured wine has a very intense ripe blackberry and bramble nose with perfume and nutty almond flavours. Medium-bodied wine with ripe dark fruitiness combined with rich supple tannins and delightful sweet spicy flavours. A very balanced and enjoyable wine capable of ageing for a short while.

1965　Barca Velha Ferreira *(Portugal)*　　*92p*

2003/2025 x3 • D 20 min / G 1 h

Nice, old looking bottle. Level was three centimetres down. Decanted 30 minutes. Bright, pale, tawny red colour. Medium-intense, a little volatile, developed bouquet with farmyard, coffee and baked aromas. Taste is better than the nose showing very balanced vivid acidity and tannins integrating well with intense ripe fruitiness. Robust and volatile style with savoury finish. Drinking well now but can hold pretty stable for another few decades.

1985　Barolo Bussia Prunotto *(Piedmont)*　　*92p*

2006/2015 x9 • D 1 h / G 1 h

Medium-pale cherry red colour. Perfumery, floral and spicy nose with ripe red berries and plums. Medium-bodied palate is structured with vivid acidity and mineral mouth-feel, ripe delicate tannins and ripe fruitiness of cherries and plums. Refined, elegant and persistent long finish. Real classic Barolo of mineral Monforte style.

1998　Brunello di Montalcino Riserva Biondi-Santi *(Tuscany)*　　*92p*

2007/2030 x3 • D 2.5 h / G 3 h

This wine was handed by Franco Biondi-Santi when we visited the winery in February 2007. He was told about the approaching great Biondi-Santi vertical Pekka Nuikki was organising in Helsinki and insisted us to include this wine in the tasting.

Moderately intense, bright ruby colour. Nose is very floral, aromatic, full of dark red fruits and oaky almond aromas. Dry and crisp wine with restrained style. Very concentrated and intense fruitiness of ripe cherries and brambles with firm well-integrated tannins. Extremely appealing wine with harmonious and balanced lingering aftertaste.

1985　Chambertin Armand Rousseau *(Côte de Nuits)*　　*92p*

2002/2020 x8 • D 1 h / G 2 h

Beautiful, bright and pale tawny-red colour with brown rim. Moderately intense developed nose with vegetal aromas, tar and ripe red berries, wild strawberries and raspberries. Earthy autumn leaves indicate it's maturing. Medium-bodied crispy taste with youthful silky tannins, intense ripe red fruits, redcurrants, strawberries, raspberries, and violet tones. Very vivid, seductive and energetic wine with harmonious finesse and superb length.

1990 Château Calon-Ségur *(Saint-Estèphe)*   *92p*

2006/2030 x12 • D 1 h / G 2 h

Fairly intensive cherry colour. Really prominent nose with blackcurrant and toffee. The abundant, medium-full taste is elegant. The subdued fruitiness of the aftertaste is overpowered by tannins and acidity in the intensive mouth-feel. The wine is not as refined and balanced as the 1989, but then it is still young. Maturing will show whether it will get balanced or remain rather robust forever.

1898 Château Pavie *(St.Emilion)*   *92p*

2006/now x3 • D 30 min / G 1 h

Négociant-bottled. Fill level top-shoulder. Decanted 15 minutes. Delicate, clear ruby colour. Delicious but one-dimensional nose - toffee, milk chocolate and mocha complemented by sweet spices. Intensively fruity taste with firm acids and tannins. Redcurrant and toffee aromas. Long, intensive aftertaste. The most youthful and sinewy wine of the tasting, not a shining example of elegance, but with a long life ahead of it.

1995 Vintage Champagne Krug *(Champagne)*   *92p*

2007/2020 x22 • D 15 min / G 2 h

Some will remember this very good vintage Krug as a farewell vintage for Remy Krug who retired in May 2007. Bright, green yellow and pale colour with rich amount of small bubbles. Persistent and fresh nose delivers green apples, lemon and steely foie gras aromas. Extremely crisp taste with mineral rich mousse. Delicate texture with moderate fruit intensity of green apples and yeasty brioche aromas. Lingering long and lemony finish being surprisingly one-dimensional but very balanced. Although the wine is crisp and fresh now, it has potential to grow in character up until the year 2020.

1968 Gran Reserva 904 La Rioja Alta *(Rioja)*   *92p*

2003/2010 x2 • D 30 min / G 1 h

Bright, pale tawny colour with a touch of brown. Opulent and developed oxidative nose express rich and intense dried fruits, plummy and nutty aromas with tobacco and some waxiness. Lively acidity together with mellow tannins and moderately intense plummy fruitiness form a nice balance with good length. A good example of how well classic Rioja Gran Reserva can keep in the bottle.

1989 Grange Penfolds *(South Australia)*   *92p*

2003/2015 x11 • D 2 h / G 2 h

Moderately deep garnet-red colour. Intense ripe wild strawberry and cassis nose married harmoniously with dark chocolate, anise, sweet spices, and hints of fresh basil. Ripe, dried dark fruitiness enlightens delicately with firm acidity and stalky tannins. Spices and herbaceous flavours stand out more in long warming finish.

1988 *Monte Bello Ridge* (Santa Cruz Mountains) 92p

2007/2015 x3 • D 30 min / G 1.5 h

Developed, bright and beautiful red colour with orange tints. The wine has a truly classic Pauillac nose with a gracefully developed bouquet. Ripe vegetal nose of blackcurrants, soy and bamboo shoots along with sweet spices, cedar, dark chocolate, and mint. Marked acidity with opulent and rich tannins on the medium-bodied palate creates the strong backbone, which is completed with ripe elegant fruitiness, chocolate, mint, and cocoa flavours. Very silky texture on the palate with seductively long finish. Drinking perfectly now!

1973 *Riesling Spätlese Schloss Gobelsburg* (Kamptal) 92p

2004/2010 x 4 • D 15 min / G 1 h

This top vintage has produced some great wines in Austria. Among these is this late harvested wine from Kamptal with pale straw yellow colour. Very mineral, less aromatic nose with waxiness and a touch of lemons and peaches. Crisp, light-bodied wine with immense mineral length and broad oily texture. Ripe apricot and apricot stone flavours with a lemony twist balance the wine superbly. Beautiful balance and surprising youthfulness for its age.

1998 *Descendant Torbreck* (Barossa Valley) 92p

2001/2015 x2 • D 2 h / G 3 h

Dave Powell established this cult winery in 1994 in the Barossa Valley. This particular single vineyard wine presents the first co-fermented wine in Australia of a blend of Shiraz and a small portion of Viognier. Both vine cuttings originate in the legendary old Runrig vineyard. Deep, dark, ruby colour. Powerful, tremendously deep and intense nose with game, white pepper and thyme aromas. Full-bodied, intensely fruity almost jammy wine with huge ripe tannins and balancing acidity. Long finish is sustained by herbaceous bramble notes. A monster of a wine!

1976 *Riesling Hugel* (Alsace) 92p

2003/2015 x2 • D 30 min / G 1 h

The vines had a good rest during the cold snowy winter. A warm, even hot, and dry summer with a little essential rain guaranteed the super quality grapes harvested in early October in ideal conditions. Moderately pale, rich yellow colour with golden tints. Pronounced, very stylish and complex nose with developing bouquet. Petrol, green apples and peaches, hints of lemon and honeyed waxiness.

Crisp, mineral light-bodied palate with concentrated apple and citrus aromas. Broad oily texture with a great length. Extremely balanced and persistent wine with lovely energy that may encourage still for further ageing.

NUMBER 824.

NUMBER 825.

NUMBER 826.

NUMBER 827.

2000   *Château Cheval Blanc* (St.Emilion)   *92p*

2006/2035 x5 • D 8 h / G 4 h

Opaque, purple colour. Opulent and intense but delicate nose of roasted coffee, toastiness and ripe dark fruits with floral tones. Medium-bodied palate charms with its delicacy - vivid acidity, firm refined tannins and intense dark fruitiness. The mid-palate shows complex spiciness and toasty oak aromas before it turns into a lingering mineral finish with cassis and coffee flavours. Drinking delicately well already although it will keep for decades in cellar.

1966   *Brunello di Montalcino Biondi-Santi* (Tuscany)   *92p*

2007/2015 x8 • D 30 min / G 1 h

Moderately intense, little hazy tawny colour. Surprisingly rich, developed and complex nose with beef stock aromas, pencil shavings, leather, flowers, dark fruits, walnuts. Medium-bodied and concentrated wine with a silky texture combined with refined acidity, round tannins, explosive fruit intensity, and delightful minerality. Hints of oxidation in the long finish adds lovely complexity into the wine. Drink up, no further ageing required!

1997   *Miserere Costers del Siurana* (Priorat)   *92p*

2007/2015 x4 • D 1 h / G 2 h

Carles Pastrana of Costers del Siurana is one of the founders of the Priorat renaissance. Miserere was created for the first time in 1990 and has performed remarkably well since. The wine's fascination lays in its elegant yet firm nature and structure capable of bottle aging. Miserere is made of a blend of Garnacha, Tempranillo, Cabernet Sauvignon, Merlot and Cariñena.

   Pale developing brick red colour. Stylish and seamlessly integrated nose that offers delicate nuances of fresh roasted coffee, tar and sweet dark berries. Fresh acidity and perfect mineral touches make this a very lively and refreshing wine. Outstanding harmony, smoothness yet structured backbone. One of the greatest Priorats, no doubt. Exquisitely enjoyable right now but its harmonious nature guarantees that there is no hurry.

1878   *Château Montrose* (Saint-Estèphe)   *92p*

2006/now x2 • D 30 min / G 20 min

By about 1878 vines covered the entire arable portion of the Château Montrose, giving a total 160 acres of vineyards. A large number of people worked on them, and Monsieur Dollfus, owner of the château, was a very 'modern' employer. He paid for all doctor's visits and medicine; pregnant women were paid a certain sum from the time they stopped work until after the birth of the baby. Moreover, a certain percentage of the profits were given out as a bonus each New Year. Such humane working conditions succeeded in producing good, long-lasting wines in 1878.

This lovely looking bottle still had the original label, capsule and cork left. It was a rare château-bottling, and the level was top-shoulder. Decanted 30 minutes. Good, dark and clear colour. Quite a clean and sound nose of red and black fruits, mushrooms, damp earth, chocolate, and mocha aromas. At first there were ripe, sweet, black cherry fruit flavours and some tannins around with a fairly good structure and balance. But as with the previous bottle, this one only lasted less than 20 minutes, and then the moment of pleasure was over, once and for all. Needs drinking within 20 minutes of opening, but then it was lovely and warm-hearted, good old-world St. Estèphe.

1968 *Cabernet Sauvignon Ridge Vineyards* (Napa Valley) 92p
2000/2010 x3 • D 1 h / G 2 h

The tasted half-bottle was in top condition. Very intense and bright, developing red colour. Unexpectedly open and sound nose. Marvellous fruit, with quite heavy tannins. A spicy, complex and fat, full wine. Good acidity and dimension. Finished well. Fantastic surprise - excellent now, and it was not even a reserve or limited-cask wine.

1970 *Vintage Port Graham's* (Portugal) 92p
2007/2025 x7 • D 5 h / G 3 h

Excellent looking, perfect bottle. Decanted five hours before the dessert. Medium-red colour. Exactly 37 years old and still very vigorous and lively. Very generous nose full of raisins, currants and wild floral aromas. Quite spirited, but still a harmonious and well balanced wine. Perhaps a bit too sweet for our taste, but a very stylish and complex wine. Round and supple, almost hot aftertaste. As good as one can expect.

1959 *Chambolle-Musigny Les Amoureuses Comte Georges de Vogüé* (Côte de Nuits) 92p
2002/2010 x3 • D 45 min / G 1 h

Domaine-bottled, ullage 4cm. Quite vigorous colour, virtually no browning at all, though the colour was getting paler towards the rim. Rich, ripe and sound nose. Firm wine with good fruit and balance. Has weight and individuality. This is a long, complex, deep, and serious wine. It is now fully mature, but has still enough ripeness to last longer.

1949 *Château Montrose* (Saint-Estèphe) 92p
2007/now x13 • D 45 min / G 1 h

The year 1949 was exceptionally dry at Montrose. The temperatures rose commonly as high as 38 °C in July and August. The harvest started on the 22nd of September, and the grapes were healthy and large in size. The yields were not as generous as expected and the total production was only just about 70,000 bottles.

Very good-looking château-bottling with base-neck level. Decanted 45 minutes. Quite dark, clear and maturing colour. Cedary, minty, earthy, and chocolaty nose. It opened beautifully in the glass. Soft and nicely rounded wine with smooth tannins. Medium-bodied and well-balanced wine, which has already lost some of its sweet fruitiness and volume. Also has some sharpness at the finish, but otherwise a splendid and very drinkable mature Montrose.

1962   Château Brane-Cantenac *(Margaux)*

2004/2010 x4 • D 1 h / G 1 h   92p

They made first-rate wine in 1962; dark colour, earthy, chocolaty, open and fine bouquet. Fairly full as opposed to the more common lighter body. Complex and in a good balance. At first it was a bit too tight and dry, but after one hour it opened up and developed richness and beautiful fruit flavours. Good and long, but a bit of an awkward and dry aftertaste. Will not improve, but will still last well. Skilfully made fine wine.

1949   Château Grand-Puy-Lacoste *(Pauillac)*

2001/2004 x3 • D 1 h / G 1 h   92p

Fine looking château-bottling. Top-shoulder. Decanted one hour. An intense, bright colour but not exceptionally attractive on the eye. On the palate, cheesy aromas, vanilla, predominantly woody with a bit of dried fruit. Still quite an intense, massive wine with tannins backed by an evident, fixed acidity. Almost too dry and tannic finish. May still be kept for several years, but will not become any better.

1999   Domaine de la Granges des Peres Rouge
(Languedoc-Roussillon)

2004/2015 x4 • D 2 h / G 2 h   92p

This small family winery with 15 hectares of vineyards is owned by Laurent Vaillé and is located in heartlands of Hérault province near Aniane village. Vaillé, who has worked formerly for Domaine de Trévallon and Chave, produced his first Granges des Peres red in 1992. The wine is made of the blend of Mourvèdre, Syrah and Cabernet Sauvignon. The yields are kept very low, only 20-25 hl/ha, to express the terroir and obtain the high concentration.

Medium intense, dark ruby colour. Rich complex nose with loads of ripe brambles and black currants, earthy, animal, tar, and pepper aromas. Full-bodied palate with moderate acidity. The rich ripe intensive fruitiness is beautifully balanced with firm tannins. High alcohol gives the wine roundness and sweet tones. Long and spicy finish with attractive intense meaty taste. Peaking now, no further ageing.

1999   Chambertin Domaine Dugat-Py *(Côte de Nuits)*

2006/2020 x1 • D 2 h / G 2 h   92p

Opaque, purple colour. Opulent, intense but delicate nose of roasted coffee, toastiness and ripe dark fruits with floral tones. The medium-bodied palate charms with its delicacy - a vivid acidity, firm refined tannins and intense dark fruitiness. The mid-palate shows complex spiciness and toasty oak aromas before it turns into a lingering, mineral finish with cassis and coffee flavours. Drinking delicately well already, although opts for decades in cellar.

1952   Château Latour-à-Pomerol *(Pomerol)*   92p
2004/2010 x2 • D 1 h / G 1 h

Nice looking old bottle of Latour-à-Pomerol. Château-bottled and level was high-shoulder. Decanted one hour. Even though the colour had turned to amber it was still deep and clear. Very adequate bouquet characterized by a scent of ripe fruit, roasted aromas and undergrowth. Plump and quite complex wine with some aggressive tannins, but not too hostile. Relatively powerful wine. Unfortunately the finish was as dry as a bone. This wine is past its best but will still be agreeable for many years to come.

1990   Femme de Champagne Duval-Leroy *(Champagne)*   92p
2004/2020 x4 • D 1 h / G 1 h

The top cuvée of Duval-Leroy is a Chardonnay dominated champagne. Soft, rich and perfumed nose of flowers, stone fruits and cream. Fruity style with some undergrowth tones. Medium-bodied with an elegant feminine feather-light feel to it. Juicy texture and well-integrated mousse. Delightful and sophisticated champagne that drinks very well today.

1995   Tinto Pesquera Reserva Alejandro Fernández *(Ribera del Duero)*   92p
2007/2015 x8 • D 1 h / G 1 h

Medium-deep brick red colour with signs of aging. The stylish and vibrant nose shows dark berry, salted liquorice and coffee bean aromas. Compared to the open and rich nose, the palate acts very restrained and youthful. Demands time in the glass to open up. Concentrated fruitiness and a firm and muscular structure. The palate corresponds to the nose, however seems lesser in nuances and more youthful in character. A further 5 years of bottle maturation will evidently help in opening up the palate. Harmonious nature and slow aging promise at least a decade of keeping potential.

1880   Château Cos d'Estournel *(Saint-Estèphe)*   92p
2006/now x3 • D 15 min / G 20 min

Château bottled. Fill level mid-shoulder. Decanted 30 minutes. Clear medium-deep cherry colour. Medium-strong, layered nose with soya, minerals, herbs, and a hint of blackcurrant. Dry, vividly acidic and medium-full taste with firm powdery tannins and a blackcurrant aroma bring the St. Estèphe properties out in a typically classic way. Excellently matured and preserved wine that will slowly wither.

1990   Salon *(Champagne)*   92p
2006/2030 x5 • D 15 min / G 1 h

Pale straw yellow colour with playful streams of small bubbles. Persistent walnutty, yeasty and biscuity nose reminiscent of Fino sherry. Hints of dried fruits. Dry, crispy, mineral, light-bodied taste with mouth-watering lemon flavoured mousse. Very persistent and long aftertaste where green apples and celery can be detected alongside charming mineral bite.

1945 Château Pichon-Longueville Baron *(Pauillac)*　　　　　92p

2004/2015 x7 • D 1 h / G 1 h

Good château-bottling with upper-shoulder level. Decanted one hour. Very dark, almost opaque mature red colour. Stylish nose is moderately intense, perfumed and roasted with nutty vanilla aromas. Full-bodied and mouth-filling wine still has a playful acidity, rich tannins and velvety texture with meatiness. Ripe dark fruitiness marries well with spicy Asian flavours and a little harsh tannin. Medium-long intense finish.

1988 Musigny Vieilles Vignes Comte Georges de Vogüé　　92p
(Côte de Nuits)

2002/2015 x2 • D 1 h / G 1 h

Lovely bright moderately pale brick-red colour. Elegant, ripe and developed nose. Very ripe strawberries, hints of tobacco and nuttiness combined with cheesy Brie aromas. Crisp acidity and refined firm tannins take hold in the mouth before delightfully intense red fruit of ripe lingonberries and raspberries forms a balance in a medium-bodied palate. Has a fresh and elegant style. The wine will be moving into its second phase of life with more open bouquet aromas. We can hardly wait.

1997 Sassicaia Tenuta San Guido *(Tuscany)*　　　　　　92p

2006/2025 x5 • D 1 h / G 2 h

Moderately deep, ruby colour. Rich, intense and ripe dark fruity nose of blackcurrants, spices, pepper, smokiness topped with an elegant touch of floral aromas. Moderately high acidity together with elegantly stalky tannins and rich mineral flavours form a typical restrained style Sassicaia. However, in this fine vintage the wine possesses intense fruitiness with cassis and red berries complemented with herbaceous flavours. Long discreet finish. Very elegant style.

1976 River West Old Vines Zinfandel Sonoma Vineyards　　92p
(Sonoma Valley)

2001/2010 x2 • D 30 min / G 45 min

This wine gave a complete new perspective to ageing potential of Zinfaldel. The year was very tough especially for young vines with a less evolved root system, since the drought caused heavy stress for wines. Thanks to 65 years old Zinfandel vines this wine succeeded apparently well. The ripeness of the grapes was immense, resulting in 27.3 Brix when harvested. The whole production of 2,863 cases of this wine was aged for 18 months in old Yugoslavian oak adding no extra spiciness or additional tannic structure to the wine. Fine looking bottle with top-shoulder level. Decanted 30 minutes. Deep, dark, clear brown colour. The powerful, rich and opulent nose has a beautiful bouquet of secondary and tertiary aromas: farmyard, leather, dates and spices with hints of jammy dark berry aromas. The ripe vintage is easily sensed in the jammy sweet fruitiness and warming high alcohol sensation on the full-bodied palate. Tealeaves, lead pencil and burnt sugar flavours are highlighted in a moderately long and round finish.

1977 *Cristal Roederer* (Champagne) 92p

2007/2010 • D 15 min x3 / G 30 min

The 1977 champagnes are rare to find and the year does not enjoy a great reputation. To us, Cristal is the most consistent champagne in both style and quality. Therefore it is no surprise that they managed to produce yet another perfect Cristal in 1977.

The bottle was in perfect condition and so was the content. A delightful experience to all the lucky tasters present. Deep golden colour with delicate effervescence in the glass. Toasty and stylish pure nose of dried fruits, marshmallow and burned sugar. Fresh and tightly-knitted wine on the palate with a linear, lean and feminine style. The mousse is gentle, velvety yet lively. A compact wine where all the elements have found their correct place. It is a privilege to enjoy this peaking Cristal now. No rush however.

1858 *Château Lafite* (Pauillac) 92p

2005/now x2 • D 15 min / G 30 min

During the 1850s many famous châteaux changed owners. The Cruse family bought Château Laujac in 1851 for 400,000 gold francs, M. E.Pereire bought Château Palmer 1853 for 425,000 gold francs, an English wine-merchant Martyns bought Château Cos d'Estournel in 1852 for 1,150.00 gold francs and the Rothschilds bought Château Branne Mouton in 1853 for 1,125,000 gold francs.

1858 was the best vintage in the fifties. It was known as the 'year of the comet' after the great comet of 1811 that was the most brilliant comet that appeared in the 19th century. It was also the first comet to be photographed. It was nearest the Earth on October 10th, 1858, approximately the same time when Château Lafite was harvested.

Fine looking old bottle, bottled by château. Level was low-mid shoulder. Decanted 15 minutes. Very dark, almost brown colour. Clear and healthy looking. Not much sediment. Sound nose, perhaps a bit oxidized, but quite complex and open. Plenty of flavours and well-balanced fruit, with some fresh acidity all-around. A rather faded beauty with just a trace of sharpness at the otherwise long and solid warm finish. Lovely, memorable wine.

1949 *Pommard Domaine Louis Latour* (Côte de Beaune) 92p

2005/now x4 • D 30 min / G 1 h

Négociant-bottled. Fill level 5cm. Decanted 30 minutes. Fairly intensive, slightly cloudy cherry red colour. Fully mature medium-strong nose with horse sweat, bouillon and a hint of tar. As the wine developed in the glass, the nose shifted toward chocolate, mocha and air-dried ham. Fresh acid and medium-full taste complemented by mineral-like, long, leathery aftertaste with mild tannins. All in all, a lush, well matured wine still in a very enjoyable condition. A nice surprise!

1970 *Château Cos d'Estournel* (Saint-Estèphe) 92p
2006/2015 x11 • D 1 h / G 1 h

We have tasted this wine various times since 1989, and it has regularly been better and more enjoyable than its reputation would suggest. Just a few months ago we arranged a full-size 1970 Bordeaux tasting with all the best wines. The whole tasting was a huge anti-climax with only a few convincingly good wines. This Château Cos d'Estournel was one of the winners.

First-rate condition, level was by the neck. Decanted for one hour. Exceptionally deep, dark and youthful colour. Quite an open, fruity and complex bouquet. Still quite tannic and as hard as many of the 1970s, but has more depth and elegance than many of them. Not much fatness or fruit here. Quite nicely balanced, perhaps a bit short and tough finish. Needs time, but we are not convinced that it makes any positive difference. Modestly priced Cos d'Estournel with some charm.

1926 *Private Cuvée Champagne Champagne Mercier* (Champagne) 92p
2004/now x2 • D - / G 20 min

Very old-looking, damaged bottle. Only remains of the label left, but it has a good level and promising colour. Deep golden colour with very few tiny bubbles left. However, enough effervescence to keep the wine alive. Fully mature nose with ripe fruitiness, honey and mushroom notes. Smooth texture and full mouth-feel. The acidity is starting to dominate over fruitiness on the palate. Long honeyed finish. Past its peak but still highly enjoyable.

1921 *Château Ausone* (St.Emilion) 92p
2005/now x3 • D 1 h / G 30 min

Old-looking bottle. High-shoulder fill. Bottled by Berry Bros. Superb and healthy colour. A clean and complex bouquet, with cedar, berries and a hint of mint, is followed by an earthy palate and a leafy flavour. The wine is well balanced, but it is not quite integrated or really succulent anymore. Quite full, but dry now. Does fall away somewhere on the finish. But still very pleasurable!

2000 *Corullón Descendientes de Jose Palacios* (Bierzo) 92p
2005/2015 x2 • D 2 h / G 2 h

The Palacios' Bierzo project yielded an outstanding single vineyard Mencia in 2000. Ruby-red colour with purple hues. Nose of spices, dark berries, leather, and Christmas spices. Full-bodied and a meaty mouth-feel. Outstanding acidity and impressive depth of flavour. Personality and class!

Schloss Gobelsburg

1997 Bancroft Ranch Howell Mountain Merlot Beringer *(USA)* 92p
2002/2010 x3 • D 1 h / G 1 h

Intense, deep purple colour. Enormous, complex nose that first gives rich cassis and wild strawberry notes then turning into leathery, tarry and smoky aromas. An opulent, full-bodied, meaty taste with mellow acidity and ripe rich tannins. A chewy wine with rich aftertaste.

1999 Cirsion Bodegas Roda *(Rioja)* 92p
2001/2020 x3 • D 3 h / G 3 h

A very good vintage in Rioja. Spring frost cut the crop size by 25 percent. The super-modern Roda winery produces this flagship wine Cirsion in very limited quantities. 100 percent Tempranillo wine produced from the best fruit of different vineyards' over 50-year-old vines.

Deep dark purple colour. Very concentrated and extracted nose with ripe blackberries, liquorice and powerful smoky flavours of bacon and spices. Full-bodied extracted structure. The ripe and intense fruiti-ness of blackberries is in harmonious balance with a moderate level of acidity and fleshy tannins. Spicy and toasty oak flavours marry well with the ripe fruit, forming a strong grip on mid-palate and a long finish. Very drinkable now but has immense structure for keeping well beyond ten years.

1970 Prado Enea Bodegas Muga *(Rioja)* 92p
2005/2010 x2 • D 30 min / G 1 h

Long and wide were the appropriate words to describe this Prado Enea 1970. The bottle was in excellent condition and had upper neck level. This wine had fully matured since we first tried it over a decade ago, and it is one of the finest Prado Eneas we have ever tasted. A dark garnet, youthful and healthy colour with a sound, intense bouquet of ripe fruit, vanilla and mineral scent. On the palate, it feels sweet, ripe, rich, and soft, but it faded quite quickly in the glass. It is a medium-bodied, marvellously lush, round and well-bal-anced wine with a likeable personality. A long and burning aftertaste. Now as ready as it is ever going to be, and ageing it any longer would be foolish.

1946 Château Mouton-Rothschild *(Pauillac)* 92p
2005/2010 x2 • D 1 h / G 1 h

This 1946 Mouton proved to be worthy of its reputation - a perfect balance between fruit and acidity, which is a typical of this vintage. An intense, sweet and ripe taste with chocolate and leather, and a full, pleasantly heavy nature. A genuinely elegant and concentrated aftertaste. Truly a great wine. We consider this to be one of the best wines of this vintage.

1962   *Viña Real Gran Reserva C.V.N.E.* (Rioja)   92p
2007/2010 x6 • D 30 min / G 1 h

This was an extremely successful vintage in Rioja ranking right behind the 1964. The winter was wet and mild. The spring frosts caused some worries for the growers. Hot summer and the autumn was favourable and the harvest yielded a moderately large but high quality crop.

All of the tasted bottles have shown extremely well preserved. The appearance of the wine is moderately pale with tawny, bright, beautiful colour. An opulent and elegant nose with red fruits, plums, cherries, herbs, and hints of sweet spicy tones. Medium-bodied harmonious taste with lovely acidity, mellow tannins and intense ripe, almost sweet fruitiness. Red berries, hints of cherry chocolate and a dash of vanilla flavours. The well-balanced, long finish delivers charming intensity and ripeness that appeal still for a few more years before declining.

2001   *Château Smith-Haut-Lafitte Blanc* (Graves)   92p
2007/2015 x5 • D 1 h / G 3 h

After a wet, mild winter, bud break took place normally in the last week of March. The cool weather in April slowed down vine growth considerably. The vines began growing vigorously during the hot, sunny weather in May and June, largely making up for the slow start to the year. Flowering took place one week later than in 2000. August was very dry and hot, especially towards the end of the month. This brought on a quick, even véraison (colour change). Both the red and white wine grapes ripened at an excellent rate. The Sauvignon Blanc grapes were picked from the 7th to the 21st of September. It was necessary to go through the vines several times to select the ripest bunches. The average potential alcohol level was nearly 13 percent. There was also good acidity, averaging 5 g/l (with variations depending on which vineyard the grapes came from). Fermentation in barrel (50% new oak) went very well. The wines were then aged on the lees and stirred (bâtonnage) once a week to bring out their richness and intrinsic elegance.

Fine bottles that came directly from the Château. Decanted 45 minutes. Very light, bright colour. On the nose nicely perfumed aromas of honey and exotic citrus fruits. Very intense, silky and well-balanced mouthfeel. Rich, concentrated and full-bodied wine with lively acidity and crisp fruit. Elegant and very long, gentle finish. One of the best white Smith-Haut-Lafitte we have tasted.

1947   *Château Haut-Brion* (Graves)   92p
2001/2008 x2 • D 1 h / G 2 h

Very dirty, old-looking bottle. Good level. Decanted one hour. Elegant, complex, delicate nose with sweet redcurrant, plum and mineral notes. Perhaps a little oxidation as well. A round, soft, still quite vigorous, and well-balanced wine. Full-bodied, but a little astringent on the palate. A bit short and dry aftertaste. Quite good but does not have the weight and intensity of the 1945. Drink now.

1966   Château Cheval Blanc *(St.Emilion)*   *92p*

2007/2010 x3 • D 1 h / G 2 h

Very good-looking bottle. Level was top-shoulder. Decanted 45 minutes. An attractive dense and bright colour. Very delicate, fragile nose. Ripe but not baked. Medium-bodied wine with some soft tannin and appealing fruit left. On the palate it is layered and quite intense, but not as rich and complex as we expected. Gentle and a bit tired aftertaste. Will not improve, but we are sure that perfectly stored bottles are still very worthy and will last well for five more years.

1947   Château Pavie *(Pomerol)*   *92p*

2003/now x5 • D 30 min / G 1 h

Van der Meulen-bottled, top-shoulder level fill, with a clear, brownish, mature colour. Quite a pleasant, open, but not very fresh bouquet. Decanted 30 minutes before tasting. A mature, ripe and fruity wine, but lacks real concentration and dimension. A soft wine with opulent fruit. Gracious, rather than powerful. Not as special as expected.

1918   Montrachet Lupé-Cholet *(Côte de Beaune)*   *92p*

2002/now x2 • D 15 min / G 30 min

Fine-looking bottle with 3 cm level. Decanted 15 minutes. Very charming golden and vibrant colour. Vigorous, fat, creamy wine with a rich, gentle oaky nose. Full and masculine style. The finish was not too short but somehow it appeared too soft, almost hidden and bland. Very good wine, but it did not have quite the grace for 'great'.

1934   Château Margaux *(Margaux)*   *92p*

2000/2004 x4 • D 30 min / G 30 min

This Margaux was bottled in Belgium. Burgundy-shaped bottle was in good condition, ullage was only 2 cm. Decanted 30 minutes before tasting. Dark, old-looking, almost brown colour. Very fragrant but close to over-mature nose with chocolate and earthy aromas. On the palate, a quite rich and sweet, well-balanced wine. Elegant and complete wine with a good level of acidity. A bit dry and short aftertaste but, even in a second-rate year like this, the famous elegance of Margaux was still present. Still holding on!

2000   Bourgogne Blanc Comte de Vogüé *(Burgundy)*   *92p*

2007/2015 x3 • D 2 h / G 3 h

The Comte de Vogüé Bourgogne Blanc is something of a rarity. At least it is the most expensive Bourgogne Blanc ever produced! The grapes come from two plots at the very top of the Musigny Grand Cru. Ever since the 1930s Comte de Vogüé has been known to produce a rare white Musigny. However, the vineyards needed to be partially replanted in 1986, 1987, 1991, and 1997. And, as there is no white Chambolle-Musigny appella-tion, the wine was downgraded to a mere Bourgogne Blanc. By law, the Grand Cru appellation could be used today but Comte de Vogüe still considers the vines to be infants for Musigny production. The quality is rising steadily vintage-by-vintage as the vines age.

Pale gold lemony colour. The nose is restrained and cool. The nose opens up with time but the palate gives a great expression of fino sherry, floral notes, oak, and hazelnuts. A tightly knit, firm and mineral struc-ture. A refined wine of medium body with some attractive oiliness on the mouth-feel. The long nutty finish has a moderate oak influence and refreshing lemony acidity. An outstanding wine today that will easily keep and develop for the next 5 to 10 years.

1934 Clos-de-la-Roche Armand Rousseau *(Côte de Nuits)* 92p
2001/now x5 • D 1 h / G 1 h

All the bottles had good levels. Only the remnants of the labels remained. We tried first the bottle with the lowest ullage – 7cm. The cork came out in one piece - the 1934 vintage was clearly legible.

Deep mature colour. Spicy, unmistakable old Pinot Noir nose. Very much alive, rich, full, quite solid. Improving in glass after 30 minutes. Soft and gentle with some sweet fruit still left. A bit short but pleasant enough. The other two bottles - ullage 4 cm – were better and more alive. Fuller and more delicious with a lovely ripe fruity flavour that seemed to extend and get richer in the glass.

1914 Le Chambertin Louis Jadot *(Côte de Nuits)* 92p
2004/2015 x2 • D 30 min / G 1 h

A fine looking bottle with 2cm level. A fully mature medium-deep brownish colour. A soft and chocolaty nose of tar, dust and plums. The aroma profile was complex with a great bundle of tertiary aromas. The palate was thick and chocolaty with low tannin and a balanced acidic backbone. The wine has still fruit to it and a structure to keep for another decade or so

1959 Château Pontet-Canet *(Pauillac)* 92p
2005/2010 x27 • D 30 min / G 1 h

Château Pontet-Canet produced many legendary wines between 1920 and 1960. During the ownership of the Cruse family, the estate had many successful years, such as 1928, 1934, 1945, 1949, 1953, and this beauti-ful 1959. But there have also been some very dramatic years since the late 1960s. The fall of Pontet-Canet quality was accelerated by the Bordeaux wine scandal of 1973. It almost bankrupted the Cruse family and led to the suicide of the head of the family. Only after 1989 have their wines been able to compare with their top-quality vintages.

Nice-looking négociant-bottling and the level was by the neck. Decanted for half an hour. An amazingly deep and dark, youthful colour for its age. Quite an elegant, open and mature nose. Relatively complex and

NUMBER 868.

NUMBER 869.

NUMBER 870.

has some lively fruit beneath. Nice ripeness. The finish was reasonably long, but somehow too dry and modest. Still very enjoyable, however.

1968   Cabernet Sauvignon Mountain Creek Louis M. Martini *(USA)*   92p
2003/now x4 • D 30 min / G 45 min

1968 was an amazingly good vintage that produced ripe, full and age-worthy wines. This Martini looked as good as new. A deep, impressive colour, even more brilliant than the 1964 Martini we tasted before it. A fabulously rich nose of sweet vanilla, cassis and herbs. On the palate it was well balanced and concentrated. It did not offer much complexity, but instead a lot of body and depth were evident. Held in the glass for an hour without drying up. A wine that has certainly survived the test of time.

1970   La Grande Dame Veuve Clicquot *(Champagne)*   92p
2005/2010 x2 • D 10 min / G 20 min

This massive vintage produced a record crop of 13,800 kg/ha. The quality was slightly compromised by the vast quantities produced. The best wines have survived well and the La Grande Dame was still in great condition: Elegant lusciously sweet appearing nose. Apple jam and nuts. Very balanced palate, refreshing acidity and voluptuous fruitiness. A stylish wine from the beginning until the very end. Enjoy now.

2006   Riesling Smaragd Singerriedel Hirtzberger *(Wachau)*   92p
2007/2020 x3 • D 30 min / G 2 h

Weingut Franz Hirtzberger and the magnificent "Singerriedel" vineyard lie on the western part of the Wachau valley in the tiny village of Spitz. The cooler microclimate of this area is able to produce some of the finest, lightest and most mineral wines of the valley. Hirtzberger is famous for the purity and elegance of its wines, and the Singerriedel is consistently the best and the most famous Riesling they produce. The 2006 vintage was warm and ripe in Austria, which is also well shown by the Singerriedel Riesling Smaragd.

Highly pronounced nose of flowers, fruits and rose oil. The palate is rich, open and stylishly mineral. Fully ripe fruitiness is supported by the steely fine acid structure. Long, intensely fruity and pure taste. A wine for prolonged bottle maturation.

1983   Château Mouton-Rothschild *(Pauillac)*   92p
2006/2015 x3 • D 1 h / G 2 h

Excellent condition and level by the neck. Brilliant deep, dark, bright, and warm colour. Fabulous rich nose, open, soft and complex. Very demanding. Good acidity and structure, not as fat and complex as 1985, but a very close match. An admirable length and finish. A lovely and memorable experience.

1959 Château de Rayne-Vigneau (Sauternes) 92p

2003/2008 x8 • D 1 h / G 2 h

This bottle was in first-class condition. Its brilliant colour and sheen of old gold were a pleasure to see after tasting numerous red wines. A most rich, full, sweet, and fascinating nose. Very honeyed, lively and seductive taste, which left a pleasant, long-lasting aftertaste. Altogether impressive and refreshing, however, it left a slightly too light impression. A well balanced but, nevertheless, not a sumptuous experience!

1908 Château Latour (Pauillac) 92p

2000/now x2 • D 30 min / G 1 h

The bottle was in decent condition, and the level was top-shoulder. Decanted for 30 minutes. A healthy looking, clear, developed colour. The bouquet was surprisingly rich and open with flavours of cedar, leather and ripe Cabernet Sauvignon fruit. Still fresh and has some attractive fruitiness left, but not much more. Fairly high acidity, but otherwise lean and solid. Long and sweet, warm finish. Enjoy now as a slow decline is already in progress.

2001 Château Rieussec (Sauternes) 92p

2007/2030 x3 • D 7 h / G 5 h

Nothing in the year's weather could foretell such a great result. The harvest began in mid-September with a preliminary sorting, and then the perfect scenario played out: light rains came on the weekend of the 22nd - 23rd of September, and botrytis was absorbed by the grapes, causing rapid and uniform concentration, enhanced by a warm and windy Indian summer. The vineyard went from a golden yellow to botrytis violet in just three days. In the eastern wind, the botrytis wavered and wrinkled, contracting and concentrating the juices. The harvest was quick and concentrated, on a single pass for certain plots, which is unprecedented at Rieussec.

Clear, bright, golden yellow colour. The very intense nose is partly closed but it still offers a peculiar complexity of aromas - apricot marmalade, coconut, toastiness, bourbon, vanilla, and alder tree. A sweet taste with a moderately high acidity and a very concentrated, glycerol-like intensity and mouth-feel. Lovely marriage of apricot marmalade and toasty oak. Very complex flavours with a silky elegance and a warming finish. By far the most fascinating flavourfully palate of all 2001 Sauternes. A great future lies ahead of this beautiful wine!

1953 Château Carbonnieux Blanc (Graves) 92p

2004/now x3 • D 30 min / G 1 h

The level was by the neck. This wine's colour reminded a Sauternes - a deep, bright golden, lively colour. A beautifully perfumed but quite light and restrained nose - very 'Carbonnieux', in the old style. A nice

balance with good crisp fruit and some phenolic astringency nicely blended. A fine, elegant and complex wine. A long and fresh finish with a kind fatness of texture.

1928 *Château Cheval Blanc* (St.Emilion) 92p

2001/now x3 • D 30 min / G 30 min

Wonderful château-bottling, the level was upper-low shoulder. Decanted 30 minutes. Deep, bright and clean colour. Very intense and powerful nose with ripe blackberries, liquorice, spices, and chocolate. The medium-bodied and soft palate is highly concentrated. Very ripe dark fruitiness, moderate-level of acidity with mature, softened, smooth tannins give the wine great structure. Delicate complexity comes from well integrated toasty earthy flavours. The finish is long but a bit dry and jumpy. A delicate and beautiful old wine that has seen its best days many decades ago. Slow degradation is evident.

NUMBER 879.

1928 *Vintage Perrier-Jouët* (Champagne) 92p

2006/now x2 • D - / G 20 min

A superb example of the greatest Champagne vintage ever. One could argue that it was solely the wonderful vintage that made this wine - it could be since Perrier-Jouët suffered a long recess period after the First World War and the death of the head of the house Henri Gallice. Anyway, this wine has wonderful appeal to it.

Bright golden colour with hardly any bubbles left. The nose is still intense with flowers, dried fruits and complex yeasty aromas. The lean, moderately light-bodied taste has sharp lemony acidity. The mousse is already weak. However, the lovely intense and long mineral aftertaste manages to convince us of the quality of Perrier-Jouël in this great vintage.

NUMBER 880.

1935 *Grands-Echézeaux Domaine de la Romanée-Conti* 92p
(Côte de Nuits)

2006/now x3 • D 15 min / G 1 h

J. Drouhin bottled this wine and the ullage was 6 cm. Decanted only for 15 minutes. Dark, and cloudy colour. At first a little diffuse and one-dimensional on the nose, but it opened up and improved a lot after an hour in the glass. Soft and round old wine intensity. Quite a developed wine that has already seen its best days. Nevertheless, it is an elegant, old, vigorous wine that is still capable of showing its class.

NUMBER 881.

1924 *Château Margaux* (Margaux) 92p

2006/now x4 • D 1 h / G 1 h

A fine vintage in spite of a relatively rainy August. The picking began on the 19th of September at Château Margaux. This bumper harvest produced pleasant, harmonious, and fine wines, which have proved to possess a remarkable capacity for ageing. Today, the wine in bottles has tired, but the magnums have retained some

NUMBER 882.

freshness and are very pleasant to drink.

Château-bottled, level was top-shoulder. Decanted one hour. The cork and capsule were in a good condition. Dark and clear colour, not much sediment. Healthy and fresh on the nose. Elegant and open, typical perfumed Margaux bouquet, which tended to grow in amplitude and articulacy. Elegant, medium-bodied and soft wine. Not much tannins, and slightly high acidity, but has some sweet fruit left. Very satisfying and charming, at least from a magnum-sized bottle. At its peak but will hold.

1991   Eileen Hardy Shiraz Hardy´s (Australia)   92p
2007/now x6 • D 1 h/ G 2 h

Hardy's Eileen Hardy was first released in 1970. The early vintages were made from Cabernet Sauvignon. It is now exclusively made from the best parcels of dry-grown Shiraz fruit sourced principally from McLaren Vale but also from Clare Valley, Padthaway and Frankland River in Western Australia. Fermentation takes place in small open concrete fermenters, which allow the winemaker to bring out the natural fruit characters of Shiraz. Since the 1995 vintage, the wine has progressively moved to being matured for approximately 18 to 20 months in 100 percent French oak.

Very dark, near-black colour. The nose is prominent and filled with fruit and overwhelming cassis, liquorice and menthol aromas. Very open and sound youthful wine. The palate is full and thick with concentrated fruitiness. An epic wine of ripe tannins, balanced acidity and warming alcohol. A voluptuous mouth-feel and an enduring finish. Needs time in the bottle for improved integration. At its peak within five years and will keep there up to ten.

1899   Château Margaux (Margaux)   92p
1999/now x2 • D 15 min / G 15 min

This was going to be a fascinating bottle, we thought. It was in fine form, recorked, relabelled and the level was top-shoulder. Decanted only 15 minutes. Light and feeble colour. Exposed and very seductive, fragrant, candied sweet bouquet. Flawless and silky, complemented by a firm backbone of minerals. Rich and soft wine with drying fruit that has echoes of chocolate and coffee. This wine offers a lot of complexity, but requires fast drinking. Long and soft at the end. Sensational, old-style refined Margaux.

1944   Vintage Port Hooper (Portugal)   92p
2003/now x2 • D 3 h / G 1 h

Decanted for three hours. A good, deep and vigorous colour. Flowery, spicy and alcoholic open nose. Full and rich, a quite forward old port wine. Not too much tannins left, but enough fruit and acidity to keep it alive and interesting. Warm and smooth finish. It lacks the depth and complexity of a really great vintage port.

1989   Château Mouton-Rothschild *(Pauillac)*   *92p*

2007/2015 x4 • D 1 h / G 2 h

Developed wine that is lively and fresh. It has a deep, dark-ruby colour that is a touch more developed than the 1986. A lovely complex nose. This is a well-designed, rich and very ripe Mouton, and not too oaky. Very good acidity and balance. Not the most concentrated and richest Mouton, but a profound drink now and in the near future.

1998   Sperss Angelo Gaja *(Piedmont)*   *92p*

2002/2020 x2 • D 2 h / G 2 h

After 1996 Angelo Gaja has classified his single vineyard Barolo along with the single vineyard Barbarescos under the Langhe IGT denomination. This legendary single vineyard wine from Barolo shines out with its moderately intense ruby colour with brick red tints. The nose explodes from the glass with underlying aromatic and perfumery aromas. Violets, ripe dark berries and some herbaceous aromas are complimented with a touch of roasted oak and dark chocolate. A very intense grip on the palate with firm acidity and supple, fresh tannins balanced well with ripe dark berries. A very fleshy, full-bodied mouth-feel, with high alcohol pushing the aftertaste to great lengths.

1967   Brunello di Montalcino Riserva Biondi-Santi *(Tuscany)*   *92p*

2007/now x3 • D 15 min / G 30 min

Fine looking bottle with by the neck level. Decanted 30 minutes. Maturing brick-red colour with browning on the rim. Open and roasted nose of sour cherries, tar and leather. Fully alive with power and persistence. Very firm with the tannins dominating the fruit. Very classical in style and great harmony. Medium long length. The wine is slightly past its peak but will remain enjoyable despite evident slow decline.

2000   Vintage Port Taylor Fladgate *(Portugal)*   *92p*

2006/2050 x6 • D 4 h / G 4 h

Opaque, purple colour with very pronounced and intense nose of medicinal tones, anise, violets, liquorice, dark fruits, blackberries, and spices. Full-bodied, moderate acidity and big stalky tannins are dominating this youngster. There is a very intense, ripe, dark fruitiness and violet-like flavours combined with spicy aromas. An immensely long and warming finish with great balance.

1964   Grands-Echézeaux Domaine de la Romanée-Conti   *92p*
(Côte de Nuits)   2004/2015 x3 • D 30 min / G 30 min

Fine looking bottle, level was three centimetres down. Decanted for one hour. Good, dark and healthy colour. Very open, tasty and intense bouquet - highly promising. A full and velvety wine, which has a lot of personal-

NUMBER 886.
NUMBER 887.
NUMBER 888.
NUMBER 889.
NUMBER 890.

ity, good fruit and a pleasant flavour, but it finished short and did not last well in the glass. After 30 minutes it suddenly became modest and basic. A fair wine if you are a quick drinker!

1999   *Château Pavie* (St.Emilion)   92p
2004/2030 x4 • D 3 h / G 3 h

The second vintage from the new Pavie owner, Gérard Perse. The wine reflects Michel Rolland's fingerprint in its enormous style. An opaque, ruby-purple colour. A rich and voluptuous nose with ripe dark fruits, butterscotch and an intense smokiness with floral aromas. Intense jammy fruit character, moderate level of acidity and chewy, juicy tannins balance well with the high alcohol. A very long warming finish with an unbelievably powerful aftertaste. A big wine!

1949   *Chianti Classico Riserva Castello di Brolio* (Tuscany)   92p
2000/now x4 • D 15 min / G 1 h

Lovely looking bottle, in good shape and the level was top-shoulder. Decanted only 15 minutes before tasting. Served blind, and our first thought was a good 1952 Pomerol. Very deep and dark colour. Wide-open, ripe nose. An unexpectedly compelling and full wine, a bit Pomerol-like. Soft and silky, and even reasonably complex. Short but pleasurable, fruity finish. It has held really impressively for 50-year-old Chianti. With the 15€ price tag this is a real bargain.

1919   *Vintage Veuve Clicquot Ponsardin* (Champagne)   92p
2007/now x3 • D - / G 20 min

The bottle looked fine with some ullage and a well-preserved label. The cork was still tight and to our relief there was a beautiful sigh at opening. A fully developed deep golden colour with orange hues. The nose is rich and mature with oxidised apple and dried fruit aromas. The nose was still very much alive awakening expectations for the taste. There were tiny amounts of fine bubbles keeping the palate alive. Concentrated dried fruit aromatics, steely acidic backbone and a long fully developed finish. No reasons to wait any longer.

1990   *Celebris Gosset* (Champagne)   92p
2004/2020 x6 • D 15 min / G 1 h

Champagne Gosset is a wonderful medium-sized champagne producer with an annual production of 1.2 million bottles. The house was founded in 1584, which makes it the oldest wine producer that has stayed in continuous production in the region. In the beginning they were involved in still wine production, which gives the title of the oldest champagne producer to Ruinart. Gosset has great tradition and its wines exemplify well that classical, elegant, fresh, and outstandingly aromatic style. Gosset belongs to the tiny minority in Champagne who do not carry out the malolactic fermentation leaving their wines crisp with green apple aromatics and great ageing potential.

The 1990 has a ripe yet high acidity making for a superb Gosset Celebris vintage. 100 percent grand cru grapes from all over the region made a wine of an expressive bouquet of ripe apple, stone fruits and lovely toasted characters. The mouth-feel is rich and velvety with lovely smooth small-sized bubbles. The fullness ties exceptionally well with the fresh acidity and concentrated fruitiness. Drinking very well now but this 1990 has the structure, power and fruit to carry on ageing for a further 15 years.

1969 *Cabernet Sauvignon Lot C-91 Heitz Cellars* (Napa Valley)   *92p*
2000/now x3 • D 45 min / G 1 h

Good neck level, decanted for half an hour. Remarkably deep, purple, lively colour. Elegant mint-eucalyptus nose. Full, solid wine, but it has lost some of its fruit. Good balance with plenty of depth and a hot, long finish. The wine was much better a decade ago, but it is still in a great form. Wine to accompany food!

NUMBER 895.

1970 *Grange Hermitage Penfolds* (South Australia)   *92p*
2007/now x3 • D 1 h / G 2 h

A very mild and dry year with 40 percent less rainfall than normal. Even though Grange has carried many different bin numbers in its early years, it has been labelled Bin 95 since the 1970 vintage. This Grange is the favourite of Don Ditter, who worked at Penfolds from 1946 onwards and succeeded Max Schubert as Chief Winemaker in 1975. The 1970 Grange is a blend of 90 percent Shiraz and 10 percent Cabernet Sauvignon. It is particularly low in alcohol for a Grange.

This bottle was bought from a Winebid's Australian auction with several other Granges from the 70s. It was in excellent condition and the level was bottom-neck. Healthy, medium-dark colour. Open, forthcoming mature nose with aromas of sweet caramel and toffee. Leathery, quite hard and a bit dry on the palate. Relatively rich and long taste with some sweet ripe fruit but, nevertheless, drying out. After tasting more than 30 different Grange vintages, it is easy to conclude that this one is certainly below the average quality of this giant and normally well-balanced wine.

NUMBER 896.

1924 *Château Grand-Puy-Lacoste* (Pauillac)   *92p*
2002/2010 x2 • D 1 h / G 1 h

This bottle was otherwise in good condition, but the label was missing. Château-bottled with top-shoulder level. Decanted for one hour. Good, healthy colour. A big black raspberry, peppery nose - very strong indeed. Full and very thick, opulent wine with remarkable concentration. A bit too powerful, alcoholic and dry finish. Was not exactly in a perfect balance, but has still some enjoyable qualities left.

NUMBER 897.

1970   Hermitage Chave J. L. *(Rhône)*   92p

2005/2015 x3 • D 1 h / G 2 h

The bottle was in decent condition with a good-looking label and by-the-neck level. Good, dark and deep colour. Quite open and clean, fresh nose with hints of ripe fruit and smoky, roasted, almost burnt flavours. Still quite powerful and tannic, and it has a lot of character and complexity. Very dynamic and meaty wine, but if it lacks something, it is charm and roundness. Powerfully spicy and satisfying finish, but the overall quality is quite far from the best vintages. Interesting wine, but not one of the greatest.

1995   Dom Pérignon Moët & Chandon *(Champagne)*   92p

2004/2025 x4 • D 30 min / G 1 h

The 1995 vintage is a blend of 48 percent Pinot Noir and 52 percent Chardonnay. A very skilful blend of the two with perfect harmony. The wine is mineral yet intense and charming. Every taste brings new subtle nuances. Cool, restrained and sophisticated. Very youthful when tasted and will need ten more years to show its full potential.

1961   CS Buena Vista Haraszthy Cellars *(Napa Valley)*   92p

2004/2010 • D 20 min / G 1 h

Good appearance, level top-shoulder. Decanted 20 minutes. Strong looking, dark and mature colour. Spicy, round blackcurrant nose, very forward. Claret style. It has some good leather aromas and black fruit flavours left, but it lacks the complexity and depth of a really great Cabernet Sauvignon. The wine is still holding well but it was not nearly as tasteful and intense as we had hoped.

1966   Château Laroze *(St.Emilion)*   92p

2004/now x2 • D 1 h / G 1 h

Brilliant level and appearance. Fully mature and healthy colour. Decanted only 15 minutes before dinner, but it had already a quite open and robust bouquet. Sweet, soft and stylish wine. Not much weight, but has an excellent balance. Still has some pleasant fruit with kind tannins left. Extensive sweet aftertaste. We enjoyed the wine very much. Ready and will not improve. A satisfying surprise!

1967   *Barolo Monfortino Riserva Giacomo Conterno* (Piedmont)   *92p*

2003/2015 x2 • D 1 h / G 1 h

This sleeping beauty came directly from Conterno's cellars, and it was in perfect condition. Decanted one hour before tasting. Lively developing brick red colour. Enchangting, layered and stylish nose. Medium-bodied with a silky mouth-feel. Softened yet still firm tannic backbone. Tar, roses and earthly notes. Long and harmonious now and in the next five to ten years.

1950   *Château Latour* (Pauillac)   *92p*

2000/2010 x3 • D 1 h / G 2 h

A severely damaged bottle, but it had a promising colour and top-shoulder level. No label or capsule. Decanted one hour. The wine exhibited full and deep colour and offered a generous and sound nose full of spices, mint and earthy flavours. Quite well balanced, but it has lost some of its fruit and concentration on the palate. Nevertheless, an elegant and soft wine with a slightly basic and hard finish. Overall, an average Latour that is pleasant to drink today, but will certainly not improve over the coming years.

1964   *Château Croizet-Bages* (Pauillac)   *92p*

2003/now x2 • D 30 min / G 1 h

Like many other châteaux, Croizet-Bages presents medals the wine has won on the labels. This bottle exhibits a silver medal from the Paris Exhibition of 1878 and a gold medal from 1889. The wine was in great condition and well worthy of the medals shown on the label.

Nice-looking bottle, level was high-shoulder. Decanted one hour. Very full, vibrant and promising colour. Open and enjoyable nose. Soft, elegant and fruity wine. Good richness. Not quite as complete as Lynch-Bages 1964, but great all the same. Clearly a wine, which had been harvested before the disreputable rainfall. Surprisingly good!

Château
Valandraud
Saint Emilion Gd cru
Château Valandraud

2005   Riesling Unendlich FX Pichler (Wachau)   92p

2006/2015 x4 • D 30 min / G 1 h

Lively and almost overwhelmingly pure fruity nose. A bodybuilder-like structure with a lot of muscle. The full mouth-feel and silky texture go well with the marked acidity and round fruitiness. The name Unendlich must refer to the unending aftertaste. Great concentration and ripeness. The wine remains very youthful with some of the particles still waiting for integration. It requires five more years to show its best and it will keep for a decade more.

1947   Château Belair (St.Emilion)   92p

2005/now x7 • D 45 min / G 1 h

These last two négociant-bottled 1947 Belairs came from Belgium, and they were both in good shape. Levels were by the neck. Good, full red colour, not much browning. Very open and sound nose with a lot of ripe fruits - very promising indeed. Not as concentrated as the 1945, but with less aggressive tannins. Light and charming, and beginning to show signs of age. Drink now. Good, but not as great as it was ten years ago.

1998   Old Vines Zinfandel Turley (USA)   92p

2001/2015 x4 • D 1 h / G 1.5 h

The legendary Zinfandel winemaker Helen Turley produces only 6,000-6,500 cases per year. The wines go through oak ageing in 75 percent French oak and 25 percent American oak. Only a quarter of the barrels are new. Although Turley has a very peculiar range of single vineyard wines, we prefer this blend of old vines for its modest level of alcohol compared to the others (only 15.1%!). The vines vary from 56-105 years of age and not more than 800 cases of the wine have been made.

Dark, intense, ruby red colour. Intense jammy nose full of mint and wild strawberries. The wine develops in the glass, giving aromas of tar, root vegetables and teak wood. The full-bodied and tightly-knit palate is dominated by high level of alcohol, firm rich tannins and very well balanced, appealing sweet fruit. The wine is rich and complex with a multitude of flavours - plums, raisins, cherries, spices, mocha, and hazelnuts. A very meaty and balanced long finish is turning towards the more restrained Old World style than overripe and jammy.

1926   Clos-des-Mouches Range Drouhin (Côte de Beaune)   92p

2000/now x1 • D 30 min / G 30 min

Good looking bottle with top-shoulder level. Decanted 30 minutes. Medium-red colour, pale rim. Spicy, complex nose of cherries, forest floor, and leather. A bit alcoholic but long, rich and full. This wine has held incredibly well for a 74-year-old Burgundy. A fully satisfying experience.

1920 Château Cheval Blanc *(St.Emilion)* *92p*

2005/now x3 • D 30 min / G 1 h

These two Belgian bottled Cheval Blancs were in quite poor condition. No capsule and the levels were low-shoulder, but the price was also very low and worth a try. Very light, dark, old looking colour. Tobacco-like, spicy, slightly herbaceous, and a bit oxidized nose. Sweet on the palate. Old but still energetic. A bit acidic and green, but quite complex. Flavourful on entry, but drying out at the finish.

1959 Viña Real Gran Reserva C.V.N.E. *(Rioja)* *92p*

2004/2010 x6 • D 1 h / G 45 min

Tasted three times with comparable notes. Decanted one hour before tasting. Good appearance, top-shoulder level. Fresh vanilla nose with blackcurrant, cherries, and herbs. A flavourful palate of roasted aromas and tar alongside berry-like and leathery nuances. A rich and round texture and a good balance. Quite a long but a bit dry aftertaste. Reached its peak a few decades ago, but it is still very pleasing.

1998 Mount Edelstone Shiraz Keyneton Vineyard Henschke *92p*
(Eden Valley) **2004/2010 x2 • D 3 h / G 2 h**

This wine is made from over 80-year-old vines in the north of the Eden Valley. The 1998 was another vintage of great concentration and blockbusting fruit. Smooth fruity nose of pepper, clove, plums, and boysenberries. Touch of vegetal nuances and farmyard notes. The alcohol is pronounced and warming, however balanced. Long and fruity finish. This wine is peaking now but will keep for another 5 years.

1970 Corton-Pougets Domaine des Héritiers Louis Jadot *92p*
(Côte de Beaune) **2006/2010 x3 • D 15 min / G 1 h**

Jadot's Grand Cru Corton Les Pougets is a great showpiece of their long history. The Grand Cru vineyard of Corton Les Pougets is directly adjacent to the Le Charlemagne climat, on the upper and mid-slope.

The bottle was in fine condition and ullage was only 2 cm down. Decanted for 15 minutes. Deep colour, maturity already showing on the rim. An immensely aromatic, wild meaty bouquet, reaching all corners of the nose. Intensive and rich on the palate. Delicate flavours of coffee, truffles and violets. Not a very robust or multi dimensional wine, but it has a lovely sweetness of soft tannins and fruit at the end. A very pleasing Burgundy from this ordinary vintage.

1834 Madeira Bual Malvasia *(Portugal)*   92p

2006/2040 x4 • D 2 h / G 4 h

Well-kept bottle with good level. Decanted two hours. Brown, fully mature colour with high viscosity. Pronounced and open raisiny nose with hazelnut and honey complexity. Luscious sweetness, which is not able to mask the lively acidity. The wine has preserved remarkably well and there is absolutely no rush to enjoy it. Well integrated high alcohol and a substantially aromatic nature. An attractive and fascinating, historical wine.

1904 Château La Mission-Haut-Brion *(Graves)*   92p

2001/now x2 • D 15 min / G 15 min

A very good-looking château-bottling with base neck level. Decanted only for 15 minutes. Quite brownish, maturing colour. Lots of cedar, mint, earth, and chocolate on the nose. It opened in five minutes. A soft and nicely rounded wine with ripe, smooth tannins. Light-bodied, well-balanced, but has already lost some of its sweet fruitiness and freshness. It also has some sharpness in the otherwise long and warming finish. It dried out displeasingly quickly in the glass. However, the first ten minutes were rewarding

1952 Château Mouton-Rothschild *(Pauillac)*   92p

2006/2010 x3 • D 2 h / G 1 h

Wonderful-looking magnum, level by the neck. Dark, good, healthy colour - looked like velvet. Quite tight and hard when first opened - closed and shy on the nose. After a while it became a lovely, open and giving wine. Meaty, rich and quite well balanced, but the fruit seemed weak, lacking intensity, making us seriously doubt if this wine is ever going to be any better than it is today. While it was certainly good, it was not nearly as great as a Mouton can be, not even in a Magnum.

1900 Château Haut-Bailly *(Graves)*   92p

2006/now x4 • D 30 min / G 1 h

Like the first bottle of Haut-Bailly 1900 we tasted, this one looked as good as new. A fine level and colour. Decanted 30 minutes. An elegant, gentle and very pleasingly well made wine. Complex and well balanced, long-lived wine with light structure soon to be forgotten. The wine is elegant and stylish. It ends quite hard and dry but with a long and warm finish.

1995 Grand Vin Signature Jacquesson *(Champagne)*   92p

2006/2015 x4 • D 15 min / G 1 h

The 1995 Signature was a blend of 55 percent Pinot Noir and 45 percent Chardonnay. This ripe vintage produced a Signature that is open and charming right now, the Chardonnay characteristics turning towards the creamier and nuttier side. Rich colour and nose. Elegant creaminess and oxidised apple nuances.

Intense and fruity palate with a delicate and charming velvety texture. Lemony acidity and a long nutty aftertaste with light mineral smokiness. A youthful and refreshing champagne that has clear future potential. Traditional and nuanced in style.

1996 *Richebourg Domaine de la Romanée-Conti* (Côte de Nuits) *92p*
2006/2020 x4 • D 3 h / G 2 h

Developing a harmonious nose of red berries, cherries and strawberries. The palate is consistent with the nose offering spiciness, burnt match aromas and nuances of undergrowth. A medium-bodied wine with a smooth and viscous texture and well-rounded, mature tannins. Stylish and balanced wine with mineral elegance and long finish. Required some time to open up in the glass but lasted well developing positive characteristics.

NUMBER 918.

1998 *Paleo Le Macchiole* (Tuscany) *92p*
2006/2015 x2 • D 2 h / G 1 h

An opaque, dark ruby colour. The upfront nose shows a whole lot of peppery spiciness and ripe dark fruits - plums and cherries mixed with floral tones. On the palate the wine is very playful with delicate but intense flavours. Rich medium-bodied palate is really subtle with an elegant, vivid acidity and moderate tannins. Intense, ripe dark fruits marry well with the spiciness from the oak ageing and the finish is very harmonious and seductive. The best Italian 100 percent Cabernet Franc wine by far.

NUMBER 919.

2003 *Meursault Genevrières 1er Cru Comte Lafon* (Côte de Beaune) *92p*
2007/2015 x3 • D 1 h / G 1 h

Youthful, medium-deep lemony colour. Soft and mild, sophisticated nose of new French oak, spices, nuts, and apple. Attractive ripe fruitiness with some bitter tones on the finish. The hotness of the vintage can be sensed in a higher than usual alcohol with a wide, oily palate. A refreshing acidity makes the wine feel lively and attractive. This vintage is not one of the longest-lived. The wine is pleasant and open now and will perform well until 2015.

NUMBER 920.

1999 *Chardonnay Giaconda* (Victoria) *92p*
2005/2010 x3 • D 1 h / G 2 h

The tiny winery run by Rick Kinzbrunner produces fabulous wines on the foothills of the Victorian Alps at 400 metres altitude. This charming Chardonnay is different from most of the New World Chardonnays by being more restrained than opulent in style. The wine with bright, moderately pale yellow colour has an extremely refined lemony and buttery nose with smokiness, toasted bread and coffee. The same flavours escort the dry gently crispy taste. The medium-bodied palate is full of tropical fruits, supported with a mouth-drying

NUMBER 921.

toastiness and warming alcohol in the spicy, delicate finish. A lovely Burgundy style wine with a sophisticated appearance and a soul full of strength.

1989   Montrachet Domaine de la Romanée-Conti *(Côte de Beaune)*   92p
2004/2015 x4 • D 1 h / G 4 h

An excellent vintage, especially for white Burgundy. We brought this bottle straight from Burgundy and it seemed to be in superb condition. Decanted one hour. The bouquet was youthful, flowery, lively, and very promising. The wine itself though was a slight disappointment, tasting edgier, thinner and less balanced compared to many other Montrachets from top producers from this great vintage. We tasted this at a blind tasting that included quite a few Montrachets from the same vintage. The DRC came in next to last with an average score of 92. This is by no means a poor wine, but a small disappointment compared to our expectations.

2000   Von den Terrassen Riesling Smaragd F.X. Pichler *(Wachau)*   92p
2007/2015 x3 • D 1 h / G 1 h

Deep developing golden colour. Some CO_2 in the bottle. Aromatic and fragrant expressive nose of flowers, honey and delicate petrol-like complexity. Epitome of a great Riesling. Very firm structure with high balanced alcohol and marked acidity. Great concentration of pure fruitiness. Long-lasting consistent finish. Drinking perfectly today but will develop positively for a few years and keep for a decade.

1996   Corton-Charlemagne Bonneau du Martray *(Côte de Beaune)*   92p
2006/2020 x3 • D 1.5 h / G 2 h

Bonneau du Martray is an exceptional winery in Burgundy. It is somehow more aristocratic than any other winery in Burgundy. One reason is of course that it is one of the few domaines focusing only on making one white and one red wine. The reason for it being such an aristocrat is that both of the wines are Grand Cru wines from the same hillside. The family Le Bault de la Morinière owns 11 hectares of Grand Cru vineyards out of the 33 hectares in the entire Grand Cru appellation. They vinify separately all 14 parcels of Chardonnay in low temperatures. The malolactic fermentation takes place very late. This very good vintage was formed by the superbly long growth period in dry and cool weather.

Moderately pale, straw yellow colour. Fresh, lean and mineral nose with rich buttery notes, tropical fruits and biscuit notes. Dry taste with crisp acidity, oily texture and very concentrated minerality. Broad taste with lemony and mineral tones and lovely depth with tropical fruitiness. Great concentration, lovely balance and lingering long aftertaste. Really aristocratic white wine with charming complexity. Drinking wonderfully now but will easily keep and evolve for the next 10-15 years.

1990 Solare Capannelle *(Tuscany)* 92p

2005/2010 x4 • D 30 min / G 1 h

This wine was officially made as an exclusive house wine for the three Michelin star restaurant Enoteca Pinchiorri in Florence. It was not until the 1996 vintage that Solare stood out from the exclusivity of Enoteca Pinchiorri being available for domestic and international markets. The wine is based on Sangiovese grapes and has been aged for almost two years in French oak. Although the wine derives from the heart of the Chianti Classico zone in Gaiole, it is still labeled as IGT Tuscany wine due to its non-traditional vinification methods.

Developed, medium-intense cherry red colour with brown tints. Wonderfully developed nose with nut, leather and cherry aromas with hints of violets and spiciness. The medium-bodied palate is completed with fresh acidity, firm powdery tannins and moderately intense fruitiness with cherries and plums. Floral and spicy flavours with hints of earthiness and black olives. Very mineral, long restrained finish – true terroir Sangiovese, authentic style for Capannelle wines. Beautifully matured and harmonious wine that will improve for few more years before starting its decline.

1996 Clos des Cistes Domaine Peyre Rose *(Côteaux du Languedoc)* 92p

2006/2015 x2 • D 1 h / G 1.5 h

Domaine Peyre Rosé winery has been owned by Marlene Soria since 1973. She became interested in winegrowing as a hobby but found herself involved in business after bottling her first vintage in 1990. This single vineyard wine from 7 hectares Clos des Cistes parcel gave name to the estate for its pink stones on the topsoil. The blend is 85 percent Syrah and 15 percent Grenache.

Deep, dark, blood red colour with mahogany hue. Rich, meaty, violet and spice nose with tar, smoke and liquorice. The well-developed nose expresses notes of horse saddle and earthiness. Truly opulent and complex in style. Big palate with broad texture, moderate acidity, refined big tannins, and ripe dark fruits of black currants, blueberries, brambles, and plums. Some herbs and delicate toasty nuances. Very long mineral finish with good tannic grip. Perfect harmony and balance. A rewarding wine, which charms with each sip. Drinking exquisitely now but this wine will develop nicely for ten more years.

1994 Opus One Mondavi & Mouton-Rothschild *(Napa Valley)* 92p

2006/2015 x5 • D 1 h / G 1 h

The longest, coolest growing season recorded in a decade, 1994 started with a sunny and dry March and an early bud break. Summer was cooler than average, extending the growing season and hang time of the grapes. Decanted two hours. A dark, deep ruby colour. Cedar and vanilla toned nose, with sound earthy and blackberry aromas. This textbook Opus One is full-bodied and more complex, richer, and more luscious than all the other vintages in the early 1990s. Well-balanced with velvety tannin and a vivid acidic presence into the long and solid finish.

1953 Clos Vougeot Blanc Phorin (Côte de Nuits) 92p

2007/2010 x3 • D 45 min / G 1 h

This real rarity of a white Clos de Vougeot was a unique experience. Judging by the performance of this wine, the appellation also deserves its status for whites. Deep, golden colour with red tints. A magnificent nose that resembles mature champagne: overwhelmingly rich aroma of toast, apples, nuts, and dried fruits. The deep and dense palate is ripe and round but the marked acidity is slightly too much for the mouth-feel. Dried fruit and wax aromatics. The palate does not reach the level of the nose. Despite this, a great white wine rarity to be consumed today. May be kept for a few more years.

1990 Cuvée Louise Pommery (Champagne) 92p

2004/2025 x9 • D 15 min / G 1 h

A stylish nose of toasty autolysis character, white flowers and fudge. A very well made, balanced and fault-less wine from this excellent vintage. Elegant yet intense and persistent. Fine mousse and a smooth velvety texture. Still at a very youthful state and will need a further 5 to 10 years to reach full potential.

2000 Château Pichon Longueville Comtesse de Lalande (Pauillac) 92p

2005/2030 x5 • D 8 h / G 3.5 h

The new millennium gave a precious gift to Bordeaux in the form of a perfect growing season and superb wines. May and early summer were cool. July continued colder than usual with occasional showers. Late July brought along sun and the warm sunny weather continued throughout most of August. The particu-larly sunny September was able to ripen the phenolics fully and to concentrate the anthocyans. At Pichon Lalande the vendange commenced on September 21st and continued until October 9th. The 2000 Pichon Lalande blend consists of 50 percent Cabernet Sauvignon, 36 percent Merlot, 6 percent Cabernet Franc, and 8 percent Petit Verdot.

Deep, purple coloured eye. Rich, layered and pronounced nose of red cherries, blackcurrants and some spicy new oak. Impressive structure of fine-grained and fully ripe tannin. Muscular and elegant at the same time. Very stylish and persistent toasty finish. Harmonious, already promising great future potential for this sensational and sensual wine.

1990 Grands-Echézeaux Domaine de la Romanée-Conti 92p
(Côte de Nuits)

2006/2025 x3 • D 2 h / G 2 h

A great vintage for premium red Burgundy. For once they had it all: phenolic ripeness, round and voluptuous fruitiness, and firm tannin. The Grand-Echezéaux is well balanced and attractive but a bit restrained for the time being. Deep dark ruby colour. Fascinating and stylish subtle nose of wild forest berries, undergrowth and oriental spices. The rich and velvety mouth-feel is firmed up by substantial tannin. A long and fine after-taste. The balanced and refined structure is perfect for ageing for another 10–20 years.

1997 *Giuseppe Quintarelli Amarone della Valpolicella* (Veneto)   *92p*

2005/2015 x3 • D 1 h / G 3 h

A clear, deep ruby red colour. The powerful spicy and jammy nose sets us up for a big wine. Ripe cherries, figs, brambles, and violets combine well with harmonious toasty oak aromas. On the palate the wine explodes! Rich full-bodied style with moderately high acidity refreshes a very concentrated texture of fruit, oak and alcohol. Astringent and chewy tannins show masculine power while delicate floral and perfumery flavours add to the delicate feminine side of the wine. A long, fleshy finish with an intense and spicy aftertaste. A classy giant!

1949 *Hermitage Chapoutier* (Rhône)   *92p*

2004/2010 x3 • D 1 h / G 1 h

1949 was an excellent vintage in the Rhône. The Chapoutier Hermitage has stood the test of time well, however it is in decline. Medium-deep brick red colour. Perfumery nose with roasted coffee beans, salted liquorice and spicy aromas. The body is viscous with the alcohol dominating slightly. Softened tannin and balanced acidity. Drink now.

1999 *Vin Santo Isole e Olena* (Tuscany)   *92p*

2007/2040 x2 • D 3 h / G 3 h

Paolo de Marchi makes an astonishing Vin Santo in Chianti Classico. Medium deep shiny amber colour. Roasted and nutty nose with light oak nuances. Soft and sweet raisiny characters on the rich and concentrated palate. Charming sufficient acidity in balance with the residual sugar. Fresh overall taste that lingers long with nut and dried fruit flavours.

1990 *Loibenberg Riesling Smaragd Alzinger* (Wachau)   *92p*

2004/2015 x4 • D 1 h / G 1 h

Sweet, soft and pronounced nose of passion fruit, petroleum and beeswax. Linear structure with oily viscosity and a full-body. Very clean, fruit driven and extremely intense taste. High alcohol and refreshing acidity. The wine has aged wonderfully and is at a great stage right now. But there is no hurry to enjoy this white wine monster.

1997 *Case Via Syrah Fontodi* (Tuscany)   *92p*

2001/2015 x4 • D 1 h / G 2 h

Moderately intense ruby colour with purple tints. Peculiar, opulent and very intense nose shows ripe dark fruits, toasty coffee aromas included with lead pencil and root vegetables. Full-bodied, seductively rich texture with ripe dark fruits, attractive toastiness and a warming sweet sensation of high alcohol. Dark chocolate and hints of liquorice flavours push through in a long, less crispy finish. Extremely pleasing wine for early consumption but will still keep for a decade.

1960 *Grange Hermitage Penfolds* *(South Australia)* 92p

2005/now x3 • D 1 h / G 1 h

Grange production officially resumed with this vintage, following a company order in 1956 to stop. Max Schubert defied the order and continued to produce Grange in secrecy for three years (1957-1959). Bottles of the 1960 Grange are becoming increasingly rare and hard to find. The year 1960 was generally hot and fairly dry, with the growing season's rainfall down 20 percent on average.

This handsome Grange was a blend of 92 percent Shiraz and 8 percent Cabernet Sauvignon. The level was only mid-shoulder. Decanted one hour. Healthy, medium-to-full red colour. Rich and powerful bouquet with layers of dark fruit and a hint of vanilla sweetness. Excellent intensity and complexity. Fresh, round and pleasant wine with layers of sweet blackberry fruits. Lots of life present, no traces of time. Long and gentle finish. Considering the low fill, the quality was fairly good.

The oldest Grange we have ever tasted was 1955. But those precious notes have vanished, and we only remember that it was already then, at the beginning of the 90s, well past it best but still quite a drinkable, soft and gentle wine.

1966 *Château Calon-Ségur* *(Saint-Estèphe)* 92p

2006/now x4 • D 1 h / G 2 h

Château Calon-Ségur produced top wines in the first half of last century. Their wines from the outstanding years 1924, 1928 (considered the wine of the vintage by many), 1934, 1945, 1947, 1949, 1953, and 1955 are often rated even higher than many Premier Cru wines from the same years. Calon-Ségur's terroir is regarded as one of the most promising in Bordeaux. It is therefore lamentable that between 1963 and 1990, somewhat decent wines could be only produced in 1966, 1970, 1975, and 1982. The older Calon-Ségur vintages have long been our favourites, and it has been particularly pleasing to notice their quality improve since 1995.

Good-looking château-bottling. By the neck level. Decanted one hour. Medium strong, brick red colour. Full, versatile, intensive nose with hints of spice, milk chocolate and plenty of bouquet from ageing. Medium-bodied, fairly intensive taste with dimensions and balance. Although the wine lacks the elegance of the 1961, it is excellently enjoyable right now.

1899 *Château Langoa-Barton* *(Saint-Julien)* 92p

2004/now x3 • D 15 min / G 30 min

The 1899 was the first really great vintage since the 1878. The summer was very dry and hot, with only a few showers during the summer period, except during the harvest when the weather was quite rainy but warm. A fine vintage with plenty of high quality wines produced.

An old bottle, still looking to be in good health with mid-shoulder level. Bottled by Calvet. Decanted 15 minutes, which was precisely the correct time. The colour was quite brown, but on the nose it has good fruit intensity and some earthy flavours. On the palate a lovely depth of flavours with some richness. Good balance and structure. This is an enjoyable, solid wine to drink. No doubt it was better about 50 years ago, but even today, 108 years after harvest, it is a very smooth and delicate wine with a kind, medium-long and gentle finish. A highly rated bottle.

1999   *Pinot Noir Vineyard Fromm Winery* (New Zealand)   92p
2005/2015 x2 • D 1 h / G 2 h

This is a boutique winery Pinot Noir from single a vineyard. A very 'old world' winery with taste of terroir in their wines. Medium-intense, bright ruby-red colour. Very refined, restrained nose full of ripe strawberries, raspberries, violets, and hints of vanilla and anise. Very Burgundian in style. The palate is medium-bodied with delightful crisp acidity, refined tannins and ripe red berry flavours. Elegant touch of French oak adds depth and complexity in the lingering mineral finish. Adorable wine just moving towards its second life, with more bouquet flavours. For fans of youthful Pinot Noirs, this is drinking beautifully now, but within the next ten years the wine will provide a great deal of appeal for fans of mature Pinot Noirs.

2000   *Reserva Real Torres* (Penedès)   92p
2007/2015 x3 • D 2 h / G 2 h

Torres Reserva Real is a minimal volume charity wine produced from a single vineyard of Cabernet Sauvignon, Merlot and Cabernet Franc grapes. The grapes from the high altitude, llicorella soil vineyard of Santa Margarida d'Agulladolç have produced Reserva Real since 1997.

Beautiful deep dark red colour. The expansive nose is stylish and layered: graphite, wet concrete, spices, cassis, and fragrant floral notes. Exceptional freshness, firmness and fruit intensity. Superbly well made and exiting wine that is starting to drink but will show its best between 2010-2015.

1996   *Rosé Jacquesson* (Champagne)   92p
2007/2020 x5 • D 45 min / G 1 h

This line of products now replaces the preceding Grand Vin Signature and Grand Vin Signature Rosé. The outstanding vintage 1996 was marked by a rapid succession of contrasting weather patterns. The atypical year produced atypical musts at Jacquesson. 11 grams of potential alcohol were combined to an exceptional acid level of 10 g/l. The rosé comprises of 61 percent Pinot Noir and 39 percent Chardonnay. The delicately hued rosé colour is attained by adding 9 percent of Dizy red wine into the blend. The bottles were disgorged after 9 years of maturation in the summer of 2006. The dosage is a minimal 3,5 g/l.

Delicate, bright, onionskin colour. The nose is expressive, toasty, mushroomy, with ripe red berry and bruised apple notes. Developed and vinous in style. The palate remains slightly closed compared to the open and charming nose. Full-bodied and silky, and the wine's CO_2 behaves very smoothly on the palate. Extremely red wine -like. Due to the richness of the palate this vinous champagne does not seem as acidic as many 1996s. This is drinking well already but will be at its peak between 2015 and 2020.

NUMBER 940.

NUMBER 941.

NUMBER 942.

1997 *Cabernet Sauvignon Hillside Select Shafer Vineyards* 92p
(Napa Valley) 2002/2020 x3 • D 1 h / G 2 h

Shafer produces one of the most sought after Cabernet Sauvignons in Napa Valley. The charm of it bases on its unique velvety tannic texture authentic to Stags Leap District. Hillside Select possesses probably the ripest Cabernet Sauvignon from the district for its unique exposure on the hillside. Only 2,200 cases were produced in 1997, which makes it very difficult to find.

Opaque, purple colour. Very concentrated nose with intense aromas of blackcurrants and wild strawberries, butterscotch, roasted coffee, together with hints of smokiness and tar nuances. Full-bodied wine with vivid acidity, very refined tannins and super-concentrated dark fruitiness. The long, 32 months' ageing in new French oak has generated dry toasty aromas of pencil shavings and roasted coffee beans. The long finish is marked with high alcohol and liquorice flavours. This wine expresses the Napa Cabernet par excellence with its sophisticated soul sensed as elegance in texture and heavily trained athlete body with its big blockbusting flavours. Wine that will age well, but serves now the qualities one might be looking for a Napa Cabernet - explosive richness with velvety texture and finesse.

1998 *Clos Fonta Mas d'En Gil* (Priorat) 92p
2007/2015 x2 • D 2 h / G 1 h

Deep and bright, beautiful dark red colour. The spicy nose shows great degree of elegance and layered characteristics. Leather, graphite and lively red berry nuances. Tightly knit structure with plenty of fruit. Perfect harmony of fruit and maturing fully ripe tannins. Full-bodied with soft yet firm texture. Long length with herbaceous notes and attractive spiciness. Very youthful wine that is starting to show its full potential. However, possesses capacity for further ten years of bottle maturation.

2002 *Dürnsteiner Kellerberg Riesling Smaragd F.X. Pichler* 92p
(Wachau) 2007/2015 x4 • D 1 h / G 2 h

Developing, bright golden lemony colour. The pronounced nose is expressively varietal: tropical fruits, lemon, mineral notes, and petrol. A very ripe and rich palate. The marked high acidity shows real grip. Balanced high alcohol and outstanding fruit intensity. A very focused and linear wine, with fruity richness tied to the firm structure in a seamless way. Exemplary expression of Wachau's greatness.

1999 *Crozes-Hermitage La Guiraude Alain Graillot* (Rhône) 92p
2005/2020 x3 • D 1.5 h / G 2.5 h

Crozes-Hermitage specialist Alain Graillot produces this special cuvée from his best Syrah wines of the vintage. Graillot is known for not using a new oak in ageing but instead the second hand oak ordered from domaines Dujac and Etienne Sauzet from Burgundy. His wines are known for expressing the purity of the

Crozes-Hermitage terroir and Syrah. This superb warm vintage helped Graillot to deliver the characteristics of Crozes to this wine better than ever before.

Deep purple colour. The intense and rich nose is dominated by smoky bacon aromas with violets, blueberries, brambles, white pepper, and tar. Full-bodied taste is extremely concentrated and tightly knit. Ripe dark fruit – blackberries and blueberries - combined smoothly with firm tannins and lively acidity. Spicy, leathery and smoky flavours are highlighted in the harmonious lingering finish. What a charming Crozes-Hermitage that knocks out many good Hermitage wines. Just reaching its optimum, but will evolve and keep well over ten years.

1964 *Royal Réserve Philipponnat* (Champagne) *92p*

2007/2010 x3 • D 15 min / G 30 min

Philipponnat's single vineyard wine Clos des Goisses is well known for its aging capacity. Therefore we had positive expectations for this vintage champagne, which it was able to live up to. Deep, golden apricot colour. Very few fine bubbles remaining. The nose is rich and toasty with beautiful dried fruit aromas opening up with time. Full body and a dry palate. Smooth silky mouth-feel with gentle mousse. Lacks great complexity but serves as a very enjoyable and fully mature glass of champagne.

1994 *Cristal Roederer* (Champagne) *92p*

2007/2015 x9 • D 30 min / G 1 h

The vintage 1994 was by no means one of the best in Champagne. However, Roederer manages to produce great Cristal also on lesser vintages. This wine was fairly open for its age and will not be one of the longest-lived Cristals. Nevertheless, a great joy to enjoy now and for the next ten years. Attractive bright yellow colour with signs of development. Small-sized elegantly behaving bubbles in the glass. The nose is pure, fruity and focused: apple, dried fruits, toast, and honey. The medium-bodied palate is structured and linear. Lacking the charm and richness of riper vintages. The wine is harmonious from the beginning until the long end. A great bottle of Champagne, however not a great bottle of Cristal.

1998 *The Dead Arm Shiraz d'Arenberg* (McLaren Vale) *92p*

2007/2015 x3 • D 3 h / G 2 h

1998 had a good amount of winter rain and plenty of warm weather around the time of berry setting. A cool start to the summer was followed by some hot days. The conditions amounted to wines with lots of fruit and plenty of tannin structure. The ripening period was mild with no rain. Crop levels were also up and in some cases this had an impact on the weight of the wine.

Decanted three hours. The nose remains quite tight, with alcohol fumes and fruit dominating. On the palate, very opulent and concentrated with blackberry and blackcurrant flavours with hints of cedar. Well balanced, but still too tannic. Drinking courteously now, but better to let it sit for a few more years.

NUMBER 947.

NUMBER 948.

NUMBER 949.

Tinto Pesquera

1999 *Corullón Descendientes de José Palacios* (Bierzo) 92p
2005/2015 x2 • D 1 h / G 1 h

Dark purple colour. Rich and nuanced nose of tar and dark berries. Pronounced palate that corresponds to the nose. Nuances of eucalyptus and herbs. Juicy, vinous mouth-feel and full body. Tannins are admirably powerful with perfect phenolic ripeness. An outstanding wine that is starting to show its full potential.

1985 *Belle Epoque Perrier-Jouët* (Champagne) 92p
2007/2010 x9 • D 10 min / G 1 h

Deep maturing yellow colour with fine bubbles. Elegant and vibrant nose of toast, cream and ripe fruitiness. Apples, white flowers and stone fruits. Rich and round harmonious mouth-feel, well integrated with the bubbles. Long taste and a refined mousse. A great wine at peak. The first experiences were from normal sized bottles but the last bottle tasted was a magnum. There was quite a difference with the magnum holding on very well, worthy of more than 92 points.

1999 *Messorio Le Macchiole* (Tuscany) 92p
2004/2020 x3 • D 1 h / G 2 h

100 percent Tuscan Merlot can be very exiting, especially if the producer is the Bolgheri-based Le Macchiole. A tiny production of 600 cases vanishes quickly into the cellars of collectors all around the world. Medium deep brick-red colour. Superb varietal characteristics of Merlot on the nose: vegetal notes, pepper, tar, chocolate, and dark berries. The nose expresses smoky new oak and a soft ripe jammy style. The palate is refreshing and firm with mouth-filling rich fruitiness. Alcohol feels high but balanced and the taste is delightfully persistent. At peak from 2010 onwards.

1945 *Barolo Riserva Borgogno* (Piedmond) 92p
2006/now x4 • D 15 min / G 1 h

The bottle was in excellent condition, and level was by the neck. Decanted one hour. Pale, light brown, unhealthy looking colour, but quite typical for old Barolos. Even a bit cloudy. Forward, but healthy and perfumed nose. Very rich, chocolaty and sweet old Barolo with a firm backbone of softened tannins. Not the most complex but filled with pleasing fruit and acidity. A little bit of edge, maybe even a hint of oxidation, although the finish was pleasant and long. A very good example of Borgogno´s old Barolos.

1921 *Château Coutet* (Barsac) 92p
2007/now x4 • D 1 h / G 2 h

This vintage can certainly be named as the vintage of the 20th century in Sauternes and Barsac regions. Although this wine does not reach the concentration and intensity of Yquem, it is still marvellous.

Bright amber colour with broad green rim. Very intense, developed and rich waxy nose shows beautiful botrytis aromas of apricot marmalade with a lemony twist. Medium-sweet taste with lovely refreshing acidity and medium intense fruitiness. The flavours of flowers, bee wax, dried fruits, such as apricots, and spices are all well presented in the lingering mineral and moderately dry finish. The wine has reached its peak way before now but is has maintained its enjoyable nature superbly well. Drinking beautifully now.

1996 *Cuvée Nicolas François Billecart Billecart-Salmon* 92p
(Champagne) 2005/2020 x2 • D 30 min / G 1 h

This cuvée was created in 1964 to honour the founder of the champagne house. It is a blend of Pinot Noir and Chardonnay grapes from Grand Cru villages. All Billecart-Salmon wines enjoy double cold settling and this part of this wine has gone through fermentation in old oak casks. It is no surprise that this wine of the great 1996 vintage is sublime but still youthful.

A medium deep golden colour with small-sized bubbles. A pronounced nose of toast and apple. An elegant mousse with a creamy and silky texture. Breadth brought on by autolysis. An elegant, lively but balanced acid structure. The aftertaste could have had more length. However, a full-bodied and rich champagne still in its youth.

1989 *Oloroso Abocado Emilio Lustau* *(Jerez)* 92p
2004/2040 x3 • D 1 h / G 1 h

This vintage sherry made a great impact with its complexity and refinement. Very stylish nose of almonds, coffee and dried fruits. Smooth, voluptuous mouth-feel with great concentration and admirable balance. Near-eternal nutty finish.

1937 *Bâtard-Montrachet Marcilly* *(Côte de Beaune)* 92p
2004/2010 x4 • D 30 min / G 1 h

Fine looking bottle with 4 cm level. Slightly hazy golden colour. Developed and nuanced nose of dried apricots, nuts, toffee, and confectionary. Astonishingly fruity for its age. A sophisticated structure with a juicy silky texture combined with warming alcohol and crisp acidity. Long nutty and fruity finish. A delightful wine with still some years ahead of it.

2000 *Cornu Bautray Non Dosé Jacquesson* *(Champagne)* 92p
2006/2020 x2 • D 20 min / G 1 h

Jacquesson's new single vineyard launch comes from a 1ha parcel in 1er Cru Dizy. The Chardonnay vines are over 40 years old. The wines are vinified in a similar manner to the rest of the Jacquesson range. Its non-dosé nature helps to maximise terroir expression. Around 5,000 bottles are produced. Old oak barrel and slight deliberate oxidation on the nose. The tight mineral Blanc de Blancs is starting to open up. Ripe fruitiness, some nutty characters and attractive steely acidity. The wine is harmonious and approachable despite the absence of residual sugar. A fantastic terroir wine that should be left to mature for at least a few more years.

1999 *Brunello di Montalcino Poliziano* (Tuscany)   *92p*
2004/2020 x2 • D 1 h / G 1 h

Developed dark-red colour. The nose is open and expressive with plenty of fruit at front: cherries, boysenberries, tobacco, leather, and oak nuances. Acidity refreshes the medium-bodied wine, fine tannic grip and balanced alcohol. Long fruity finish with Christmas spices and pepper. Fairly open and developed, enjoyable today showing layers of aromas and good depth. Will peak within a decade.

1874 *Château Lagrange* (Saint-Julien)   *92p*
2002/now x4 • D 15 min / G 30 min

In 1875 Château Lagrange became the meeting place for 'high society' on great festive occasions. It was this year that de Muicy Louys bought the château. This Briton from the Colonies, who installed his collection of exotic birds in the great hall of the château, became heir to the property at a very bad time since the Bordeaux vineyards were the victim of two terrible disasters: phylloxera (appeared in the Médoc towards 1876) and mildew. Thanks to its imposing size, Lagrange resisted better than other châteaux.

Fine looking bottle with mid-shoulder level. Decanted 15 minutes. Pale, brick red to brown colour. Very fragrant earthy nose with menthol aromas and hints of root vegetables. Crisp acidity with vigorous and complex palate with vibrancy and richness. Virtually no tannins left, but very supple and round taste that has surprisingly long mineral finish.

1992 *Clos des Goisses Philipponnat* (Champagne)   *92p*
2006/2015 x4 • D 45 min / G 1 h

This vintage was not generally declared in Champagne. High yields created some thin wines without great fruit intensity or firmness. As on most off-vintages Clos des Goisses made an exception. The particularity and enhanced ripeness of this single vineyard allows Philipponnat to produce superb vintage champagne nearly every year. Based on vintage quality the production can vary from 3,000 to 42,000 bottles. The hillside of Clos des Goisses is 800 metres long. It is very narrow, barely 100 metres deep, but the maximum altitude difference is 60 metres, giving an inclination of up to 45 percent. The sun strikes the soil in a perpendicular fashion, maximizing heat and exposure to rays. The soil is nearly pure chalk, thus soaking up the heat efficiently. The slope enhances the flow of cold air toward the plain, whereas the proximity of the Marne Canal moderates night time temperatures.

Bright, light yellow colour with refined small bubbles. Rich and complex nose reveals butterscotch, creaminess and apple aromas. Dry, delicate acidity, intense flavours of cooked peaches. Long, lingering finish. Drinking well already but will keep at its peak another 5-10 years.

2003 *Grüner Veltliner Tradition Schloss Gobelsburg* (Kamptal) *92p*

2007/2020 x10 • D 0 h / G 1 h

This exclusive wine has been vinified with ancient methods. Michael Moosbrugger introduced this spectacular style in 2001 after heavy research on the topic. Harvesting grapes late in mid November, high natural fermentation temperatures with natural yeasts in open tanks. Moderately intense, bright yellow colour with golden hints. Reserved, less aromatic, but very complex buttery nose with oxidative style and waxiness, very ripe white fruits and hints of spiciness. Dry, moderate level of acidity, rich minerality together with very ripe white fruits almost tropical one. The oily texture with rich medium-bodied structure has a very elegant and long mineral finish reminding of the grand cru Chablis of the same hot year.

1987 *Côte-Rôtie La Mouline Guigal* (Rhône) *92p*

2007/2015 x4 • D 1.5 h / G 1.5 h

This wine really expresses the greatness of Guigal. The poorest vintage of 1980's with constant rain in August, and Guigal was capable to produce this adorable wine which shows still good potential for further ageing!

Very intense and deep garnet colour. The nose reveals extremely deep and intense spicy and smoke bacon aromas with dark fruits and earthiness. Powerful palate with moderate acidity, ripe rich tannic structure and fleshy dark fruit flavours with elegant toasty spiciness. Refined and supple but big wine with lovely youthful tones. Pure pleasure for drinking now, but will keep and evolve wonderfully for the next ten years.

2002 *Pinot Gris A360P Domaine Ostertag* (Alsace) *92p*

2005/2020 x7 • D 30 min / G 2 h

An unusual Pinot Gris from the very dedicated biodynamic wine grower André Ostertag. Vines are located on a block called A360P in Muenchberg grand cru vineyard. Since making wine in Burgundian style with the methods André has adopted from his great friend Dominique Lafon, the wine does not fit into the standards of Alsace Grand Cru. Thus, he is not allowed to label the wine with the grand cru standards and uses for this reason the block name.

Intense golden yellow colour. Pronounced, rich and intense nose shows seductive mixture of ripe peaches and pineapple, flowery aromas with honeyed overtones. Spices, vanilla and delicate toastiness add special complexity to the nose. On the palate the wine is extremely playful and complex. Dry, vivid acidity with loads of ripe tropical fruits. Delicate toasty oakiness adds firmness to the broad oily texture. Very long, lingering finish with lemony bite and minerals. Complex and big white wine reminding of classic Meursault style. Drinking now but will keep another five years.

2002 *Pinot Gris Grand Cru Hengst Josmeyer* (Alsace) *92p*
2006/2015 x2 • D 15 min / G 45 min

Josmeyer is without a doubt one of the best producers in Alsace. The estate is one of the leading domaines in France with its organic and biodynamic production since 1999. Hengst is a steep southeast facing Grand Cru vineyard with soil rich in marl.

Bright, moderately pale lemony colour. Intense, ripe and deep nose with plenty of apricot aromas enhanced with hints of spiciness. Off-dry palate shows vivid acidity of medium level, elegant mineral flavours with honey. High alcohol is very well-integrated to the intense fruitiness, forming a rich and expressive wine with great length. Drinking nicely now but will evolve showing more complexity of flavours in the next 5–7 year period.

1928 *Corton Domaine Louis Latour* (Côte de Beaune) *92p*
2004/2015 x6 • D 30 min / G 30 min

Fully mature see-through brick-red colour. The nose seems youthful for its age with herbaceous, forest-like nuances to it. Tar and roasted aromas complement the wine. Balanced medium-bodied structure with a smooth silky mouth-feel, some tannic backbone and warming alcohol. This wine has lasted well and shows no signs of deterioration.

1982 *Zinfandel Swan* (Sonoma) *92p*
2004/2010 x5 • D 1 h / G 2 h

The old Zinfandel vines on this Laguna Road farm in Sonoma's Russian River Valley were planted as early as 1880. Joe Swan made his first Zinfandel here in 1968. This 1982 vintage has his fingerprint on it. His last vintage was 1987 as he passed away in 1989. This 1982 seems surprisingly youthful for its age. Developing deep colour. Fascinating mix of aromas on the nose: Christmas spices, leather, cedar, pepper, and vegetal notes. The fresh acidity lifts the wine up, balanced high alcohol and plenty of fully ripe tannin. This wine is peaking now but it can handle some more years in the bottle.

1990 *Nec Plus Ultra Bruno Paillard* (Champagne) *92p*
2004/2020 x4 • D 15 min / G 1 h

A one-of-a-kind champagne from an equal blend of Chardonnay and Pinot Noir. Fascinating nose of tart red berries, dough, bread, and citrus elements. High concentration and weighty masculine style with some deliberate oxidation signs. Requires some time in the glass to open up. Balanced acidity and fine persistence on the finish. The aftertaste reveals mineral and lemony tones. More a wine than a champagne.

1993 Mount Edelstone Shiraz Keyneton Vineyard Henschke 92p
(Eden Valley)
2004/2010 x2 • D 1.5 h / G 2 h

This was the most difficult growing season since 1974 in most parts of Australia. The period from October to January was unusually cool and wet, the result of a south-easterly drift of tropical high-pressure, which brought moist air and cloudy conditions to the southern part of the continent.

The abnormally wet spring led to widespread disease problems, principally from downy mildew, and the lack of heat delayed budburst, flowering and veraison by up to three weeks. The rainfall eased in late January and autumn was generally fine, although temperatures remained cool. The harvest period was dry in most regions, apart from scattered rain in the Hunter Valley. The long autumn enabled full sugar and flavour ripeness to be achieved. Overall quality was very good, but yields were disappointing and losses to pests and disease, mostly downy mildew, were reported at between 5 percent and 35 percent. This was particularly frustrating, coming at a time of rapid growth in exports, and created upward pressure on prices.

Deep maturing colour. Jammy nose of dark berries, salted liquorice, spices, and vegetal notes. Huge extract on the palate, full and smooth. Extremely soft, fully mature tannin and high yet balanced alcohol. The texture is juicy and vinous and the finish fruity and persistent. A fully mature dense and concentrated wine.

2000 Masseto Tenuta dell'Ornellaia (Tuscany) 92p
2007/2010 x5 • D 5 h / G 2 h

Medium-intense ruby colour, with tints of brick red. A round, intense and opulent nose pleases with spicy, chocolate and toasty aromas. The full-bodied palate shows a fine harmony of ripe intense dark fruits, moderate acidity and firm powdery tannins. Rich earthy aromas in the mid-palate with leather and cherry liqueur express evolvement. The high level of alcohol guarantees a long warming finish.

2001 Blanco Remelluri (Rioja) 92p
2006/2010 x3 • D 30 min / G 1 h

Taste this wine blind and you will end up most certainly in Condrieu. It is an unbelievable mixed bag of varieties that beats even Mas de Daumas Gassac Blanc. The wine is a blend of Viognier, Moscatel, Garnacha Blanca, Chardonnay, Sauvignon Blanc, Roussanne, and Marsanne.

Medium intense straw yellow colour. Very pronounced and complex nose full of tropical fruits, mango, peaches, and apricots, flowers, hints of butter, vanilla, along with delicate toasty aromas and lovely honeyed overtones. Dry, opulent, full-bodied white wine with oily texture and intense ripe tropical fruitiness. Buttery mid-palate with toasty oak flavours and long floral and spicy finish with a great dose of well-integrated alcohol rounding up the long aftertaste. The wine has such a great balance and complexity, that it makes you wonder why there are no more Spanish wines like this. Well, at least there is Remelluri!

NUMBER 969.

NUMBER 970.

NUMBER 971.

1998 *York Creek Ridge* (Santa Cruz Mountains) **92p**

2001/2010 x4 • D 30 min / G 1.5 h

This splendid wine is a blend of 88 percent Zinfandel and 12 percent Petite Syrah. Moderately deep ruby-red colour with tawny rim. Very elegant nose with a reserved elegant style - ripe wild strawberries and blueberries combine with smoked bacon aromas and barbeque spices. Full-bodied palate shows extremely well-balanced ripe dark fruitiness combining perfectly with ripe tannins. The finish is long and harmonious with smoky oak tones. Faithful Ridge style with elegance and opulence. Enjoy now.

1996 *Cloudy Bay Sauvignon Blanc* (New Zealand) **92p**

2006/2010 x19 • D 30 min / G 30 min

In its first year, Cloudy Bay had no buildings or cultivations of its own. The grapes were bought from other vineyards and produced in rented premises. Kevin Judd, winemaker of Cloudy Bay, remembers how he supervised the making of the first vintage over the telephone! Today, Kevin Judd is one of the most respected winemakers in New Zealand. The success of the Cloudy Bay winery has introduced the country's wine industry to the world. When Kevin's 1996 Cloudy Bay Sauvignon Blanc received the title of the world's best white wine in the highly regarded American magazine Wine Spectator, the winery's success story really took off. These days, Cloudy Bay has more than 45 hectares of vines, and it produces more than 600,000 bottles a year. Cloudy Bay is in Wairau Valley in the Marlborough region. This unique wine-growing region enjoys a cool maritime climate and the sun ripens the grapes longer than anywhere else in New Zealand. The name of the winery has its origins in a bay in Wairau Valley, named Cloudy Bay by Captain Cook in 1770.

A bright, pale lime green colour. Explosive and very lean fresh nose of ripe currant leaves, gooseberries and passion fruit. Crisp, mineral palate with fresh fruitiness and oily texture. Long lingering finish with lovely concentration of herbaceousness and delicate fruit. The first benchmark Sauvignon Blanc from Cloudy Bay. The New Zealand's Sauvignon Blancs are not valued for their longevity. However, this wine proves that the best of them are worthy of a wait.

1996 *Château Pichon-Longueville Baron* (Pauillac) **92p**

2006/2020 x5 • D 3 h / G 2 h

A great Cabernet vintage. The regularity of the weather allowed perfect ripening. Picking started on September 23rd at Pichon-Longueville. For the Merlot, the weekend of September 21st and 22nd marked a turning point in the phenolic maturity. The early parcels were picked on the 23rd and the 24th. Heavy rain during the night of the 24th forced them to stop on the 25th and to start again on the 26th. The young Cabernet Sauvignon was harvested on September 29th and 30th in a perfect healthy state and in magnificent sunshine. The 1995 is blended from 80 percent Cabernet Sauvignon and 20 percent Merlot. The old Cabernet Sauvignons on the plateau, which are particularly voluminous, fatty and fleshy, make up the essence of Pichon-Longueville. The 1996 spent around 15 months in oak, 70 percent of it in new oak barrels, 30 percent in one-year old barrels. Decanted three hours. Pure, focused, concentrated blackcurrant on the nose with chocolate, hints of minerals and tobacco aromas. Silky and full on the palate. Very concentrated, with good structure and balance. Medium-long, dry finish. This is more 'international' in style than some earlier vintages, and quite a distance away from the quality and style of 1989 vintage.

1992 *Turriga Argiolas* (Sardegna)   *92p*
2004/2010 x2 • D 30 min / G 1.5 h

Flagship wine from Argiolas family winery from Sardegna. Very peculiar blend of Carignano, Bovale Sardo, Cannonau, and Malvasia Nera grown on chalky soils in Selegas area near Piscina Trigus. After low temperature fermentation the wine is blended and aged 18 months in new French barriques.

Medium intense, cherry red colour with tawny tints. Multilayered, rich and ripe nose shows ripe black currants, black cherries, vanilla, and toastiness. Rich, full-bodied taste with very refined acidity, velvety tannins and ripe dark fruitiness. Elegant and opulent taste with warm sweet spiciness and finesse thanks to moderate level of 12,5% alcohol. Absolutely harmonious wine with toasty chocolate notes in the lingering finish. One of the best-hidden treasures of Italy! At it's best now, but will keep another 5-10 years.

1990 *Comtes de Champagne Taittinger* (Champagne)   *92p*
2007/2015 x2 • D 15 min / G 1 h

Comtes de Champagne is not reputed as a champagne that requires time. However, this 1990 shows the capacity and charm of a mature Comtes. Crystal clear golden colour. Toasty wide-open nose of pineapple, toffee and dried fruits. Excellent fruit ripeness and perfumery charm. Rich and round palate with firm acidic backbone. Long lasting finish. A charming example of a mature Chardonnay aged with grace. At a great drinking age but will continue to age beautifully.

1974 *Georges de Latour Beaulieu Vineyard* (Napa Valley)   *92p*
2007/now x2 • D 30 min / G 1 h

This vintage can be considered one of the best ever in California! The keys to success were the moderately cool temperatures throughout the growing season and plenty of sun.

A moderately dark, ruby red colour. The very intense and pronounced, ripe, almost jammy cassis nose is highlighted by a herbaceous mint character with coconut and chocolate aromas. A firm and intense mouthfeel with very jammy and juicy fruitiness. A supple structure, rich in texture, and a long warming aftertaste with cassis and menthol flavours. The aftertaste shows some raisiny and less elegant characters, suggesting the wine is beginning to decline rather than improve with further ageing. This wine is so charmingly opulent that why wait longer anyway?

1990 Cuvée William Deutz Champagne Deutz *(Champagne)* 92p

2004/2025 x8 • D 25 min / G 1 h

The trademark balance of Champagne Deutz is evident in this harmonious and complex wine. An intense nose of red berries, toast, rye bread, and apple. The structure is like a tightly woven fabric: smooth, and firm. Refreshing lemony acidity and a crisp youthful style. Drinking wonderfully now but will continue to evolve and improve for over another decade.

1998 Domaine de l'Aigulière Côte-Dôrée *(Languedoc-Roussillon)* 92p

2002/2015 x2 • D 1 h / G 2 h

This unique wine comes from the Montpeyroux village in l' Hérault in Languedoc. It is made from the Syrah grapes from 66-year-old vines in the 7 hectares of the Côte Dôrée vineyard owned by the Commeyras family. This sun-drenched vineyard yields only 15,000 bottles per year.

Deep, dark ruby-red colour. Strong and intense gamey nose with tar, smoked ham, white pepper, and dried herbs very reminiscent of classic Côte-Rôtie flavours. Very sophisticated medium-bodied palate shows great balance between moderately high acidity, ripe intense fruit and really meaty powerful tannins. Ripe brambles, spicy, peppery, and smoky flavours highlight a long, chewy finish. Very diverse wine with both sensual and wild sides to it. This wine will be tamed to become tender, delicate and fully sensual in ten year's time.

1990 Châteauneuf-du-Pape Cuvée Réservée Domaine du Pegau 92p

(Rhône)

2001/2015 x2 • D 1 h / G 1.5 h

Bright, moderately intense, brick-red colour. Beautifully complex and deeply intense nose with fragrances of ripe wild strawberries, flowers, white pepper, and coffee. Full-bodied on the palate serving big ripe fruitiness combined superbly with big ripe tannins. Moderate acidity with volatile flavours adds complexity to the long afterlaste. All flavours are very concentrated and still surprisingly vibrant and youthful for the wine's age. Wonderfully enjoyable now but will still keep for a decade.

1924 Château Cheval Blanc *(St.Emilion)* 92p

2007/now x2 • D 1 h / G 1 h

The 1924 vintage was only average on the Right Bank, although summer was beautiful and there was hot weather during the harvest. A fine looking château-bottling. Level was top-shoulder. Decanted 30 minutes. A fine dark colour. Quite an open and sound nose. A lighter wine than many other wines from 1924, but has a good medium-body and a well-balanced structure. Not much tannin left and quite acidic but, nevertheless, an attractive and smooth wine with a long and intense ending that still drinks beautifully.

1995   Clos de la Roche Joseph Drouhin (Côte de Nuits)   92p

2001/2020 x6 • D 3 h / G 2.5 h

Very good vintage for red Burgundy, limited in quantity but high in quality. A mild winter turned into a cool spring delaying bud-break. Then came the frost, interrupting the flowering. Luckily the hot summer gave some relief until the rain ruined hopes of a dream vintage. Thanks to the rapid harvesting the vintage turned out to be very good with non-diluted grapes.

Moderately pale cherry-red colour. Opulent and deep nose with plenty of ripe cherries, raspberries and brambles, violets, liquorice, and smokiness. Medium-bodied palate delivers rich flavours of ripe dark fruits, refined toastiness, crisp acidity, and rich velvety tannins. Very aromatic and complex taste with a long lingering finish.

1990   Cabernet Sauvignon Reserve Robert Mondavi (Napa Valley)   92p

2003/2010 x4 • D 30 min / G 1.5 h

This was a cool vintage producing elegant style wines. A cool winter delayed bud break and cool temperatures with rain affected the flowering and fruit set in May, reducing the crop size. After a good summer, conditions were ideal throughout the harvesting. Dry and cool mornings with gradually warming days ensured fresh acidity and delicate ripe fruitiness and tannins. The celebrated 25th harvest of the winery resulted in the blend with 77 percent Cabernet Sauvignon, 17 percent Cabernet Franc and 6 percent Merlot.

Medium intense, bright and beautiful brick-red colour. Elegant, moderately intense ripe cassis nose is peculiarly refreshed with herbaceous leafy aromas. Delightful toastiness and spiciness of anise and tobacco adds complexity into the nose. Medium-bodied palate enjoys vivid acidity, very elegant tannins and a good amount of ripe dark fruit. Very intense wine with great length.

1996   Cornas Auguste Clape (Rhône)   92p

2005/2020 x2 • D 1.5 h / G 3 h

Auguste Clape is without a doubt the king of Cornas. He manages year after year to produce great wines from his 5.5 hectare plot on the steep hills of Cornas. The wines express always the purity and concentration of old Syrah vines from a unique terroir of limestone, marl, sand, and granite.

Very deep violet and ruby colour. Pronounced explosive nose full of ripe dark fruits, wild strawberries and blueberries enhanced with smoky, spicy, liquorice, and tar aromas. Full-bodied palate shows many layers of flavours with great structure formed by moderately high acidity, big ripe tannins and intense dark fruitiness. The aromas shown on the nose are repeated on the palate along with hints of white pepper, smoked ham and leathery flavours. A lingering long chewy finish with minerality and spiciness. A big terroir wine drinking well now but keeping over a decade still.

1977 Grange Penfolds 92p

2007/2010 x2 • D 45 min / G 1 h

Fine looking bottle with top-shoulder level. Decanted one hour. Dark, opaque crimson. Very deep, concentrated fruit on the nose: a seam of rich blackcurrant and mulberry dusted with spice and black coffee. Still quite tight, very focused. Background of cedar and pencil-shavings. On the palate very densely-textured with fine tannins that are ripe and of high quality. The mouth-feel is creamy and the wine has a lovely balance. Good length, with drying tannins coating the tongue as it finishes. Surprisingly good still.

1996 Cuvée William Deutz Rosé Deutz (Champagne) 92p

2007/2020 x2 • D 30 min / G 1 h

Beautiful pale orange onionskin colour with fine bubbles. Subtle and elegant nose of spices, minerality and extreme purity. Ethereal nuances and dried fruit characters brought extra dimensions to the wine. Classical and very fine in style. The steely acidity is a benchmark to this terrific vintage. Extremely glamorous and harmonious already but will improve significantly with extended cellaring.

1966 Château La Mission-Haut-Brion (Graves) 92p

2005/2015 x12 • D 45 min / G 1.5 h

A moderately dry and cool summer followed a mild winter and an early spring. The growing season remained stable until September when the sunny weather with hot temperatures took place boosting the ripening of the grapes. The result was a very good vintage, which has shown good ageing potential. This wine is a brilliant example of this.

Moderately intense brick red colour. Very developed and pronounced nose with plenty of flavours: leather, dark fruit, chocolate, cedar, and strong volatile aromas. Medium-bodied palate with high level of acidity and minerals. Firm tannic structure gives still good backbone to this restrained wine. Floral and smoky flavours with blackberry and blackcurrant notes. Volatile flavours take a hold on the lingering finish reducing the elegance of the wine but adding at the same time vividness to it. Does not benefit from further ageing, although, the wine will keep for another ten years. Perfect time to drink up.

NUMBER 985.

NUMBER 986.

NUMBER 987.

1986 *Cuvée Sir Winston Churchill Pol Roger* (Champagne) 92p

2005/2020 x7 • D 20 min / G 1 h

Deep maturing golden colour with fine lively bubbles. The nose is super rich and exotic in style. Heavy leesy autolytic tone and attractive tropical and spicy fruit. Very concentrated and open on the palate, enormous depth, length and density. A monstrous wine that is refreshed significantly by the stylish and pronounced acidity. Blockbuster wine that manages to be extremely nuanced and stylish at the same time. The mousse is smooth highlighting the creamy rich style. Long finish and positive development in the glass promise an even greater future to come for this wine.

1997 *Grande Siècle Cuvée Alexandra Rosé Laurent-Perrier* 92p
(Champagne)

2007/2020 x5 • D 1 h / G 1 h

Medium-deep orange colour that has a delicate amber tinge. The nose is spicy and developed, cool and elegant, with great harmony. The gastronomic and charming style continues on the vinous palate. Linear acidity, smooth velvety mousse and great body weight. Cuvée Alexandra starts to be enjoyable now, but will benefit greatly from a decade of maturation. An exceptional rarity.

1990 *Cuvée Syrah Château de Fonsalette* (Rhône) 92p

2004/now x3 • D 30 min / G 1 h

Perhaps the best Côtes du Rhône wine ever produced! The Reynaud family, the owners of Château Rayas, have created two red wines Cuvée Syrah and Réservé from 11 hectares of wines in Côtes du Rhône appellation. This wine is made of a blend of two different Syrah parcels. The other ones grow on a gravel sticky soil and the others on lighter, less clayey soil. Blended together and aged one year in barrels.

Moderately intense ruby colour with cherry red tints. Very opulent, wild and animally nose with manure, tar, smoke, spices, liquorice, and loads of dark fruits. Full-bodied opulent taste with moderate acidity, firm tannins and intense dark fruitiness. Great depth and complexity. Long mineral finish. Drinking perfectly now but will keep still for five years, although not improving.

1896 *Vintage Port Martinez* (Portugal) 92p

2003/2010 x3 • D 1 h / G 2 h

The vintage of the decade in Douro. No wonder 24 shippers declared the vintage among them was Martinez. The company was first established in London in 1797 by a Spaniard D. Sebastian Gonzalez Martinez, but in 1834 the company took place also in Portugal's Vila Nova de Gaia.

Excellent bottle with perfect level. Moderately pale orange tawny colour. Intense nose with sweet dried fruit flavours, figs, apricots, and dates. Delicious aromas of liquorice, chocolate and nuts. Sweet, medium-bodied taste with moderate level of acidity and loads of dried fruits, nuts and liquorice flavours on intense palate. In the warming aftertaste, milk chocolate and walnut flavours are more apparent. The wine has been far better decades ago, but is still extremely enjoyable and a wonderful taste of history from 19th century.

1996   Dom Pérignon Rosé Moët & Chandon *(Champagne)*   92p
2007/2030 x2 • D 45 min / G 1 h

An elegant, glowing pale rosé colour. Stylish and charming nose of tart red berries: lingonberries, cherries and cranberries. The nose is open and expressive, however, relatively primary still in style. Not much autolysis character detectable yet. Very promising palate: powerful, dense and velvety with layered spicy and fruity characteristics. The outstanding acid structure of 1996 is well captured into this seriously vinous champagne. Its structure and intensity propose the wine to be nearly immortal.

1888   Tokaji Essence Berry Bros *(Tokaj)*   92p
1999/2010 x2 • D 1 h / G 2.5 h

This rare Tokaji was imported to England by Berry Bros in 1938. Originally it derived from Baron Beust Tallya Negyalya Estate. As an Essencia of Tokaji the wine is produced fully botrytised grape must, which has fermented naturally over decades to reach only few percents of alcohol.

Very deep dark amber colour. Hugely concentrated nose with immense depth of honey, raisins, prunes, and wax. Luscious taste with great concentration and crisp acidity. The nectar-like taste shows rich range of flavours - burnt sugar, raisins, apricot marmalade, honey, and spicy waxiness. The high viscosity of the wine forms a foil-like sensation in the mouth that lasts long. A wine that seems to be immortal!

2000   Chryseia Prats & Symington *(Portugal)*   92p
2003/2015 x5 • D 3 h / G 3 h

This interesting project of the Symington family and ex-owner of Château Cos d'Estournel Bruno Prats began in 1998. The wine represents the first Chryseia ever produced with the blend of Touriga Nacional, Touriga Franca, Tinta Roriz and Tinta Cão. Very hot weather led to a very small quantity.

Opaque purple colour. Rich concentrated flavours of blueberry, smokiness and tar, hints of floral aromas. Full-bodied, very intense palate with moderate acidity, extremely muscular tannic structure and very ripe blackberries and blueberries. Very concentrated wine with persistent long finish.

1997   Roda I Reserva Bodegas Roda *(Rioja)*   92p
2001/2015 x6 • D 1.5 h / G 1.5 h

This is a 100% Tempranillo wine made from grapes grown on over 30-year-old vines. Deep, intense cherry red colour. Pronounced spicy nose with bacon and brambles with hints of chocolate. A full-bodied, rich and intense dark fruit palate is balanced by refined acidity and firm tannins. Mid-palate shows meaty and delicately toasty flavours, which escort the lingering finish. Superb showcase of modern Rioja style – rich and concentrated with vibrancy.

1994 Quintet Cabernet Blend Mount Mary (Australia) 92p

2006/2015 x2 • D 2 h / G 2 h

Mount Mary commands a mythical status among wine collectors. Quintet is a blend of Cabernet Sauvignon, Cabernet Franc, Malbec, Merlot, and Petit Verdot. The vineyard faces north and captures optimum sunlight during the growing season. New French Oak plays an underlying role in the style. Owing to the age of the vines, the wine became richer and more complex during the 1990s. Quality is usually outstandingly good, although as a single vineyard wine, the vagaries of vintage can come into play. Quintet resonates an individuality of place and Dr John Middleton's fastidious respect of the landscape.

Bright, medium-intense, dark ruby colour with elegantly pronounced nose. Ripe dark berries, cherries, flowers, rosebuds, all in a bouquet, which combined well with dry spicy aromas from new oak. Full-bodied palate with lively acidity, refined but big, ripe, powdery tannins, crispy mineral twist with intense fresh red fruit and long mouth-drying finish. Big, modern but elegant Mount Mary benefitis from further ageing.

1998 Ab Ericio Hans Igler (Burgenland) 92p

2005/2015 x4 • D 1.5 h / G 2 h

The second vintage of this flagship red wine is a tribute to the great Austrian red wine pioneer Hans Igler. He became known in Austria and Burgenland for developing and introducing new red wine making techniques since the 1960's. He introduced French barrels imported from Château Latour in 1981. This great wine is made of Merlot (40%), Blaufränkisch (40%) and Zweigelt (20%) aged 21 months in French oak.

Very deep, purple colour. Intense, extracted, spicy, and toasty nose with blueberries, blackberries, plums, and cherries. Very intense full-bodied wine with lovely acidity and extremely refined powdery tannins. Ripe and intense dark fruit with mineral and spicy tones. A concentrated and powerful wine with very elegant toastiness and a long intense finish. Still a youthful wine that can handle 3-5 year bottle ageing well. Wine that reminds miraculously the great Super Tuscans with its style!

1975 *Cuvée William Deutz Vinothéque Deutz* (Champagne) 92p

2005/2010 x2 • D 10 min / G 45 min

The 1975 Cuvée William Deutz comprises of 60 percent Pinot Noir, 30 percent Chardonnay and 10 percent Pinot Meunier. This bottle was a prime example of the 1975 vintage's ageing potential. Balanced, harmonious and surprisingly young at heart:

Youthful bright yellow colour. Floral and aromatic nose promising a great deal: toasted bread, mushrooms, dried fruits, and honey. Very lively structure with marked acidity and pleasant effervescence. Surprisingly youthful wine for its age. However, will not greatly improve with further aging.

2000 *Grands-Echézeaux Domaine de la Romanée-Conti* 92p
(Côte de Nuits)

2006/2030 x2 • D 3 h / G 3 h

Youthful, bright ruby colour. Primary fruitiness still dominates the first closed nose. Mild and soft red berry aromatics and sweet cherry nuances. Lacks dimension at first but half an hour in the glass reveals layers of spicy and earthy notes. New oak aromatics are still detectable but well balanced. Warming palate has marked acidity and broad ripe tannin. Fine structure and supple texture. At the moment a restrained wine with a great future ahead.

1832 *Château Lafite* (Pauillac) 92p

2007/now x5 • D 10 min / G 30 min

This château-bottled wine was recorked at château in 1986. Regardless, the cork seemed to leak a little and the wine was at top shoulder condition. After decanting, the wine showed out well. The colour was medium–intense and brick red. The nose was etherised with a broad range of tertiary aromas: soy, meat stew, cooked vegetables, red fruits, cassis, and herbaceous nuances plus a strong hold of Asian spices. The medium-bodied palate revealed crisp mineral freshness, moderately intense flavour of red fruits, mostly cherries, a touch of tar, and a still noticeable, although declining, tannic structure. Sweet cooked vegetable aromas with a juicy mouth-feel and a lingering mineral finish. The concentration is getting loose at the end but the wine is performing still amazingly well!

Old and rare wines have been a popular target for wine fraud over the past few decades. As there may be an element of uncertainty about the authenticity of old bottles, we only accept tasting notes from wines of known origin or from wines that have been tasted with similar notes from several bottles that derive from different origins. We feel obliged to add at the end of the book tasting notes of a few wines that clearly would belong to the 1000 Finest Wines Ever Made, but of which authenticity we have no quarantee.

1784 *Château Brane-Mouton* *(Pauillac)* *98p*

D 10 min / G 15 min

This estate used to be part of the Lafite estate under the de Ségur family until 1720 when Joseph de Brane purchased it. He changed the name to Brane-Mouton and formed the basis of what was yet to become the legendary Mouton-Rothschild. Joseph de Brane worked hard for this estate and made it very successful, acknowledged as one of the best estates in Médoc just behind the first growths. Brane was also one of the highly esteemed pioneers of Cabernet Sauvignon in Médoc. This particular vintage of Brane-Mouton must have been one of the best ever made under this name.

The appearance did not promise much - hazy brown colour with orange hue on the rim. The nose gave such a lovely, surprisingly rich aromas of earthiness, spices and delicate balsamic aromas. Medium-bodied taste with very silky texture. Balsamic notes but still elegant showing hints of spiciness and woodiness in the moderately long finish. Absolutely astonishing experience!

1784 *Château Lafite* *(Pauillac)* *98p*

D 15 min / G 10 min

Beginning in 1716, Marquis Nicolas Alexandre de Ségur would consolidate Lafite's initial successes. He improved the winemaking techniques and above all enhanced the prestige of fine wines in the foreign markets and the Versailles court. He became known as the 'Wine Prince' and Lafite's wine became 'the King's Wine'. The Marquis Alexandre de Ségur did not have any sons and his property was divided between his four daughters. Lafite was thus separated from Latour, despite remaining in the family and being governed by the same steward until 1785. Lafite was inherited by Count Nicolas Marie Alexandre de Ségur, the son of the Marquis' oldest daughter, who had married a cousin, Alexandre de Ségur, provost of Paris. In 1785, the anonymous author of a memoir on the 'Lafite Lordship' spoke of the "finest vineyard in the Universe". Things did not turn out so well for the Count de Ségur, though. With outstanding debts, he was forced to sell Château Lafite in 1784. As a relative of the seller, Nicolas Pierre de Pichard, the first president of the Bordeaux Parliament, used the 'kinship rights' legislation to purchase the estate.

Luckily, this was tasted twice since the first bottle was already way over the top. The second bottle was still incredibly drinkable, although it fell rapidly into pieces in the glass. The appearance is hazy and brown with an intense balsamic nose. Medium-bodied wine shows surprisingly rich palate with beef stock, cooked vegetables and great deal of balsamic flavours. Moderately short finish but the wine amazes with its condition compared to its age.

1787 Château Lafite (Pauillac)   *97p*

D 10 min / -

On the eve of the French revolution, Lafite was at the height of its winemaking legacy, as witnessed in the exceptional authorship of Thomas Jefferson, future President of the United States. While serving as ambassador for the young United States Republic to the Versailles Court, this multi-faceted individual - farmer, businessman, politician, lawyer, architect, diplomat, and founder of the University of Virginia - acquired a passion for winemaking and thought about developing it in his own country. He stayed in Bordeaux in May 1787, and five days would be time enough for him to visit the major Chartrons merchants and gather a mass of information that he would report in his travel memoirs. He detailed the hierarchy of the growths, highlighting those that would go on to be the four leading wines. Château Lafite was among them. Jefferson remained a steadfast customer of Bordeaux wines until the end of his days. Lafite 1787 was the first of the 'Jefferson' wines to come on to the market when a single bottle was sold at Christie's London auction house in December 1985. Starting bid was around £2000, then the bidding went quite quickly up to £7000, then to £10,000 until finally two bidders, Christopher Forbes and Marvin Shanken, were left in the running. The winning bidder was Christopher Forbes. The final price was £105,000, at the time a world record auction price for a single bottle of wine.

The 1787 Lafite showed moderately dark brown colour with lots of sediment flakes. Very evolved acetic nose delivering hints of preserved fruits and cooked vegetables. Medium-bodied palate with dominance of acidity and sweet tones. High content of volatile aromas with an acetic finish. Still an amazingly good structure.

I N D E X

I N D E X

FRANCE

BORDEAUX

640	1945	Château Cos d'Estournel (Saint-Estèphe)	93p	2000/2010 x4
411	1953	Château Cos d'Estournel (Saint-Estèphe)	95p	2003/2012 x4
718	1961	Château Cos d'Estournel (Saint-Estèphe)	93p	2007/2020 x6
852	1970	Château Cos d'Estournel (Saint-Estèphe)	92p	2006/2015 x11
507	1986	Château Cos d'Estournel (Saint-Estèphe)	94p	2005/2020 x3
954	1921	Château Coutet (Barsac)	92p	2007/now x4
320	1934	Château Coutet (Barsac)	96p	2003/2015 x7
904	1964	Château Croizet-Bages (Pauillac)	92p	2003/now x2
388	1961	Château Ducru-Beaucaillou (Saint-Julien)	95p	2004/2010 x22
702	1970	Château Ducru-Beaucaillou (Saint-Julien)	93p	2004/2010 x38
157	1947	Château l'Eglise Clinet (Pomerol)	97p	2001/2015 x11
268	1950	Château l'Eglise Clinet (Pomerol)	96p	2004/2010 x12
392	1952	Château l'Eglise Clinet (Pomerol)	95p	2003/2010 x11
685	1928	Château L'Evangile (Pomerol)	93p	2005/2010 x3
496	1945	Château L'Evangile (Pomerol)	94p	2004/2008 x6
43	1947	Château L'Evangile (Pomerol)	99p	2004/2020 x7
138	1961	Château L'Evangile (Pomerol)	97p	2005/2020 x3
756	1947	Château Figeac (St.Emilion)	93p	2007/2015 x17
230	1949	Château Figeac (St.Emilion)	97p	2006/2020 x11
800	1890	Château Filhot (Sauternes)	92p	2005/2010 x2
431	1935	Château Filhot (Sauternes)	95p	2003/2020 x2
382	1961	Château La Gaffelière (St. Emilion)	95p	2007/2020 x13
897	1924	Château Grand-Puy-Lacoste (Pauillac)	92p	2002/2010 x2
186	1945	Château Grand-Puy-Lacoste (Pauillac)	97p	2001/2015 x5
506	1947	Château Grand-Puy-Lacoste (Pauillac)	94p	2003/2010 x3
837	1949	Château Grand-Puy-Lacoste (Pauillac)	92p	2001/2004 x3
701	1961	Château Grand-Puy-Lacoste (Pauillac)	93p	2005/2015 x4
484	1871	Château Gruaud-Larose (Saint-Julien)	94p	2002/now x4
517	1945	Château Gruaud-Larose (Saint-Julien)	94p	2001/2010 x15
781	1950	Château Gruaud-Larose (Saint-Julien)	93p	2004/now x3
379	1959	Château Gruaud-Larose (Saint-Julien)	95p	2005/2015 x14
356	1961	Château Gruaud-Larose (Saint-Julien)	95p	2002/2020 x23
916	1900	Château Haut-Bailly (Graves)	92p	2006/now x4
571	1898	Château Haut-Brion (Graves)	94p	2006/2015 x3
642	1921	Château Haut-Brion (Graves)	93p	2000/now x2
255	1924	Château Haut-Brion (Graves)	96p	2000/2010 x2
487	1928	Château Haut-Brion (Graves)	94p	2004/2010 x4
50	1929	Château Haut-Brion (Graves)	98p	2004/2015 x13
17	1945	Château Haut-Brion (Graves)	100p	2006/2010 x17
862	1947	Château Haut-Brion (Graves)	92p	2001/2008 x2
341	1949	Château Haut-Brion (Graves)	96p	2001/2008 x2
601	1950	Château Haut-Brion (Graves)	94p	2002/2015 x3
406	1953	Château Haut-Brion (Graves)	95p	2001/2015 x8
251	1959	Château Haut-Brion (Graves)	96p	2004/2020 x11

78	1961	Château Haut-Brion (Graves)	98p	2006/2020 x23
185	1982	Château Haut-Brion (Graves)	97p	2006/2020 x9
53	1989	Château Haut-Brion (Graves)	98p	2007/2030 x29
147	1990	Château Haut-Brion (Graves)	97p	2005/2020 x22
115	1929	Château Haut-Brion Blanc (Graves)	98p	2004/2010 x2
550	1962	Château Haut-Brion Blanc (Graves)	94p	2004/2010 x6
162	1985	Château Haut-Brion Blanc (Graves)	97p	2002/2025 x3
275	1945	Château Lafaurie-Peyraguey (Sauternes)	96p	2001/2015 x3
	1784	Château Lafite (Pauillac)	98p	
	1787	Château Lafite (Pauillac)	97p	
254	1812	Château Lafite (Pauillac)	96p	2006/now x3
1000	1832	Château Lafite (Pauillac)	92p	2007/now x5
850	1858	Château Lafite (Pauillac)	92p	2005/now x2
243	1864	Château Lafite (Pauillac)	96p	2000/2010 x3
9	1870	Château Lafite-Rothschild (Pauillac)	100p	2001/2010 x6
274	1874	Château Lafite-Rothschild (Pauillac)	96p	1999/now x2
643	1892	Château Lafite-Rothschild (Pauillac)	93p	2005/now x4
634	1899	Château Lafite-Rothschild (Pauillac)	93p	2005/now x2
605	1900	Château Lafite-Rothschild (Pauillac)	94p	2007/now x2
739	1945	Château Lafite-Rothschild (Pauillac)	92p	2007/2015 x11
461	1947	Château Lafite-Rothschild (Pauillac)	95p	2007/2010 x1
412	1949	Château Lafite-Rothschild (Pauillac)	95p	2005/2025 x18
31	1953	Château Lafite-Rothschild (Pauillac)	99p	2007/2020 x24
98	1959	Château Lafite-Rothschild (Pauillac)	98p	2007/2020 x23
723	1961	Château Lafite-Rothschild (Pauillac)	93p	2006/2015 x32
64	1982	Château Lafite-Rothschild (Pauillac)	98p	2005/2020 x9
146	1986	Château Lafite-Rothschild (Pauillac)	97p	2005/2025 x24
674	1989	Château Lafite-Rothschild (Pauillac)	93p	2007/2020 x11
276	1945	Château Lafleur (Pomerol)	96p	2004/2015 x15
21	1947	Château Lafleur (Pomerol)	100p	2007/2020 x16
458	1950	Château Lafleur (Pomerol)	95p	2006/2020 x7
597	1955	Château Lafleur (Pomerol)	94p	2004/2010 x4
327	1966	Château Lafleur (Pomerol)	96p	2006/2030 x4
156	1975	Château Lafleur (Pomerol)	97p	2003/2015 x14
119	1982	Château Lafleur (Pomerol)	98p	2006/2025 x5
960	1874	Château Lagrange (Saint-Julien)	92p	2002/now x4
613	1900	Château La Mission-Haut-Brion (Graves)	94p	2003/now x1
914	1904	Château La Mission-Haut-Brion (Graves)	92p	2001/now x2
778	1918	Château La Mission-Haut-Brion (Graves)	93p	2000/now x3
641	1926	Château La Mission-Haut-Brion (Graves)	93p	2000/now x2
33	1945	Château La Mission-Haut-Brion (Graves)	99p	2000/2015 x19
271	1950	Château La Mission-Haut-Brion (Graves)	96p	2006/2015 x16
353	1952	Château La Mission-Haut-Brion (Graves)	95p	2006/2015 x22
729	1953	Château La Mission-Haut-Brion (Graves)	93p	2006/2010 x8
408	1955	Château La Mission-Haut-Brion (Graves)	95p	2007/2015 x10
59	1959	Château La Mission-Haut-Brion (Graves)	98p	2006/2010 x24
76	1961	Château La Mission-Haut-Brion (Graves)	98p	2004/2020 x32
967	1966	Château La Mission-Haut-Brion (Graves)	92p	2005/2015 x12
69	1975	Château La Mission-Haut-Brion (Graves)	98p	2007/2030 x21
301	1978	Château La Mission-Haut-Brion (Graves)	96p	2007/2010 x18

63	1982	Château La Mission-Haut-Brion (Graves)	98p	2006/2035 x16
28	1989	Château La Mission-Haut-Brion (Graves)	99p	2006/2035 x17
939	1899	Château Langoa-Barton (Saint-Julien)	92p	2004/now x3
901	1966	Château Laroze (St.Emilion)	92p	2004/now x2
713	1870	Château Latour (Pauillac)	93p	2007/now x4
466	1897	Château Latour (Pauillac)	95p	2005/now x2
876	1908	Château Latour (Pauillac)	92p	2000/now x2
536	1911	Château Latour (Pauillac)	94p	2007/now x2
264	1921	Château Latour (Pauillac)	96p	2005/2015 x13
245	1924	Château Latour (Pauillac)	96p	2005/2015 x13
523	1926	Château Latour (Pauillac)	94p	2003/now x2
58	1928	Château Latour (Pauillac)	98p	2007/2025 x7
61	1929	Château Latour (Pauillac)	98p	2001/2020 x17
364	1934	Château Latour (Pauillac)	95p	2004/2010 x5
133	1945	Château Latour (Pauillac)	97p	1998/2030 x10
498	1948	Château Latour (Pauillac)	94p	2003/2010 x4
161	1949	Château Latour (Pauillac)	97p	2006/2025 x21
903	1950	Château Latour (Pauillac)	92p	2000/2010 x3
632	1953	Château Latour (Pauillac)	93p	2006/2010 x5
44	1959	Château Latour (Pauillac)	99p	2005/2030 x33
1	1961	Château Latour (Pauillac)	100p	2007/2030 x73
744	1962	Château Latour (Pauillac)	93p	2002/2015 x3
249	1964	Château Latour (Pauillac)	96p	2006/2015 x24
555	1966	Château Latour (Pauillac)	94p	2006/2015 x25
107	1970	Château Latour (Pauillac)	98p	2007/2030 x26
36	1982	Château Latour (Pauillac)	99p	2006/2040 x17
805	1986	Château Latour (Pauillac)	92p	2003/2020 x16
211	1990	Château Latour (Pauillac)	97p	2005/2025 x9
573	1998	Château Latour (Pauillac)	94p	2006/2025 x4
465	1945	Château Latour-à-Pomerol (Pomerol)	95p	2006/2015 x4
191	1950	Château Latour-à-Pomerol (Pomerol)	97p	2006/2020 x14
840	1952	Château Latour-à-Pomerol (Pomerol)	92p	2004/2010 x2
113	1961	Château Latour-à-Pomerol (Pomerol)	98p	2007/2015 x10
495	1966	Château Laville Haut-Brion (Graves)	94p	2007/2015 x3
500	1948	Château Léoville Barton (Saint-Julien)	94p	2002/2020 x2
604	1949	Château Léoville Barton (Saint-Julien)	94p	2007/2010 x4
702	1970	Château Léoville Barton (Saint-Julien)	93p	2004/2010 x38
452	1900	Château Léoville-Las Cases (Saint-Julien)	95p	2004/now x2
572	1926	Château Léoville-Las Cases (Saint-Julien)	94p	2004/2015 x2
118	1928	Château Léoville-Las Cases (Saint-Julien)	98p	2004/2010 x5
129	1945	Château Léoville-Las Cases (Saint-Julien)	97p	2004/2020 x12
666	1947	Château Léoville-Las Cases (Saint-Julien)	93p	2003/2015 x12
505	1961	Château Léoville-Las Cases (Saint-Julien)	94p	2007/2010 x21
253	1982	Château Léoville-Las Cases (Saint-Julien)	96p	2006/2020 x24
474	1986	Château Léoville-Las Cases (Saint-Julien)	95p	2006/2020 x12
261	1900	Château Léoville Poyferré (Saint-Julien)	96p	2004/now x3

603	1959	Château Lynch-Bages (Pauillac)	92p	2004/2015 x3
722	1961	Château Lynch-Bages (Pauillac)	93p	2004/2015 x7
201	1989	Château Lynch-Bages (Pauillac)	97p	2006/2020 x17
777	2000	Château Lynch-Bages (Pauillac)	93p	2004/2030 x9
775	1877	Château Margaux (Margaux)	93p	1999/now x2
646	1884	Château Margaux (Margaux)	94p	2006/now x4
72	1893	Château Margaux (Margaux)	98p	2001/2010 x3
884	1899	Château Margaux (Margaux)	92p	1999/now x2
5	1900	Château Margaux (Margaux)	100p	2005/now x15
882	1924	Château Margaux (Margaux)	92p	2006/now x4
188	1928	Château Margaux (Margaux)	97p	2003/2010 x12
866	1934	Château Margaux (Margaux)	92p	2000/2004 x4
758	1945	Château Margaux (Margaux)	93p	2003/2010 x3
599	1947	Château Margaux (Margaux)	94p	2007/2015 x13
608	1949	Château Margaux (Margaux)	94p	2006/2015 x9
409	1953	Château Margaux (Margaux)	95p	2001/2015 x2
381	1959	Château Margaux (Margaux)	95p	2007/2020 x11
447	1961	Château Margaux (Margaux)	95p	2007/2025 x7
163	1982	Château Margaux (Margaux)	97p	2006/2020 x3
316	1983	Château Margaux (Margaux)	96p	2005/2025 x9
218	1990	Château Margaux (Margaux)	97p	2006/2030 x12
449	1995	Château Margaux (Margaux)	95p	2003/2025 x9
221	1996	Château Margaux (Margaux)	97p	2006/2035 x15
512	2000	Château Margaux (Margaux)	94p	2004/2050 x4
433	1996	Château La Mondotte (Saint-Emilion)	95p	2007/2020 x5
831	1878	Château Montrose (Saint-Estèphe)	92p	2006/now x2
354	1929	Château Montrose (Saint-Estèphe)	95p	2000/2010 x13
510	1945	Château Montrose (Saint-Estèphe)	94p	2003/2015 x3
835	1949	Château Montrose (Saint-Estèphe)	92p	2007/now x13
198	1990	Château Montrose (Saint-Estèphe)	97p	2006/ 2025 x7
796	1945	Château Mouton d'Armailhac (Pauillac)	92p	2004/2006 x4
	1784	Château Brane-Mouton	98p	
51	1875	Château Mouton-Rothschild (Pauillac)	98p	2006/now x3
366	1924	Château Mouton-Rothschild (Pauillac)	95p	2007/now x3
623	1926	Château Mouton-Rothschild (Pauillac)	94p	2003/2010 x4
627	1929	Château Mouton-Rothschild (Pauillac)	93p	2003/2010 x4
2	1945	Château Mouton-Rothschild (Pauillac)	100p	2007/2025 x34
859	1946	Château Mouton-Rothschild (Pauillac)	92p	2005/2010 x2
192	1947	Château Mouton-Rothschild (Pauillac)	97p	2004/2020 x19
812	1948	Château Mouton-Rothschild (Pauillac)	92p	2007/2015 x2
42	1949	Château Mouton-Rothschild (Pauillac)	99p	2006/2020 x25
635	1950	Château Mouton-Rothschild (Pauillac)	93p	2006/2015 x4
915	1952	Château Mouton-Rothschild (Pauillac)	92p	2006/2010 x3
280	1953	Château Mouton-Rothschild (Pauillac)	96p	2007/2020 x25
246	1955	Château Mouton-Rothschild (Pauillac)	96p	2006/2015 x7
23	1959	Château Mouton-Rothschild (Pauillac)	100p	2007/2020 x33
91	1961	Château Mouton-Rothschild (Pauillac)	97p	2006/2030 x15
651	1962	Château Mouton-Rothschild (Pauillac)	93p	2006/2015 x7
717	1966	Château Mouton-Rothschild (Pauillac)	93p	2007/2015 x4

57	1982	Château Mouton-Rothschild (Pauillac)	99p	2007/2032 x7
630	1985	Château Mouton-Rothschild (Pauillac)	93p	2007/2015 x11
266	1986	Château Mouton-Rothschild (Pauillac)	96p	2007/2030 x35
483	1988	Château Mouton-Rothschild (Pauillac)	94p	2006/2015 x5
886	1989	Château Mouton-Rothschild (Pauillac)	92p	2007/2015 x4
639	1994	Château Mouton-Rothschild (Pauillac)	93p	2007/2015 x10
336	1995	Château Mouton-Rothschild (Pauillac)	96p	2006/now x3
423	1998	Château Mouton-Rothschild (Pauillac)	95p	2006/2030 x7
764	1999	Château Mouton-Rothschild (Pauillac)	93p	2006/2015 x3
731	2000	Château Mouton-Rothschild (Pauillac)	93p	2006/2040 x4
277	1959	Château Palmer (Margaux)	96p	2007/2015 x9
45	1961	Château Palmer (Margaux)	99p	2006/2020 x22
80	1966	Château Palmer (Margaux)	98p	2006/2015 x23
902	1982	Château Palmer (Margaux)	92p	2006/2020 x9
586	1983	Château Palmer (Margaux)	94p	2007/2015 x9
675	1990	Château Palmer (Margaux)	93p	2000/2020 x8
659	1949	Château Pape-Clément (Graves)	93p	2004/2006 x3
820	1898	Château Pavie (St.Emilion)	92p	2006/now x3
864	1947	Château Pavie (St.Emilion)	92p	2003/now x5
811	1949	Château Pavie (St.Emilion)	92p	2006/2010 x8
390	1961	Château Pavie (St.Emilion)	95p	2004/2010 x3
891	1999	Château Pavie (St.Emilion)	92p	2004/2030 x4
34	1921	Château Pétrus (Pomerol)	99p	2005/2015 x15
170	1928	Château Pétrus (Pomerol)	97p	2007/2025 x3
153	1929	Château Pétrus (Pomerol)	97p	2001/2015 x11
451	1934	Château Pétrus (Pomerol)	95p	2006/now x2
587	1937	Château Pétrus (Pomerol)	94p	2003/2020 x4
760	1943	Château Pétrus (Pomerol)	93p	2005/now x4
70	1945	Château Pétrus (Pomerol)	98p	2007/2025 x6
7	1947	Château Pétrus (Pomerol)	100p	2007/2015 x34
645	1948	Château Pétrus (Pomerol)	93p	2006/2015 x5
398	1949	Château Pétrus (Pomerol)	95p	2004/2010 x11
150	1950	Château Pétrus (Pomerol)	97p	2005/2025 x8
418	1952	Château Pétrus (Pomerol)	95p	2007/2015 x7
358	1955	Château Pétrus (Pomerol)	95p	2007/2015 x8
56	1959	Château Pétrus (Pomerol)	98p	2006/2020 x39
14	1961	Château Pétrus (Pomerol)	100p	2007/2020 x19
297	1964	Château Pétrus (Pomerol)	96p	2001/2010 x21
196	1966	Château Pétrus (Pomerol)	97p	2006/2020 x3
87	1970	Château Pétrus (Pomerol)	98p	2007/2015 x22
179	1971	Château Pétrus (Pomerol)	97p	2006/2025 x12
225	1975	Château Pétrus (Pomerol)	97p	2006/2020 x6
54	1982	Château Pétrus (Pomerol)	98p	2007/2040 x7
19	1989	Château Pétrus (Pomerol)	100p	2006/2040 x22
49	1990	Château Pétrus (Pomerol)	99p	2006/2030 x12
460	2000	Château Pétrus (Pomerol)	95p	2006/2045 x4
845	1945	Château Pichon-Longueville Baron (Pauillac)	92p	2004/2015 x7
242	1989	Château Pichon-Longueville Baron (Pauillac)	96p	2006/2030 x5
974	1996	Château Pichon-Longueville Baron (Pauillac)	92p	2006/2020 x5

236	1953	Château Pichon Longueville Comtesse de Lalande (Pauillac)	97p	2006/2030 x3
625	1959	Château Pichon Longueville Comtesse de Lalande (Pauillac)	94p	2006/2010 x12
174	1961	Château Pichon Longueville Comtesse de Lalande (Pauillac)	97p	2005/2015 x7
726	1964	Château Pichon Longueville Comtesse de Lalande (Pauillac)	93p	2005/2015 x8
86	1982	Château Pichon Longueville Comtesse de Lalande (Pauillac)	98p	2005/2025 x15
930	2000	Château Pichon Longueville Comtesse de Lalande (Pauillac)	92p	2005/2030 x5
101	1979	Château Le Pin (Pomerol)	98p	2006/2020 x5
60	1982	Château Le Pin (Pomerol)	98p	2006/2020 x7
204	1998	Château Le Pin (Pomerol)	97p	2005/2030 x3
488	2000	Château Le Pin (Pomerol)	94p	2006/2025 x3
788	1879	Château Pontet-Canet (Pauillac)	93p	2004/now x6
870	1959	Château Pontet-Canet (Pauillac)	92p	2005/2010 x27
638	1945	Château de Rayne-Vigneau Crème de Tête (Sauternes)	93p	2003/2010 x3
875	1959	Château de Rayne-Vigneau Crème de Tête (Sauternes)	92p	2003/now x8
435	1918	Château Rausan-Ségla (Margaux)	95p	2003/now x1
497	1937	Château Rieussec (Sauternes)	94p	2003/2010 x4
602	1949	Château Rieussec (Sauternes)	94p	2000/2015
877	2001	Château Rieussec (Sauternes)	92p	2007/2030 x3
421	1921	Château Sigalas-Rabaud (Sauternes)	95p	2003/now x3
861	2001	Château Smith-Haut Lafitte Blanc (Graves)	92p	2007/2015 x8
135	1921	Château Suduiraut (Sauternes)	97p	2003/2015 x3
149	1928	Château Suduiraut (Sauternes)	97p	2002/2010 x2
751	1961	Château Talbot (Saint-Julien)	93p	2004/2020 x6
591	1975	Château Trotanoy (Pomerol)	94p	2007/2015 x15
504	1994	Château Valandraud (St.Emilion)	94p	2007/2015 x3
220	1945	Vieux Château Certan (Pomerol)	97p	2003/2040 x3
11	1811	Château d'Yquem (Sauternes)	100p	1996/2010 x13
20	1819	Château d'Yquem (Sauternes)	100p	2004/now x2
84	1847	Château d'Yquem (Sauternes)	98p	2000/now x13
252	1861	Château d'Yquem (Sauternes)	96p	2005/2010 x3
99	1882	Château d'Yquem (Sauternes)	98p	2005/2020 x2
240	1896	Château d'Yquem (Sauternes)	96p	2007/2010 x6
127	1900	Château d'Yquem (Sauternes)	97p	2002/2030 x3

588	1918	Château d'Yquem (Sauternes)	92p	2007/2015 x3
6	1921	Château d'Yquem (Sauternes)	100p	2006/2030 x18
172	1928	Château d'Yquem (Sauternes)	97p	2007/2020 x2
308	1937	Château d'Yquem (Sauternes)	96p	2005/2015 x2
22	1945	Château d'Yquem (Sauternes)	100p	2001/2030 x7
456	1947	Château d'Yquem (Sauternes)	95p	2004/2015 x5
344	1949	Château d'Yquem (Sauternes)	96p	2001/2025 x7
797	1950	Château d'Yquem (Sauternes)	92p	2007/2015 x3
583	1955	Château d'Yquem (Sauternes)	94p	2004/2020 x3
79	1959	Château d'Yquem (Sauternes)	98p	2005/2030 x11
104	1967	Château d'Yquem (Sauternes)	98p	2002/2050 x16
120	1975	Château d'Yquem (Sauternes)	98p	2006/2030 x4
95	1990	Château d'Yquem (Sauternes)	98p	2007/2030 x17
780	1996	Château d'Yquem (Sauternes)	93p	2005/2030 x12
337	2001	Château d'Yquem (Sauternes)	96p	2007/2030 x5
748	1961	Ygrec Y, Château d'Yquem (Bordeaux)	93p	2004/2010 x2
574	1916	Domaine de Chevalier Rouge (Graves)	94p	2005/2010 x2

BURGUNDY

501	1945	Ruchottes-Chambertin Thomas Bassot (Côte de Nuits)	94p	2000/now x2
742	1955	Chambertin Clos-de-Bèze Jules Belin (Côte de Nuits)	93p	2004/now x11
754	1875	Chambertin Bouchard Père & Fils (Côte de Nuits)	93p	2006/now x3
355	1906	Romanée St.Vivant Bouchard Père & Fils (Côte de Nuits)	95p	2004/now x4
210	1921	Le Montrachet Bouchard Père & Fils (Côte de Beaune)	97p	2000/now x3
328	1966	La Romanée "Réserve du Paul Bouchard" Bouchard Père & Fils (Côte de Nuits)	96p	2007/2015 x2
924	1996	Corton-Charlemagne Bonneau du Martray (Côte de Beaune)	92p	2006/2020 x3
671	2002	Corton-Charlemagne Bonneau du Martray (Côte de Beaune)	93p	2006/2020 x3
867	2000	Bourgogne Blanc Comte Georges de Vogüé	92p	2007/1015 x3
834	1959	Chambolle-Musigny Les Amoureuses Comte Georges de Vogüé (Côte de Nuits)	92p	2002/2010 x3
351	1937	Musigny Comte Georges de Vogüé (Côte de Nuits)	95p	2007/2010 x2
82	1990	Musigny Comte Georges de Vogüé (Côte de Nuits)	98p	2004/2010 x2
607	1983	Musigny Vieilles Vignes Comte Georges de Vogüé (Côte de Nuits)	94p	2004/2020 x1
846	1988	Musigny Vieilles Vignes Comte Georges de Vogüé (Côte de Nuits)	92p	2002/2015 x1

151	1989	Meursault ler Cru Charmes Comtes Lafon (Côte de Beaune)	97p	2007/2015 x4
720	1994	Meursault 1er Cru Charmes Comtes Lafon (Côte de Beaune)	93p	2007/2020 x3
920	2003	Meursault 1er Cru Gevevrieres Comtes Lafon (Côte de Beaune)	92p	2007/2015 x3
154	1929	Chambertin Joseph Drouhin (Côte de Nuits)	97p	2002/2010 x4
650	1926	Chambertin Joseph Drouhin (Côte de Nuits)	93p	2006/now x4
908	1926	Clos-des-Mouches Rouge Drouhin (Côte de Beaune)	92p	2000/now x1
982	1995	Clos de la Roche Joseph Drouhin (Côte de Nuits)	92p	2001/2020 x6
117	1978	Musigny Joseph Drouhin (Côte de Nuits)	98p	2005/2015 x2
88	1996	Griotte-Chambertin Claude Dugat (Côte de Nuits)	98p	2004/2025 x4
839	1999	Chambertin Domaine Dugat-Py (Côte de Nuits)	91p	2006/2020 x1
735	1918	Corton-Charlemagne Faiveley	93p	2006/now x3
260	1990	Clos des Corton Faiveley (Côte de Beaune)	96p	2006/2010 x4
401	1945	Richebourg Louis Gros (Côte de Nuits)	95p	2005/2015 x1
703	1969	Bonnes-Mares Domaine Dujac (Côte de Nuits)	93p	2004/now x3
429	1997	Clos-St. Denis Domaine Dujac (Côte de Nuits)	95p	2007/2020 x3
75	1985	Richebourg Henri Jayer (Côte de Nuits)	98p	2000/2015 x6
132	1966	Richebourg Henri Jayer (Côte de Nuits)	97p	2007/2015 x4
534	1964	Pommard Premier Cru Camille Giroud (Côte de Beaune)	94p	2001/2015 x4
578	1971	Chambertin Camille Giroud (Côte de Nuits)	94p	2001/2020 x2
593	1978	Volnay Premier Cru Les Frémiets Camille Giroud (Côte de Beaune)	94p	2001/2015 x3
570	1979	Chablis Premier Cru Montmains Camille Giroud (Côte de Nuits)	94p	2001/2020 x2
584	1949	Nuits-St-Georges 'Les St. Georges' Henri Gouges	94p	2004/2015 x3
269	1898	Grand-Chambertin Gresigny (Côte de Nuits)	96p	2006/now x2
427	1919	Clos-de-Vougeot Grivelet-Gusset (Côte de Nuits)	95p	2001/2008 x1
626	1888	Clos-de-Vougeot Louis Jadot (Côte de Nuits)	93p	2004/now x4
481	1892	Clos-des-Ursules Louis Jadot (Côte de Nuits)	94p	2003/now x2
455	1896	Le Chambertin Louis Jadot (Côte de Nuits)	95p	2005/now x7
629	1898	La Romanée Louis Jadot (Côte de Nuits)	93p	2005/now x1
548	1900	Cuvée Nicolas Rolin Louis Jadot (Côte de Beaune)	94p	2004/now x2

430	1911	Le Chambertin Clos de Beze, Louis Jadot (Côte de Nuits)	95p	2005/now x3
869	1914	Le Chambertin Louis Jadot (Côte de Nuits)	92p	2004/2015 x2
513	1929	Le Chambertin Louis Jadot (Côte de Nuits)	94p	2004/now x2
180	1964	Chevalier-Montrachet Les Demoiselles Louis Jadot (Côte de Beaune)	97p	2004/2015 x2
556	1985	Le Chambertin Clos St. Jacques Louis Jadot (Côte de Nuits)	94p	2002/2020 x2
293	1986	Bâtard-Montrachet Louis Jadot (Côte de Beaune)	96p	2004/2020 x2
912	1970	Corton-Pougets Domaine des Héritiers Louis Jadot (Côte de Beaune)	92p	2006/2010 x3
410	1985	Chevalier-Montrachet Leflaive	95p	2007/2015 x6
966	1928	Corton Domaine Louis Latour (Côte de Beaune)	92p	2004/2015 x6
851	1949	Pommard Domaine Louis Latour (Côte de Beaune)	92p	2005/now x4
142	1959	Corton-Charlemagne Domaine Louis Latour (Côte de Beaune)	97p	2000/2010 x3
761	1937	Chapelle-Chambertin Domaine Leroy (Côte de Nuits)	93p	2005/2010 x3
801	1937	Romanée St.Vivant Domaine Leroy (Côte de Nuits)	92p	2000/2008 x3
294	1959	Chambertin Domaine Leroy (Côte de Nuits)	96p	2005/2015 x3
350	1964	Musigny Domaine Leroy (Côte de Nuits)	95p	2000/2015 x2
375	1969	Le Montrachet Domaine Leroy (Côte de Beaune)	95p	2002/2015 x4
262	1976	Clos de Vougeot Leroy (Côte de Nuits)	96p	2004/2010 x11
333	1985	Corton-Charlemagne Leroy (Côte de Beaune)	96p	2007/2015 x6
159	1990	Richebourg Domaine Leroy (Côte de Nuits)	97p	2005/2020 x5
592	1996	Musigny Domaine Leroy (Côte de Nuits)	94p	2006/2030 x2
478	1996	Chambolle-Musigny 1er Cru Les Charmes Leroy (Côte de Nuits)	94p	2006/2030 x4
865	1918	Le Montrachet Lupé-Cholet (Côte de Beaune)	91p	2002/now x2
90	1949	Romanée-St.Vivant Domaine Marey-Monge (Côte de Nuits)	98p	2005/now x4
681	1969	Romanée-St.Vivant Domaine Marey-Monge (Côte de Nuits)	93p	2003/now x2
957	1937	Bâtard-Montrachet Marcilly (Côte de Beaune)	92p	2004/2010 x4
654	1964	Clos-de-Tart Mommessin (Côte de Nuits)	93p	2000/now x4
448	2002	Bâtard-Montrachet Domaine Ramonet (Côte de Beaune)	95p	2007/2015 x3
589	1997	Montrachet Domaine Ramonet (Côte de Beaune)	94p	2006/2025 x6
382	2004	Montrachet Domaine Ramonet (Côte de Beaune)	95p	2006/2015 x3

661	2001	Chablis Premier Cru Montée de Tonnerre Raveneau (Chablis)	93p	2006/2015 x3
560	1921	Clos-de-Vougeot Regnier (Côte de Nuits)	94p	2001/now x1
309	1998	Bâtard-Montrachet Domaine de la Romanée-Conti (Côte de Beaune)	96p	2006/2015 x1
762	1947	Echézeaux Domaine de la Romanée-Conti (Côte de Nuits)	93p	2007/2015 x3
463	1989	Echézeaux Domaine de la Romanée-Conti (Côte de Nuits)	95p	2006/2015 x3
881	1935	Grands-Echézeaux Domaine de la Romanée-Conti (Côte de Nuits)	92p	2006/now x3
426	1937	Grands-Echézeaux Domaine de la Romanée-Conti (Côte de Nuits)	95p	20072010 x2
296	1959	Grands-Echézeaux Domaine de la Romanée-Conti (Côte de Nuits)	96p	2004/2010 x2
890	1964	Grands-Echézeaux Domaine de la Romanée-Conti (Côte de Nuits)	92p	2004/2015 x3
931	1990	Grands-Echézeaux Domaine de la Romanée-Conti (Côte de Nuits)	92p	2006/2025 x3
999	2000	Grands-Echézeaux Domaine de la Romanée-Conti (Côte de Nuits)	92p	2006/2030 x2
769	1947	La Tâche Domaine de la Romanée-Conti (Côte de Nuits)	93p	2005/2010 x4
105	1949	La Tâche Domaine de la Romanée-Conti (Côte de Nuits)	98p	2000/2010 x2
440	1950	La Tâche Domaine de la Romanée-Conti (Côte de Nuits)	95p	2007/now x2
749	1952	La Tâche Domaine de la Romanée-Conti (Côte de Nuits)	93p	2005/2015 x5
515	1953	La Tâche Domaine de la Romanée-Conti (Côte de Nuits)	94p	2006/2015 x2
32	1959	La Tâche Domaine de la Romanée-Conti (Côte de Nuits)	99p	2000/2020 x8
16	1962	La Tâche Domaine de la Romanée-Conti (Côte de Nuits)	100p	2005/2015 x4
145	1969	La Tâche Domaine de la Romanée-Conti (Côte de Nuits)	97p	2006/2030 x8
581	1971	La Tâche Domaine de la Romanée-Conti (Côte de Nuits)	94p	2007/2020 x7
445	1976	La Tâche Domaine de la Romanée-Conti (Côte de Nuits	95p	2007/2015 x6
37	1978	La Tâche Domaine de la Romanée-Conti (Côte de Nuits)	99p	2007/2020 x6
27	1985	La Tâche Domaine de la Romanée-Conti (Côte de Nuits)	99p	2006/2020 x4
13	1990	La Tâche Domaine de la Romanée-Conti (Côte de Nuits)	100p	2006/2025 x9
373	1999	La Tâche Domaine de la Romanée-Conti (Côte de Nuits)	95p	2006/2030 x8
40	1966	Montrachet Domaine de la Romanée-Conti (Côte de Beaune)	99p	2001/2020 x5
47	1986	Montrachet Domaine de la Romanée-Conti (Côte de Beaune)	99p	2004/2015 x1
575	1987	Montrachet Domaine de la Romanée-Conti (Côte de Beaune)	94p	2006/2015 x3
922	1989	Montrachet Domaine de la Romanée-Conti (Côte de Beaune)	92p	2004/2015 x4
616	1997	Montrachet Domaine de la Romanée-Conti (Côte de Beaune)	94 p	2004/2020 x4
663	2000	Montrachet Domaine de la Romanée-Conti (Côte de Beaune)	93p	2007/2015 x3
454	2002	Montrachet Domaine de la Romanée-Conti (Côte de Beaune)	95p	2006/2030 x2
582	2003	Montrachet Domaine de la Romanée-Conti (Côte de Beaune)	94p	2007/2015 x3
92	1929	Richebourg Domaine de la Romanée-Conti (Côte de Nuits)	98p	1998/2010 x4
112	1937	Richebourg Domaine de la Romanée-Conti (Côte de Nuits)	98p	2007/now x1
209	1964	Richebourg Domaine de la Romanée-Conti (Côte de Nuits)	97p	2001/2020 x2
918	1996	Richebourg Domaine de la Romanée-Conti (Côte de Nuits)	91p	2006/2020 x4
680	1997	Richebourg Domaine de la Romanée-Conti (Côte de Nuits)	93p	2002/2020 x3
24	1923	Romanée-Conti Domaine de la Romanée-Conti (Côte de Nuits)	99p	2007/now x7

434	1927	Romanée-Conti Domaine de la Romanée-Conti (Côte de Nuits)	95p	2005/now x2
102	1929	Romanée-Conti Domaine de la Romanée-Conti (Côte de Nuits)	98p	2000/2015 x10
124	1934	Romanée-Conti Domaine de la Romanée-Conti (Côte de Nuits)	97p	1999/2010 x2
48	1937	Romanée-Conti Domaine de la Romanée-Conti (Côte de Nuits)	99p	2000/2015 x12
446	1940	Romanée-Conti Domaine de la Romanée-Conti (Côte de Nuits)	95p	2004/now x2
425	1941	Romanée-Conti Domaine de la Romanée-Conti (Côte de Nuits)	95p	2004/now x2
407	1943	Romanée-Conti Domaine de la Romanée-Conti (Côte de Nuits)	95p	2007/2015 x4
3.	1945	Romanée-Conti Domaine de la Romanée-Conti (Côte de Nuits)	100p	1995/2020 x4
706	1952	Romanée-Conti Domaine de la Romanée-Conti (Côte de Nuits)	93p	2007/2010 x5
376	1957	Romanée-Conti Domaine de la Romanée-Conti (Côte de Nuits)	95p	2007/2010 x2
171	1962	Romanée-Conti Domaine de la Romanée-Conti (Côte de Nuits)	97p	2006/2020 x5
743	1967	Romanée-Conti Domaine de la Romanée-Conti (Côte de Nuits)	93p	2004/2010 x2
619	1976	Romanée-Conti Domaine de la Romanée-Conti (Côte de Nuits)	94p	2006/2020 x1
93	1978	Romanée-Conti Domaine de la Romanée-Conti (Côte de Nuits)	98p	2007/2020 x3
18	1985	Romanée-Conti Domaine de la Romanée-Conti (Côte de Nuits)	100p	2004/now x3
284	1988	Romanée-Conti Domaine de la Romanée-Conti (Côte de Nuits)	96p	2004/2020 x2
227	1989	Romanée-Conti Domaine de la Romanée-Conti (Côte de Nuits)	97p	2006/2035 x2
30	1990	Romanée-Conti Domaine de la Romanée-Conti (Côte de Nuits)	99p	2004/2030 x6
541	1997	Romanée-Conti Domaine de la Romanée-Conti (Côte de Nuits)	94p	2002/2020 x3
482	1999	Romanée-Conti Domaine de la Romanée-Conti (Côte de Nuits)	94p	2005/2040 x4
443	1985	Romanée St Vivant Domaine de la Romanée-Conti (Côte de Nuits)	95p	2002/2015 x4
590	1988	Romanée St Vivant Domaine de la Romanée-Conti (Côte de Nuits)	94p	2007/2015 x3
543	1958	Chambertin Armand Rousseau (Côte de Nuits)	94p	2000/2010 x3
554	1966	Chambertin Armand Rousseau (Côte de Nuits)	94p	2000/2010 x3
121	1978	Chambertin Armand Rousseau (Côte de Nuits)	98p	2004/2020 x2
818	1985	Chambertin Armand Rousseau (Côte de Nuits)	92p	2002/2020 x8
85	1990	Chambertin Armand Rousseau (Côte de Nuits)	98p	2005/2015 x3
868	1934	Clos-de-la-Roche Armand Rousseau (Côte de Nuits)	91p	2001/now x5
540	1955	Clos-de-la-Roche Charles Vienot (Côte de Nuits)	94p	2005/now x3
928	1953	Clos Vougeot Blanc Phorin (Côte de Nuits)	92p	2007/2010 x3
237	1947	Le Montrachet Van der Meulen (Côte de Beaune)	97p	2003/2010 x5

RHÔNE

567	1989	Châteauneuf-du-Pape Hommage à Jacques Perrin Château de Beaucastel (Rhône)	94p	2005/2007 x3
83	1990	Châteauneuf-du-Pape Hommage à Jacques Perrin Château de Beaucastel (Rhône)	98p	2005/2020 x2
509	1983	Châteauneuf-du-Pape Château de Beaucastel (Rhône)	94p	2005/2015 x3
557	1986	Châteauneuf-du-Pape Château de Beaucastel (Rhône)	94p	2001/2015 x2
804	1990	Châteauneuf-du-Pape Château de Beaucastel (Rhône)	92p	2001/2015 x4
696	1990	Châteauneuf-du-Pape Réserve des Celestins Henri Bonneau (Rhône)	93p	2006/2020 x3
933	1949	Hermitage Chapoutier (Rhône)	92p	2004/2010 x3
165	1991	Ermitage le Pavillon Chapoutier (Rhône)	97p	2006/2020 x4
469	1998	Ermitage L'Ermite Chapoutier (Rhône)	95p	2006/2030 x3

898	1970	Hermitage J.L. Chave (Rhône)	92p	2005/2015 x3
176	1990	Hermitage J.L. Chave (Rhône)	97p	2005/2020 x3
231	1990	Hermitage Cuvée Cathelin J.L. Chave (Rhône)	97p	2004/2025 x2
984	1996	Cornas Auguste Clape (Rhône)	92p	2005/2020 x2
539	1999	Côte-Rôtie Les Grandes Places Domaine Clusel-Roch	95p	2002/2020 x1
787	1961	Châteauneuf-du-Pape Devigneau (Rhône)	93p	2004/2015 x5
235	1945	Hermitage Delas Frères (Rhône)	95p	2003/2008 x2
990	1990	Cuvée Syrah Château de Fonsalette	92p	2004/now x3
946	1999	Crozes-Hermitage La Guiraude Alain Graillot (Rhône)	92p	2005/2020 x3
167	1990	Côte-Rôtie La Landonne Guigal (Rhône)	97p	2003/2020 x2
494	1999	Côte-Rôtie La Landonne Guigal (Rhône)	94p	2006/2040 x3
81	1969	Côte-Rôtie La Mouline Guigal (Rhône)	98p	2006/2010 x3
108	1976	Côte-Rôtie La Mouline Guigal (Rhône)	98p	2003/2020 x3
272	1985	Côte-Rôtie La Mouline Guigal (Rhône)	96p	2005/2020 x2
963	1987	Côte-Rôtie La Mouline Guigal (Rhône)	92p	2007/2015 x4
136	1988	Côte-Rôtie La Mouline Guigal (Rhône)	97p	2005/2025 x9
474	1999	Côte-Rôtie La Mouline Guigal (Rhône)	95p	2006/2030 x4
774	2000	Côte-Rôtie La Mouline Guigal (Rhône)	93p	2007/2020 x2
46.	1985	Côte-Rôtie La Turque Guigal (Rhône)	99p	2003/2025 x2
144	1988	Côte-Rôtie La Turque Guigal (Rhône)	97p	2004/2025 x9
791	1996	Côte-Rôtie La Turque Guigal (Rhône)	93p	2004/2025 x3
730	1955	Hermitage La Chapelle Paul Jaboulet Aîné (Rhône)	93p	2003/2010 x4
8	1961	Hermitage La Chapelle Paul Jaboulet Aîné (Rhône)	100p	2007/2030 x17
646	1964	Hermitage La Chapelle Paul Jaboulet Aîné (Rhône)	93p	2007/2015 x2
480	1966	Hermitage La Chapelle Paul Jaboulet Aîné (Rhône)	93p	1998/2008 x5
535	1970	Hermitage La Chapelle Paul Jaboulet Aîné (Rhône)	94p	2001/2010 x9
74	1978	Hermitage La Chapelle Paul Jaboulet Aîné (Rhône)	98p	2005/2030 x3
291	1990	Hermitage La Chapelle Paul Jaboulet Aîné (Rhône)	96p	2006/2025 x6
980	1990	Châteauneuf-du-Pape Cuvée Réservée Domaine du Pegau (Rhône)	92p	2001/2015 x2
518	1978	Châteauneuf-du-Pape Château Rayas (Rhône)	94p	2001/2020 x2
77	1990	Châteauneuf-du-Pape Château Rayas (Rhône)	98p	2004/2030 x3
683	1990	Domaine de Trévallon (Rhône)	93p	2007/2015 x3

CHAMPAGNE

690	1995	Clos Saint Hilaire Billecart-Salmon (Champagne)	93p	2005/2030 x3
295	1996	Cuvée Elisabeth Salmon Rosé Billecart-Salmon (Champagne)	96p	2006/2020 x3
955	1996	Cuvée Nicolas François Billecart Billecart-Salmon (Champagne)	92p	2005/2020 x2
615	1990	Grande Cuvée Billecart-Salmon (Champagne)	94p	2004/2030 x4
318	1996	Grande Cuvée Billecart-Salmon (Champagne)	96p	2006/2025 x2
694	1990	Grande Année Bollinger (Champagne)	93p	2004/2025 x3
639	1970	R.D. Bollinger (Champagne)	93p	2007/now x3
173	1975	R.D. Bollinger (Champagne)	97p	2007/2015 x3
486	1976	R.D. Bollinger (Champagne)	94p	2007/2020 x7
522	1979	R.D. Bollinger (Champagne)	94p	2004/2015 x6
617	1996	R.D. Bollinger (Champagne)	94p	2006/2025 x3
39	1969	Vieilles Vignes Françaises Bollinger (Champagne)	99p	1999/2010 x1
374	1970	Vieilles Vignes Françaises Bollinger (Champagne)	95p	2002/2010 x2
111	1985	Vieilles Vignes Françaises Bollinger (Champagne)	98p	2006/2015 x3
230	1990	Vieilles Vignes Françaises Bollinger (Champagne)	97p	2004/2020 x7
660	1992	Vieilles Vignes Françaises Bollinger (Champagne)	93p	2003/2020 x5
212	1996	Vieilles Vignes Françaises Bollinger (Champagne)	97p	2007/2020 x4
621	1999	Vieilles Vignes Françaises Bollinger (Champagne)	94p	2006/2020 x3
103	1928	Vintage Bollinger (Champagne)	98p	2005/now x2
325	1945	Vintage Bollinger (Champagne)	96p	2005/now x2
721	1952	Vintage Bollinger (Champagne)	93p	2006/2010 x5
699	1953	Vintage Bollinger (Champagne)	93p	2007/now x4
395	1955	Vintage Bollinger (Champagne)	95p	2006/now x2
790	1990	Comte Audoin de Dampierre Réserve Familiale (Champagne)	93p	2004/2015 x8
978	1990	Cuvée William Deutz Champagne Deutz (Champagne)	92p	2004/2025 x8
998	1975	Cuvée William Deutz Vinothéque Champagne Deutz (Champagne)	92p	2005/2010 x2
986	1996	Cuvée William Deutz Rosé Deutz (Champagne)	92p	2007/2020 x2
322	1959	Carte d´Or Brut Champagne Drappier (Champagne)	96p	2005/2010 x4
841	1990	Femme de Champagne Duval-Leroy (Champagne)	92p	2004/2020 x4

894	1990	Celebris Gosset (Champagne)	92p	2004/2020 x6
724	1998	Celebris Gosset (Champagne)	93p	2006/2020 x4
422	1996	Celebris Rosé Gosset (Champagne)	95p	2006/2015 x4
29	1907	Champagne Goût American Heidsieck & Monopole (Champagne)	99p	2005/now x3
549	1966	Vintage Heidsieck & Monopole (Champagne)	94p	2004/2010 x5
753	1979	Charles Heidsieck Rosé (Champagne)	94p	2005/2010 x2
958	2000	Cornu Bautray Non Dosé Jacquesson (Champagne)	92p	2006/2020 x2
807	1990	Grand Vin Signature Jacquesson (Champagne)	92p	2004/2015 x8
917	1995	Grand Vin Signature Jacquesson (Champagne)	92p	2006/2015x4
942	1996	Rosé Jacquesson (Champagne)	92p	2007/2020 x5
52	1979	Clos du Mesnil Champagne Krug (Champagne)	98p	2005/2020 x3
106	1983	Clos du Mesnil Champagne Krug (Champagne)	98p	2006/2020 x4
96	1985	Clos du Mesnil Champagne Krug (Champagne)	98p	2007/2020 x5
519	1992	Clos du Mesnil Champagne Krug (Champagne)	94p	2006/2020 x4
15	1928	Krug Collection Champagne Krug (Champagne)	100p	2004/2010 x3
399	1953	Krug Collection Champagne Krug (Champagne)	95p	2007/now x4
177	1966	Krug Collection Champagne Krug (Champagne)	97p	2003/2010 x2
166	1973	Krug Collection Champagne Krug (Champagne)	97p	2007/2015 x3
794	1981	Krug Collection Champagne Krug (Champagne)	93p	2002/2010 x4
128	1926	Vintage Champagne Krug (Champagne)	97p	2006/now x2
214	1945	Vintage Champagne Krug (Champagne)	97p	2006/now x5
357	1953	Vintage Champagne Krug (Champagne)	95p	2006/2010 x3
160	1955	Vintage Champagne Krug (Champagne)	97p	2004/now x2
200	1959	Vintage Champagne Krug (Champagne)	97p	2002/2010 x2
444	1961	Vintage Champagne Krug (Champagne)	95p	2006/2012 x2
725	1962	Vintage Champagne Krug (Champagne)	93p	2001/2010 x4
193	1964	Vintage Champagne Krug (Champagne)	97p	2007/2015 x3
686	1966	Vintage Champagne Krug (Champagne)	93p	2002/2015 x3
270	1969	Vintage Champagne Krug (Champagne)	96p	2007/2010 x2
140	1971	Vintage Champagne Krug (Champagne)	97p	2005/2015 x4
352	1973	Vintage Champagne Krug (Champagne)	95p	2006/2015 x3
533	1975	Vintage Champagne Krug (Champagne)	94p	2006/2015 x5
183	1979	Vintage Champagne Krug (Champagne)	97p	2006/2018 x9
359	1982	Vintage Champagne Krug (Champagne)	95p	2007/2018 x4
283	1988	Vintage Champagne Krug (Champagne)	96p	2007/2010 x12
349	1989	Vintage Champagne Krug (Champagne)	95p	2007/2010 x8
821	1995	Vintage Champagne Krug (Champagne)	92p	2007/2020 x22
989	1997	Grande Siècle Cuvée Alexandra Rosé Laurent-Perrier	92p	2007/2020 x5
765	1921	Vintage Champagne Fred Lerouix (Champagne)	92p	2006/now x5
773	1941	Vintage Champagne Mercier (Champagne)	92p	2005/now x2
853	1926	Private Cuvée Champagne Champagne Mercier (Champagne)	92p	2004/now x2
257	1947	Brut Impérial Moët & Chandon (Champagne)	96p	2005/2008 x3
313	1952	Brut Impérial Moët & Chandon (Champagne)	96p	2004/2010 x3
768	1959	Brut Impérial Moët & Chandon (Champagne)	93p	2004/now x3

100	1921	Dom Pérignon Moët & Chandon (Champagne)	98p	2006/now x3
450	1928	Dom Pérignon Moët & Chandon (Champagne)	95p	2005/2010 x2
516	1929	Dom Pérignon Moët & Chandon (Champagne)	94p	2006/now x3
116	1934	Dom Pérignon Moët & Chandon (Champagne)	98p	2005/now x4
393	1937	Dom Pérignon Moët & Chandon (Champagne)	95p	2006/now x1
164	1947	Dom Pérignon Moët & Chandon (Champagne)	97p	2006/now x3
559	1949	Dom Pérignon Moët & Chandon (Champagne)	94p	2005/now x5
708	1952	Dom Pérignon Moët & Chandon (Champagne)	93p	2006/now x3
288	1955	Dom Pérignon Moët & Chandon (Champagne)	96p	2006/2010 x3
324	1959	Dom Pérignon Moët & Chandon (Champagne)	96p	2006/now x16
41	1961	Dom Pérignon Moët & Chandon (Champagne)	99p	2007/now x45
673	1962	Dom Pérignon Moët & Chandon (Champagne)	93p	2005/2010 x8
405	1964	Dom Pérignon Moët & Chandon (Champagne)	95p	2006/now x7
305	1966	Dom Pérignon Moët & Chandon (Champagne)	96p	2006/now x7
545	1973	Dom Pérignon Moët & Chandon (Champagne)	94p	2006/2020 x8
340	1976	Dom Pérignon Moët & Chandon (Champagne)	96p	2007/now x8
663	1982	Dom Pérignon Moët & Chandon (Champagne)	93p	2007/2020 x16
899	1995	Dom Pérignon Moët & Chandon (Champagne)	92p	2004/2025 x4
745	1996	Dom Pérignon Moët & Chandon (Champagne)	93p	2006/2030 x7
529	1998	Dom Pérignon Moët & Chandon (Champagne)	94p	2007/2025 x9
273	1966	Dom Pérignon Rosé Moët & Chandon (Champagne)	96p	2001/now x11
992	1996	Dom Pérignon Rosé Moët & Chandon (Champagne)	92p	2007/2030 x2
554	1958	Cordon Rouge G.H. Mumm (Champagne)	94p	2006/2010 x3
538	1969	Cordon Rouge G.H. Mumm (Champagne)	94p	2003/2010 x2
968	1990	Nec Plus Ultra Bruno Paillard (Champagne)	92p	2004/2020 x4
360	1969	Belle Epoque Perrier-Jouët (Champagne)	95p	2004/now x3
951	1985	Belle Epoque Perrier-Jouët (Champagne)	92p	2007/2010 x7
771	1990	Belle Epoque Perrier-Jouët (Champagne)	93p	2004/2020 x6
532	1996	Belle Epoque Rosé Perrier-Jouët (Champagne)	94p	2006/2015 x2
880	1928	Vintage Perrier-Jouët (Champagne)	92p	2006/now x2
547	1951	Clos des Goisses Philipponnat (Champagne)	94p	2006/2015 x2
125	1952	Clos des Goisses Philipponnat (Champagne)	97p	2006/2010 x4
190	1964	Clos des Goisses Philipponnat (Champagne)	97p	2000/2010 x2
229	1966	Clos des Goisses Philipponnat (Champagne)	97p	2004/2020 x2
203	1975	Clos des Goisses Philipponnat (Champagne)	97p	2006/2010 x3
298	1979	Clos des Goisses Philipponnat (Champagne)	96p	2006/2010 x5
485	1989	Clos des Goisses Philipponnat (Champagne)	94p	2006/2010 x5
378	1990	Clos des Goisses Philipponnat (Champagne)	95p	2005/2025 x5
961	1992	Clos des Goisses Philipponnat (Champagne)	92p	2006/2015 x4
542	1996	Clos des Goisses Philipponnat (Champagne)	94p	2006/2025 x8
947	1964	Royal Réserve Philipponnat (Champagne)	92p	2007/2010 x3
659	1880	Extra Cuvée Réserve Pol Roger (Champagne)	91p	2005/now x3
55	1911	Vintage Pol Roger (Champagne)	98p	2002/2010 x2
365	1921	Vintage Pol Roger (Champagne)	95p	2001/now x2
67	1928	Vintage Pol Roger (Champagne)	98p	2007/now x5
551	1955	Vintage Pol Roger (Champagne)	94p	2003/now x3
178	1959	Blanc de Blancs Pol Roger (Champagne)	97p	2003/2015 x2
709	1961	Vintage Pol Roger (Champagne)	93p	2004/now x4

988	1986	Cuvée Sir Winston Churchill Pol Roger (Champagne)	92p	2005/2020 x7
436	1996	Cuvée Sir Winston Churchill Pol Roger (Champagne)	95p	2007/2020 x7
929	1990	Cuvée Louise Pommery (Champagne)	92p	2004/2025 x9
187	1953	Cristal Roederer (Champagne)	97p	2001/2010 x3
233	1955	Cristal Roederer (Champagne)	97p	2006/2010 x3
234	1969	Cristal Roederer (Champagne)	97p	2007/2010 x9
688	1971	Cristal Roederer (Champagne)	93p	2006/2010 x4
371	1975	Cristal Roederer (Champagne)	95p	2006/2020 x3
849	1977	Cristal Roederer (Champagne)	92p	2007/2010 x3
223	1988	Cristal Roederer (Champagne)	97p	2007/2030 x5
310	1990	Cristal Roederer (Champagne)	96p	2004/2030 x3
948	1994	Cristal Roederer (Champagne)	92p	2007/2015 x5
380	1996	Cristal Roederer (Champagne)	95p	2007/2030 x5
290	1997	Cristal Roederer (Champagne)	96p	2007/2020 x8
26	1961	Cristal Rosé Roederer (Champagne)	99p	2005/2010 x3
719	1979	Cristal Rosé Roederer (Champagne)	93p	2006/2020 x2
755	1982	Cristal Rosé Roederer (Champagne)	93p	2005/2020 x3
372	1988	Cristal Rosé Roederer (Champagne)	95p	2001/2020 x3
216	1995	Cristal Rosé Roederer (Champagne)	97p	2006/2020 x4
712	1955	Vintage Champagne Louis Roederer (Champagne)	93p	2003/now x4
644	1966	Vintage Champagne Louis Roederer (Champagne)	93p	2004/2010 x2
89	1969	Dom Ruinart Rosé Ruinart (Champagne)	98p	2007/2010 x3
525	1979	Dom Ruinart Rosé Ruinart (Champagne)	94p	2007/2010 x5
317	1988	Dom Ruinart Rosé Ruinart (Champagne)	96p	2007/2020 x8
464	1990	Dom Ruinart Rosé Ruinart (Champagne)	95p	2007/2020 x2
226	1976	Salon (Champagne)	97p	2006/2015 x3
281	1988	Salon (Champagne)	96p	2006/2020 x11
844	1990	Salon (Champagne)	92p	2006/2030 x5
747	1995	Salon (Champagne)	93p	2005/2020 x12
416	1961	Comtes de Champagne Taittinger (Champagne)	95p	2005/2010 x3
976	1990	Comtes de Champagne Taittinger (Champagne)	92p	2007/2015 x3
143	1971	Comtes de Champagne Rosé Taittinger (Champagne)	97p	2005/2010x2
872	1970	La Grande Dame Veuve Clicquot (Champagne)	92p	2005/2010 x2
803	1995	La Grande Dame Veuve Clicquot (Champagne)	92p	2003/2020 x7
241	1900	Veuve Clicquot Ponsardin (Champagne)	96p	2006/now x2
181	1923	Veuve Clicquot Ponsardin (Champagne)	97p	2004/now x5
893	1919	Vintage Veuve Clicquot Ponsardin (Champagne)	92p	2007/now x3
334	1942	Vintage Veuve Clicquot Ponsardin (Champagne)	96p	2005/now x2
808	1997	Coeur de Cuvée Vilmart (Champagne)	92p	2007/2015 x6

ALSACE

827	1976	Riesling Hugel (Alsace)	92p	2003/2015 x2
526	1989	Pinot Gris Sélection de Grains Nobles Josmeyer (Alsace)	95p	2006/2020 x3
965	2002	Pinot Gris Grand Cru Hengst Josmeyer (Alsace)	92p	2006/2015 x2
964	2002	Pinot Gris Muenchberg A360P Domaine Ostertag (Alsace)	92p	2007/2015 x6
763	1997	Gewurtraminer Sélection des Grains Nobles Rimelsberg Marc Tempé	93p	2002/2015 x1
332	1983	Riesling Clos Ste Hune Domaine Trimbach	96p	2001/2015 x2
667	1999	Gewurtraminer Heimbourg Zind-Humbrecht (Alsace)	93p	2003/2010 x3
264	1990	Riesling Brand Vendange Tardive Zind-Humbrecht (Alsace)	96p	2005/2015 x3
402	1994	Riesling Rangen de Thann Clos St Urbain Zind-Humbrecht (Alsace)	95p	2003/2010 x2

LANGUEDOC-ROUSSILLON

292	1929	Banyuls Grand Cru (Banyuls)	96p	2006/2040 x4
979	1998	Domaine de l'Aigulière Côte-Dôrée (Languedoc-Roussillon)	92p	2002/2015 x2
838	1999	Domaine de la Granges des Peres Rouges (Languedoc-Roussillon)	92p	2004/2015 x4
926	1996	Clos des Cistes Domaine Peyre Rose (Coteaux du Languedoc)	92p	2006/2015 x2

LOIRE

672	1997	Coteaux du Layon SGN Aprés Minuit Domaine de la Coeur d'Ardenay (Loire)	93p	2001/2030 x3
544	1997	Coteaux du Layon 'Anthologie' Pierre Delesvaux	94p	2001/2040 x1
789	1964	Vouvray Clos du Bourg Moelleux Huet (Loire)	92p	2002/2020 x3
224	1919	Vouvray Haut-Lieu Moelleux Huet (Loire)	97p	2002/2015 x1
562	1959	Vouvray Le Haut Moelleux Huet (Loire)	94p	2005/2010 x2
563	1997	Bonnezeaux Cuvée Zenith René Renou	94p	2005/2015 x3

ITALY

612	1990	Solaia Antinori (Tuscany)	94p	2006/2015 x8
287	1997	Solaia Antinori (Tuscany)	96p	2006/2025 x5
746	1970	Tignanello Antinori (Tuscany)	93p	2006/now x2
610	1971	Tignanello Antinori (Tuscany)	94p	2007/now x3
975	1992	Turriga Argiolas (Sardegna)	92p	2004/2010 x2
577	1994	Vin Santo Avignonesi (Tuscany)	94p	2005/2015 x4
561	1959	Amarone della Valpolicella Bertani (Veneto)	94p	2002/2015 x2
829	1966	Brunello di Montalcino Biondi-Santi (Tuscany)	92p	2007/2015 x8
25	1891	Brunello di Montalcino Riserva Biondi-Santi (Tuscany)	99p	2000/now x2
692	1945	Brunello di Montalcino Riserva Biondi-Santi (Tuscany)	93p	2007/now x2
397	1955	Brunello di Montalcino Riserva Bionti-Santi (Tuscany)	95p	2007/2020 x6
552	1964	Brunello di Montalcino Riserva Biondi-Santi (Tuscany)	94p	2007/2015 x8
888	1967	Brunello di Montalcino Riserva Biondi-Santi (Tuscany)	92p	2007/now x3
817	1998	Brunello di Montalcino Riserva Biondi-Santi (Tuscany)	92p	2007/2030 x3
946	1945	Barolo Riserva Borgogno (Piedmont)	92p	2006/now x4
467	1947	Barolo Riserva Borgogno (Piedmont)	95p	2007/2020 x6
569	1952	Barolo Riserva Borgogno (Piedmont)	94p	2003/2015 x4
470	1974	Barolo Riserva Borgogno (Piedmont)	95p	2007/2010 x3
925	1990	Solare Capannelle (Tuscany)	92p	2005/2010 x4
892	1949	Chianti Classico Riserva Castello di Brolio (Tuscany)	92p	2000/now x4
314	1996	Barolo Bricco Rocche Ceretto (Piedmont)	96p	2001/2020 x3
330	1974	Barolo Granbussia Riserva Aldo Conterno (Piedmont)	96p	2006/2015 x1
611	1979	Barolo Granbussia Riserva Aldo Conterno (Piedmont)	94p	2006/now x2
321	1937	Barolo Monfortino Riserva Giacomo Conterno (Piedmont)	96p	2007/now x2
606	1943	Barolo Monfortino Riserva Giacomo Conterno (Piedmont)	94p	2003/2010 x2
228	1945	Barolo Monfortino Riserva Giacomo Conterno (Piedmont)	97p	2006/2015 x3
123	1952	Barolo Monfortino Riserva Giacomo Conterno (Piedmont)	98p	2006/2010 x4
902	1958	Barolo Monfortino Riserva Giacomo Conterno (Piedmont)	93p	2003/now x2
215	1964	Barolo Monfortino Riserva Giacomo Conterno (Piedmont)	97p	2006/2020 x6

402	1967	Barolo Monfortino Riserva Giacomo Conterno (Piedmont)	92p	2003/2015 x1
622	1994	Barolo Monfortino Riserva Giacomo Conterno (Piedmont)	94p	2004/2020 x2
468	1995	Barolo Monfortino Riserva Giacomo Conterno (Piedmont)	95p	2006/2020 x3
936	1997	Case Via Syrah Fontodi (Tuscany)	92p	2001/2015 x4
415	1961	Barbaresco Angelo Gaja (Piedmont)	96p	2007/now x3
528	1974	Barbaresco Angelo Gaja (Piedmont)	94p	2007/now x3
740	1978	Barbaresco Costa Russi Angelo Gaja (Piedmont)	93p	2004/2010 x2
141	1967	Barbaresco Sori San Lorenzo Angelo Gaja (Piedmont)	97p	2007/2010 x5
265	1985	Barbaresco Sorí San Lorenzo Angelo Gaja (Piedmont)	96p	2005/2019 x6
471	1989	Barbaresco Sorí San Lorenzo Angelo Gaja (Piedmont)	95p	2004/2015 x4
887	1998	Sperss Angelo Gaja (Piedmont)	92p	2006/2020 x2
802	2000	Cepparello Isole e Olena (Tuscany)	92p	2007/2015 x9
580	1997	Vin Santo Isole e Olena (Tuscany)	94p	2003/2020 x4
934	1999	Vin Santo Isole e Olena (Tuscany)	92p	2007/2040 x2
945	1999	Messorio Le Macchiole (Tuscany)	92p	2004/2020 x3
919	1998	Paleo Le Macchiole (Tuscany)	92p	2006/2015 x2
715	1968	Barolo Giuseppe Mascarello (Piedmont)	93p	2000/now x2
232	1991	Masseto Tenuta dell'Ornellaia (Tuscany)	97p	2005/2015 x5
473	1994	Masseto Tenuta dell'Ornellaia (Tuscany)	95p	2004/2020 x3
197	1997	Masseto Tenuta dell'Ornellaia (Tuscany)	97p	2007/2015 x4
687	1998	Masseto Tenuta dell'Ornellaia (Tuscany)	93p	2007/2015 x6
970	2000	Masseto Tenuta dell'Ornellaia (Tuscany)	92p	2007/2010 x5
795	1998	Acininobili Fausto Maculan (Veneto)	92 p	2002/2015 x2
677	1952	Vin Santo Fattoria Montaquari	93p	2003/2015 x1
682	1997	Brunello di Montalcino Pertimali (Tuscany)	93p	2002/2015 x4
609	1958	Barolo Pio Cesare (Piedmont)	94p	2005/2010 x3
624	1967	Brunello di Montalcino Riserva, Il Poggione (Tuscany)	94p	2007/2020 x3
959	1999	Brunello di Montalcino Poliziano (Tuscany)	92p	2004/2020 x2
816	1985	Barolo Bussia Prunotto (Piedmont)	92p	2006/2015 x9
595	1998	Barbera d'Asti Quarum (Piedmont)	94p	2001/2010 x2
932	1997	Giuseppe Quintarelli Amarone della Valpolicella (Veneto)	92p	2005/2015 x3

732	1999	Vigna d'Alceo Castello dei Rampolla (Tuscany)	93p	2003/2020 x4
420	1990	Barolo Cannubi Boschis Luciano Sandrone (Piedmont)	95p	2006/2025 x4
658	1997	Barolo Cannubi Boschis Luciano Sandrone (Piedmont)	93p	2002/2030 x4
614	1996	Barolo Le Vigne Luciano Sandrone (Piedmont)	94p	2007/2020 x3
648	1968	Sassicaia Tenuta San Guido (Tuscany)	93p	2006/now x3
400	1978	Sassicaia Tenuta San Guido (Tuscany)	95p	2006/2010 x4
384	1979	Sassicaia Tenuta San Guido (Tuscany)	95p	2006/2010 x6
35	1985	Sassicaia Tenuta San Guido (Tuscany)	99p	2006/2020 x8
697	1992	Sassicaia Tenuta San Guido (Tuscany)	92p	2005/2010 x5
847	1997	Sassicaia Tenuta San Guido (Tuscany)	92p	2006/2025 x5
475	2000	Barolo Sarmassa Roberto Voerzio (Piedmont)	95p	2007/2030 x4
809	2000	Barolo La Serra Roberto Voerzio (Piedmont)	92p	2005/2020 x2

SPAIN

814	1999	Aalto Bodegas Aalto (Ribera del Duero)	92p	2002/2010 x3
655	1997	Lapsus Abadia Retuerta (Sardon del Duero)	93p	2002/2020 x5
258	1995	Viña El Pison Artadi (Rioja)	96p	2000/2015 x3
637	1928	Imperial Gran Reserva C.V.N.E. (Rioja)	93p	2004/2010 x1
784	1949	Viña Real Gran Reserva C.V.N.E. (Rioja)	93p	2007/now x9
910	1959	Viña Real Gran Reserva C.V.N.E. (Rioja)	92p	2004/2010 x6
860	1962	Viña Real Gran Reserva C.V.N.E. (Rioja)	92p	2007/2010 x6
263	1885	Sherry Amontillado González Byass (Jerez)	96p	2002/2010 x1
956	1989	Oloroso Abocado Emilio Lustau (Jerez)	92p	2004/2040 x3
428	1917	Castillo Ygay Marqués de Murrieta (Rioja)	95p	2000/now x2
705	1959	Castillo Ygay Gran Reserva, Marqués de Murrieta (Rioja)	93p	2005/2010 x1
766	1922	Reserva Marqués de Riscal (Rioja)	93p	2005/2010 x5
704	1958	Reserva Marqués de Riscal (Rioja)	93p	2007/now x8
944	1998	Clos Fonta Mas d'En Gil (Priorat)	92p	2007/2015 x2
733	1968	Prado Enea Bodegas Muga (Rioja)	93p	2006/2010 x4
858	1970	Prado Enea Bodegas Muga (Rioja)	92p	2005/2010 x2
472	1995	Clos de l'Obac Costers del Siurana (Priorat)	95p	2004/2015 x2
830	1997	Miserere Costers del Siurana (Priorat)	92p	2007/2015 x4
943	1999	Corullón Descendientes de Jose Palacios (Bierzo)	92p	2005/2015 x2
855	2000	Corullón Descendientes de Jose Palacios (Bierzo)	92p	2005/2015 x2

244	1890	Gran Reserva 890 La Rioja Alta (Rioja)	96p	2002/now x1
566	1958	Gran Reserva 890 La Rioja Alta (Rioja)	94p	2003/2010 x6
493	1982	Gran Reserva 890 La Rioja Alta (Rioja)	94p	2007/2015x14
822	1968	Gran Reserva 904 La Rioja Alta (Rioja)	92p	2003/2010 x2

329	1994	Janus Pesquera Alejandro Fernández (Ribera del Duero)	96p	2003/2015 x3
772	1978	Tinto Pesquera Alejandro Fernández (Ribera del Duero)	93p	2007/2010 x3
842	1995	Tinto Pesquera Alejandro Fernández (Ribera del Duero)	92p	2007/2015 x8

289	1995	Pingus Dominio de Pingus (Ribera del Duero)	96p	2004/2020 x3
342	1999	Pingus Dominio de Pingus (Ribera del Duero)	96p	2006/2025 x3

971	2001	Remelluri Blanco (Rioja)	92p	2006/2010 x3

857	1999	Cirsion Bodegas Roda (Rioja)	92p	2001/2020 x3
995	1997	Roda I Reserva Bodegas Roda (Rioja)	92p	2001/2015 x6

657	1970	Gran Coronas Black Label Torres (Penedès)	93p	2004/now x3
462	1971	Mas La Plana Torres (Penedès)	95p	2005/2010 x2
941	2000	Reserva Real Torres (Penedès)	92p	2007/2015 x3

73	1917	Unico Bodegas Vega Sicilia (Ribera del Duero)	98p	1999/2010 x1
256	1922	Unico Bodegas Vega Sicilia (Ribera del Duero)	96p	2002/2010 x1
152	1941	Unico Bodegas Vega Sicilia (Ribera del Duero)	97p	2001/2010 x2
741	1942	Unico Bodegas Vega Sicilia (Ribera del Duero)	93p	2003/2010 x4
600	1953	Unico Bodegas Vega Sicilia (Ribera del Duero)	94p	2006/now x8
799	1957	Unico Bodegas Vega Sicilia (Ribera del Duero)	92p	2001/2010 x3
150	1958	Unico Bodegas Vega Sicilia (Ribera del Duero)	97p	2007/2015 x4
437	1959	Unico Bodegas Vega Sicilia (Ribera del Duero)	95p	2002/2010 x2
94	1962	Unico Bodegas Vega Sicilia (Ribera del Duero)	98p	2003/2015 x6
199	1964	Unico Bodegas Vega Sicilia (Ribera del Duero)	97p	2003/2010 x2
403	1965	Unico Bodegas Vega Sicilia (Ribera del Duero)	95p	2002/2010 x2
531	1970	Unico Bodegas Vega Sicilia (Ribera del Duero)	94p	2002/2020 x4
527	1973	Unico Bodegas Vega Sicilia (Ribera del Duero)	94p	2003/2020 x5
361	1975	Unico Bodegas Vega Sicilia (Ribera del Duero)	95p	2006/2010 x3
302	1982	Unico Bodegas Vega Sicilia (Ribera del Duero)	96p	2005/2015 x2
668	1987	Unico Bodegas Vega Sicilia (Ribera del Duero)	93p	2005/2015 x9

GERMANY

707	1990	Rauenthaler Nonnenberg Riesling Spätlese Georg Breuer (Rheingau)	92 p	2005 / 2020 x2

182	1921	Niersteiner Riesling Hermannshof (Germany)	97p	2003/2010 x2
537	1929	Niersteiner Riesling Hermannshof (Germany)	94p	2003/2010 x4

767	1876	Geisenheimer Rothenberg Auslese Weingut Langwerth von Simmern	93p	2004/now x2

785	1949	Riesling Auslese Scharzhof Egon Müller (Mosel-Saar-Ruwer)	93p	2005/2010 x2

323	1959	Riesling Auslese Scharzhof Egon Müller (Mosel-Saar-Ruwer)	96p	2005/2010 x5
175	1959	Riesling Trockenbeerenauslese Scharzhofberger Gold Capsule Egon Müller (Mosel-Saar-Ruwer)	97p	2000/2020 x3
414	2003	Scharzhofberger Riesling Auslese Egon Müller (Mosel-Saar-Ruwer)	95p	2006/2020 x4
508	1976	Scharzhofberger Riesling Auslese Egon Müller (Mosel-Saar-Ruwer)	94p	2006/now x2
439	1959	Riesling Oestricher Gottesthal Ferdinant Pierot (Germany)	95p	2002/2010 x4
757	1929	Hermannshof Auslese Franz Schmitt (Germany)	93p	2004/now x5
432	1934	Beerenauslese Robert Weil (Rheingau)	95p	2007/now x2
184	2001	Kiedricher Gräfenberg Riesling Auslese Robert Weil (Rheingau)	97p	2006/2030 x4
312	2001	Kiedricher Gräfenberg Riesling Eiswein Robert Weil (Rheingau)	96p	2006/2015 x3
546	1967	Weingut Robert Weil (Rheingau)	94p	2007/2010 x4

AUSTRIA

935	1990	Loibenberg Riesling Smaragd Alzinger (Wachau)	92p	2004/2015 x4
873	2006	Riesling Smaragd Singerriedel Hirtzberger (Wachau)	92p	2007/2020 x3
453	1998	TBA No. 13 Chardonnay "Nouvelle Vague" Alois Kracher	95p	2005/2050 x4
491	2000	TBA No. 8 Welschriesling "Zwischen den Seen" Alois Kracher	94p	2005/2025 x5
304	1999	TBA No. 10 Welschriesling "Nouvelle Vague" Alois Kracher	96p	2006/2025 x3
155	2000	TBA No. 10 Welschriesling "Zwischen den Seen" Alois Kracher	97p	2006/2030 x3
442	1997	Grüner Veltliner Smaragd Ried Loibenberg Emmerich Knoll (Wachau)	95p	2005/2020 x3
792	1995	Ried Pfaffenberg Steiner Riesling Beerenauslese Emmerich Knoll (Wachau)	93p	2001/2030 x5
300	1990	Riesling Loibner Vinothekfüllung Emmerich Knoll (Wachau)	96p	2005/2010 x12
394	2000	Riesling Loibner Vinothekfullung Emmerich Knoll (Wachau)	95p	2005/2010 x2
728	1960	Gewürztraminer Lenz Moser	93p	2006/2010 x2
391	1994	Riesling Trockenbeerenauslese Achleiten Prager	95p	2007/2010 x3

396	1994	Riesling Smaragd Steinertal FX Pichler (Wachau)	95p	2006/2010 x3
596	1997	Riesling Smaragd Durnsteiner Kellerberg FX Pichler (Wachau)	94p	2007/2015 x2
438	2000	Riesling Unendlich FX Pichler (Wachau)	95p	2006/2015 x2
905	2005	Riesling Unendlich FX Pichler (Wachau)	92p	2006/2015 x4
923	2000	Von den Terassen Riesling Smaragd F.X. Pichler (Wachau)	92p	2007/2015 x3
945	2002	Riesling Smaragd Dürnsteiner Kellerberg F.X. Pichler (Wachau)	92p	2007/2015 x4
530	2000	Opitz One Willi Opitz (Neusiedlersee)	94p	2006/2015 x10
628	1969	Grüner Veltliner Spätlese Schloss Gobelsburg (Kamptal)	93p	2007/now x3
750	1975	Grüner Veltliner Schloss Gobelsburg (Kamptal)	93p	2007/2010 x2
825	1973	Riesling Spätlese Schloss Gobelsburg (Kamptal)	92p	2004/2010 x4
962	2003	Grüner Veltliner Tradition Schloss Gobelsburg (Kamptal)	92p	2007/2020 x10
511	2005	Riesling Tradition Schloss Gobelsburg (Kamptal)	95p	2006/2015 x6

HUNGARY

565	1957	Grown Estate Tokaji Essencia (Tokaj)	94p	2004/now x3
679	1999	Tokaji Aszú 6 puttunyos István Szepsy (Tokaj)	95p	2005/2040 x2
993	1888	Tokaji Essence Berry Bros (Tokaj)	92p	1999/2010 x2

PORTUGAL

DOURO

195	1890	Vintage Port Burmester (Portugal)	97p	2007/2025 x3
66	1878	Vintage Port Cockburn (Portugal)	98p	2006/2020 x3
247	1896	Vintage Port Cockburn (Portugal)	96p	2005/2020 x6
311	1908	Vintage Port Cockburn (Portugal)	96p	2005/2030 x3
286	1927	Vintage Port Cockburn (Portugal)	96p	2001/2020 x2
649	1922	Vintage Port Croft (Portugal)	93p	2004/2010 x3
492	1904	Vintage Port Dow's (Portugal)	94p	2005/now x6
520	1927	Vintage Port Dow's (Portugal)	94p	2003/2015 x3
370	1887	Vintage Port Graham's (Portugal)	95p	2005/now x1
319	1945	Vintage Port Graham´s (Portugal)	96p	2007/2015 x1
206	1947	Vintage Port Graham's (Portugal)	97p	1999/2020 x2
386	1966	Vintage Port Graham's (Portugal)	95p	2000/2020 x3
833	1970	Vintage Port Graham's (Portugal)	92p	2007/2025 x7
579	1994	Vintage Port Graham's (Portugal)	94p	2000/2040 x4
528	2000	Vintage Port Graham's (Portugal)	94p	2006/2040 x6

426	1820	Vintage Port Guilherme (Portugal)	95p	2007/now x2
636	1957	Barca Velha Ferreira (Portugal)	93p	2006/2015 x3
815	1965	Barca Velha Ferreira (Portugal)	92p	2003/2025 x3
618	1983	Barca Velha Ferreira (Portugal)	94p	2007/now x4
424	1927	Vintage Port Fonseca (Portugal)	95p	2001/2020 x3
885	1944	Vintage Port Hooper (Portugal)	92p	2003/now x2
991	1896	Vintage Port Martinez (Portugal)	92p	2003/2010 x3
222	1900	Colheita Niepoort (Portugal)	96p	2000/now x3
489	1904	Colheita Niepoort (Portugal)	94p	2004/2010 x2
362	1912	Colheita Niepoort (Portugal)	95p	2006/2020 x2
477	1934	Colheita Niepoort (Portugal)	95p	2007/2025 x2
689	1952	Colheita Niepoort (Portugal)	93p	2002/2020 x4
553	1962	Colheita Niepoort (Portugal)	93p	2004/2015 x2
303	1931	Garrafeira Niepoort (Portugal)	96p	2006/2015 x2
110	1927	Vintage Port Niepoort (Portugal)	98p	2006/2030 x2
786	1942	Vintage Port Niepoort (Portugal)	93p	2004/2010 x3
994	2000	Chryseia Prats & Symington (Portugal)	92p	2003/2015 x5
783	1896	Colheita Quinta do Noval (Portugal)	93p	2001/now x2
285	1937	Colheita Quinta do Noval (Portugal)	96p	2006/2020 x5
338	1962	Nacional Vintage Port Quinta do Noval (Portugal)	96p	2007/2025 x3
12	1963	Nacional Vintage Port Quinta do Noval (Portugal)	100p	2007/2020 x5
259	1964	Nacional Vintage Port Quinta do Noval (Portugal)	96p	2006/2020 x4
134	1970	Nacional Vintage Port Quinta do Noval (Portugal)	97p	2005/2030 x2
413	1975	Nacional Vintage Port Quinta do Noval (Portugal)	95p	2006/2030 x2
217	1994	Nacional Vintage Port Quinta do Noval (Portugal)	97p	2005/2040 x8
208	1997	Nacional Vintage Port Quinta do Noval (Portugal)	97p	2006/2050 x4
343	1966	Vintage Port Quinta do Noval (Portugal)	96p	2007/2020 x11
813	1927	Vintage Port Sandeman (Portugal)	92p	2001/now x4
219	1963	Vintage Port Taylor Fladgate (Portugal)	97p	2007/2020 x2
326	1977	Vintage Port Taylor Fladgate (Portugal)	96p	2001/2025 x4
363	1992	Vintage Port Taylor Fladgate (Portugal)	95p	2004/2030 x5
691	1994	Vintage Port Taylor Fladgate (Portugal)	93p	2007/2030 x5
889	2000	Vintage Port Taylor Fladgate (Portugal)	92p	2006/2050 x6
476	1931	Vintage Port Warre's (Portugal)	95p	2003/2020 x3

MADEIRA

68	1792	Madeira Extra Réserve Solera 'Napoléon Réserve' Blandy's	98p	2006/2060 x6
239	1792	Madeira Bual	96p	2005/2020 x7
479	1795	Madeira Terrantez	94p	2005/2040 x8
913	1834	Madeira Bual Malvasia	92p	2006/2040 x4
798	1848	Madeira Bual Barbeito	92p	2003/2030 x2
656	1863	Madeira Bual Barbeito	93p	2005/2040 x3

USA

539	1997	Madrona Ranch Cabernet Sauvignon Abreu (Napa Valley)	94p	2002/2020 x3
669	1949	Georges de Latour Beaulieu Vineyard (Napa Valley)	93p	2003/now x2
779	1970	Georges de Latour Beaulieu Vineyard (Napa Valley)	93p	2002/2010 x4
977	1974	Georges de Latour Beaulieu Vineyard (Napa Valley)	92p	2007/now x2
856	1997	Bancroft Ranch Howell Mountain Merlot Beringer	92p	2002/2010 x3
564	1959	CS Buena Vista Haraszthy Cellars (Napa Valley)	94p	2004/now x5
900	1961	CS Buena Vista Haraszthy Cellars (Napa Valley)	91p	2004/2010 x1
202	1997	Cabernet Sauvignon Bryant Family Vineyard (Napa Valley)	97p	2006 /2030 x5
377	1995	Cabernet Sauvignon Bryant Family Vineyard (Napa Valley)	95p	2005/2020 x2
148	1976	Cabernet Sauvignon Special Selection Caymus (Napa Valley)	97p	2004/2015 x3
194	1985	Cabernet Sauvignon Special Selection Caymus (Napa Valley)	97p	2004/2015 x2
389	1990	Cabernet Sauvignon Special Selection Caymus (Napa Valley)	95p	2007/2020 x5
652	1981	Estate Chardonnay Reserve Chalone (California)	93p	2000/2010 x1
806	1997	Estate Cabernet Sauvignon Château Montelena (Napa Valley)	92p	2002/2015 x6
521	1992	Cabernet Sauvignon Herb Lamb Vineyard Colgin (Napa Valley)	94p	2004/2015 x2
282	1995	Cabernet Sauvignon Herb Lamb Vineyard Colgin (Napa Valley)	96p	2004/2020 x2
299	1992	Maya Dalla Valle (Napa Valley)	96p	2003/2015 x4
267	1996	Maya Dalla Valle (Napa Valley)	96p	2005/2019 x2
700	1997	Cabernet Sauvignon Howell Mountain Dunn Vineyards (Napa Valley)	93p	2002/2030 x4
459	1978	Cabernet Sauvignon Volcanic Hill Diamond Creek (Napa Valley)	95p	2000/2010 x1

387	1987	Proprietary Red Wine Dominus (Napa Valley)	95p	2002/2020 x3
457	1994	Proprietary Red Wine Dominus (Napa Valley)	95p	2004/2020 x3
189	1991	Proprietary Red Wine Harlan Estate (Napa Valley)	97p	2003/2020 x3
895	1969	Cabernet Sauvignon Lot C-91 Heitz (Napa Valley)	92p	2000/now x3
383	1968	Martha's Vineyard Cabernet Sauvignon Heitz (Napa Valley)	95p	2000/2010 x2
568	1970	Martha's Vineyard Cabernet Sauvignon Heitz (Napa Valley)	94p	2000/2010 x2
38	1974	Martha's Vineyard Cabernet Sauvignon Heitz (Napa Valley)	98p	2004/2010 x16
598	1986	Martha's Vineyard Cabernet Sauvignon Heitz (Napa Valley)	94p	2004/2010 x3
684	1996	Martha's Vineyard Cabernet Sauvignon Heitz (Napa Valley)	93p	2002/2015 x3
130	1946	Cabernet Sauvignon Inglenook (Napa Valley)	97p	2002/2010 x2
737	1897	Pinot Noir Inglenook (Napa Valley)	92p	2005/now x3
810	1949	Cabernet Sauvignion Charles Krug (Napa Valley)	92p	2003/now x2
871	1968	Cabernet Sauvignon Mountain Creek Louis M. Martini	92p	2003/now x4
710	1961	Special Selection Cabernet Sauvignon Louis M. Martini	93p	2004/2010 x3
279	1992	Chardonnay Alexander Mountain Estate Marcassin (Sonoma)	96p	2005/2015 x5
207	1993	Chardonnay Lorenzo Vineyard Marcassin (Sonoma)	97p	2002/2015 x4
782	1999	Chardonnay Three Sisters Vineyard Marcassin (Sonoma)	93p	2005/2015 x4
620	1979	Opus One Mondavi & Mouton-Rothschild (Napa Valley)	94p	2007/2010 x3
927	1994	Opus One Mondavi & Mouton-Rothschild (Napa Valley)	92p	2006/2015 x5
594	1998	Opus One Mondavi & Mouton-Rothschild (Napa Valley)	94p	2002/2020 x7
678	1968	Cabernet Sauvignon Private Reserve Robert Mondavi (Napa Valley)	93p	2003/2010 x3
983	1990	Cabernet Sauvignon Reserve Robert Mondavi (Napa Valley)	92p	2003/2010 x4
759	1995	Cabernet Sauvignon Reserve Robert Mondavi (Napa Valley)	93p	2003/2015 x2
503	1974	Insignia Joseph Phelps (Napa Valley)	94p	2000/2010 x1
793	1984	Insignia Joseph Phelps (Napa Valley)	92p	2002/2010 x4
248	1997	Merlot Pahlmeyer (Napa Valley)	96p	2005/2020 x3
404	1984	Zinfandel Dickerson Vineyard Ravenswood (Napa Valley)	95p	2001/2010 x3
832	1968	Cabernet Sauvignon Ridge Vineyards	91p	2000/2010 x3

369	1974	Monte Bello Ridge (Santa Cruz Mountains)	95p	2005/2010 x4
824	1988	Monte Bello Ridge (Santa Cruz Mountains)	92p	2007/2015 x3
736	1996	Monte Bello Ridge (Santa Cruz Mountains)	93p	2006/2015 x2
588	1999	Monte Bello Ridge (Santa Cruz Mountains)	94p	2007/2020 x3
972	1998	York Creek Ridge	91p	2001/2010 x4
191	1997	Cabernet Sauvignon Screaming Eagle (Napa Valley)	97p	2004/2025 x7
205	1994	Cabernet Sauvignon Hillside Select Shafer Vineyards (Napa Valley)	97p	2003/2020 x6
943	1997	Cabernet Sauvignon Hillside Select Shafer Vineyards (Napa Valley)	92p	2002/2020 x3
848	1976	River West Old Vines Zinfandel Sonoma Vineyards	92p	2001/2010 x2
727	1962	Chardonnay Stony Hill Vineyard (Napa Valley)	93p	2005/now x1
647	1981	Zinfandel Swan (Sonoma)	93p	2004/2010 x2
967	1982	Zinfandel Swan (Sonoma)	92p	2004/2010 x5
499	2000	Incognito Sine Qua Non (California)	94p	2007/2025 x2
568	1997	Syrah Imposter McCoy Sine Qua Non (California)	94p	2005/2015 x4
676	1998	Black Sears Vineyard Zinfandel Turley	93p	2001/2015 x4
907	1998	Old Vines Zinfandel Turley	92p	2001/2015 x4

AUSTRALIA

714	1995	The Dead Arm Shiraz d'Arenberg (McLaren Vale)	93p	2006/2020 x4
949	1998	The Dead Arm Shiraz d'Arenberg (McLaren Vale)	92p	2007/2015 x3
770	1999	The Dead Arm Shiraz d'Arenberg (McLaren Vale)	93p	2005/2015 x2
213	1996	Astralis Clarendon Hills (South Australia)	97p	2005/2015 x5
662	1991	Chardonnay Giaconda (Victoria)	93p	2006/2015 x2
921	1999	Chardonnay Giaconda (Victoria)	91p	2001/2010 x3
662	1998	Shiraz Roennfeldt Road Greenock Creek (Barossa Valley)	93p	2005/2015 x8
883	1991	Eileen Hardy Shiraz Hardy's (McLaren Vale)	92p	2007/now x6
137	1962	Hill of Grace Henschke (Eden Valley)	97p	2001/2015 x2
331	1998	Hill of Grace Henschke (Eden Valley)	96p	2005/2025 x2
367	1981	Mount Edelstone Henschke (Eden Valley)	95p	2007/2015 x9
969	1993	Mount Edelstone Shiraz Keyneton Vineyard Henschke (Eden Valley)	92p	2004/2010 x2

911	1998	Mount Edelstone Shiraz Keyneton Vineyard Henschke (Eden Valley)	92p	2004/2010 x2
653	1998	Black Sock Magpie Estate (Barossa Valley)	93p	2002/2015 x3
996	1994	Quintet Cabernet Blend Mount Mary	92p	2006/2015 x2
801	1955	Grange Hermitage Penfolds (South Australia)	92p	2002/now x3
664	1959	Grange Hermitage Penfolds (South Australia)	93p	2006/2015 x2
937	1960	Grange Hermitage Penfolds (South Australia)	92p	2005/now x3
169	1961	Grange Hermitage Penfolds (South Australia)	97p	2001/2010 x3
109	1962	Grange Hermitage Penfolds (South Australia)	98p	2002/2010 x8
711	1965	Grange Hermitage Bin 95 Penfolds (Australia)	93p	2001/now x3
896	1970	Grange Hermitage Penfolds (South Australia)	92p	2007/now x3
230	1971	Grange Hermitage Penfolds (South Australia)	97p	2004/2015 x3
97	1976	Grange Hermitage Penfolds (South Australia)	98p	2003/2010 x3
985	1977	Grange Hermitage Penfolds (South Australia)	92p	2007/2010 x2
514	1981	Grange Penfolds (South Australia)	94p	2004/2010 x4
585	1986	Grange Penfolds (South Australia)	94p	2003/2020 x9
823	1989	Grange Penfolds (South Australia)	92p	2003/2015 x11
734	1998	Grange Penfolds (South Australia)	93p	2006/2025 x7
346	1879	Seppelt Para Liqueur Port (Barossa Valley)	95p	1999/2040 x1
826	1998	Descendant Torbreck (Barossa Valley)	92p	2001/2015 x2
752	1996	Run Rig Torbreck (Barossa Valley)	93p	2006/2015 x4
441	1996	Three Rivers Shiraz (Barossa Valley)	95p	2005/2020 x3
693	1997	Duck Muck Shiraz Wild Duck Creek (Heathcote)	93p	2005/2015 x4
776	1990	Cabernet Sauvignon Coonawarra John Riddoch Limited Release Wynns	93 p	2007/2020 x4

NEW ZEALAND

940	1999	Pinot Noir Vineyard Fromm Winery (New Zealand)	92p	2005/2015 x2
973	1996	Cloudy Bay Sauvignon Blanc (New Zealand)	92p	2006/2010 x19

SOUTH AFRICA

62	1870	Vin de Constance (South-Africa)	98p	1998/2020 x2

CHILE

698	1996	Almaviva (Maipo)	93p	2006/2010 x3

RUSSIA

368	1938	Ai-Daniel Tokay Massandra Collection (Crimea)	95p	2006/2010 x4
490	1928	Livadia White Muscat Massandra Collection (Crimea)	94p	2006/2010 x2
126	1895	Red Port Livadia Massandra Collection (Crimea)	97p	2005/2020 x4
307	1937	Tavrida Black Muscat Massandra Collection (Crimea)	96p	2006/2010 x4

LEBANON

738	1960	Château Musar (Lebanon)	92p	2003/2010 x3